Reading the World

Reading the World

Cormac McCarthy's Tennessee Period

Dianne C. Luce

THE UNIVERSITY OF SOUTH CAROLINA PRESS

© 2009 University of South Carolina

Cloth edition published by the University of South Carolina Press, 2009
Paperback edition published in Columbia, South Carolina,
by the University of South Carolina Press, 2010

www.sc.edu/uscpress

Manufactured in the United States of America

19 18 17 16 15 14 13 12 11 10   10 9 8 7 6 5 4 3 2 1

The Library of Congress has cataloged the cloth edition as follows:

Luce, Dianne C.
  Reading the world : Cormac McCarthy's Tennessee period / Dianne C. Luce.
    p. cm.
  Includes bibliographical references and index.
  ISBN 978-1-57003-824-2 (cloth : alk. paper)
  1. McCarthy, Cormac, 1933– —Criticism and interpretation. I. Title.
  PS3563.C337Z76 2009
  813'.54—dc22

                              2009004279

One section of chapter 3 previously appeared as "The Cave of Oblivion: Platonic
Mythology in Child of God," in *Cormac McCarthy: New Directions*, ed. James D. Lilley
(Albuquerque: University of New Mexico Press, 2002). It is substantially revised here.
With gratitude, the author acknowledges permission for the use of the following
materials:

   Quotations from *The Orchard Keeper* reprinted by permission of International Creative Management, Inc. © 1965 by Cormac McCarthy.
   Quotations from *Outer Dark* reprinted by permission of International Creative Management, Inc. © 1968 by Cormac McCarthy.
   Quotations from *Child of God* reprinted by permission of International Creative Management, Inc. © 1973 by Cormac McCarthy.
   Quotations from *Suttree* reprinted by permission of International Creative Management, Inc. © 1979 by Cormac McCarthy.
   Quotations from *The Tennessee* by Donald Davidson, © 1946, 1948 by Donald David-
son, © 1991 by Thomas Daniel Young, © 1992 by Mrs. Eric Davidson Bell, by permission of Ivan R. Dee, Publisher.
   From *The Gnostic Religion* by Hans Jonas. © 1958 by Hans Jonas. Reprinted by permission of Beacon Press, Boston.
   Quotations from *Gnosticism in Modern Literature* by Josephine Donovan. © 1990.
Reprinted by permission of Josephine Donovan.

ISBN: 978-1-57003-988-1 (pbk)

Contents

Preface / vii
Acknowledgments / xi
Abbreviations / xiii

Chapter 1. Landscape of Memory: *The Orchard Keeper* (1965) / 1

    Consuming the Wilderness: Dispossessing the Mountain People / 3
    The TVA: Eviction in the Valley / 18
    Evading the Law: Whiskey Blockading / 23
    The Voice of the Land / 28
    Defending the Orchard: Arthur Ownby / 37
    Defending the Orchard: Marion Sylder / 49
    Defending the Orchard: John Wesley Rattner / 55

Chapter 2. Cosmic Estrangement: *Outer Dark* (1968) / 62

    The Cosmic Shadowland: Culla / 75
    Amnion of Light: Rinthy / 79
    Flood, Mud, and Swamp: Turbid Water / 83
    Bound by Nothin: Outlaws and Archons / 87
    The Dark Necessity of Psyche / 92
    Rinthy, Tinker, Culla, Seer: Gnosis and Nothingness / 100
    The Wilderness Nightmare: Gnostic "Ecology" / 113
    Current Ferries, Rural Squires, and Hog Drives:
       Realistic Underpinnings / 124

Chapter 3. The Cave of Oblivion: *Child of God* (1974) / 134

    James Blevins, Lookout Mountain Voyeur / 138
    Ed Gein, Plainfield Necrophile / 144
    Voyeur, Necrophile, *Psycho:* Novel, Script, and Film / 146
    McCarthy in Sevier County / 153

The Cave as Leviathan / 156

Platonic Intimations: The Descent into Materialism / 158

Failure of Vision and the Love of Material Bodies / 160

Voyeurism, Narcissism, and the Opportunity for Self-Recognition / 165

Celestial Intimations and the Oracles of Dreams / 169

The Heedless Blacksmith and the Origin of Evil / 172

Chapter 4. Stranger in the Garden of Industry: *The Gardener's Son* (1977) / 176

The Weaver God and the Material Factory / 178

The Revolt / 182

The Trial and the Lie of the World / 185

The Condemned Man and the Question of Gnosis / 189

Chapter 5. Prisoner in Babylon: *Suttree* (1979) / 194

Gnostic/Existentialist *Suttree* / 198

The Dream-Frame: Suttree as Narrator / 202

Hallucinated Recollections: The Album of the Dead / 217

"This obscure purgatory" / 226

Apprentice Felons, Apprentice Predators / 234

The Prison of Erotic Attraction / 238

The Rage for Justice / 251

"Babbling gospelarity" and the Spiritual Wound / 256

Notes / 271

Works Cited / 293

Index / 303

NOVELIST CORMAC MCCARTHY is a philosopher and a poet. One of the most fundamental observations to be made about him is that his deepest engagement with the world is represented obliquely and yet concretely in his fiction. Issues of value and vision concerning humanity's understanding of its very nature, of its history and culture, and of its place within the natural environment inform all his work. But they are seldom presented overtly, sociologically, politically. The concrete texture of McCarthy's works reflects his close observation of the empirical reality of the world. But the deeper structure of his works—their engagement with specific questions of value in a given time and place in human and natural history or, more essentially, with the universal questions of humanity's place within the cosmos and the relation of our spiritual nature to our psychological and material being—carries his bedrock philosophical concerns. The integration in McCarthy's works of the surface texture, of *seeing* the world, with his allegorical or metaphorical delving beyond the transitory and the mundane constitutes his essential vision: his *reading* of the world. For McCarthy this reading involves observation and experience, a sharp eye for the realities of nature, the tools and crafts of human endeavor, and the nuances of human interaction as well as an acute ear for human speech. It also involves literal reading, of newspapers, of national and local history, and of works of philosophy and religious history. But beyond these, his reading of the world is the engagement of a writer who is awake in all his faculties: an eye that looks into the past and the future, an ear that is open to the unspoken mystery of the world, a mind that seeks insight.

By exploring the still relatively neglected Tennessee period, we can see the beginnings and evolution of McCarthy's vision. The first four novels are deeply grounded in McCarthy's experience in East Tennessee, and it is fruitful to bring to a reading of these works an understanding of the social, historical, cultural, and environmental issues evoked by the subtly presented nuances of time and place in them. McCarthy expects so much from his readers that his works sometimes seem to be written for a specialized local audience, an audience of insiders. Read with a knowledge of place, the works open out in unsuspected ways, and what may seem merely a realistic detail relegated to the hazy background of McCarthy's fiction—the displacement of a small landowner, a

temperance parade, a flooded river, a passing reference to White Caps, a comi-
cally corrupt justice of the peace—comes into focus as a newly perceived foreground, one that was always there to be recognized. An oscillation between
field and ground is ever at work in McCarthy's fiction. It is there in the interplay between the realistic and the philosophical. The realistic designation of
place is essential in most of McCarthy's work, functioning to evoke a world
of cultural realities that impinge on his characters' lives and choices. But
McCarthy's settings and topography are typically metaphorical as well, reflecting the metaphysical positioning of his characters.

Two works in the Tennessee period, *The Orchard Keeper* (1965) and *Suttree*
(1979), were most likely conceived at the outset of McCarthy's writing career,
in about 1959, and he seems to have worked on them concurrently until each
was published in its turn. *Outer Dark* (1968), *Child of God* (1974), and *The Gardener's Son* (filmed in 1976) were begun later, and each manifests McCarthy's
interest in particular philosophical mindsets and systems of metaphors correlative to these mindsets that derived from his readings and continued to
inform the Tennessee novels he completed later. Of these five works, the first
published is the least philosophical and the most deeply informed with
the social, economic, and cultural history of East Tennessee. In *Outer Dark*,
which had its genesis in about 1963, McCarthy's engagement with gnosticism
comes to the fore; here he delineates a nightmarish dreamworld that derives
largely from the myth and symbol systems of ancient gnosticism, a technique
he employs again in later novels, most notably *Blood Meridian*. *Child of God*,
too, has its gnostic implications, but for its metaphorical topography and its
meditation on vision and materialism it is most indebted to Plato, whose philosophy fed into ancient Christianity and gnosticism in interesting ways, sometimes involving a reversal or repudiation. With *The Gardener's Son* and *Suttree*,
the gnostic turn asserts itself anew, now blended with the neo-gnosticism of
twentieth-century existentialism. These varieties of religious/philosophical experience are ways of encountering the world for McCarthy's characters, ways
of reading the world for his narrators. His works engage with their symbols,
myths, parables, or fictions (such as Camus's absurdist novels) to establish the
fictional worlds and ontologies his characters inhabit. His narrators read the
characters and their worlds through the lenses of these systems. Although one
philosophical/mythic system predominates in some early pieces, McCarthy's
mind and method are syncretic, and in his subsequent works he often blends
systems. Recognizing these influences does not and should not lead us to identify McCarthy the thinker as a gnostic, a Platonist, or an existentialist, but to
read his works in this way is to read, in a sense, his intellectual biography—no
mean compensation for the dearth of reliable biographical information about
this intensely private man.

Certain other perceptions and principles developed over my thirty years of attention to McCarthy's work inform this study. A few readers have mentioned (and exaggerated) the psychological opacity of McCarthy's characters, sometimes concluding with Vereen Bell that his characters are "virtually without thoughts" (*Achievement* 8) or with Denis Donoghue that they have no inner life at all (260). It is true that McCarthy is subtler and more reticent about his characters' psychology than many modernist and contemporary novelists, but the psychological dimension is always a significant factor, even when it is not foregrounded. And the characters' inner lives are usually quite active and turbulent indeed (although this inner activity is of an entirely different nature for his spiritually oblivious characters than for his awake and seeking ones). McCarthy handles psychology much as he does the implications of his realistic time and place settings: he seems not interested in laying out the workings for us; rather, he expects us to bring our own insights and understanding to bear on objectively observed behaviors. The psychology of the characters, while important, is usually not the engine that drives McCarthy's works. For McCarthy it is the spiritual status of the characters, as opposed to their psychological experience, that is most at stake. Nevertheless, to open oneself to the possibility that human psychology is at work in the lives of McCarthy's characters is to read them in their full dimensionality. Often the inner life is conveyed through the interplay between the narrator's impressions and those of the focalized character, or suggested through dreams, or hinted at the level of gesture or imagery. Indeed, to read McCarthy on his own terms is to be alert to his poetic image patterns and the metaphorical or metaphysical or psychological hints they convey.

From the beginnings of McCarthy's career, he has evidenced strong interest not only in metaphysical ways of reading the world but also in the concrete experience of the individual in relation to authority and hierarchy. Issues and agents of law and other forms of culturally imposed order appear in each work of the Tennessee period, and these pieces comprise an extended exploration of antinomianism, sometimes unique to the individual, sometimes raised to the metaphysical level. Further, in these works, as throughout most of McCarthy's novels, a markedly antimaterialistic stance is tempered by an evident love and reverence for the natural world and a vibrant curiosity about manual skills and the practical sciences.

The ideal reader of McCarthy's works would be, I suppose, McCarthy himself—or someone who shared his knowledge and reading. This study has been driven by the perception that reading what McCarthy has read, reading about the places he has experienced deeply, helps to open the reader to his work by preparing us to understand what he understands and to see the world in the same contexts as he does. My work here draws eclectically on philosophy, literature, film, local histories, and newspaper accounts from the time when

McCarthy lived in Tennessee in an attempt to contextualize and provide informed readings of his early novels and screenplay. Given the range of McCarthy's interests, this contextualizing is rather different for each work, sometimes explicating the various socio-economic matters evoked, sometimes exploring the issues of social and spiritual outlawry raised by a specific murder case that informs his work, often emphasizing the philosophical myths and symbols they engage. Always I have taken my cue from the work itself and sought out contexts to illuminate the mysteries they inherently pose.

Acknowledgments

IN ONE SENSE, THIS BOOK is the end result of fourteen years of interchange with the diverse members of the Cormac McCarthy Society, whose conference presentations, emails, internet postings, responses to my own presentations, and casual conversations about McCarthy's work have provided constant stimulation and inspiration. Foremost among these scholars is Edwin Arnold, a longtime friend and collaborator who has generously shared information, suggestions, and encouragement and has ever been a staunch advocate of the highest scholarly and professional standards. Our conversation about McCarthy began in the mid-1970s and continues unabated. For urging me to read McCarthy three decades ago, my gratitude goes equally to Edwin Arnold and Shelby Foote, two readers of impeccable taste.

Other McCarthy scholars whose ideas and suggestions have influenced the shape or execution of this book include James Lilley, who read and edited one section of it in a previous form. I also thank Douglas Canfield, Christine Chollier, Georg Guillemin, Susan Hawkins, William Prather, Paul Ragan, Nell Sullivan, John Sepich, Rick Wallach, and John Wegner; their influence, by suggestion or example, is apparent to me even though they may not be aware of it. Several specific acknowledgments to scholars are detailed in the text that follows. All have my gratitude. I have benefited too from the energy, insights, and curiosity of the students in my fiction classes, who have studied *The Orchard Keeper, Outer Dark, Blood Meridian,* and *All the Pretty Horses* with me at Midlands Technical College in Columbia, South Carolina, and from the focused discussions of *The Stonemason* and *The Crossing* with my former colleagues in the English department there.

My research has been generously encouraged and supported by the administration of Midlands Technical College with funding for travel and expressions of enthusiastic interest and celebration. For this I am appreciative of Jean Mahaffey, former vice president for educational affairs; Ronald Drayton, vice president of arts and sciences; and Diane Carr, former department chair of English. I thank Dr. Mahaffey, too, for breaking with precedent by approving my leave in the spring of 1996. During that semester, I was a Visiting Fellow at the Australian National University, where some of my focused research for this book began. For that support, my thanks go to the ANU's acting head of the

Department of English, Fred Langman, and to his successor as department head, Iain Wright.

The professional staffs of several libraries and archives have graciously and efficiently assisted me in my research. These include the librarians of the University of South Carolina's Thomas Cooper Library, South Caroliniana Library, and Law Library; the University of Tennessee's James D. Hoskins Library and Special Collections Library; Midlands Technical College Library (with special thanks to Marilyn Hook for her assistance with research on the James Blevins law case); the Australian National University Library in Canberra; the Albert B. Alkek Library at Southwest Texas State University in San Marcos; Knox County's Lawson McGhee Public Library and the Calvin M. McClung Historical Collection in Knoxville's East Tennessee Historical Center; and the public libraries of Blount and Sevier Counties in East Tennessee. I am also indebted to the staffs of the Knox County Archives and the Knox County Courthouse and to Carole Wunderlich, communications director of Knoxville's Immaculate Conception Church. For copying and mailing me materials essential to my work, special thanks go to Joe Rader, head of the University of Tennessee Archives, to the Local History Department of the Bicentennial Library in Chattanooga, Tennessee, and to Danette Mullinax of the Cherokee Regional Library in Lafayette, Georgia.

For conversations about Knoxville that provided a range of insights, my thanks go to Bob Gentry, Steve Horton, Bill Kidwell, Richard Marius, Bill McCarthy, Dennis McCarthy, Wesley G. Morgan, and Don Williams.

For advice, encouragement, patience, and steadfast support, my deepest gratitude goes to my husband Harvey Starr, scholar, soldier, good heart and true.

Finally, I am grateful to Cormac McCarthy, whose love of this dark world is a fire illuminating it.

Abbreviations

APH	*All the Pretty Horses*
BM	*Blood Meridian*
C	*The Crossing*
CoG	*Child of God*
CoP	*Cities of the Plain*
GS	*The Gardener's Son*
OD	*Outer Dark*
NCOM	*No Country for Old Men*
S	*Suttree*

Chapter One

Landscape of Memory   *The Orchard Keeper* (1965)

The Orchard Keeper is set primarily in a partially fictionalized but often geographically and topographically accurate southeastern Knox County and northeastern Blount County, Tennessee—in the area near Brown Mountain and the town of Vestal, where Cormac McCarthy, born Charles Joseph McCarthy, Jr., lived with his family when he was a child. Knoxville, to the north, would become the primary setting of *Suttree*, and Sevier County, to the east, is the setting of *Child of God*. These three novels seem consciously designed to exploit, in sequence, his familiarity with the Tennessee locales in which he lived or attended school between the 1930s and the 1960s. *Suttree* is a novel of urban life; *Child of God* emphasizes the main character's anachronistic life in a near-wilderness situation; and the setting of *The Orchard Keeper* mediates between the two. Its characters both resist and benefit from modern technology: Marion Sylder and John Wesley Rattner travel with ease between the traditional community of Red Branch and the city, and Arthur Ownby, the oldest of the three, lives contentedly in Red Branch but feels the encroachment of modern life most. "If I was a younger man," he thinks longingly, "I would move to them mountains" (55); when the government hounds him, he does just that, dragging his sledge with his meager belongings on foot south and east across Chilhowee Mountain in hopes of settling in the Hurricane, an old logging camp just outside of the Great Smoky Mountains National Park in Blount County (*History of Blount County* 5, 11).[1] His retreat toward the mountains marks his choice of nature, traditional mountain culture, and personal freedom over civilization, modern technology, and governmental regulation. It is also an informed retreat to the lost world of his youth. But the tragic resolutions of his and Sylder's narrative arcs leave both of them imprisoned in the city and the world of modern bureaucracy. McCarthy's first novel establishes metaphorical implications for Knox, Blount, and Sevier counties, then, that remain fairly consistent across his Tennessee works and that largely reflect the socio-geographical reality of mid-twentieth-century East Tennessee. The physical move toward the mountains always signifies a movement toward the primitive and toward the past. In *The Orchard Keeper,* Blount County is a liminal space that mediates geographically and culturally between the urban and the wild, manifesting elements of both.

Despite its physical location near Knoxville, Red Branch is not suburban, nor was the area where the McCarthy children grew up on Martin Mill Pike at its intersection with Neubert Springs Road near Vestal, an area that had more in common with rural Blount County than with Knoxville. The Tennessee Historical Records Survey indicates that in 1940, the time in which sections II and III of the novel are set, the whole of Blount County had a population of only 41,116, up from 33,981 in 1930 following a decade of rapid expansion driven by such factors as the advent of the Tennessee Valley Authority (TVA). Its economy was predominantly agricultural, with a farming population of 16,787 in 1935, nearly all Caucasian; most farms were under one thousand acres in size. Maryville, the county seat west of Vestal from which Kenneth Rattner moves his family in the Depression year 1933, was Blount's largest town but still just a village by absolute standards. Her population grew from 4,958 in 1930 to 5,609 in 1940 (Tennessee Historical Records Survey 12). With Alcoa Aluminum and the Knoxville Municipal Airport nearby, Maryville has continued to grow, but the area near McCarthy's boyhood home has not been transformed by suburban sprawl—even today it retains its pastoral and semi-developed feel.

The biographical sketch provided on the dust jacket of the first edition indicates that McCarthy "grew up in a rural area similar to that described in *The Orchard Keeper.*" Edwin T. Arnold has photographed the old McCarthy house and its rural surroundings, and he and others have identified some likely local analogues to key sites in the novel (Arnold, "World" 7). South of the former McCarthy home on Martin Mill Pike, a dirt road branches off, leading to an abandoned orchard and some fenced-off TVA property (Arnold, "World" 5, 7). In a letter to the editor of *Metro Pulse* in response to Mike Gibson's article about East Tennessee locales in McCarthy's works, Frank E. Bourne of Knoxville writes that on Brown Mountain (which in McCarthy's novel became Red Mountain) stands a five-hundred-thousand-gallon water tank still in working condition after one hundred years, a tank he associates with the government installation in *The Orchard Keeper.* In the woods near the McCarthy house is an old rectangular pit, which may have influenced McCarthy's conception for the spray pit where Rattner's corpse lies (Arnold, World" 7). McCarthy's boyhood friend Jerry Anderson believes that some of the book's details and incidents reflect the adolescent experiences of McCarthy and himself with two other friends, Hugh Winkler and Jerry Reed. He recalled that "on one occasion, the boys were roaming a thicket of honeysuckle when they spotted a green-striped frog, a turtle, and a pit four feet deep and bottomed with green slime[, which] had been excavated so as to allow the orchard's caretakers a natural vat for mixing insecticides" (Gibson 26). On Neubert Springs Road, not far from the McCarthy house, stood a country store built in the early 1900s. "According to locals, a boarder who roomed with a boy named Warn Smith and his mother would come into Doyle's store once a week, on Fridays, remove his socks and buy a new pair to last him for seven days more, just as Marion Sylder does" (Arnold, "World" 5). Other nearby locations that figure in the book are Bay's Mountain Road, where Constable Jefferson Gifford lives, and the Green Fly Inn, reputed to have been on Brown Mountain (Arnold, "World" 5; Gibson 26). Indeed, in a tour Wesley Morgan conducted for the 2004 Cormac McCarthy Society's conference in Knoxville, he demonstrated that much of the activity in and around Red Branch in *The Orchard Keeper* can be superimposed on the actual roadways and terrains near McCarthy's home. Like John Wesley's, McCarthy's boyhood activities in this environ included hunting and trapping, sleeping on the screened porch in summer, and escaping the house at night to roam the countryside. And his next-door neighbor, Homer Garland Winkler, who was probably the father of McCarthy's friend Hugh, sometimes took young Cormac hunting with him, accompanied by his dogs Buster and Scout (Arnold, "World" 4–5; "Winkler, Homer").[2]

Consuming the Wilderness: *Dispossessing the Mountain People*

In his essay "Commercial and Industrial Trends since 1865," local historian C. P. White identifies four phenomena that by the mid–twentieth century had made the greatest impact on the economy of Knox County and East Tennessee: the opening of the Alcoa Aluminum plant fifteen miles south of Knoxville near Maryville; the establishment of the Great Smoky Mountains National Park in southern Blount and Sevier counties; the advent of the TVA, headquartered in Knoxville; and the development of atomic energy facilities at Oak Ridge northwest of Knoxville in Roane and Anderson counties (224). Of these four factors, the first three had an immediate effect on Blount County. Characteristically McCarthy makes no fictional use of the particular industrial company, Alcoa, but *The Orchard Keeper* alludes pointedly to the other two: the national park and the TVA. Indeed Blount County's economic history and the drastic changes that wrenched East Tennessee into the modern world lie behind much of the novel's depiction of the conflict between the mountain culture and the progressive order. In 1946, two years before John Wesley's return to Red Branch, Harvey Broome wrote that the entire history of the white settlement of the area, "from the rude palisading at Fort Loudoun to the radioactive piles at Oak Ridge," had occurred within a mere nineteen decades: "Few regions, anywhere, have moved so rapidly from primitive conditions. When Knox County was organized this was a land of primeval forests, of high barrier mountains, and of unbridged rivers with almost impassable shoals. . . . Scarcely more than one hundred years ago, the people were burning coal for the first time; ninety years ago they were witnessing the arrival of the first train. . . . Fifty years ago horse-cars were plying the streets of Knoxville. Thirty years back the County was pouring rock into the mud and mire of its roads to make way for the automobile; and only twenty years ago, the County Court was first extolling the glories of the Great Smoky Mountains" (359). When they moved from the Northeast in 1937, the McCarthy family was part of the new order of outsiders arriving in East Tennessee to marshal in abrupt modernization, and young Cormac (or Charlie, as his family and friends called him then) observed first-hand the developments of the final decade Broome addresses and absorbed at second hand the reminiscences of the older residents who had lived through more of this change.

Arthur Ownby, born in 1857 or '58, remembers eight of these decades. His history captures indirectly much of the fate of both the mountain dwellers and the forested wilderness of Blount County in the late nineteenth and early twentieth centuries; and the economic history of the region goes far toward illuminating the antinomian attitudes of Ownby and Sylder. Donald Edward Davis's environmental history of the southern mountains offers a particularly relevant discussion of the post–Civil War period of land speculation in the southern Appalachians, when "politicians, businessmen, and prominent journalists promoted the region as a New South mecca, encouraging northern capitalists to exploit the mountains' remaining mineral and timber reserves" (163). Less dispassionately, in his 1948 two-volume history of the Tennessee River, Donald Davidson, a Southern Agrarian, assessed what these "benevolent agents of Progress" meant to the traditional cultures of the South and revealed how they were viewed by some Tennesseans.[3] The northern capitalists were "subtle utopians . . . who came bringing plentiful cash or credit and often enough large funds of honest good will. Their great armies had ruined the country, but now, come to think about it, they did not hate the southern people. . . . They begged to be permitted to assist in the humane task of restoring the devastated regions. . . . While offering the genial right hand of fellowship and reconcilement, they thought it only common sense to point out that the rebuilding of railroads, the exploitation of mineral and timber rights, and the development of manufacturing might be so arranged as to confer mutual benefits" (2:147–48).

Before 1870, around Ownby's twelfth year, the remoteness of the area had discouraged lumber barons from venturing into the mountains of East Tennessee, but the advent of railroad lines there and the dwindling timber reserves in the North and the Midwest led to the era of industrial railroad logging, "the single greatest human activity to affect environmental and cultural change in the southern Appalachians" (Davis 165–66). The railroad logging industry, which would reach maturation by the 1880s, had already begun in the mid-1870s, when Arthur Ownby was a young man hoping to support a wife and baby on the way. He grew up in Tuckaleechee (59), one of the old coves in the mountainous region of eastern Blount County, just outside the Great Smoky Mountains National Park area and east of the "Harrykin" where Ownby plans to hide from the authorities. In the late nineteenth century, Tuckaleechee was the site of several prerailroad logging operations. Its locale was a practical one for logging before the advent of the railway because the timber could be floated down the Little River to mill at Rockford (Carberry, "Blount County" section). The Little River Lumber Company, an offshoot of a northern company, was chartered there in 1901, and it began buying timberland in both Blount and Sevier counties, ultimately obtaining over seventy thousand acres. The company was led by a powerful executive, Col. W. B. Townsend, who was "sent south to breathe life into the new enterprise." In 1903 Tuckaleechee was renamed Townsend for him, and it is still known by that name (*Gentle Winds* 114).[4] Associated with the lumber company was the Little River Railroad, chartered at the same time, which in 1903 began to construct rail connections to the Knoxville and Augusta Railroad not far away, in Walland, Tennessee (Carberry, "Blount County" section; *Gentle Winds* 118).

Thus Ownby's childhood home would not have become associated with industrial railroad logging until the early twentieth century, and it is not in Tuckaleechee but in nearby Wear's Valley in Sevier County that he works on a railroad crew in 1876 or '77, blasting into the mountains to construct railbeds (151). At the same time, he cultivates a little twenty-acre "side-hill" farm five miles west of Sevierville because neither occupation is very profitable (152).[5] Davis records that logging in the southern Appalachians offered at best subsistence wages. Although the national average was nearly 20 cents per hour, the average North Carolina logger worked a 62.7-hour week and earned only 12 cents an hour (177). Statistics for the Tennessee side of the mountains were likely similar, and Arthur's manual labor on the railroad that supports the logging endeavor cannot pay much more. One worker who cleared land for the railroad, Lemuel Ownby, a partial model for Arthur Ownby, recalled that his pay for each eleven-hour work day was a dollar and a half (Dumas, "Lem Ownby" 1:12).

As Davis shows, industrial railroad logging facilitated the harvesting of forests in areas previously untouched: "Narrow-gauge railroad beds . . . could now be laid along the contours of steep hillsides in places once thought inaccessible by lumbermen. From there, logs of all sizes were 'skidded' by cables across steep slopes to awaiting railroad cars for loading and transport. The end result was, in effect, a clear-cut since the skidded logs destroyed everything in their path" (168). In her 1955 book *The French Broad*, a popular history of the

French Broad River in Sevier County, Tennessee, and adjoining Buncombe County, North Carolina, Wilma Dykeman observes that clearing the land in the southern Appalachians had always been a wasteful "slaughter of the trees": "From days of the first ax-wielding settlers through . . . the arrival of the band sawmill and the really big operators, the policy has been almost completely one of cut out and get out" (255–56). But industrial railroad logging took clear-cutting to a larger scale and into more remote wilderness areas.

The clear-cutting and skid trails led to erosion and wildfires, to which sparks from the locomotives and brushpiles of logging refuse contributed. The erosion of the topsoil in logged areas reduced the amount of rainwater that could soak into the mountain soil, depleting the water tables, drastically increasing runoff, and aggravating flooding (Davis 168–69). And of course the deforestation, worsened by the devastating chestnut blight, an imported disease that hit the Smoky Mountains by the 1920s, constituted extensive destruction of wildlife habitats. The blight was so rampant that by 1940 virtually all the American chestnuts in the entire Appalachian chain were dead or diseased (Davis 193–94)—a reality reflected in the "barren" chestnuts of *The Orchard Keeper* (172). Thus after Ownby has struggled to the crest of Chilhowee Mountain in the spring of 1941, he rests against the trunk of a "broken chestnut the color of stone," the sole tree in a field of sedge, not spared the blight even in its isolation from other trees (190). The loss of habitat resulting from logging industry practices and careless international trade lies behind the declining numbers of mink, muskrats, and panthers noticed by John Wesley and Ownby as well as their abiding perception of a diminished world.

Although it introduced an industrial economy to the mountains, the railroad work itself was conducted in rather primitive fashion. Dykeman writes that "it was work done by hand and sweat and, yes, even blood. There was no machinery. . . . There were only heavy picks swung in a rhythm of near desperation, shovels loading leaden masses of Appalachian mud, and horses and mules straining under the long haul of the wagons. Even the dynamite was homemade. All the drilling of rock was done by hand, and sometimes the old pioneer method of fire and water (fire built on rock to heat it, then doused with cold water to make it crack) was used" (*French* 161). The hard and primitive nature of his labor against the land may initially blind young Arthur Ownby to the fact that his attempt to support his family by working for the railroad implicates him in the progressive destruction of the wilderness. But Arthur soon comes to recognize and regret his participation in this assault that had far-reaching effects not only on the land and wildlife but also on the human culture of the region, culminating in the mountain folks' loss of their "semi-agrarian and intimately forest-dependent way of life" (Davis 198). "By the end of the Great Depression," Davis writes in his final summation of the effects of industrial railroad logging, "farmers had, in many ways, become less rather than more self-sufficient, causing many residents to leave their marginal farms for logging or coal camps or migrate into neighboring towns and cities where textile mills and tanneries had begun to dominate the local economy" (205). Among the changes were a move toward monoculture among those who continued to farm and a reduction in family size (Davis 197). Further, as Dykeman writes,

> The rails were laid, leading almost like the tracks of some animate monster, both into and out of isolation.
>
> Now the tallow candles on mountain tables could give way to oil lamps, New England factory cloth—gingham and muslin and percale—could replace rough linsey-woolsey, and the expansive agents for sewing machines and organs, lightning rods and enlarged pictures, would travel over the watershed, penetrating creeks and coves with their own particular symptom of "civilization." (*French* 164)

K. Wesley Berry rightly points out that the mail-order or store purchases of the novel's characters reflect this new dependence on manufactured goods and consumption of processed foods (52). Sylder buys his boots from a catalogue and wears a pair of store-bought socks for a week, then burns and replaces them, signaling his involvement in the new, throw-away culture. "Looms and spinning wheels largely became things of the past," Davis writes (197)—a phenomenon that figures in *The Orchard Keeper*. In the attic of the Rattners' old log house was a loom, but since East Tennessee families no longer make their own clothing, they have burned it as firewood (62).

The resulting changes in home-building techniques and materials are also reflected in the novel. The ancient but still sound log house in which the Rattners settle persists as a reminder of the passing mountain way of life. Its logs are "hand-squared and chinked with clay, the heavy rafters in the loft pinned with wooden pegs." The structure is reputed to be "the oldest house in the county," yet its rafters still exhibit "a yellow newness," and only its roof shakes fail to contribute to the dwelling's overall appearance of being "impervious to weather and time" (62–63). But this log house seems unique in Red Branch of the 1930s and early '40s. Due to the logging industry, "'Boxed' houses—that is, frameless structures made exclusively with sawn planks and boards—gradually replaced log cabins as residents working seasonally for lumber companies had less time and help to build traditional log homes" (Davis 197). And with the advent of the steam-powered sawmills early in the twentieth century, the availability of sawn lumber accelerated the transition away from log structures (Shields 58, photo caption). The boxed house has become the new norm in Red Branch. Accommodating Increase Tipton's clan are the "jerrybuilt shacks" he constructs with Sylder's help. In contrast to the Rattners' log dwelling, these more modern houses are "endowed with an air transient and happenstantial as if set there by the recession of floodwaters. Even the speed with which they were constructed could not outdistance the decay for which they held such affinity" (11). Old as it is, the "box-shaped" Green Fly Inn also lacks the stability of the log house, which does not creak in the wind. Nailed to a tree, the saloon sways with each gust, impressing the drinkers with its "precariousness" (12–13). And Ownby's loss of his earlier way of life is hinted in his already shabby boxed cabin in Red Branch, "a small board shack with the laths curling out like hair awry, bleached to a metal-gray" and missing a front step (56). When John Wesley revisits the log house in the novel's final chapter, he finds that the wind has finally invaded this solid structure through its broken windows and its fallen roof shakes. This once-impervious shelter, emblem of the mountaineers' vanished way of life, no longer shelters any human and seems in a limited way to be returning to nature. When John Wesley acknowledges that "it was never his house anyway," he alludes not only to his family's status as squatters but also to his recognition that he was born too late to have inherited the way of life once known by Ownby, the forest-dependent life of the mountaineers for which he feels such affinity (244).

In his classic 1913 description of the mountain culture of North Carolina and Tennessee, *Our Southern Highlanders*, Horace Kephart wrote that in the "snort" of the logging train he could hear the death knell of the mountain environment and the culture of the mountain people:

> Slowly, but inexorably, a leviathan was crawling into the wilderness and was soon to consume it.
>
> "All this," I apostrophized, "shall be swept away, tree and plant, beast and fish. . . . The simple-hearted native men and women will scatter and disappear. In their stead will come slaves speaking strange tongues.
> . . . Let me not see it! No; I will
>
> > "Get me to some far-off land
> > Where higher mountains under heaven stand . . .
> > Where other thunders roll amid the hills,
> > Some mightier wind a mightier forest fills
> > With other strains through other-shapen boughs."
> > (104–5)

Kephart's prophecy and lament echo eerily in *The Orchard Keeper*, both in Ownby's desire to retreat to the mountains to escape the agents of modernity and in the lament of the "narrator," John Wesley, for the vanquished mountain people in the closing frame.

It had begun in the 1880s, in a time of peace, but industrial railroad logging eventually became part of "war's machinery," "disinherit[ing]" the mountain people, to quote *Cities of the Plain* (204), the third novel of McCarthy's post-nuclear Border Trilogy. According to Davis, despite growing recognition of the ecological damage it caused, railroad logging increased during World War I, peaking just after 1920, and the postwar building boom kept the demand for timber high. Such war-driven demand motivated the industry to press into even the most remote areas of the mountains. These outposts of remaining wilderness, the "higher mountains" for which Kephart yearns, were, Davis writes, "in effect" the Great Smoky Mountains, where over two billion board feet of lumber were harvested from 1900 to 1938 (Davis 172), a year that mediates between the end of Section I and the beginning of Section II of *The Orchard Keeper*.

Logging in the Great Smoky Mountains is intimately connected with the creation of the national park there, and the history of the park further illuminates Ownby's stance with regard to government and the modern world. The park movement began at a local level in 1923 with the efforts of Knoxville businessman Willis P. Davis and his wife, state congresswoman Ann Davis, who were prompted by their desire to preserve the natural beauty of the mountains and protect the remaining virgin timberlands from logging (Campbell 6, 13–14). But Carlos C. Campbell pointed out that at that time few in Knoxville were aware of the appeal of the wilderness area near their city (13), and it seems clear from all accounts that much of the support for the park movement in Knoxville was engendered through economic arguments. Soon many influential businesspeople in the urban center added their voices, so much so that in his interpretation of Knoxville history, William J. MacArthur Jr., asserted in a rather celebratory tone, "In many ways the park seems to have been the creation of Knoxville's commercial-civic elite" (55). He pointed out that the movement had substantial support in the newspapers and among civic leaders. In his early, extended history of the park movement, Campbell, himself manager of the Knoxville Chamber of Commerce during the early years of the park movement, chronicled in a self-effacing way the involvement of that body in the creation of the park.[6] Under his management, among other initiatives, the Chamber of Commerce raised funds to bring state legislators and officials to see at first hand the attractions of the park region (32). Campbell's account reveals the complicated mixture of motives that drove the park movement in Knoxville: the promise of economic development in the urban area that would accrue from the creation of the park, the desire to preserve the natural environment that had already been endangered by the logging industry, and also to a lesser degree, the hope to preserve East Tennessee's "pioneer history" (16).

Except for those individuals who had financial interests in logging and preferred to see the area designated a national forest, which would have favored
continued commercial harvesting of timber, the Knoxville "elite was united in
support of the project which became the basis of East Tennessee's tourist industry and ultimately paid the city's businesses great dividends" (MacArthur 56).
In the park-versus-forest debate, Colonel David C. Chapman, who emerged as
the local park movement's chief spokesman, argued that neither "advertising,"
nor "prestige," nor the requisite profit would come from yet a third national
forest in East Tennessee (Dunn 242). The development of a national park, on
the other hand, would bring tourism dollars to Knoxville and the area. As
Campbell put it in the 1960s,

> Park advocates . . . predicted that the national park would soon provide
> a still greater dollars-and-cents value [than would a national forest]. After
> decades of hindsight, it is easy to see that, although the aesthetic facet of
> the Great Smokies remains the most important consideration, the national
> park also has a far greater economic value than a national forest could
> have provided.
>
> A national forest is a high-character commercial enterprise. A national
> park is essentially a cultural agency, with incidental but important eco-
> nomic benefits. (56)

Members of the Knoxville elite, organized as the Great Smoky Mountains Con-
servation Association, approached the Southern Appalachian National Park
Committee, urging it to consider the Tennessee side of the Great Smoky
Mountains for its proposed park in addition to the several locations in North
Carolina it had already planned to study (Broome 356; Campbell 16, 22–23).
These citizens also proposed legislation and raised money for the purchase of
the required lands. Durwood Dunn's study of the Cades Cove community,
which was taken over by the park, looks at the history from the very different
perspective of the mountaineers who were dispossessed by its creation. Yet he
agrees that the impetus behind the park's formation came largely from influential Knoxville businessmen, who, while they may have had a genuine conservationist interest in the project, also anticipated that it would promote the
economic development of East Tennessee through tourism, which would lead
to commercial profits for Knoxville. Dunn writes that the potential for substantial profit was a key selling point in the promotional literature soliciting
private donations for the purchase of land for the park.

As Roderick Nash observes in *Wilderness and the American Mind*, "The laws
creating National Parks and Monuments deliberately left the way open for the
construction of roads and tourist accommodations" (222). The missions of a
park, as established by the National Park Service Act of 1916, were not only to

preserve nature but to facilitate human recreation, an uneasy mixture of goals that adumbrated the more recent debate between bio-centric and anthropo-centric approaches to wilderness management. In his 1960 history, Campbell observed that the national park system served "both aesthetic and economic values," noting that the federal parks drew more than 150 million tourists each year and that seventy-four million dollars were expended annually to develop park facilities "so that they may be enjoyed without damage to their primeval character" (1). Although it may seem naive from today's ecological perspective, Campbell and, one gathers, the fellow park promoters for whom he spoke, endorsed the National Park Service's goal of providing "enjoyment without impairment": "The national parks are developed so as to permit their use and enjoyment without destroying their original splendor or historic values" (Campbell 10). Campbell's stance is consistent with Nash's observation that "in general before 1960 the national parks leaned toward anthropocentrism. Hotels were built, roads extended, trails improved, toilets provided, and lakes stocked with fish—all in the name of aiding the recreating public in its pursuit of what the 1916 act called 'enjoyment'" (325–26).

For this public good—conservation, development, tourism, and profit—to come into being, the privately owned lands within the proposed park bound-aries had to be acquired. By 1930, according to Davis, industrial interests held fully 62 percent of the privately owned timberlands in the entire Appalachian range (176). But the statistics are even higher for the area that would become the Great Smoky Mountains National Park, where 18 pulpwood and lumber companies held 85 percent of the acreage (Campbell 12). Of the land in Blount County, only 15 percent was still virgin, untouched by logging (*History of Blount County* 9). But, as Campbell wrote, one third of the entire 515,226-acre park tract, which included the higher elevations in Sevier County, could still be con-sidered "primeval forest"; some of the rest had been subjected to selective har-vesting; and much of the remainder was in various stages of reforestation (12). The initial part of the acquisition process involved buying some of these large tracts from the lumber companies. In 1925 state legislator Ann Davis intro-duced a bill authorizing the state's initial purchase of land for the park—the 76,507-acre tract owned by the Little River Lumber Company—contingent on Knoxville's contribution of one third of the price (Campbell 31–33; MacArthur 55). Soon after, the city council agreed to issue bonds for this purpose (MacArthur 55). However, the terms of the agreement allowed the Little River Lumber Company rights to harvest trees of over ten inches in diameter for a period of fifteen years after the sale, a controversial provision that led the edi-tor of the *Knoxville News*, Edward J. Meeman, to criticize the park movement's leaders in a series of editorials and to rechristen the Great Smoky Mountains Conservation Association the "Conservation-with-an-Axe Association." The contract was also problematic because the Department of the Interior would not accept as part of the park those acres on which logging was still under way. The association defended its decision by arguing that insufficient funds were available to buy the timber rights from the company and that the success of the park movement depended on this large early land acquisition. Meeman eventually accepted this as a necessary tradeoff and continued to support the park movement. Nevertheless, the cutting of timber on these lands remained a sore point among park supporters, especially when it was reported that the company was clear-cutting in some areas. Finally the Conservation Association again made a tradeoff, returning some of the land to the Little River Lumber Company in exchange for timber rights on 3,300 acres and a sixty-five-acre tract at Elkmont. The company ceased harvesting in 1938 (Campbell 48–49, 72–74).

Despite these problems, promoters of the endeavor spread "the park gospel far and wide" and raised over three hundred thousand dollars in contributions within Tennessee, mostly from Knoxville (MacArthur 56). The state passed its definitive park bill in 1927 (Campbell, 54; Dunn 243), creating a Park Commission of seven members, mostly from the communities of East Tennessee (Campbell 52–54). The commission received power to condemn property for the park since it was considered "impractical to buy so much land as was required . . . without the right to condemn any tracts for which the asking price was too high" (Campbell 52–53). So the efforts to buy the park land pushed forward. This required the purchase of 6,600 individual parcels in North Carolina and Tennessee, most of them small lots and summer residences, with about 1,200 farms (Campbell 12). Half the funds came from the Laura Spelman Rockefeller Memorial Foundation, and the other half was made up of contributions from the citizens of Tennessee, North Carolina, and other states (Campbell 61; *History of Blount County* 9). By 1931 the 150,000 contiguous acres required for the National Park Service to assume administrative responsibility had been deeded to the federal government, and the Maryville Post Office housed the park's headquarters briefly before they were moved to Gatlinburg (Broome 355–56; *History of Blount County* 9; Campbell 97). In 1933 President Roosevelt allocated over 1.5 million dollars of Public Works monies to acquire the necessary acreage to develop the park facilities (Broome 356; Campbell 117, 119–20), and the United States Congress officially approved the park on June 15, 1934 (*History of Blount County* 9; Campbell 138).

The experience of the people who would eventually be displaced by the park through the intervention of neighboring Knoxville's business interests, the states of Tennessee and North Carolina, and the federal government can be appreciated through the example of Cades Cove, a historic farming community of about six hundred residents not far southwest of Tuckaleechee Cove in Blount County, and which became one of the 251 "ghost towns" within the park's borders (*History of Blount County* 9–10; Dunn 251). The history of Cades Cove is invoked in *The Orchard Keeper* through its references to the Tiptons. Tennessee issued the first land grant in Cades Cove, for 640 acres, to William "Fighting Billy" Tipton, a veteran of the American Revolution, in 1821, and he sold parcels of the grant to family and friends who settled there (*History of Blount County* 10; Shields 68). The Tipton family remained prominent in Cades Cove into the twentieth century (Shields 68–70), and people named Tipton sold at least seven parcels of land for the creation of the Great Smoky Mountains National Park (Shields, Appendix B). The presence in Red Branch of Increase Tipton, who rapidly throws up cabins for his extended family in 1929, of Sylder's friend June Tipton, and of John Wesley's provocative acquaintance Wanita Tipton are thus understated reminders of the displacement of Cades Cove people into other parts of the county.

Initially, outsiders' interest in developing a national park was not entirely unwelcome to the people of the Smoky Mountain coves. They too hoped the park would increase tourism and improve transportation. Some, such as John Oliver of Cades Cove, also hoped that the park would bring an end to the destructive logging practices of the Little River Lumber Company and the resulting forest fires and erosion. But Cades Cove residents did not at first anticipate what Dunn calls the "death by eminent domain" that was to destroy their mountain community (ch. 10). They expected to stay in their homes even though it quickly became clear that Cades Cove would be within the boundaries of the park, and this expectation was encouraged by Knoxville Chamber of Commerce manager and Park Commissioner Carlos C. Campbell, Senator Lawrence D. Tyson, Governor Austin Peay and other park promoters, who assured them between 1923 and 1927—sometimes publicly—that their farms would not be taken (Dunn 243–46). As late as 1926, Governor Peay told the worried citizens of Elkmont, "'As long as I am a member of the Park Commission . . . I wish to assure these people that there will be no condemnation of their homes.' Such evictions 'for the pleasure and profit of the rest of the state . . . would be a blot upon the state that the barbarism of the Huns could not match'" (quoted in Dunn 247; see also Campbell 105). Dunn believes that such public assurances "lulled [Cades Cove residents] into a false sense of security" but that their hope to save their cove was doomed by 1927, when the state's General Assembly passed its appropriations bill creating the Park Commission. Cades Cove had missed the chance seized by some larger communities, including Townsend in Tuckaleechee Cove, Walland, Wear's Valley, and others, to campaign to keep their coves outside of the boundaries of the park; given Cades Cove's location in the interior of the proposed park area, such protest would not have availed in any case (Dunn 246–47).

As the Park Commission stepped up its efforts to buy the farms of Cades Cove, the reactions of residents varied, some selling readily enough, most reluctantly facing removal. Campbell argued that the very promotional materials that aroused interest in preserving the area as a park gave residents an exaggerated sense of the value of their property. Thus the commissioners found that in order to buy at "reasonable prices" they had to persuade owners that "their mountain land was relatively worthless for other purposes" (19). This was a hard sell, since the land held familial and cultural value for those whose kin had lived for generations on the same farms. But the Park Commission was powerful and persistent, doggedly fighting many condemnation battles in the courts (Campbell 97). One by one, the properties came into the fold. Dunn writes, "A pervasive feeling of helplessness in light of the coercive power of eminent domain seemed to preclude any effective community opposition. Who could withstand the power of the state or federal government?" (247–48). Blount County had been a Republican stronghold during the Civil War and remained so through the Depression years and Roosevelt's New Deal (Tennessee Historical Records Survey 12). Residents' sense of confusion and betrayal over their dispossession was exacerbated by the threat now confronting their community and long-established way of life from "their own beloved federal government! For the first time in anyone's experience, loyalty to the cove community was directly at odds with loyalty to the United States" (Dunn 248). East Tennesseeans' bewildered disaffection from the federal government over their eviction, combined with their longstanding bitterness against federal alcohol regulation and taxation and the cultural disruptions brought about by the federally mandated Tennessee Valley Authority, quietly echoes in Warn Pulliam's comment to his friends that their region used to be "the North" (145), and it underlies the attitudes promoting resistance to the new order in Ownby, Sylder, and finally John Wesley.

In 1927 John Oliver and a few other Cades Cove inhabitants began a letter-writing campaign in protest, but this was met with denial that the community had been designated for takeover. Ultimately Oliver, a descendent of William Tipton (Campbell 98), decided that he would take his protest to the courts. According to Dunn, "The critical issue . . . was whether one sovereignty, the state of Tennessee, could exercise the power of eminent domain to secure land for the public use of another sovereignty, the federal government" (249). Campbell, on the other hand, characterized the dispute as predominantly a matter of purchase price, complicated because Oliver, "a man of deep religious and moral convictions, bitterly resented the fact that a certain land-buyer who was personally objectionable to him had been assigned to work in the Cove" (98). The proceedings to determine the legality of the state's seizure of private lands were complex and went through appeals before the Tennessee Supreme Court, but the question was finally settled in favor of the state in 1932, a decision that gave the Park Commission the go-ahead to seize other lands in Cades Cove. Oliver struggled on, contesting the state's valuation of his property in further legal proceedings, but the larger battle was already lost.

Unlike Oliver many residents did not contest the value placed on their lands, and in return for selling below the appraised value they were allowed to lease their homesteads or were granted permission to continue living on them (Campbell 70; Dunn 251). However, the Park Commission had overstepped its authority in making such promises, which were not legally binding on the National Park Service (Dunn 251). Finally, then, most families were displaced in the middle of the Depression years, the years of section I of *The Orchard Keeper*. Many, like the Tiptons who resettle in Red Branch, had been relocated by 1934, and the twenty-one households remaining in Cades Cove were warned that they must move by January 1, 1936, or be evicted. Eventually twelve families were in fact permitted to stay on as lessees, but the experience left a legacy of bitterness about "broken promises" and "the destruction of their community" (Dunn 253).[7] Given the economic condition of the country and of the county, the timing of the removals was disastrous for the displaced families. As Dunn explains: "The economy throughout Blount County and East Tennessee was collapsing by 1930. Unemployment was rising at a catastrophic rate; a more hostile or unwelcome environment for newcomers could scarcely be imagined. Not only were most cove families unable to re-create their prosperous farms, but in their new homes they were now scattered and isolated from their former neighbors and friends. . . . Finally, many banks to which cove people entrusted money from their farms collapsed in 1932–33. Especially devastating was the failure of First National Bank in Maryville in January 1933" (251–52).

One of the men who resisted displacement from his ancestral land was Lemuel Ownby, known as "Uncle Lem," who was ninety-five years old when he died in 1984. Ownby was born in Elkmont on Jakes Creek, in Sevier County. Two years later his family moved to the farm two miles away where he lived the rest of his life (Dumas, "Lem Ownby" 1:12). In his final decade and a half Ownby was well known in East Tennessee and beyond as the last leaseholder still living within the Great Smoky Mountains National Park. Numerous newspaper articles about Ownby—interviews with photographs of him—appeared throughout the East Tennessee region in the 1970s and '80s.[8] He was a raconteur who recalled the old times in East Tennessee, and among his stories were memories of White Cap Bob Catlett and of a logging train wreck that killed engineer Daddy Bryson—tales that resonate with McCarthy's southern novels (Dumas, "Lem Ownby" 1:12).

Like most men of the East Tennessee coves, Ownby was a farmer. He cultivated his hilly land with horses and oxen and raised cattle following the old practice of herding them up to the mountain balds to graze in the summer and bringing them down in the fall ("We Just Pass" 3; Brewer, "This Is Your Community" F1). Ownby's eyesight, which was always poor, kept him from enlisting in World War I ("We Just Pass" 3). In the 1920s he farmed during the growing season and worked as a lumberman for the Little River Lumber Company's operation in Elkmont in fall and winter (Brewer, "This Is Your Community" F1; Dumas, "Lem Ownby" 1:12), but he told one reporter that he had been "here before the lumber company even thought about being" (Wilkinson A9). Among his first logging assignments was clearing trees for the railroad line that connected the lumber company to Knoxville. He also drove the ox teams that dragged the logs to the rail docks for loading on flatcars (Dumas, "Lem Ownby" 1:12).

In 1933 the park commission offered Ownby the options of selling his forty-four-acre farm or deeding it to the park and staying for the rest of his natural life.[9] According to one feature writer, "He didn't like either option. But Lem had no real choice. 'They lawed me,' he recalled, the edge in his voice betraying an old bitterness" (McKamey C1). Ownby chose to stay, selling his land for less than it was worth to ensure that he could do so (Brewer, "Last Smokies" B2).

But his life changed even so. During World War II, his last remaining neighbors moved away and he was forced to close the log grist mill his father had built because he could not acquire lumber to repair it; and when the park prohibited cattle-grazing on the mountain balds, he gave up raising them (Brewer, "This Is Your Community" F1; McKamey C1). His freedom to hunt bear had been curtailed as early as 1931, when the Park Service assumed administration of the Great Smoky Mountains (Wilkinson A9; Campbell 97). Although his grape vines and the few apple trees in front of his house were still fruitful in 1982, his apple orchard had ceased producing by then (McKnight). But he continued to keep chickens and raise tobacco until he became too old to do the work (Wilkinson A9; Brewer, "This Is Your Community" F1). And fulfilling his namesake Arthur Ownby's wish, he raised bees and sold honey—often to tourists who stumbled upon his homestead while hiking in the park and who returned later to buy more and to listen to stories of his life (McKnight; Brewer, "This Is Your Community" F1). At one time, following a family tradition, he managed nearly one hundred and fifty hives, but in the last decades of his life he kept fewer (Brewer, "Last Smokies" B2).

Lemuel Ownby's house was a mountain cabin made not of logs but of board and batten. When Carson Brewer described it in January 1973, the exterior was "an aged natural gray." In the center of the interior room that functioned as both living room and bedroom stood a big Warm Morning iron stove (Brewer, "This Is Your Community" F1; Jenkins), for which Ownby chopped the kindling (Dumas, "Lem Ownby" 1:12).[10] The stove was a concession to modern convenience, but "a creek rock chimney, daubbed [*sic*] with red clayish mud . . . [gave] evidence of a fireplace" (McKnight). The house had one electric light, installed after World War II (Dumas, "Lem Ownby" 1:12), but Ownby still kept kerosene lamps "filled and ready to burn" (McKnight).

Like McCarthy's Arthur, Lemuel Ownby remained remarkably strong even as he aged. The approach to his house was steep and rocky, but when he climbed it "in the old days," he told Wilkinson, "I used to carry 100 pounds up on my back without stopping. I couldn't carry near' that much today." However, when a friend commented, "I bet you could if it was something you really needed," he did not dispute this and appeared pleased (Wilkinson A9). He remained self-reliant throughout his life. "'I never was on relief,' he said proudly, 'and I never went hungry'" (McKamey C1). "I don't have anything against relief for folks who need it," he told another reporter, "but I never thought I needed it and I sure wouldn't have taken it" ("We Just Pass" 3). Arthur Ownby shares this perspective.

Lemuel Ownby married late in life and explained that he thought it wise to wait to marry "till we had good sense" (Wilkinson A9). Unlike Arthur, Lemuel had a happy marriage that lasted forty-three years until the death of his wife Gemima—"Mymie"—in 1968 (Brewer, "This Is Your Community" F1; Fields, "Lifetime"). After Mymie's death, Ownby lived alone in the mountains with his dogs for company. Hikers would drop in, and friends and relatives would check on him and deliver things he needed. He became legendary. According to one obituary, he had received visits from reporters as far away as New York (Dumas, "Fabled"). He was slowly going blind, but he did not choose to live anywhere else. When he had to stay in a Knoxville hospital for a short time, he couldn't drink the water, and he asked a friend to bring some from his own spring. Late in his life, a nephew lived in a trailer on his property and looked after him (Dumas, "Fabled"). But in 1973 Brewer recorded the impression Ownby made on visitors when he was still relatively independent: "Lem has lived alone, with the sounds of the creek, the bees, the ticking of the old clock, birdsong, the roosters crowing" ("This Is Your Community" F1).

Ownby was remembered not only for his keeping alive an older, forgotten way of life but also for his resistance to government. As neighborly as he usually was, he refused to see two justices of the United States Supreme Court, Harry Blackmun and Potter Stewart, when they were in the area for a legal conference in Gatlinburg. "I don't want to talk to them. Let them go back to Washington," he called through the door to embarrassed Knoxville lawyer Foster Arnett, who had escorted them to Ownby's cabin. When Arnett returned the following week, Ownby demanded to know if the "fellers from Washington" were with him before he would join him in his yard ("94-year-Old"

C12). "Intelligent and alert to the end," Jim Dumas wrote in his 1984 obituary, "Ownby had set views and never hesitated to tell all who listened—in the set ways of his long life, that politicians could not be trusted. Probably the last to hear Ownby's outspoken belief that public officials elected to high office, left less than honest, was Gov. Lamar Alexander who stopped by Lem's cabin recently to help build up the Park's 50th Anniversary. 'I ain't heard nothing on you yet,' Ownby told Alexander in the presence of stunned listeners" ("Fabled"). Alexander took this in good humor, retelling the story in a statement about Ownby on the occasion of his death in which he remarked that Ownby was "a link with what makes East Tennessee special" (Brewer, "Last Smokies" B2). Similar impulses to mythologize the evicted mountain dwellers were evident two decades earlier, just two years before the publication of *The Orchard Keeper*, when Assistant Park Superintendent David deL. Condon asserted that "although their homes are gone from within [the park's] boundaries, [they] have left behind them an aura of mystery and a lore and history of outstanding appeal" (57).

The TVA: *Eviction in the Valley*

The United States Congress approved the act creating the Tennessee Valley Authority, a governmental corporation, in May 1933, just about the time when the Rattner family moves to Red Branch, and when the development of the Great Smoky Mountains National Park was moving forward. This New Deal program of unprecedented scope and power was to coordinate regional planning for the entire Tennessee River Valley, from Knoxville to Paducah, Kentucky, where the Tennessee joins the Ohio River. Flood control and the river's transformation into a navigation channel of still lakes via dams and locks were two of its chief objectives. The dam system would also provide hydroelectric power to run TVA facilities, and the legislation authorized the TVA to sell the surplus to customers in the region (Davidson 2:217–19). The availability of electricity would promote industrial development throughout the valley, it was thought, although by 1976 no such industrial boom had been stimulated in Knoxville itself (MacArthur, 61, 63). Also in the initiating legislation was the charge to manufacture nitrate fertilizer in factories that would be refitted to make explosives in wartime. Further, the bill called for TVA oversight of "proper use of marginal lands, reforestation, and economic and social well-being" (Davidson 2:219). Thus, according to skeptic Donald Davidson, the TVA was apparently given broad powers to "take notice of any item of valley life that could be included under the term 'general welfare' or 'physical, economic, and social development'" (Davidson 2:220). The actual extent of the TVA's authority would be worked out gradually in a series of hearings and court cases, but the agency was a powerful force introduced from outside the

region that would profoundly recast the lives of the valley residents. In Knoxville, where the agency would soon move its headquarters from Muscle Shoals,
Alabama, the TVA brought more dramatic change than the Depression itself.
According to local historian William J. MacArthur, Jr., "The economic cata-
clysm . . . did not destroy the economic base of Knoxville, although the demise
of some businesses was certainly sped by the Depression. With no single industry to be affected, the city probably felt the national disaster no more than
other places. The great effect of the Depression on Knoxville was the rise of
the federal government's activities in the area" (60–61). As an attorney for the
TVA, McCarthy's father was a participant in the changes it wrought.

Local histories laud the economic benefits the TVA brought to East Tennessee, some of which were apparent almost immediately. With the construction of Norris Dam just north of Knoxville from 1933 to 1936 (Davis 184),
recent "high school and college graduates from Tennessee were hired by the
authority at a time when jobs were almost unobtainable, and the TVA money
tempered the wind in various ways to many Depression-stricken Knoxvillians"
(MacArthur 62). Although questions were raised about whether it was appropriate for the federal government to own public power facilities, local people
took a pragmatic approach: "Not too many people bothered whether the water
behind the dams was constitutional or not, or whether it was public water or
private, or even New Deal water. They quickly found that it would support a
boat and that the fish that swam therein were immune to ideologies, if not to
lures. They found that the triple phosphate produced at Muscle Shoals would
add fertility to their soil; that the power would flow out along the lines to the
farms, and that it would reduce aluminum to go into bombers. The [*sic*] found
that the dams would hold back floods from saint and sinner, employer and
employee, white, black, Republican and Democrat" (Broome 357).

The TVA issued glowing reports of its successes, but some local people
resented the changes and could not view the agency, with its agenda of mod-
ernizing the region, as a savior. Southern Agrarian Donald Davidson speaks for
the less articulate Tennesseeans whose lives and traditional culture were forever altered by its programs. Like the history of industrial railroad logging and
the eviction of the cove residents for the formation of the Great Smoky Mountains National Park, dissenting attitudes such as those Davidson expresses about
the TVA illuminate Arthur Ownby's resistance to government. First of all, with
the advent of the TVA, Republican East Tennessee found itself facing dramatic
federal intrusion from a Democratic regime after a period of sixty years of
mostly Republican control of the federal government (Davidson 2:222). Suddenly it was on the receiving end of unprecedented "hunks of favor" from the
"Democratic pork barrel," social welfare it had not requested and perhaps did
not feel it needed. In putting its programs into effect, the TVA worked closely

with local agencies, advising and prompting, but often letting the local agents work directly with valley residents in the hopes that they would be more sensitive to the values and assumptions of the people, and thus that the programs would be more readily accepted (Davidson 2:213).[11] But Ownby is hard pressed to understand the county social worker who is sent to evaluate him, and he complains that he "talks like a God-damned yankee" (219). It is not the young man's accent he means.

Even more troubling was that the TVA was free of state and local oversight and largely free of federal red tape as well. It could do pretty much whatever it thought wise without having to answer to the people it affected. Davidson writes, "The people of the valley, although ruled in certain ways by [the TVA's] three directors, could not elect them. . . . Nor could [they] . . . in any way control or influence the policies of TVA, except through the roundabout process of federal legislation" (2:221). Thus the TVA constituted a form of nonrepresentative and nonparticipatory governmental control imposed from above. Furthermore, in bringing its engineering and technological improvements to the river, the agency's directors "could change the natural environment to such an extent that the natural order might be deeply and even permanently affected; and in changing the natural order they might change the course of human life in the . . . Tennessee Valley" (Davidson 2:224). In Davidson's view, the TVA was "playing God" with the lives of the local people, full of the utopian zeal of its self-promotion as "uplifter" to a region it denigrated in "new legend[s]" of its "social depravity" and "economic bad habits" (2:224, 211). The arrogant certainty of the TVA, everywhere implied in Davidson's treatment, is reflected in the complacence and "infinite contempt" Ownby perceives in the "coldly gleaming" and "sinister" tank likely serving one of the TVA's engineering projects, erected and maintained by the federal government at the end of the orchard road (93). Davidson gives little credit to the TVA's attempts to be sensitive to local traditions and to deal compassionately with the pain its physical and social engineering brought to the valley, ridiculing its gestures toward tempering modernization with a stance of "cherish[ing] with fond care the individualism, the homeliness, the folkways, the crafts of the old time in Tennessee." Davidson implies that with characteristic hubris, the TVA thought that "it could do both" (2:231).

In fact the TVA's engineering decisions destroyed the farmlands of hundreds of families and permanently altered the traditional culture of the region. Its engineers debated between constructing a high-dam or a low-dam system on the river but finally chose the former because it would maximize production of cheap electricity (Davidson 2:236). But this marvel of engineering for flood control, navigation, and power production also flooded vast acres of the most fertile and prized farmland of the region and, like the Great Smoky

Mountains National Park, displaced thousands of people and their old cemeteries. With his typical irony, Davidson comments: "It was . . . too bad that, in
order to achieve flood control, they would have to create a permanent flood
in the valley itself—a permanent flood that would put the main river always
beyond its banks in the wide reservoir stretches and that would back far up into
smaller rivers and creeks—a permanent flood locked up under watchful eyes
and instruments" (Davidson 2:237). The plan was all the more acceptable to
the TVA because little industrial or transportation infrastructure would be
inundated. The burden would be borne primarily by small communities and
farmers. These losses "inflicted upon a sizable and innocent minority," Davidson comments, "weighed less in the TVA scales than the benefits that would
accrue, in terms of industrial and social engineering, to the nearby or the distant majority who sacrificed only tax money" (2:237–38). Together with the
national park, then, the construction of the TVA's high-dam system could be
seen as another way in which the nation and East Tennessee citizens partici-
pated in the offense that prompts Sylder's deepest scorn, that of *"sell[ing] . . .
[one's] own neighbors out for money"* (2 15).

By 1935, Congress mandated that the TVA construct a navigation channel
at least nine feet deep along the entire Tennessee River, a charge that committed the agency to developing its coordinated system of dams and locks (Davis
184). The first major project to be completed was Norris Dam above Knoxville
in 1936. Fort Loudoun Dam, which made a lake of the Knoxville waterfront,
was completed in September 1943—a decade before the time setting of *Suttree*
(Ezzell 110). By the end of the second world war, the TVA had built more than
a dozen dams (Davis 184), and by 1946, five years after the protagonists of *The
Orchard Keeper* are expelled from Red Branch, the agency owned or administered twenty-six dams in the Tennessee River watershed (Davidson 2:249). By
June of that year, "in the sixteen areas where it had erected high dams, TVA
had acquired, with easements and certain special purchases included, over
1,129,000 acres of land, or approximately one-twenty-third of the valley area"
and had moved 13,449 families, with another thousand still slated for removal.
Davidson claims that a conservative estimate would equate this to at least
72,000 individuals, at five members per family (Davidson 2:254–55), and Davis
sets the total number of evicted people at over eighty thousand (186).

The Norris Dam alone displaced three thousand families (fourteen thousand individuals) and over five thousand graves from the Cove Creek area
(Wilson 73; Davis 186). The TVA hired James W. Cooper as director of land
acquisition. He was uniquely qualified for the job because he also managed
land acquisition for the Great Smoky Mountains National Park as its leading
attorney until his death in 1942 (Wilson 29; Campbell 118, 128). But the chief
attorney responsible for processing the condemnation of these properties was

none other than Charles Joseph McCarthy, Sr. (Prather, "'Color of this life'" 32).[12] The TVA reported that only 5.4 percent of all its acquisitions as of 1946 were contested in court, a figure which, according to Davidson, the agency interpreted "to mean that the population in general considered [its] appraisal methods fair" (2:256). In his reminiscences of his work for the Authority, Marshall Wilson reports that at Norris Dam the TVA paid landowners slightly above market value for their property, "but that . . . included owners of small plots of little value, so poor that their opportunities for purchasing other decent homes were severely limited" (73). Davidson asserts that these land acquisitions constituted "forcible evictions," since if the landowner did not accept the TVA offer at the land's appraised value, the agency would initiate condemnation proceedings. "Tears might be shed, and angry words might be passed, but the only questions worth discussion were: How much will you pay? Where do we go next?" (2:256). Local county agents or TVA case workers such as Marshall Wilson arranged for the relocation of most families near their old farms or communities but on higher ground that had to be farmed differently than the fertile bottom land they had lost (Davidson 2:257). And at Norris Dam 41 percent of the displaced were "tenants or squatters who owned nothing that TVA would buy and were not eligible for any material assistance or compensation from TVA for their removal expenses nor their anguish, loss of time and opportunities" (Wilson 73).

By the mid-1940s, according to Davidson, "TVA had modernized a region scolded for its backwardness—had greened its fields [through its agricultural and erosion-control programs], put money in its pocket, taught it to fix itself up and behave." As a primary means to effecting these changes, the TVA "had tamed the Tennessee River, and in so doing had made the name of that river, the world over, a symbol of what technology might accomplish for man's material good" (2:270). But to Davidson and some residents of the valley, "the managed river . . . had taken on the dullness that inevitably attends a reduction to a state of pure economic function" (2:285). In addition the TVA's agricultural program, perhaps the best-received locally of all its initiatives, had further "remodeled" the "very landscape" and the lives of those who lived there (Davidson 2:289). And the agency had displaced thousands of people from their homes and communities, creating profound ruptures in the traditional culture of the region. The changes the TVA wrought, then, were not without considerable costs to the people who were to be "saved" by this federal initiative. They are passionately limned in Donald Davidson's river history, but they are also stressed in Donald Davis's environmental history of the southern Appalachians. About the construction of dams alone, Davis concludes:

> The environmental, social, and cultural effects . . . cannot be underestimated. Collectively, these hydroelectric and navigation projects inundated

more than a million acres of mountain lands, submerged over a thousand miles of natural flowing streams and rivers, and permanently flooded hundreds of important cultural and historical sites significant to the region's history. The overall water quality of the region's rivers greatly diminished, as did the number of species dependent upon the native river ecosystem. . . . By far the best agricultural land in the region was taken out of the agriculture land base, resulting not only in a decline in farming as a primary occupation but also in the loss of millions of dollars' worth of valuable property that was permanently removed from the local tax base. (191)

These costs to the land and people are central to McCarthy's concerns in *The Orchard Keeper*.

Evading the Law: *Whiskey Blockading*

In the Southern Appalachian Mountains, "an illicit distiller is called a blockader, his business is blockading, and the product is blockade liquor," writes Horace Kephart. "Just as the smugglers of old Britain called themselves freetraders, thereby proclaiming that they risked and fought for a principle, so the moonshiner considers himself simply a blockade-runner dealing in contraband" (126). Sylder and the other mountain whiskey-makers' and runners' preference for the term "blockading" (see *Orchard Keeper* 214) is significant, then, in that it reveals the attitudes of the mountain people toward their lawbreaking and the makers and enforcers of the law. Kephart traces the history of blockading to its roots in the seventeenth-century Scots-Irish ancestors of the southern mountain settlers and their hatred of British excise laws.[13] The resentment arose in reaction to a tax on one's subsistence imposed by outsiders who had no understanding or sympathy for the point of view of those being taxed. Exacerbating such feeling was the fact that whiskey was the traditional drink of Scotland and Ireland, where distilling it was a common household practice, each family making enough to supply its own requirements. "A tax, then, upon whiskey was as odious as a tax upon bread baked on the domestic hearth." When these excise taxes increased, they promoted "a spirit of defiance and resistance among the great body of the people" (Kephart 146–47).

Deriving a genealogy of southern blockading, Kephart explains that when the Scots-Irish emigrated from northern Ireland to the American colonies, largely to western Pennsylvania, they brought with them a tradition of tough independence and resistance to excise laws. These settlers expelled the Indians from the Alleghenies and were staunch supporters of the new government in its fight for independence from Great Britain. But when the young federal government itself imposed an excise tax on distilled spirits in 1791, they rebelled. The difficulty of farming in the mountains and the lack of good roads on which to transport grain to markets made distilling seem an economic necessity if the mountain farmers were to enter the cash economy at all: "A horse could carry about sixteen gallons of liquor, which represented eight bushels of grain, in weight and bulk, and double that amount in value" (150–54). This whiskey could be sold at a profit in the eastern markets, but only if no tax were imposed on it. The excise tax put the mountain farmers at an economic disadvantage since it made New England rum cheaper for the consumer and lowland farmers could, as always, market their grain profitably without processing it into liquor.

In 1794 agitation against the tax erupted in an insurrection in which the "Whiskey Boys" marched on Pittsburgh and President Washington marshaled a militia against them. Through negotiation the revolt was settled without bloodshed, and resistance was further quieted with the election in 1800 of Thomas Jefferson, who had always opposed the excise tax and who quickly repealed it (Kephart 156–58, 161).

Kephart argues that the cultural tradition of resistance to excise taxation imposed on the home distillery passed from the seventeenth-century Scots-Irish to eighteenth-century Allegheny mountain pioneers and then down the Appalachian Mountain migration routes to the highlands of North Carolina and Tennessee. Although the mountain people themselves might not remember the specifics of this history, the cultural attitudes were still intact when Kephart lived among them in the early twentieth century (159). These attitudes had resurfaced dramatically in the Reconstruction years, when the Internal Revenue Service turned its attention to the whiskey-making practice in the southern mountains. The conflict between federal agents and mountain whiskey blockaders peaked in about 1877, approximately the time when Arthur Ownby takes his job constructing the railroad. The IRS commissioner complained in his report for 1876–77 that there were at least three thousand stills in the region, each producing ten to fifty gallons of illicit spirits daily. "They are usually located at inaccessible points in the mountains, away from the ordinary lines of travel, and are generally owned by unlettered men of desperate character, armed and ready to resist the officers of the law" (quoted in Kephart 167). Despite his unsympathetic characterization of the southern mountain people, the commissioner recognized that the law was unpopular in the region and that its enforcement was only increasing the citizens' resistance: "Many citizens not guilty of violating the law themselves were in strong sympathy with those who did violate, and the officers in many instances found themselves unsupported in the execution of the laws by a healthy state of public opinion. The distillers . . . were, I have no doubt, at times treated with harshness. This occasioned much indignation on the part of those who sympathized with the lawbreakers" (quoted in Kephart 168–69).

Resistance to what was perceived as an unfair law led to bitterness against the enforcers, and both are evident in the values of the rebels in *The Orchard*

Keeper. Sylder treats blockading as a sport and a profession until Constable Gifford tries to elicit evidence against him by threatening the fatherless John Wesley, after which Sylder feels not only justified but obligated to assault him. Gifford's threats and his cowardly retaliatory beating of Sylder, together with the perhaps excessive three-year prison sentence imposed on Sylder, condition John Wesley's awakening rebellion against the impositions of law and bureaucracy. Kephart indicates that in 1904, before Prohibition and the modernization of the mountain region, the penalty for blockading was only a month or two in prison (119, 122n). As a local constable, Gifford is not an IRS agent, and his persecution of Sylder seems self-determined—perhaps motivated by the hope of a reward. Nevertheless, Kephart's conversation with an old mountain man about local attitudes toward revenue officers is also relevant to McCarthy's depiction of Gifford: "We ain't all blockaders," said Kephart's informant, "yet you can search these mountains through with a fine-tooth comb and you wunt find ary critter as has a good word to say for the revenue. The reason is't we know them men from 'way back; we know whut they uster do afore they jined the sarvice, and why they did it. Most of them were blockaders their own selves, till they saw how they could make more money turncoatin'. They use their authority to abuse people who ain't never done nothin' nohow" (170). Kephart adds that "there is no denying that there have been officers in the revenue service who, stung by the contempt in which they were held as renegades from their own people, have used their authority in settling private scores, and have inflicted grievous wrongs upon innocent people" (172). We are given no hint that Gifford has ever been a blockader, but the old men gathered around Mr. Eller's stove, who carefully avoid answering Gifford's questions, seem to regard him as a turncoat, and Sylder detests him as one who *"sells his own neighbors out for money"*—one of the few who *"lie that deep in the pit, that far beyond the pale"* (215).

The traditional reasons for resistance to the excise law still held in the southern mountains when Kephart interviewed his neighbors. Primary among them was that the tax was excessive and unjust. An informant told him that the mountain people "believe in supportin' the Government, because hit's the law. Nobody refuses to pay his taxes, for taxes is fair and squar'. Taxes cost mebbe three cents on the dollar; and that's all right. But revenue costs a dollar and ten cents on twenty cents' worth o' liquor; and that's robbin' the people with a gun to their faces" (120–21). The farmer was obligated to subsist on the products of his land, so "why can't I make some o' my own corn into pure whiskey to drink, without payin' tax?" (122). He believed that he ought to be free to make the whiskey needed for his family's medicinal use: "Whiskey means more to us mountain folks than hit does to folks in town, whar thar's drug-stores and doctors. . . . We can't git a doctor up hyar less'n three days; and it costs scand'lous.

The only medicines we-uns has is yerbs, which customarily ain't no good 'thout a leetle grain o' whiskey" (121). Finally the difficulty and cost of transporting their corn to market was as troublesome for Kephart's Smoky Mountain informant in the early twentieth century as it was for the Allegheny Mountain pioneers of the eighteenth: "The only farm produce we-uns can sell is corn. You see for yourself that corn can't be shipped outen hyar. . . . Corn *juice* is about all we can tote around over the country and git cash money for. Why, man, that's the only way some folks has o' payin' their taxes!" (123).

A considerable proportion of an East Tennessee farmer's corn crop traditionally went into the making of whiskey. From tax records Davis estimates that the annual per capita production of legal whiskey for the entire region was about fifty gallons, representing between a quarter and half of the corn crop. In Blount County forty-seven stills paid taxes on whiskey in 1820 (Davis 140). Shields writes that in Cades Cove, "when government-licensed distilleries existed . . . , corn whiskey was the principal product," and it was still produced after the state enacted severe restrictions on the sale of liquor in the 1870s, "but at a much greater effort" (25). In 1919 Congress approved Prohibition, and in 1920 an agricultural depression caused farm prices to plummet so that a bushel of corn brought only twenty-five cents on the market. In Sevier County and, presumably, the other farming counties of East Tennessee, the hard economic times made whiskey-making an economic lifeline even though both local and national prohibition were in full swing (*Gentle Winds* 93). Dunn reports that with the advent of federal prohibition and the destruction of stills in the more populous portions of the state, normally law-abiding Cades Cove residents increasingly grasped the economic benefits of whiskey blockading: "Law enforcement officials commented on the growing size of stills and the increased volume of whiskey seized in 1921 in and around the cove" (234). Indeed, Dunn writes, "Compared to the total population of Blount County, cove citizens in the 1920s were not frequently before the circuit court for misdemeanors or felonies other than for those offenses associated with illicit distilling" (240). Even some revenue agents perceived blockaders "less as criminals than as economically desperate men" (*Gentle Winds* 94). Ray Cline, an agent with the Knoxville office of the Alcohol, Tobacco and Firearms Bureau, recalled that blockading crested in the decades of the 1930s and '40s—the decades of *The Orchard Keeper*—when the economic pressures were toughest. Its decline was finally brought about by the improved economy of the region and rising prices of the sugar required to make whiskey (Julian B1).

According to Kephart, national Prohibition, instituted with the Eighteenth Amendment and the Volstead Act in 1919, was actually supported by southern blockaders because it would eliminate their competition, the legal distilleries and saloons (187–88)—a fact that illuminates Sylder's complaint that with the repeal of Prohibition his blockading job in the gulf "had gone off the market December fifth 1933" (32). As a result of Prohibition, blockading in the southern Appalachians became even more profitable. More and more blockaders emerged, and informing also spiked, with feuds and bloodshed as the inevitable result.[14] At the height of Prohibition, Kephart predicted dire consequences for the moral fiber and cohesiveness of the mountain communities. And although he did not foresee the repeal of federal Prohibition, he envisioned the modern mountain South that has become reality in the pre–World War II East Tennessee of *The Orchard Keeper:* "Our new highways will make the distant marketing of blockade liquor a veritable line of trade. 'Mountain dew' will be collected by fly-by-night cars and carried to a far extended market" (190).

Federal Prohibition was repealed during the Depression, when it was argued that the money spent on enforcement could better be devoted to unemployment relief and that legalizing the manufacture of liquor would create jobs (Kobler 353). The repeal actually costs Sylder his well-paying illegal job with Jimenez, but his services as a blockader remain in demand in East Tennessee because of its longstanding state and local prohibition laws. In 1877 Tennessee had enacted its four-mile law stating that no liquor could be sold within four miles of a school. This law would hold everywhere in the state except in incorporated municipalities.[15] As a result, Maryville repealed its charter in 1879 "to make the town safe from the evils of the traffic in alcoholic beverages" (Tennessee Historical Records Survey 10). Amendments in 1899 and 1903 extended the four-mile rule to all towns of two thousand and five thousand people, respectively; with the passage of the Pendleton Bill in 1907, the four-mile rule applied to all towns and cities with a population lower than 150,000. This prompted a public debate in Knoxville punctuated by temperance meetings and antisaloon parades (such as the one John Wesley observes three decades later). A referendum was held to decide whether the Knoxville city charter should be abolished for the purpose of reincorporating without saloons. It passed in March 1907 (Gray and Adams 106–7), and Knoxville remained more or less a dry city until the sale of liquor was legalized there in 1961 (MacArthur 65).

In response to the temperance movement, speakeasies cropped up in Knoxville, and Ed Hooper reports that "by the time of national prohibition, the city was a leader across the nation in the illegal liquor trade, in both moonshine and the 'stamped variety'" (109). Local columnist Bert Vincent recalled that "gentlemen bootleggers" strolled Gay Street in downtown Knoxville in the 1920s and '30s, taking soft-spoken orders from the professional men they passed (13). In *Inside U.S.A.,* visitor John Gunther described the Knoxville of 1946 as "an extremely puritanical town . . . [which] serves no alcohol stronger than 3.6 per cent beer, and its more dignified taprooms close at 9:30 P.M. . . . Perhaps as a result," Gunther added, "it is one of the least orderly cities in the

South—Knoxville leads every other town in Tennessee in homicides, automobile thefts, and larceny" (761). Selling liquor by the drink did not became legal there until 1972, seven years after the publication of *The Orchard Keeper*—a change that MacArthur describes as "hardly less shocking than the fluoridation of the city's water which was approved in a referendum in the same year" (65). If Knoxville citizens were to drink anything harder than beer in the 1930s and '40s, whiskey-makers such as the Hobies and blockaders such as Sylder or the "gentlemen bootleggers" of Vincent's memory would have to provide it. Before Sylder begins whiskey running for Garland Hobie, he haunts the Knoxville "beer taverns" on Friday and Saturday nights, but on Sundays even these saloons must remain closed, "their glass fronts dimmed and muted in sabbatical quietude," and Sylder returns "to the mountain to join what crowds marshaled there beyond the dominion of laws either civil or spiritual" (16). Thus the Green Fly Inn provides an illicit service to the men of Red Branch, attracting "thiefs and drunks," as Mrs. Eller disapprovingly announces (26), and its mysterious burning is likely the result of temperance sentiment.

The Voice of the Land

The ecocentric vision that so crucially shapes the Border Trilogy (1992–98) is already manifest in *The Orchard Keeper*. The hawk bounty John Wesley claims and then repudiates adumbrates the wolf extermination Billy Parham naively embraces and then opposes in *The Crossing*. The owl crucified on Billy's windshield (*CoP* 34) refigures the first novel's electrified owl hanging dead from lightwires "in an attitude of forlorn exhortation" (*Orchard Keeper* 143). Even the abject dogs, uneasy mediators between nature and civilization, similarly challenge man's relation to his fellow creatures: Ownby's abandoned dog Scout is "like some atavistic symbol or brute herald of all questions ever pressed upon humanity" (205), and the nameless dog that Billy drives from his shelter—"repository of ten thousand indignities and the harbinger of God knew what"—howls "as if some awful composite of grief had broke through from the preterite world" (*C* 424). As in McCarthy's later works, nature is no silenced subject in *The Orchard Keeper* (though it is both silent and invisible to some of the characters): the text privileges it in both naturalistic and lyric imagery, giving it presence and voice. The text itself is a "watcher of the seasons" (90).

In the world of *The Orchard Keeper* we find an uneasy alliance of nature and material culture, from the fence *"growed all up"* in the tree at the cemetery (3) and the Green Fly Inn, nailed to a living tree for support and voiding its waste down the mountainside it overhangs, to Sylder's series of assertive cars silencing or drowning out the natural voices of the mountain nights as he negotiates between the orchard and the city. Red Branch represents a kind of "middle ground," to use Leo Marx's term for the pastoral ideal prevalent in American literary tradition, but a very complex and ambiguous one (*Machine in the Garden*). Located across the river from urban Knoxville and at the base of Red Mountain, the first ridge from which "on a clear day you can see the cool blue line" of the Appalachian Mountains to the east "like a distant promise," Red Branch geographically mediates between city and wilderness (10). However, it is neither a pastoral ideal in the literary, Arcadian sense nor the Jeffersonian hope of an agrarian utopia in the new world, but rather a micro-frontier where mechanized civilization and "official" progressive culture meet and combat both what is left of the natural environmental matrix and the mountain pastoral world. Red Branch is contested ground, repeatedly invaded by the machine in accordance with the archetypal pattern Marx traces, and thus it is appropriate to consider its pastoral qualities. But if *The Orchard Keeper* is a pastoral novel, it too, like most of Marx's major examples, embodies the complex pastoralism that transcends the merely conventional, escapist, nostalgic, and sentimental tradition of the pastoral and that recognizes environmental and biological facts, death (*et in Arcadia ego*), and history. Indeed, in *The Pastoral Vision of Cormac McCarthy*, Georg Guillemin finds the novel in many ways antipastoral, and he too places it in the more contemporary category of eco-pastoralism.

History is key here, for the history of Red Branch and the orchard defines another axis on which the land and culture at the center of the book are located in middle ground. The orchard kept by Arthur Ownby in his role as guardian and steward, and in another sense *kept* or habituated by John Wesley, Marion Sylder, and even the dead Kenneth Rattner, is the novel's dominant pastoral image. In its remembered healthiest state, before the opening of the novel, it was an emblem of the fruitful collaboration between man and nature, specifically of the traditional, forest-dependent, pastoral culture of East Tennessee's mountain people. As a pastoral image, the orchard's Edenic connotations link it to humanity's old dream of the return to the garden, sanctuary from labor, history, change, and death. But history has invaded this garden. The orchard is in fact a ruin. Its peaches are small and hard, though still edible for an old man with good teeth. And the life depicted in Red Branch, self-sufficient though Ownby seems to be, is far from the ideal of Jeffersonian agrarianism. The orchard has gone to ruin "twenty years before when the fruit had come so thick and no one to pick it that at night the overborne branches cracking sounded in the valley like distant storms raging," an echo of the storms in Europe that have taken the valley's young men away to war (51). But the orchard, we understand, was doomed anyway. If not World War I, then the expansion of machine culture, already introduced to East Tennessee in the industrial railroad logging era and continued with the advent of the TVA, would draw the agrarian workers away from farms and into the factories and offices of the 1930s and '40s. Like the assaulted wilderness, the orchard has fallen into ruin because of the march of progress and the machinery of war and government. There is hunting and gathering in Red Branch, but agriculture is declining. (In fact the doomed cattle culture of the Border Trilogy is more truly pastoral than the community foregrounded in *The Orchard Keeper.*) Country women may still take eggs and the produce of their cottage gardens to market in Knoxville, but the novel's most prominent images of farming are the neglected orchard and the moonshine processed from corn, the prohibited fruit of pastoral enterprise that has primary currency in the markets, albeit illicit, of men. Red Branch's "decline" from a pastoral ideal it may never have precisely exemplified is manifest in Sylder's job options: he can help Increase Tipton construct boxed cabins—a development in 1929 that prefigures the looming wave of materialistic, throwaway culture; or work in the TVA fertilizer plant—emblem of federal encroachment on the traditional ways of East Tennessee and of the centralization and mechanization of farming; or become, literally, the middle man transporting processed "corn" from the mountain stills to the urban market. Especially after the debacle at the fertilizer plant, the one kind of job Sylder never considers is an "official" one as the arm or tool of the urban and governmental machine.

The liminal world of *The Orchard Keeper*—always more a mountain, forest-dependent community than a classically pastoral one—is thus partly a regressive frontier. The novel depicts a semi-pastoral way of life carved out of and still intimately nestled within the wilderness, with its mixture of low technology and traditional values: cooperation, self-reliance, reverence, respect for neighbors—an anthropocentric culture for good and ill, but a culture from which a nascent ecocentrism emerges in its most conscious members. The novel challenges the observation of Nash and others that an appreciation for wilderness and a desire to preserve it occurs most often in the nostalgic urban dweller who somewhat sentimentally imagines himself cut off from his old home in nature (44, 57, 63, 249–54, 265–68). The ecocentric vision of the novel is most associated with those rural characters who have experienced all their lives an intimate connection with nature, naively exploiting her plenitude, and who have experienced the guilt and repudiation of exploitive relations to the environment that Annette Kolodny traces as part of the American heritage from the earliest European settlement. Red Branch is partially reverting to wilderness ways at the same historical moment(s) when it is challenged by the intrusion of the machine and materialistic, technocentric culture. If forced to abandon the orchard to one of these contesting forces, Arthur Ownby and John Wesley Rattner clearly would choose wilderness.

Nash identifies the ever-westering American frontier as the arena of battle between civilization and wilderness, with the goal being to convert the wilderness or "waste" to a garden (32). In the eighteenth and nineteenth centuries, this frontier contest was repeated over and over on the American continent until wilderness was conquered from Atlantic to Pacific: "Insofar as the west-ward expansion of civilization was thought good, wilderness was bad. It was construed as much a barrier to progress, prosperity, and power as it was to god-liness. On every frontier intense enthusiasm greeted the transformation of the wild into the civilized" (40). However, the ominous note that points to the archetypal intrusion of the machine into the garden, an event ironically prefig-ured by the pioneer's hacking the garden from the wilderness, was also already sounded in the nineteenth century: "The . . . pioneer's emphasis on material progress did not entirely exclude the older idea of conquering wilderness in the name of God. William Gilpin, an early governor of Colorado and trumpeter of America's Manifest Destiny, made clear that 'Progress is God' and that the 'occupation of wild territory . . . proceeds with all the solemnity of a providen-tial ordinance'" (Nash 41). The fable of *The Orchard Keeper* demonstrates that if progress is God, then the march of civilization and its machinery does not stop with the garden's cultivation; it drives through the garden too, leaving it in ruin and erecting new icons in its place. *Blood Meridian*'s Judge Holden echoes Gilpin when he claims that "War is god" (249), and in McCarthy's work, beginning with *The Orchard Keeper*, material progress is often equated with war's machinery. McCarthy's war-ruined orchard, then, is the locus of an anachronistic and regressive frontier in which twentieth-century mechano-centric culture contests simultaneously both the garden and the natural wilder-ness to which the garden tends to revert—a frontier that reflects the unique characteristics of East Tennessee in the 1930s and 1940s when McCarthy was growing up there, when communities were flooded by the TVA or taken over for the creation of the Great Smoky Mountains National Park, with its devel-opment of roads and facilities as magnets for tourists, and when wilderness itself was invaded by the industrial machine in continuation of the process introduced with industrial logging. *The Orchard Keeper* joins the ranks of other American novels such as *Moby-Dick*, *Huckleberry Finn*, and *The Great Gatsby* as a fable that enacts what Marx calls "the dilemma of technological progress" (340).

In the early twentieth century, Kephart reminded his readers that "full three-fourths of our mountaineers still live in the eighteenth century, and that in their far-flung wilderness, away from large rivers and railways, the habits, customs, morals of the people have changed but little from those of our old colonial frontier" (285). But Kephart was already seeing with uncanny pre-science the transformations under way, and his melancholy description of them reads like a synopsis of much of *The Orchard Keeper*: "Suddenly the mountaineer is awakened from his eighteenth-century bed by the blare of steam whistles and the boom of dynamite. He sees his forests leveled and whisked away; his rivers dammed by concrete walls and shot into turbines that outpower all the horses in Appalachia. He is . . . awed by vast transfers of property, incensed by rude demands. Aroused, now, and wide-eyed, he realizes with sinking heart that here is a sudden end of that Old Dispensation under which he and his ancestors were born, the beginning of a New Order that heeds him and his neighbors not a whit" (454–55).[16] The Great Smoky Mountains and to some extent even the Tennessee Valley of McCarthy's childhood belatedly underwent Marx's archetypal experience of nineteenth-century America, when, "within the lifetime of a single generation, a rustic and in large part wild landscape was transformed into the site of the world's most productive industrial machine"—a transformation that made for "profound contradictions of value or meaning" and that haunts American fiction in the "recurrent image of the machine's sudden entrance into the landscape" (343). *The Orchard Keeper* encompasses many such images—not only the striking antipastoral image of the government tank brooding over the neglected orchard, but also those that capture the machine's penetration of wilderness itself.[17] For example, one image that captures this direct juxtaposition of wild nature and industrialism occurs in one of Sylder's night rides through the mountains, when he drives "through the gap with the moon riding low over the pines that edged the long and barren slash of white beneath the power lines," an allusion not only to the construction of new roads through the landscape but also to the energy production of the TVA, its impact on the land characterized as "a barren slash" (162–63). Similarly, when Ownby escapes into the wilderness, or the closest approximation he can still find in East Tennessee, he follows a Civilian Conservation Corps fire trail to reach Huffaker's store (200), an evocation of the New Deal program that employed thousands of young men during the Depression to develop the Appalachian Trail and to construct paths and roads, firetowers, telephone lines, bridges, retaining walls, stone "comfort stations," and drinking fountains throughout the National Park, transforming the wilderness and making it accessible by foot, automobile, and telephone (see Jones 112–16; Campbell 125).[18]

In McCarthy's dynamic, the garden is a precarious and fleeting middle ground, contested on both sides by its natural wilderness state and by the machine. In fact the garden is largely defeated when the novel opens, the ruined orchard and all it stands for merging toward wildness; but the war continues toward total conquest of nature and of the orchard keepers who would preserve an anthropocentric pastoral/mountain culture or even overlay it with ecocentrism. The novel's end announces the victory of the new breed of unneighborly men and women, muffled in their cars and regulated by stoplights, who have displaced the orchard keepers as surely as they themselves had displaced the Indians, and who complete the process of supplanting the wilderness.[19]

Nash demonstrates that pioneers frequently used military language to express their determination to impose civilization on "empty" North American wilderness: "Countless diaries, addresses, and memorials of the frontier period represented wilderness as an 'enemy' which had to be 'conquered,' 'subdued,' and 'vanquished' by a 'pioneer army'" (27). Many scenes in *The Orchard Keeper* explicitly demonstrate the machine culture's militancy. Gifford and Legwater invade the cozy communal setting of Eller's store with "martial" steps, and the federal officials who tend the government installation dress in the camouflage fatigues and drive the "olivecolored truck" of war (116, 98). Even the youth of Red Branch contribute a "militant air" to Eller's store when they arrive armed to buy shells by "fours and sixes" (142). This is an assaulted landscape, blasted for roads and railroads, quarried, trashed. The natural environment of Red Branch is depicted in imagery stressing its repeated penetration by the paramilitary machine or, in a corollary image pattern, its enclosure or containment by the mechanical.

Sylder's car is prominent among such images. Its association with the panther it has displaced emphasizes the youthful Sylder's own predatory qualities when he and June Tipton use it to hunt down young women hiking along the road—emblem of man's use of the machine to "progress" in imposing his will on nature or other humans. But more frequently Sylder is presented as the victim of his machine. It is the vehicle of his encounter with the more egregious predator Kenneth Rattner, who honors no human connection and who prowls the night highways seeking victims to assault and rob. And just as Ownby has earlier worked on the railroad, Sylder, too, is implicated in the mechanized world. Invested in both Red Branch and Knoxville, he employs his car to bridge the two environments, traveling the roads that link town and country, even while his illegal activities repudiate the codes of the official culture. Ultimately, though, his bravado is ineffectual against the new regime. As an emblem of this, he runs into his worst difficulties on bridges, first the one over Red Branch when he loses control of his machine, overshoots the bridge, and overturns the car in the creek, nearly drowning himself; and then the Henley Street bridge crossing north into Knoxville, where his car simply fails him (its gas is diluted with natural rain water), and the police arrest him with a trunk full of whiskey. Furthermore, Sylder's perception of nature is largely muffled by his containment within his car. He is less a watcher of seasons than either Ownby or John Wesley, who together carry most of the ecocentric values of the novel. His appreciation of the land has become an avocation. Yet released from his car Sylder is redeemed by the hunt, his dogs, and his willingness to sponsor John Wesley in hunting and trapping—and by his sharing the value of ethical personal relations exemplified in Ownby and taught to John Wesley through his contact with both mentors.

The orchard's pesticide pit is another Marxian image of the machine in the garden, emphasizing that the orchard was never an absolute Eden but rather a cultivated landscape already regulated by mechanized culture. Its pesticides bespeak man's tendency to divide creatures into the beneficial and the harmful according to his anthropocentric view of the world, reminding us that the garden is an artificial construct that comes into being via the rigorous expulsion of plants humans designate weeds and creatures we designate pests.

Adding commodification to this utilitarian value structure is the bounty theme of this book, picked up again in *Outer Dark* with the snakehunter's career; in *Suttree* with Gene Harrogate's attempt to redeem bat corpses for cash; in *Blood Meridian* with the Glanton gang's application of a similarly ethnocentric approach to native Americans; and in *The Crossing* with Billy Parham's futile attempt to counter the extermination of the Mexican wolf. In *The Orchard Keeper*, the bounty trope is most explicit in John Wesley's shocked rejection of the notion that the dead sparrow hawk he has innocently redeemed for cash has no value "other than the fact of [its] demise" (233). His act of repudiation is partially conditioned by his final conversation with Ownby, devalued by the progressive, urban bureaucracy even as it places him within its system of social welfare. Embittered with the new order, Ownby tells John Wesley, "They's even a bounty on findin dead bodies, man over to Knoxville does pretty good grapplehookin em when they jump off of the bridge like they do there all the time. They tell me he gets out fast enough to beat anybody else to em only not so fast as they might stit be a-breathin" (228).

The bounty trope appears in a grim parable just before Ownby's arrest, when any idyllic aura of his retreat into relative wilderness (the automobile has preceded him there and follows easily to carry him back to progressive civilization) is substantially tempered as he and Scout walk down the mountain trail blazed by the CCC: "Brogan and cane and cracked pad clatter and slide on the shelly rocks and stop where a snake lies curled belly-up to the silent fold and dip of a petal-burst of butterflies fanning his flat and deadwhite underside. Scout smells cautiously at the snake, the butterflies in slow riot over his head, flowery benediction of their veined and harlequin wings" (201). In a dialogic moment, the text invites us to read this scene through Judeo-Christian and American pioneer biases, describing the snake, archenemy of man and dog, and the anomalous benediction of the butterflies before shocking and shaming us with an ecocentric alternative to this reading: "With his cane the old man turns the snake, remarking the dusty carpet pattern of its dull skin, the black clot of blood where the rattles have been cut away" (201). Following Kolodny's discussion of the serpent in William Gilmore Simms's *The Forayers*, we may recognize in the snake an avatar, like the she-panther, of the threatening face of nature: "the mythic power of the Great Mother protecting her own" (121). The genuine evil in this environment is revealed to be man, who in his rage to control his environment kills the creature he codes as pariah and scapegoat, claiming its rattles as trophy. The pointlessness of the snake's killing is suggested by Kephart's comments that although rattlers are "common" in the mountains, "the chance of being bitten by one is about as remote as that of being struck by lightning" (70). Yet once the trail exists, bringing tourists into the rattlesnake's domain, the snake must be eradicated.

In *The Orchard Keeper,* the absence of an extended focus on endangered species—whales or wolves—paired with the lyricism and animism of nature in passages mediated by either Ownby's or John Wesley's vision might suggest that the ecocentrism of McCarthy's first novel is more an aesthetic ecology than the deep ecology of "Whales and Men" or *The Crossing,* but there is more consistency across McCarthy's career than first appears. The depiction of Red Branch is also unflinchingly naturalistic, and the novel reflects the shared environment of a wide range of wildlife attempting to withstand the incursions of technologically aggressive civilization—muskrat, mink and raccoon, hawk and owl, squirrel and rabbit, gar and leech, rattlesnake and butterfly, pine and cedar and hickory and Indian Pipe and ginseng. The episode that follows the cat to the creek, where she tries to take the mink from John Wesley's trap and then is carried off by the owl, briefly escapes anthropocentric narrative perspective and privileges the creature's experience, prefiguring the long passages focalized through the she-wolf in *The Crossing.* John Wesley's education is accomplished as much through his observations of wildlife and natural cycles as it is through his brief associations with Ownby and Sylder. The boy is interested in it all, flinching less at the leech on Wanda Tipton's leg than at her engulfing sexuality and sharing none of the courthouse clerk's squeamishness about handling the ripe sparrow hawk or the dead mink beginning to slue in its skin. He soberly studies the dead rabbit trapped in the well and the reduction to bones of the dead squirrel he inters in a jar. And when we consider that the novel is framed as his imaginative reconstruction of the past, we may recognize that the ventures into the perspectives of nonhuman creatures represent John Wesley's own emergent ecocentrism.[20] McCarthy projects on his older alter ego Ownby a lyricism not so much romantic in a sentimentalized, aesthetically selective sense as druidical, embracing both the terror and the beauty of nature, recognizing that its wonders are predicated on death and change. There is no squeamish repudiation of predation here but an informed respect for the creatures and processes of nature.

In *The Orchard Keeper* as in the Border Trilogy, one test of a male character's values and ethics is his practicing of right or profane versions of the hunt. Critiquing Americans' domination over the natural world, our neglect of stewardship or enlightened coexistence in favor of utilitarian ownership and even paramilitary assault, *The Orchard Keeper* demonstrates the childish irresponsibility of "official" culture through implicit comparison with boys' games. In their wasteful and self-indulgent trapping or dynamiting of the creatures who are their neighbors, Warn, Johnny, and Boog model their acts on and unconsciously parody the adult culture they are preparing to join, contrasting markedly with John Wesley even as he befriends them. Their mindless, militant approach to wildlife is comparable to that of the settlers in Cooper's *The Pioneers*, "a people who grasp only weapons of destruction" and who are themselves parodied in Richard Jones's attack on the passenger pigeons with "the gadget technology of cannon warfare" (Kolodny 92). The boys' adult counterparts are everywhere in the "official" culture. Their use of dynamite against wild animals directly comments on Ownby's railroad work, which he repudiates with more maturity. But the most pointed adult parody of the unmindful, progress-obsessed, and materialistic culture's pernicious tendencies is Legwater, whose behavior makes an oxymoron of the term "humane officer." By implication, *The Orchard Keeper* extends this critique to all the "officers" of the novel, who have lost their humanity in their thoughtless allegiance to civilization's norms.

In addition to images of nature's penetration by the machine, a pattern of possession, entrapment, or containment is at work here, as with Sylder's containment within his rocket-like car. The rabbit that dies in the Rattner family's well is entombed by the machine just as surely as is Kenneth Rattner in the pesticide pit. Two of the panther cubs are mangled by the dynamite blast, but the one Ownby keeps is buried alive when his den collapses. Warn flies a buzzard on a tether and traps a skunk in a cave tunnel before blazing at it with his rifle, an incident that also suggests the most violent of vaginal penetrations of the land. The cultural machine imprisons, and this trope extends to the human contest at the book's core: the inexorable attempt by aggressive, technology-based culture to contain/detain the more nature-based culture of Red Branch's "orchard keepers." Thus Marion Sylder ends up in prison, and Arthur Ownby is sealed away behind the fence and walls of the state mental hospital, where he is as surely imprisoned as Sylder—indeed, more indefinitely so. John Wesley asks Ownby with naive hope where he plans to live after his release, while outside the ominous "mowers" pass and return "in martial formation drowning the babble of voices" (223). Like the representatives of the older mountain culture, wilderness itself is contained by the federal government, under "official" control, tamed as a national park or as a dammed navigational waterway.

However, in *The Orchard Keeper* the vanquishing of the orchard and its keepers is presented with aching sadness but without ecological despair. The novel evokes the persistence of the natural world despite the vanishing human generations and the ruin of their material artifacts—even nature's answering impingement on human culture. Its power is evident in the spring floods that engulf the land and the human structures imposed on it. The pine tree to which the Green Fly Inn is anchored rocks it in the wind like a ship at sea. The contest between the iron fence and the tree is a draw: the tree contains and distorts the fence to the same extent that the fence penetrates and distorts the tree. Though the panther has gone from the mountains, wasps nest in the Rattner family's house. Weeds reclaim the orchard and yard. The creek submerges Sylder's car, the owl carries off the half-domestic cat, and the big raccoon survives and nearly drowns Sylder's dog, Lady.

Like *The Crossing*, *The Orchard Keeper* closes ambiguously with the sun also rising (or setting) on the now fully mechanized post–World War II world. But John Wesley escapes containment through a "gap in the fence" to reenact the archetypal retreat to the west (246). On the other hand, we know that the American frontier is gone and the last pockets of wilderness—whether the Hurricane or the Mexican Sierra—offer no lasting sanctuary to Arthur Ownby or Billy Parham. Any sanctuary John Wesley attains is in his mind. His truest act of civil disobedience is his imaginative re-creation, the "hallucinated recollection" of the vanished world that he experiences as he seeks his mother's grave and that he carries in his heart as he sojourns in a diminished modern world.

Defending the Orchard: *Arthur Ownby*

The resistance of *The Orchard Keeper*'s three protagonists to law and the progressive order may best be perceived in context of the cultural, economic, and ecological history of East Tennessee from Reconstruction through World War II. A strain of antinomianism runs through many of McCarthy's works, but in his first novel he anchors it in the specific historical challenges to the traditional mountain culture detailed in the preceding pages and develops it in less insistently metaphysical fashion than in his later southern works. The antinomian influences most evident in *The Orchard Keeper* are Henry David Thoreau and such defenders of East Tennessee culture as Donald Davidson and Horace Kephart. This is not to deny that an existentialist reading, for example, can be fruitful. However, *The Orchard Keeper*'s strategies point toward, but are not identical with, those of McCarthy's more thoroughly existentialist work such as *The Gardener's Son*, in which the cultural and economic history of the Graniteville textile mill is seamlessly integrated with gnostic/existentialist plot structure and imagery. Such systematic employment of imagery and archetypal incident drawn from philosophical sources is not yet apparent in McCarthy's first novel.

The unifying conflict in *The Orchard Keeper* is the contention between traditional mountain culture and the modern, commercial, and technocentric culture of "mainstream" America, endorsed by the federal government. The invasion comes largely from the north via excise taxes on whiskey, industrial railroad logging, and the projects of the TVA—manifestations of a cultural imperialism that threatens to displace the mountain people and their way of life, not only through evictions but also through dilution of the population with newcomers from other parts of the country and through the defection of those mountain people who abandon their traditional values for the cash flow and catalogue goods of the new economy. In addition to the novel's ecocentric depiction of the *agon* of the land and wilderness, which Guillemin finds to be the novel's "principal protagonists" (*Pastoral Vision* 22), this conflict is developed through the three human protagonists, who represent three generations of the mountain culture and who, because of their ages and circumstances, enjoy differing relationships to it. Through these "heroes" the narrative voice, structurally identified with the perspective of John Wesley, allies itself with the traditional culture and sings its lament. For all three the story is of resistance to inevitable loss.

The oldest protagonist, Arthur Ownby, was raised in a Blount County cove where he lived a mountain-dependent life inherited with little change from eighteenth-century pioneers, a life which by modern standards comes close to "maintaining the precarious balance between intimacy and exploitation," which Kolodny concludes has always been difficult in the American experience of the land (73). When he was a child, a witch placed milfoil drops on Arthur's tongue and told him that this would bring him vision. Her pronouncement appalled his Christian mother, but he internalized it nonetheless. The woman moved to the Smoky Mountains, exiling herself from other black people, because there she could feel "the movements and significations" (59). And the text supports her conviction that the mountains are a realm of mystical wonderment, at least for those who are attuned to them. Sylder recognizes it even as he drives resentfully toward Atlanta after losing his job in the fertilizer plant: "The high country rolled lightless and uninhabited, the road ferruling through dark forests of owl trees, bat caverns, witch covens" (31). This playful progression of images from the naturalistic to the supernatural suggests that the land works a sort of magic on Sylder, soothing his anger and disclosing its powers, not necessarily nurturing but nonetheless enchanting him. With similar progression from realism to mysticism, but with even less reassuring effect, John Wesley watches night deepen in the valley: "Sound of voices close and urgent on the acoustic night air, doors falling to, laughter. . . . An encampment settling for rest, council fires put out. . . . In caverns by torchlight a congress of fiends and warlocks rattling old dry bones in wistful hunger" (66). Ownby's perception of the natural world's wonder is frequently evoked. For example, on the day after the snowstorm, he notices that "the trees were all encased in ice, limbless-looking where their black trunks rose in aureoles of lace, bright seafans shimmering in the wind and tinkling with an endless bell-like sound, a carillon in miniature, and glittering shards of ice falling in sporadic hail everywhere through the woods and marking the snow with incomprehensible runes" (137). Again the passage builds—from the realistic to the metaphoric to the mystical culmination in the runic characters inscribed by nature, characters which Ownby, with his special vision, recognizes for their mystery, their resistance to human reading.

The witch who grants Ownby vision specifically implies that he will be able to discern the magical "wampus cats with great burning eyes and which left no track even in snow" (59–60). His vision is also manifested in his attunement to nature, his mystical intuition about the seven-year cycles governing nature and the spirit, and his serene conviction that his own life is regulated by such cycles: that if he does not die at eighty-four (at twelve seven-year cycles), he will live to one hundred and five (fifteen seven-year cycles). Crucially Ownby's belief in his vision becomes a self-fulfilling prophecy, and he observes attentively the signs of disasters on the way. But his vision is not perfect, and his story encompasses his failure to see soon enough to prevent his own losses but also his developing insight into the meanings of the changes in the mountains.

Growing up in Tuckaleechee, Ownby witnesses the intrusion of the machine into the pastoral/wilderness realm in post–Civil War logging operations. Because logging is familiar, he does not immediately grasp the implications of the railroad newly penetrating into the mountains. So when he marries and must provide for his family, he moves to a small farm in Sevier County and takes on hourly work building rail beds for the lumber company. The move amounts to an almost accidental choice of the cash economy, modernism, and exploitation of the wilderness on a scale his pioneer forebears could not have imagined; but this choice quickly leads Ownby to the regret and repudiation that Kolodny detects in many American texts when a man assaults the land, perceived as the feminine principle of nurturing plenitude either as Mother or as Virgin. Kolodny writes that such events typically rupture the pastoral dream because "the guilt incurred by such violations [of the land] will not allow . . . man to experience [its] maternal embrace . . . as permanently receptive" (86). Ownby's assignment is to dynamite the landscape to clear the way for the railroad. His blasting destroys the den of a she-panther, killing two kits and injuring the third. The act exemplifies the railroad logging industry's destruction of habitat. It also is a classic assault on the land as mother, figured in the she-panther and her womb-like den, associated with the nurturing of her offspring. Ownby compounds his offense when he naively separates the living cub from its mother by "rescuing" it and taking it home. He accepts responsibility for it, an indication of the guilt and remorse he already feels. But in doing so, he usurps the nurturing role that rightly belongs to the she-panther, to wilderness. Stealing it from its natural mother, he consigns it to a human surrogate, his wife Ellen, an act of adoption that will compromise its wild nature or, more likely, doom it to imprisonment or destruction within the human culture to which, by nature, it cannot assimilate.[21] Thus the cub is also emblematic of the displaced mountain people themselves, imprisoned within the newly imposed, perhaps well-intentioned but inimical progressive culture of outsiders.

When the she-panther comes after her kit, invading Ownby's farm and killing his livestock, he understands this as the rightful vengeance of the wilderness for civilization's intrusion, for which Ownby himself has been agent. In her discussion of Cooper's *The Pioneers*, Kolodny writes that the panther in association with her cub incorporates "both the angry and threatening mother as well as the protective and nurturing aspect" (93). Both come into play in *The Orchard Keeper* as well, and Ownby begins to understand that he cannot be an innocent child of nature and exploit it too, that the land does not nurture her sons of the soil at the expense of her other creatures. In reclaiming her kit, the panther frightens Ellen so badly that she miscarries Arthur's child (theirs has been a shotgun wedding), robbing him of generative powers and costing him his marriage. These facts are somewhat elided in his memory, suggesting that they comprise his deepest grief. However, Ownby interprets the panther's effects on his family as a kind of natural justice. It is a terrible moment of recognition, and he frees the cub to appease its mother who is, in his perception, "no common kind of painter," but one of the mystical cats the conjure woman has foretold (157). In the she-panther Ownby recognizes something like the very spirit of the wilderness. He respects not only her knowledge and persistence in reclaiming her own but also her uncanny retributive power, manifested in her destroying his domestic life. When Ellen leaves him, he sees that his rape of the land has further emasculated him by indirectly provoking Ellen to cuckold him. To assault the land is to make it barren and to introduce sterility to human endeavors, which are always grounded in nature.

His memory's emphases suggest that Ownby's participation in the building of the railway was a crime against the wilderness that cost him his livestock, his unborn child, and his marriage. Moreover, he comes to understand that the mountain people's complicity with the railroad has cost them their own habitat and treasured way of life. His conclusion that the she-panther is no common "painter" is a statement of her mythic significance to him. Her retribution prompts in Ownby no superstitious fear of the wild, however. As one who is old enough to have experienced the frontier, when plentiful panthers stood off man's invasion, Ownby exhibits a healthy respect for the animal's nature, telling John Wesley and Warn that "anybody ceptin a fool'd be skeered of . . . a full-growed one" (148). But he pokes fun at others' terror of panthers, mere figments of their relatively citified imaginations, and this emphasizes that Ownby strives to hear and see nature's reality. The anecdote he tells the boys may be informed by his own sense of foolishness for mistaking a sickle moon shining in his window for the panther who has traumatized him, taking the moon for "a white mark on its face like an inverted gull wing" and shooting at it blindly so that he blasts the wall of his own domicile—a notable lapse in his powers of vision that recapitulates his original error in blasting the mountain that nurtures the panther (60). After this, Ownby no longer sleeps with his shotgun near his bed, and he merely listens for night sounds that may be panthers instead of fearfully peering out the window after them.

Although his worst dreams are of panthers invading his small cabin in endless retribution, the pioneer's archetypal dread, of all the novel's characters Ownby is most at home in wild nature. His dreams do not derive from the generalized hysteria that *Saturday Evening Post* correspondent Robert Wernick described in 1965: the perception that wilderness "is the dark, the formless, the terrible, the old chaos which our fathers pushed back. . . . It is held at bay by constant vigilance, and when the vigilance slackens it swoops down for a melodramatic revenge" (quoted in Nash 27). Rather, Ownby's dreams of the avenging wilderness manifest deep regret for the role he has played in destroying the habitat of the panther and of the mountain people, his sense that nature is not a dread enemy, calling for increased vigilance and aggression, but rather the impartially nurturing realm for all her creatures, a realm he has violated, for which action he deserves punishment. By the time of the novel's main action, the panther as a species has been evicted from Red Branch, displaced by the machine; when Ownby listens for cats in the night, it is the whine of the motor he is most likely to hear. The only predatory feline left in Red Branch is the half-feral domestic cat who scavenges pork ribs from the Rattners' smokehouse in a diminished parody of the she-panther's preying on Ownby's hogs, and the cat herself falls prey to the wild owl.

Kolodny's observation that "the desire to experience at least some kind of punishment . . . seems . . . a part of the pattern of pastoral experience in America" resonates with Ownby's response to losing his wife when the she-panther avenges her cubs (94). He waits for Ellen for six days, allowing his farm to go to ruin and his livestock to die of thirst and starvation in an extreme act of neglect and self-punishment, as if he himself, in his grief and guilt, would abet the she-panther's vengeance against the man who violates the bonds of balanced coexistence between the wilderness and the mountain farmer (155–56). For Guillemin, "The violence of letting his livestock perish . . . is directed more against Ownby's own ego than against the beasts, for it copies the destruction of his pastoral and romantic self," and these scenes mark "the death of Ownby's pastoral dream" and the "onset of [his] lifelong melancholia" (*Pastoral Vision* 33, 32). Only when his uncle reminds him that Ownby owes him two hundred dollars—presumably to repay the loan that enabled him to purchase his now neglected farm—does Ownby pull himself out of his self-destructive depression and resume normal responsibilities (156). But it is doubtful that he ever goes back to this farm; Guillemin believes that he repudiates farming altogether (*Pastoral Vision* 32–33).

Ownby "scout[s] the bushes" for nine years after he has killed someone (228, 229)—probably the Bible drummer he suspects has seduced Ellen. Quite likely he has hidden out in the wilder portions of the Smoky Mountains he knows from his childhood, a retreat from the pastoral into wilderness that holds compensatory appeal for Ownby because the wilderness, in a Kolodnian sense, wraps him in her protective embrace, promising him shelter from the persecutions of civil institutions. The retreat, then, is a rejection of both the pastoral realm and civilization, or it marks an eschewing of the site where the machine penetrates the garden to break the illusion of harmony between the land and civilization. It suggests that Ownby considers his pastoral inheritance tainted by the tragic relationship between man and nature, the conflict that Kolodny identifies as "locked into the heart of American pastoral: that which is contained within the matrix of the feminine [the land as Mother or Virgin] . . . must inevitably fall helpless victim to masculine activity" (24).

However, Warn Pulliam tells John Wesley that Ownby worked with his grandfather "cuttin sleepers" for the railroad, apparently for years (145); so it seems that, paradoxically, despite his shock and guilt over his offenses against the land, Ownby does not permanently abandon railroad work. It seems likely that after nine years of self-imposed exile in the wilderness he has no farm or money with which to start again. Probably he has sold his farm in Sevier County to repay his uncle and to rid himself of this reminder of his failed domestic life. His return to the railroad is complicated by necessity, then, but it amounts to an exile from the land and seems further perverse self-punishment imposed out of guilt.

Ownby's continued exile is evident in his living in Red Branch, neither the home of his childhood nor the location of his uncle's farm. Somehow he has lost the family farm in Tuckaleechee: perhaps his family were tenants rather than owners; perhaps his father died young, so young Arthur had to turn to his uncle for help when he married; or perhaps the marriage itself, which prompted his father-in-law's threats of violence, was enough to put in motion the sequence of removals that comprise Ownby's dispossession. For whatever reasons, Ownby has moved northwest to Red Branch, away from his beloved mountains and closer to the urban center of Knoxville. In Red Branch he may be a squatter like the Rattners, since the young social worker says that the county has no record of him. In this locale he re-creates much of the traditional life he knew as a child in the Smoky Mountains, living close to nature and observing her seasons, all the while yearning to return to the mountains and raise bees, an activity that in "Paradise (To Be) Regained," Thoreau singles out as a "nobler and finer relation to nature than we know" because it "is a very slight interference" (776).

But in the course of the novel, his nostalgic yearning becomes compounded by anger redirected from himself to the new order. Long exiled from his mountain birthplace and living among other exiles such as the Tiptons, Ownby longs to return to the distant mountains not just to raise bees but to regain his freedom from the law—to scout the wilderness again. After his evasion of the law as a young man, the first manifestation of Ownby's overt antinomianism is that he conceals the corpse he finds in the abandoned pesticide pit rather than report it to authorities. His trust in his visionary abilities seems a determining factor. It is clear enough that the corpse has suffered a violent death and that the killer wants to avoid revealing his deed to the law. Sylder kills Rattner in self-defense, but the evidence Ownby sees would ordinarily suggest some deeper level of foul play. Yet Ownby intuits that the killer had good reasons and that the victim somehow needed killing. Ownby's decision partly derives from his empathy with a man who might, like himself, kill in self-reliant pursuit of justice. And partly it reflects cool-headed appraisal of the men who function as agents of law and order in Red Branch—men such as Constable Gifford. Perhaps, too, Ownby intuits the significance of the killer's dumping the corpse in a pesticide pit, a choice that identifies the victim as the moral equivalent of a pest and thus hints at the motives of the killer. When Ownby interprets the cat's cry as that of the dead man's spirit, he intuits that the man is "*bound most probably for hell and I hope they don't nobody hear no more from him never.*" Ownby guards the corpse for seven years, believing that this is the legal statute of limitations on prosecuting the man's killer. A lawyer has told him that Ownby himself hid from the law "*two year longer than needful,*" and it may have surprised him to discover that the law has thus encoded the seven-year period that carries such mystical import for him. But the legal and the mystical meanings come together in his relief at the spirit's flight to hell: "*That man put him there either justified or not is free too afore God because after that seven year they cain't nobody bother you*" (228).

Ownby's compassion for the killer and his reluctance to let law officers bother him—the pestilential implication applies to lawmen as well as highwaymen in this book—are consistent with the antinomian attitudes and behaviors of the traditional mountain people described by Kephart. On a pragmatic level, Ownby's tactic of camouflaging the corpse with a cut cedar reprises the mountain whiskey-maker's method of screening his still: "A great hemlock tree may be felled in such position as to help the masking, so long as its top stays green, which will be about a year" (Kephart 131). Ownby's cedars are a subtle reminder of the mountain people's resistance to excise taxes on their whiskey, and thus they connect him with the whiskey-runner Sylder, who, unbeknownst to Own-by, has secreted the corpse in the pit. Kephart observes that while theft was rare, highlanders often viewed the killing of another as a by-product of "private wars," and it was so common that almost every adult he met in the mountains had been "directly interested in some murder case, either as principal, officer, witness, kinsman, or friend" (266–67). He explains that the Scots-Irish pioneers who settled the southern Appalachian mountains and experienced a weak presence of organized law held to their traditions of clan loyalty as in northern Ireland. They looked to one another in times of conflict and refused to testify in law courts about the illegal actions of their kin and neighbors. In the mountain culture, Kephart writes, clan loyalty lies "outside of and superior to the law. . . . The law itself, in many of these localities, is but a feeble, dilatory thing that offers practically no protection to those who would obey its letter. So, in an imperfectly organized society, it is good to have blood-ties that are faithful unto death" (387, 389). This casual approach to the letter of the law as opposed to private judgments of right and wrong was related to the tradition of the outlaw as popular hero in the mountains. "This is not due to any ingrained hostility to law and order as such," Kephart observes, "but simply to admiration for any men who fight desperately against overwhelming odds. . . . Whoever has the reputation of being a dangerous man to cross—the 'marked' man, who carries his life upon his sleeve, but bears himself as a smiling cavalier—he is the only true aristocrat among a valorous but primitive people" (393).

Thus Ownby's culturally ingrained predisposition is not to report what may be a murder to agents of law and order but rather to regard it as a personal matter between the two combatants, a matter that they and their families, if need be, will work out in their own way. He does not assume that the killer is a danger to others or to his society. And he may feel a certain admiration for this man who has had the nerve to solve his own problems outside of the constraints of an imperfect legal system. Ownby is pledged within himself to watch over the corpse out of respect not only for the killer but also for the spirit of the dead man who has not yet attained release. But it may well be that his empathy and respect for the man who has rid himself and his community of a "pest" reinforces his own resolve to protest the government's intrusion on the land and people of Red Branch. And his conviction may strengthen further when he thinks of the young boys of his community—boys like Warn and John Wesley, to whom he stands in the relation of "uncle," and whose birthright to the land and the mountain culture is denied by the technocentric modern culture imposed by outlanders.

Even more directly is Ownby's assault on the government tank related to his guilt for his work on the railway. He has had years to think about the machine's penetration of the mountain wilderness and the displacement of the mountain people, now repeated and escalated in the TVA's encroachment; and when he ponders the tank, he has another kind of vision, a revelation of what the installation signifies for the traditional culture of East Tennessee: "*I seen them fellers never had no business there*" and "*knowed what they was up to,*" Ownby thinks. Moreover, he knows what needs "*attendin to*" (229). The tank's purpose is never specified, but it is official, tended by men in martial fatigues; it is a mechanical presence, penetrating and dominating the pastoral scene. To Ownby, this "bald and sinister" phallic icon stands "complacent, huge, seeming older than the very dirt, the rocks, as if it had spawned them of itself and stood surveying the work, clean and coldly gleaming and capable of infinite contempt" (93).[22] The contempt is that of the now-dominant machine culture, arrogant to the point of claiming sovereignty and even precedence over the materials of nature from which it wrests its being.

The intuitive seeds of Ownby's overt act of civil disobedience have been planted earlier, in the moment when he sees lightning strike the installation in an emblem of natural repudiation, "the domed metal tank on the peak illuminated, quivering in a wild aureole of light . . . , the image burning white hot in . . . [his] lenses" (58). However, not until the subsequent scene, when Ownby slowly contemplates the contemptuous icon, does he consciously formulate his gesture of ecological and cultural defiance. He does not do this for himself, as he anticipates that he will be identified as the perpetrator and will have to evade the law again, now in his eighties. Nor does his action lay to rest the old guilt that he carries for participating in the railroad's assault on the wilderness. Even after he has shot the tank, he feels rightly hounded by nature in the spring storms of 1941, a deserving victim of nature's retribution when the blighted chestnut explodes in a lightning strike and brings him down to the sound of Valkyries descending "to bear him away." The "cats' cries" emitted by the Valkyries evoke the scream of the panther, Ownby's symbol of avenging wilderness, and he experiences his injury, which proves not fatal after all, as being swooped upon by the predator who will carry him to death—an inner experience that prefigures and conditions his interpretation of the cat preyed upon by winged death as Rattner's spirit justly subjected to retribution (172).[23] Ownby likely has no hope that his gesture of defiance can atone for his youthful transgression against the land. Rather, he commits this act out of a sense of confederation with and responsibility to the people of the older order, all the inheritors of the mountain traditions who are being disinherited by the machinery of the modern world. Reaffirming his decision later, Ownby thinks, "*I knowed if they could build it they could build it back and I done it anyway*" (229). It is essential, he believes, to make the gesture, to brand the tank with an X, symbolically mark it for cancellation. His is a gesture of conscientious protest that he knows in advance will be ineffective in a practical sense and that will call out the agents of government against him.

Interestingly, Ownby does not react similarly against Sylder's car, which breaks the mountain peace every night. Nor does he repudiate his own shotgun or the stove and kerosene lamps that bring comfort to his modest cabin. Ownby is no mere primitivist, despite his attunement to nature, his druidical associations, and his enactments of the archetypal retreat to wilderness. Rather, while remaining the novel's most ecocentric character, equaled only by the enlightened John Wesley (who in a sense is Ownby's author), Ownby seems to acknowledge man's tragic nature, his drive toward civilization and progress (often motivated by the need for survival and economic security), and his contradictory impulse to value for itself the natural world that is the very foundation of his life and culture. Ownby and the text itself distinguish the private acts of individuals from those of governmental agents, stripped of ethical conscience by their automated participation in the machine. Ownby values social cooperation and kindliness and is remarkably tolerant of his neighbors, as his observation that what an old man loves best is peace attests (229). His acceptance of Sylder's "howling" and "rocket[ing]" (91–92) down the mountain road in his cars is of a piece with his respect for the corpse in the pesticide pit and the unknown man who has put it there. Ownby's is an ethic that ordinarily neither judges nor attempts to control the actions of others, for he assumes that individuals are actuated by conscience. But his encounters with anonymous representatives of a new order, characters who seem not to share his values and motives, fill this peace-loving old man with anger and disgust. Especially relevant seems the passage in "Civil Disobedience" in which Thoreau writes, "The mass of men serve the state . . . not as men mainly, but as machines. . . . They are the standing army, and the militia, jailers, constables, *posse comitatus*, etc." (791). In his disdain for Constable Gifford, his Knoxville jailers, and the sleepy guardians of the installation on the orchard road, Sylder shares this perception.

The violent reaction of the agents who try to arrest Ownby for his vandalism is craven and excessive. He resists, so they send an escalating arsenal against him, perhaps because his standing them off with a shotgun leads them to conclude he is protecting an illegal still. Wrongly expecting violence from him, they overreact, strafing his home and meager belongings with a "cannonade of shots," any one of which could kill him (186). On their third visit, in their frenzy they recklessly shoot one of their own, whose instinct is to blame Ownby, who has abandoned the cabin the night before (188). Ownby has offended the government, but the officers' response is tantamount to government's running "amok" against him, to use Thoreau's terminology ("Walden" 359). They do not know how to "cherish [the] wise minority" among them ("Civil Disobedience" 796). Thoreau asks in "Civil Disobedience" how a government official shall "ever know well what he is and does as an officer of the government, or as a man, until he is obliged to consider whether he shall treat me . . . as a neighbor and well-disposed man, or as a maniac and disturber of the peace" (797). The agents who approach Ownby's house do not communicate and cannot empathize with this old man who lives by his own principles, and they in fact do regard him as a "maniac." But with good reason Ownby perceives that what "they" are up to with the installation amounts to the federal government's running amok against the citizens and the land of East Tennessee—waging a war of cultural and technological imperialism that must be resisted. He is akin to Thoreau's heroes or martyrs or reformers who serve the government with conscience and "so necessarily resist it for the most part" and consequently "are commonly treated as enemies by it" ("Civil Disobedience" 791). Ownby's restraint from firing at his opponents until he himself is fired upon and his careful aiming not to kill emphasize his good faith in comparison with them (186–87).

Ownby leaves Red Branch because the government agents there have declared him their enemy. As in Cooper's *The Pioneers*, the officers who drive Ownby, like Natty Bumppo, from his home represent the same forces that have driven the wilderness creatures from the land. Ownby's escape into the mountains is motivated by self-protection but is also his further repudiation of the government that sponsors the progressive order. His personal freedom to resist government owes much to his freedom from the materialism of modern culture. As Thoreau says, to be thus free, "You must hire or squat somewhere, and raise but a small crop, and eat that soon. You must live within yourself, and depend upon yourself always tucked up and ready for a start, and not have many affairs" ("Civil Disobedience" 800); or as he puts it in "Walden," "It is desirable that a man . . . live in all respects so compactly and preparedly that, if an enemy take the town, he can, like the old philosopher, walk out the gate empty-handed without anxiety" (259–60). Packing his few possessions onto the traditional mountain man's sledge (see Kephart 42) and settling his failing dog Scout on top, Ownby serenely sets off for the Hurricane in hopes of placing himself beyond the reach of the law. But an agent pursues him there.

No legal or governmental official in this antinomian book is depicted as an admirable character. This officer, ever crisp in pressed chinos, elicits the storekeeper Huffaker's "suspicion" of the outlander, the law agent (196); and his relentless presence so disrupts the "conviviality" of the "idlers" in the store "that they took on the look of refugees grimly awaiting bulletins of some current disaster, the news of flood or fire or plague"—metaphors for the new order's disastrous impact on their culture (197–98). Huffaker is reluctant to inform this stranger about Ownby, and he dreads the old man's return with his harvest of wild ginseng. When the day comes, the officer watches his approach "with the composed disinterest of a professional assassin" (202). He treats the mild and reasonable Ownby rudely, even roughly, and seems incapable of understanding the importance the old man places on his responsibility for his dog. Given the positive valuation placed throughout the novel on the mutual loyalty between dog and human, the officer's refusal to take the aged hound to a new home constitutes a further indictment, in Ownby's eyes and in the reader's, of the inhumane efficiency—or the "expediency," as Thoreau identifies it in "Civil Disobedience" (792–93)—motivating the agents of governmental bureaucracies.

"Wherever a man goes, men will pursue and paw him with their dirty institutions, and, if they can, constrain him to belong to their desperate odd-fellow society," writes Thoreau in the section of "Walden" dealing with his civil disobedience (359). Ownby's irritation grows as he is increasingly pawed by the institutions of this new civil order. He tries to carry on a cordial conversation with the social worker from the county Welfare Bureau, but the young man does not seem to understand conventions of sharing information in mutual exchange. Chained to his paper forms, he rudely cuts off Ownby's conversational answers to his questions. His insistence on cold efficiency wearies the older man, who quickly recognizes in this young bureaucrat another avatar of the law officers who have treated him with such hostility. "Why not jest up and ast me?" Ownby challenges him. "Why I done it. Rung shells and shot your hootnanny all to hell? Where *you* from, heh? You talk like a Goddamned yankee" (221). These queries are very much to the point, from Ownby's perspective. No one has asked the crucial question of his intent in firing on the tank; no one has considered that he might have a motive of conscience. These conformist agents represent the points of contact between the citizen and the institutions of government, but they are utterly alien to him and his culture. Though the young man may well be from Tennessee, that Ownby calls him a "yankee" indicates just how estranged the old Unionist East Tennesseans have come to feel from their own federal government. The social worker is well-intentioned, mild, even polite by his own standards; but trapped within his role he is incapable of detecting just what in his demeanor and values provokes Ownby's outrage. Their interchange is emblematic of all the relations between the mountain people and the newcomers who have imposed their own cultural order on East Tennessee. Offended by Ownby and encouraged by the careless jailer, who exaggerates the number of people Ownby has shot and tells him that his prisoner is "mean as a snake," the case worker decides the old man is pathologically "anomic," sealing his fate as an inmate of the insane hospital until death. Ownby intuits something like this as the social worker leaves his cell, one in a "row of cages," feeling "the circle of years closing" in on him, "the final increment of the curve returning him again to the inchoate . . . flux . . . wherein he had drifted once before and now beyond the world of men" (222). He foresees his physical death, but first his looming imprisonment "beyond the world of men"—a death in life.

In the asylum, Ownby is not chastened and has not changed his mind about either his enemies or his resistance. He is yet again manhandled by the state, this time in the person of the physician who examines him as if he were inanimate meat, prompting Ownby to remind him of his own dignity by asking *"quietly if he intended to kill him"* (230). When John Wesley visits and tells him Sylder has been arrested, Ownby remarks, "I hope he fares better'n me. I cain't get used to all these here people" (226). Then he curbs his tongue lest he incite the boy to self-destructive resentment. Nevertheless he returns to his statements of disaffection: "The ways of these people is strange to me," he remarks to John Wesley when the boy wonders how it can be that sane people are incarcerated (230). Ownby's comments are not assessments of the other inmates but expressions of his confirmed alienation from the culture of progress that now controls the land of his birth. Thoreau writes that prisons are "that separate, but more free and honorable, ground, where the State places those who are not *with* her, but *against* her" ("Civil Disobedience" 798). But in *The Orchard Keeper*, Ownby and Sylder's imprisonments mark the defeat of a culture that had nourished a proud and principled people for generations. The text holds up such "outlaws" for admiration as popular heroes, courageous adherents to values that are out of conformity with the dominant culture, but Ownby's story ends in his removal from the world of men where he might have any influence. The protest of this single individual does not seem to have the awakening effect on government agents and complacent citizens that Thoreau predicted. But it does profoundly affect John Wesley, the young man who feels himself the rightful heir to the mountain culture.

Defending the Orchard: *Marion Sylder*

Considerably younger than Ownby, Sylder has experienced less of wilderness and seems less painfully attuned to its loss. He has grown up in Red Branch, closer to urban Knoxville than to Ownby's home in Tuckaleechee; industrial logging and the railroad have always been a part of Sylder's world. Although it is not mentioned in the novel, Alcoa Aluminum's presence in Blount County dates from 1913 (Tennessee Historical Records Survey 11), the year of his birth, and by the time he returns to Red Branch as a young man in 1934, the TVA is already established in East Tennessee. In addition, he has embraced the world of the machine, exemplified in his fast cars. Nevertheless, Sylder shares some of Ownby's antinomian mindset and the mountain people's attitudes about whiskey laws, neighborliness, and outsiders. We don't know how much he may have shared in the pastoral experience, but his leaving school to do construction work for Increase Tipton marks his entry into the cash economy, much like Ownby's work on the railroad does. Sylder's friendship with the Tiptons also makes him aware of the displacement of the mountain people, and this may combine with his resentment of whiskey regulation to promote his outlawry as much as his recognition that blockading is the most lucrative employment he can find during the Depression. Thus although it is complicated by personal profit in ways that Ownby's protest is not, Sylder's outlawry is at least partly a principled resistance to the encroachments of federal and local government on his and his neighbors' freedoms. He is not the sociopath Mark Royden Winchell sees in him (295). On the contrary, he combines an insouciant courage to flout unjust laws with an ethic that defends the rights and welfare of his neighbors. Although he does not understand the old man's specific motives, he is no more inclined to report Ownby's firing on the tank than Ownby is to report the corpse in the spray pit. Kephart's characterization of the local moonshiner as opposed to organized crime syndicates seems for the most part applicable to Sylder: "He fights fair, according to his code, and single-handed against tremendous odds. He is innocent of graft. There is nothing between him and the whole power of the Federal Government, except his own wits and a well-worn Winchester or muzzle-loader. . . . This man is usually . . . of decent standing in his own community, and a right good fellow toward all the world, save revenue officers. . . . He is soundly convinced that the law is unjust, and that he is only exercising his natural rights. Such a man . . . suffers none of the moral degradation that comes from violating his conscience; his self-respect is whole" (127). Interestingly, unlike the owner of a still who might warn off revenuers with a shotgun, Sylder carries no weapons on his whiskey runs.

Sylder is not the stereotypical gangster of the northern cities but the free-wheeling highlander who courageously breaks certain laws based on his and his culture's assessment of their merits. He is a popular figure in Red Branch, free-handed with his wealth, buying rounds for the men in the Green Fly Inn and providing youngsters rides to town. His first name, Marion, recalls an earlier southern rebel, Francis Marion, the Swamp Fox, the guerilla partisan of the American Revolution who harassed the British from his position of greater familiarity with the wilderness of South Carolina; Marion is a central figure in some of the Revolutionary War novels of William Gilmore Simms and in the television series "Swamp Fox" that aired on *Disneyland* in 1957–58 (Brooks and Marsh 1092). Nevertheless, in his rollicking youth, Sylder is poised precariously between the roles of conscientious resister and true outlaw, and much of his story before he meets John Wesley has to do with his refining his identity in relation to others and to governmental institutions.

As owner of a car, Sylder places himself in a haphazard relation to the people and events of the road. In contrast to his employing his car hospitably to provide transportation for the boys, as a young man he and his buddy June Tipton use it to stalk the girls Jack the Runner has left on the mountain road, hunting them opportunistically for casual sex, a pastime that becomes a source of ribald humor when they discuss it afterwards, enjoying their conquest but failing to register the terror that one girl's wetting herself implies. Sylder's callous predation in this scene seems out of character for the man he becomes by the time John Wesley knows him, when he has settled into a stable and loving marriage; even he recognizes the change when he thinks of June and himself in 1940 as "old married men" (163). Between the ages of twenty-one and twenty-seven, Sylder has matured, as well he should, but the novel also suggests that the shock of being assaulted by his dark double, Kenneth Rattner, has led him to reject behaviors that could have hardened him as Rattner's kind of highwayman.

Indirectly, Sylder's choice to work in the fertilizer plant and his resulting alienation bring him into contact with Rattner. Since the production of nitrates and superphosphates is so linked with the TVA initiatives, Sylder's work in the plant subtly alludes to the TVA's presence. McCarthy's decision to locate a fertilizer plant near Red Branch is an uncharacteristic liberty and seems an invention meant to evoke the TVA without direct reference to it. Local histories make no mention of a fertilizer plant in Knox, Blount, or Sevier counties, and the TVA's plants were located in Muscle Shoals, Alabama, and Columbia, Tennessee, far from the setting of the novel. Yet when his Prohibition-era blockading money runs out in 1934, Sylder of Red Branch takes a job in such a plant—his first legitimate employment since his work for Increase Tipton. The decision suggests that he has no aversion to the new economic opportunities in East Tennessee and that his earlier work as a whiskey blockader did not derive from a confirmed position of generalized outlawry. But Sylder's brief experience in the fertilizer plant embitters him in ways that will determine the direction of his life.

The plant is managed by an outsider, Mr. Petree, who exhibits no tolerance for the rough ways of his young local employees. In his memoir Wilson identifies a U.S. marshal, Edgar Petree, as the leader of several delegations to enforce evictions from the Norris Dam area (94, 97, 100). McCarthy's use of the surname for the plant manager emphasizes his status as the outsider who expels East Tennessee's native sons. After Sylder allows himself to be provoked into a fistfight at work, Petree summarily fires him. Sylder believes that the dock foreman or the supervisor, probably both native to East Tennessee, merely "would have said Break it up." But Mr. Petree disdains to communicate with the combatants at all, spinning "on his square leather heel and stalk[ing] briskly back down the aisle," then dispatching word through the foreman that Sylder is fired and sending his pay along to eliminate the need for any personal contact (30). The job loss is harsh for an uneducated and inexperienced worker in the Depression, and that alone might drive Sylder back to the outlawry of whiskey running. But it also gives him a distaste for the outsiders that the TVA is bringing in to remake the river valley, and his anger consolidates the aliena-tion from government that had already become personal when the Coast Guard opened fire on him. Petree's firing him drives home to Sylder one of the most profound local effects of the TVA according to MacArthur, the "new wave of outsiders"—technicians, engineers, and certainly lawyers such as Charles J. McCarthy Sr.—who settled in the Knoxville area in the 1930s: "There was, of course, a deep and abiding resentment in many quarters against the outsiders who came with the TVA and against all they seemed to stand for. Thirty years after the fact [in the 1960s, when *The Orchard Keeper* was written] some older Knoxvillians still voiced this antagonism" (62). The uncommunicative Petree, the sleepy officials who tend the installation on the orchard road, and the unre-sponsive couple whose movement is regulated by the stoplight and who do not return John Wesley's salute all represent this influx of the TVA outsiders who bring a culture of technological progress to the region but whose ways are alien.

Outraged at his rude dismissal, Sylder broods over some beers (the only alcohol he can buy legally) and then leaves Red Branch, as if in repudiation of what his home has become. He drinks more beer on the road, nursing his grudge all the way to the Atlanta city limits; then he stops at Jim's Hot Spot, where at last he can buy whiskey. His reflection in the bar mirror appears "sin-ister," as if providing him a glimpse of the violent outlaw Rattner in himself. But as he consumes four shots, he becomes not more oblivious but less, com-ing to himself even before he returns to his car. Watching two drunken men brawling and then turkey-trotted out of the bar by the bored bouncer, Sylder apparently recognizes the humor in his and Conatser's own fight—even the reasonableness of his being bounced from the fertilizer plant, for as he feels "waves of fatigue roll from him," he "didn't even think he was mad any more" (32). He heads to his car, wondering why he has left Red Branch, ready to return and reconstruct his life at home.

But this healthier state of mind is shattered when Sylder discovers Rattner "installed beneath his steering wheel," as if some craven and grotesque reflec-tion of himself. He recognizes with a knowledge deeper than presentiment that this man is evil and that he will be "for a certainty called upon to defend at least his property" from Rattner, if not his life (33). This unforeseen invasion re-awakens the rage Sylder has laid to rest. For him Rattner is not only evil but also specifically the correlative of the usurping intrusions under which he and his neighbors suffer at the hands of agents such as Petree. Sylder rudely orders Rattner from his car, but Rattner's blithe disregard of Sylder's meaning, his ploy of claiming the relation of neighbor ("I knowed you wouldn't turn down nobody from home"), and Sylder's reluctance to lay violent hands on Rattner induce Sylder to tolerate his presence (34).

From the first, Rattner provokes in Sylder "a terrific need to be clean," to rid himself of contamination (34). He senses a certain fatedness in their convergence, as he begins to feel that he has driven to Atlanta specifically for the purposes of confronting this alter ego and defending himself from what he represents. Anticipating their pending violent confrontation, he perceives a threat to his very sanity and integrity: "This son of a bitch will have me crazy" (35). Rattner functions not only as a realistic character, husband to Mildred and father to John Wesley, but also as an allegorical figure comparable to the triune in *Outer Dark* and the judge in *Blood Meridian*—a psychic and spiritual threat that rises up from within and yet is manifest in flesh and blood. With the overlaying of gnostic imagery and myth, these later characters are rendered even more mysterious and threatening. But in his first novel, McCarthy was already experimenting with the double who ambiguously represents a main character's darkest self, yet who also menaces him physically.

In this sense the fatal confrontation between Rattner and Sylder—Rattner assaults Sylder and Sylder kills him in self-defense—is an allegory of the defeat of corruption within Sylder: he conquers the impulse toward true outlawry that his rage over his job loss might have called forth. The imagery in which Sylder perceives Rattner as they fight to the death extends and heightens Sylder's initial, instinctive equation of Rattner with corruption. In "Disgust in the Early Works of Cormac McCarthy," Arnold (77–78) comments on the profound revulsion Rattner evokes in Sylder (and the reader) as he perceives his "cheesy neck-flesh" (38), his jaw "like a mass of offal, some obscene waste matter uncongealing and collapsing in slow folds over the web of [Sylder's] hand," and the sensation that strangling the man is "like squeezing a boil" (39). But the disgust he projects onto Rattner also reflects Sylder's profound revulsion against his own violence. The scene suggests that the fight, in which Sylder is forced to lay violent hands on another, has a shattering psychological impact. The events unfold in slow motion, "as in a nightmare" (38), and only after the murder is over does Sylder feel that normal "time was coming back" (40). He is far from cavalier about his act of savagery. He sits stunned for fifteen minutes before he can move at all. Then he staggers to the running board of his car, where he stares "unblinking into the brass eye of the sun ponderous and unreal on the red hills until he lost consciousness" (40). Not the pain of his broken shoulder causes his loss of consciousness but rather the trauma of having murdered this repulsive man with his bare hands—of having been capable of it and having accomplished it with more ferocity than may have been necessary. This isolated image of the personified sun adumbrates the patterns of gnostic and existentialist solar imagery that prevail in *Outer Dark*, *The Gardener's Son*, and

Blood Meridian.[24] Here it reprises Sylder's struggle with a personification of evil hostility. Further, it hints at Sylder's mirroring in the glare of the sun's eye, which contests his gaze, and recalls the incident in the car when Rattner strikes a match and his eyes, reflected in the windshield, meet Sylder's. The two face "each other over the cup of light like enemy chieftains across a council fire" (36). Sylder's loss of consciousness suggests his psychological pain not only at the act of murder but also at his recognition that his instinct to kill is shared with this corrupt highwayman. And this pain does not quickly subside: late that night when he drives away from the spray pit where he has dropped the body, Sylder is so shaken, so absorbed in processing his horrific experience, that he forgets he has left the trunk lid up (46).

Sylder's self-doubting response to killing another in self-defense adumbrates the reactions of John Grady Cole in *All the Pretty Horses*, explicitly articulated in the boy's conversation with the Texas judge (*APH* 290–93), and of Black in McCarthy's play *The Sunset Limited*, for whom murder is a profoundly life-changing experience that reconnects him with his spirituality. Both John Grady and Black follow their violent acts with attempts to rescue others: White for Black, Magdalena for John Grady (in *Cities of the Plain*). Sylder's decision to nurture the son of the man he has killed may well be motivated by a similar psychological dynamic. His subsequent actions reveal that the murder initiates a process of self-examination that curbs his own feral qualities that might thoughtlessly be directed against others in sexual or economic predation or physical aggression. Although he continues to break state and local prohibition laws, never again does he confront another individual with mindless aggression. His only other act of violence is when he strikes the sleeping Constable Gifford a single time with his fist, but this gesture, rather like Ownby's shooting the tank, is a conscious protest of injustice prompted by his care for his young friend John Wesley.

Sylder's urgency to conceal the corpse of Rattner, that "rotten son of a bitch," is not only the self-preservation of a man who distrusts institutions of law and justice but also a psychological necessity (45). Rattner is the suppressed tendency to prey on others that Sylder must put away from him. Ominously, when the men who stop on the road to offer help do not want to leave Sylder alone, he thinks threateningly, like the murderous Lester Ballard, "Get your dead ass out of here" (42). But Sylder desperately wants not to kill again, even in self-preservation. What he intensely desires is to rid himself of the corruption within, to bury it where it will not resurface. This is not simple repression and denial. Never again will Sylder be unconscious of his innate feral qualities skulking just below the surface—his dark shadow. His killing Rattner, like Ownby's dynamiting the panther's den, has led to an awakening into greater ethical consciousness. In an important passage, Sylder is distinguished from the agents of mechanized culture who approach the tank in the early morning "looking serious and official, but somewhat sleepy." In contrast, Sylder is "genial, unofficial, and awake"—a statement that captures the opposing values driving the novel's plot (98). "The millions are awake enough for physical labor; but only one in a million is awake enough for effective intellectual exertion," wrote Thoreau in "Walden." "To be awake is to be alive. I have never yet met a man who was quite awake" (304). Sylder is no Thoreauvian philosopher, but he has awakened into a heightened consciousness of his own nature and a reconfirmed willingness to rely on his own moral and ethical intuition rather than acting in drowsy conformity to societal institutions and conventions, like the "sleepy" officials at the tank or the "numbed traffic officers" in Knoxville, whom Sylder observes with "insolent bemusement" (164).

Though he and Kenneth Rattner are both outlaws, ironically the mature Sylder is at least partly outlawed by virtue of his ethical awareness of human relations, an awareness superior to that of the agents of law and government. This consciousness is expressed in his scorn for those who sell out their neighbors and in his generous mentoring of John Wesley, even though he probably has heard enough of the family's story to recognize the boy's father as his assailant and may even have seen the photograph of Rattner Mildred keeps on her mantel. Sylder's thought that John Wesley's susceptibility to poison ivy betokens his "bad blood" suggests that he has figured out the dead highwayman's relation to the boy (183). If so, the decision to keep this dreadful secret from John Wesley, like his lie to prevent the boy from avenging Sylder's beating by Gifford, is prompted at least as much by compassion as by self-protection. By the time John Wesley meets him, Sylder's antinomianism is restrained and principled, directed thoughtfully against injustice in legal institutions and their officials. On the other hand, Rattner, the alleged "officer" and warrior, comes to represent not only Sylder's repudiated violent impulses but also the madness of a commodified and mechanized culture—craven, egocentric, and rotten. Throughout his life, then, Sylder continues to combat Rattner both internally and externally. In doing so, he defends those values of the traditional culture that he deems worthy of preservation and passes them on to the young man who remembers him even after he has been "banished in . . . exile" from Red Branch (246). In resisting Rattner, he expunges him not only from himself but from John Wesley. In atonement he refathers John Wesley and replaces Rattner's example with that of healthy self-reliance and conscious, ethical nonconformity in dealings with institutions and individuals.

Defending the Orchard: *John Wesley Rattner*

On a metaphorical level, then, Sylder and Ownby together bury John Wesley's corrupt father, acting as salvific agents in the boy's life. This is what he honors as he remembers these two mentors beside his mother's grave. In "finding" the men who took away his father, who expunged the opportunist outlaw from John Wesley's natural makeup, the young man completes an important psychological process, confirming as the dominant parts of his identity the admirable if risky values of his newly claimed fathers. He rejects his mother's program of vengeance for the loss of his biological father, which amounts to his violent heritage, and replaces it with a healthy pattern of mindful, ethical, and self-reliant dealings with the world. In electing his fathers, then, John Wesley repudiates not only his biological father but also his death-seeking mother.

As Prather points out, the grotesque imagery in which John Wesley as narrator presents both his parents exposes his alienation ("Like Something Seen" 42–43). His antinomianism thus begins with repudiation of the parent as given in favor of finding his own way and identifying those to whom he can conscientiously give his allegiance. This narrative disloyalty to his parents functions both realistically, as a gauge of his emotional trauma as an essentially orphaned child, and more metaphysically, as an emblem of his psychological and spiritual self-reliance, his dedication to re-creating himself. Lester Ballard in *Child of God* is similarly orphaned but does not consciously repudiate his neglectful parents, which leaves him more vulnerable to the toxic emotions that keep him in thrall, forever acting out his repossession of those who have abandoned him.

The rebellious streak in young John Wesley is not as immediately apparent as Sylder and Ownby's antinomian tendencies, but incipient in this compassionate and earnest child is the principled and conscious man he will become. At fourteen, he seems naive and unsure of himself, overwhelmed by the program of vengeance his mother imposes on him, unsettled by witnessing a couple having sex in a field, panicked by the advances of the precocious Wanita Tipton, terrified at the smell of death he perceives in Sylder's wrecked car. Poised on the brink of manhood but without a living father or a healthy mother to guide him, he is bewildered by the realities of sex and death and does not seem sure enough of anything to rebel against the world's injustices. Although he attends school, it plays no role in his narrative and seems insignificant for his emotional growth. So when he instinctively turns to the natural world for education about life and death, he turns away from both his schoolteachers and his self-absorbed mother, rejecting their influence or relegating it to the category of the irrelevant. His escaping from the house at night to explore the land or to tend his traps is emblematic of his rejection of his mother's domestic influence, his rebellion from her rule.[25] Further, it seems clear even before he meets Sylder and Ownby that he will evade her attempt to make him avenge his father's death. "How can I?" he asks her, and behind this response lies not only his sense of impotence in the face of an impossible task but also his repugnance to the taking of another's life (66). He swears to fulfill her mandate under the duress of her painful grip and in empathy for her pain over "innumerable dreams laid to death upon the hearth" (67). But as he grows in courage and reliance on his own judgment, he will abjure this coerced promise, never forgetting it but never fulfilling it in the sense he has promised his mother.

The boy's ambiguous relationship to the natural world, accepting its nurturing tuition but also naively engaging in utilitarian muskrat trapping, reenacts the early history of Arthur Ownby and of the Kolodnian archetype of the American male who must eventually confront his guilt over his violation of the land. John Wesley conceives the idea of trapping through conversations with Warn Pulliam, hardly an enlightened environmentalist. As his bargaining with the kindly old clerk in the Knoxville hardware store suggests, John Wesley has given more thought to the economics of his enterprise than to his relation to the creatures he will trap. Indeed, accounting tropes partially pattern his thinking throughout the novel. Like the pioneer, like young Arthur Ownby, the boy sees his use of the natural world as a means to his own survival and well-being. The traps allow him to enter the cash economy, and his immediate spending plans do not extend beyond buying yet more traps. But his efforts to earn constitute a bid for the self-sufficiency of manhood, perhaps an attempt to become the "man" of the Rattner household that so clearly needs a responsible and capable adult. Mildred burdens and challenges her son with her idealized portrayal of Kenneth as a proud "provider" (73). By becoming the breadwinner for his bereft mother, John Wesley might fulfill his promise to her in an alternative way, replacing his father and thus compensating in part for her terrible loss. His stake in this endeavor comes through an accident involving a natural creature, when he finds the injured sparrow hawk in the road—probably the victim of a car (77). With the best of intentions, he tries to nurse it back to health, but to do this he imprisons it within a cardboard box, where it dies. John Wesley innocently sells the bird's body to the county, and the windfall bounty allows him to buy his first traps. From nature's providence and plenitude—and exploitation, he will provide for himself and his mother.

Throughout most of the book, John Wesley is serenely unconscious that he is thus incurring a debt he will later feel compelled to repay: "this dollar which he hadn't even known that he owed" (232). He sets traps for mink and muskrat with so little success that it does not occur to him that he may affect the land he so loves. He enthusiastically learns to hunt raccoons with Sylder, treasuring the activity as a masculine bonding ritual that earns him the respect of the older men of his community—validation that the fatherless boy craves. The hunting is corollary to his trapping, and again it seems to him that wild nature has the upper hand: the big coon is more than a match for the little hound Lady with whom John Wesley is linked—both of them exhibiting admirable "heart" (126). If he is repelled by the other boys' callous treatment of wild animals, he does not challenge them about it. And when he shows Warn the dead mink mauled by the cat, and Warn consoles him by telling him it is only a "cotton mink," which would have brought half the price of a "first-class mink," John Wesley slings its body carelessly to the top of the woodpile—enacting the utilitarian approach to nature he has learned from his culture (206).

Moving into the world of nature, John Wesley breaks through the strange isolation that has seemed to dominate his life before the autumn of his fourteenth year. We know that he and his mother arrive in Red Branch as outsiders, kin to "the stranger" Kenneth Rattner, and the text is almost silent about any social contacts either of them has enjoyed before 1940. As John Wesley escapes the circle of solitude imposed by his parents, he not only turns to the land for fellowship but begins there to encounter others via the agency of nature. He meets all of his new friends out of doors—Sylder and the other coon hunters, Warn, Johnny, Boog—or through the agency of those he has met in a natural setting, as when Sylder introduces him to the Tiptons and Warn takes him to visit Ownby. And his development of an extended family of friends and mentors oscillates between outdoor scenes and those in the warming homes of his new companions, scenes in which he is always welcomed into an intimate circle and nurtured with food or wine. Such communion with others is crucial to his breaking free of his mother's stifling influence. With the death of his father he has not exactly won the Oedipal contest since his mother remains obsessively devoted to the iconic memory of her husband. Yet she threatens to draw him into the closed circuit of her grief. He is in danger of remaining in lifelong thrall to her destructive tutelage, and his adolescent intuition that he needs to pull away from her is sound. One implication of the book's ending, when John Wesley steps through the gap in the fence that encloses the graveyard where his mother lies, is that he is conclusively declaring his freedom from the death-in-life his parents represent.

John Wesley's awakening into conscious rebellion results from his loyalty to his two mentors—an allegiance deepened by his great need for masculine acceptance and role models. His new consciousness combines Ownby's respect for the natural world with the ethical defiance of governmental institutions and agents displayed by both Ownby and Sylder. On the very day when John Wesley helps Sylder out of his overturned car, he is already choosing his new friend over Constable Gifford. He does not agonize about this decision. And it is not because Sylder has given him one of Lady's puppies, which is a simple act of gratitude and friendship untainted by bribery. Like the other men of his culture, the boy is reluctant to turn in his law-breaking neighbor. Sylder seems to take this culturally instilled value for granted from the beginning. So when Gifford asks questions about the blockader's abandoned car, threatening John Wesley for trapping without the license the boy didn't know he needed and confiscating his traps in hopes of pressuring him to give evidence against Sylder, John Wesley's allegiance to his friend only solidifies, and resentment of the law enters his awareness for the first time (159–60).

The one-two punch of seeing both mentors incarcerated unjustly for relatively minor offenses drives John Wesley into his conscious repudiation of the powers attempting to hold his people in subjugation. In his initial outrage, he is ready to pledge himself to avenge the severe and cowardly beating Gifford has given Sylder, embracing for the first time his mother's code of vengeance but transferring it from his natural father to his adopted one. Crucially, in their interview in the county jail, Sylder acts the genuine father to John Wesley, countering Mildred's dangerous teaching with his somewhat specious argument that balance and justice already have been achieved with his imprisonment: that he feels obligated to pay with jail time for the blockading that has financially rewarded him for that time in advance (214). He presents the law as a kind of contractual game of tag, with the consequences of playing readily accepted on both sides. But John Wesley cannot move past his sense that he is indebted to Sylder, that the man has suffered on the boy's account, and he wants to settle these accounts to make it "square" (212–13). The young man feels a rage for justice, for balancing the books, and Sylder can quiet his rage only by cruelly ridiculing John Wesley's desire "to be some kind of a goddamned hero" (214). He has seen the boy's attraction to playing the rescuer twice already, when John Wesley pulled him from the wrecked car and when he pulled the nearly drowned Lady from the creek. Sylder's concern for John Wesley, still only fifteen, leads him to chastise his own kind of antinomianism in the boy in the hopes of protecting him from the legal harassment he has been willing to risk for himself. The shame Sylder induces in John Wesley has the desired effect: it prevents the boy from jumping rashly into the icy waters of rebellious outlawry. But it does not really temper the new awareness John Wesley is formulating. His will to disbelieve Sylder's repudiation is manifest in the "wan" farewell smile he gives to his advisor. And if we read the novel as John Wesley's hallucinated recollection, it becomes clear that Sylder's final thoughts rescinding what he has told the boy represent the mature John Wesley's own conclusions: "*That's not true what I said. It was a damned lie ever word. He's [Gifford's] a rogue and a outlaw hisself and you're welcome to shoot him, burn him down in his bed, any damn thing, because he's a traitor to boot*" (214–15).

Despite these aggressive thoughts, however, John Wesley has not pledged himself to a life of violent revenge for the wrongs done to his friends and neighbors. He honors Sylder by listening to his advice and not playing the hero. In doing so, he also frees himself from his mother, from mindlessly fulfilling his coerced promise to avenge his father's death. And in remembering Sylder he celebrates the life of this "outlaw" who has set him free of the law, whether laid down by civil or parental authority, and attuned him instead to the law of conscience.

The shock of seeing Ownby's fate within the civil institutions of progressive East Tennessee amplifies and confirms the alienation John Wesley has already felt in his farewell conversation with Sylder. The incarceration of both men repeats the primal loss of parents with which John Wesley has been struggling much of his young life. Sylder may calm his resentment temporarily, but John Wesley's understanding a few weeks later that the new order has casually discarded the life of Ownby, the venerable old man of the country, reawakens his outrage. Nevertheless, his reckless desire to lash out at the agents of such law is now curbed, appropriately deflected away from violence and toward symbolic protest. John Wesley has arrived at his mature stance of conscientious, nonviolent revolt, manifested in his returning the hawk bounty to the county courthouse and in his leaving Red Branch, refusing either to witness further or to take part in the destruction of the land and the mountain culture. In leaving, he does not "go west" into an unspoiled paradise; the narrative offers no hope that such islands of wilderness or uncorrupt communities of men exist within the modern world. In fact the chronology of the novel emphasizes that John Wesley leaves Red Branch to enter the world of America at war, the era of the atomic bomb developed at Oak Ridge and Los Alamos, when the progressive order of modern America is exposed as a monstrous will to thrive at any expense to humanity and nature. But John Wesley sets himself in opposition to this order, refusing, like Thoreau, to support it in conscience or deed.

The law's harsh treatment of his mentors confirms John Wesley in his resistance to any order that functions without conscience; and the recognition that the hawk bounty is paid simply because the county prefers that the hawk not exist shatters his own complacency about nature, pushing him to articulate the new conception that wild creatures have "some value or use commensurate with a dollar other than the fact of their demise" (233). His response is still formulated in the utilitarian terms of his own hunting and trapping: one kills what can be used for fur or food, and that use justifies and in a sense dignifies the animal's death. But questions of value come with his recognition that in commodifying the hawk's demise, in setting an exchange "value on death and annihilation" (Chollier 172), the civic order does not justify its killing by dignified use, that it kills to reorder the world according to its convenience. And this hints at his moving toward the more ecocentric and reverent view of nature exemplified in Ownby. His very "narration" of Ownby's development of a more enlightened view of nature confirms that he himself, by the time of the imaginative act, has made the same journey.

The tragic endings of the narrative strands concerning Sylder and Ownby, in which these awakened and free men are caged and defeated, is tempered by the novel's celebration of their lasting impact on John Wesley. With their imprisonment and with the official devaluing of the land as represented by the sparrow hawk, he loses much of what has made Red Branch his home, but his mature values and his mindful approach to life cannot be stripped from him. His narrative after seven years reaffirms them, and his unfettered escape from the cemetery of Red Branch, from the old community that has become a grave-yard, is a movement into life. John Wesley carries with him his old allegiances and memories and a thoughtful resistance to orders and agents that function in sleepy unawareness of their ethical responsibility to the land and to other humans. Like the elderly Billy Parham of *Cities of the Plain*, he carries them into an alien and diminished world. But John Wesley's narrative act is itself a gesture of rebellion, as Prather has argued ("Like Something Seen"). It is his "Walden"—his assertion of a more authentic way of being in the world—as, quite possibly, *The Orchard Keeper* is McCarthy's.

Chapter Two

Cosmic Estrangement *Outer Dark* (1968)

Outer Dark represents a significant departure from McCarthy's almost trade-mark tendency of grounding his fictions in an actual time and place, a practice begun in *The Orchard Keeper* and maintained in all of his other novels except *The Road*, where it is significantly modified. Even while the second novel invokes a rich texture of realistic imagery of rural life and deploys McCarthy's research into cultural aspects of nineteenth-century Tennessee, its deliberately under-determined and ambiguous locale contributes to the novel's parabolic qualities; and the gothic imagery—surprising, fabulous, fraught with significance—is the stuff of dreams overlaid with fairy tale and Dantean or, most prominently, gnostic myth. The dream is a significant structuring device, marking the novel as an early venture with techniques and ideas McCarthy later exploited most strikingly in *Blood Meridian*, where the kid's encounter with the judge in the San Diego jail, an ambiguous dream of self-accusation and denial of responsi-bility, retroactively calls into question the nature of the kid's progress in vio-lence, as well as in the epilogue of *Cities of the Plain*, with its evocation of a Chinese box of embedded dreams and lives. Culla's frightening dream of bear-ing responsibility for engulfing all the dream-supplicants in his darkness, for making it *outer* dark and thus capturing them within his nightmare, establishes the subsequent experience of the novel as a kind of dream and suggests the ambiguous and paradoxical relationships between dreamer and dreamed that are explored in the epilogue of *Cities of the Plain*. The surrealistic imagery of *Outer Dark* frequently suggests that not only does the novel occur in a dream-scape, not only are the triune and their avatars manifestations of Culla's initial framing dream, but the "real" characters Culla confronts are also "figures wan-dered from a dream" (146) or "toilers in a dream stunned and without purpose" (134). Thus we are encouraged to read Culla the dreamer as the "narrator" of the novel, recalling the meta-narrational way in which the frame of *The Orchard Keeper* intimates that John Wesley is the "narrator" of its hallucinated recollec-tion even as we confront it as a narrative with its own autonomy.

We witness Rinthy's experience as a separate life and yet one that the darkness of Culla's dream impinges upon. She is a presence in his dream, as he is in hers. She is simultaneously the author of her own dream/life and a figment of his, and yet the two worlds touch, suggesting a notion revisited impressively in McCarthy's next three novels, that our inner life is always manifest in the world around us: our experience of the world is always a projection of our inner grace or darkness, and the world of "reality" is largely subjective. The differing experiences of Culla and Rinthy as they travel the "same" surreal world are central to this. The "dream-roads" in *Outer Dark*, like Dante's visions of the inferno, purgatorio, and paradiso, are metaphors for states of being, of spirit: whether it be the frail and grief-stricken grace of Rinthy, the hounded guilt and denial of Culla, or the aggrieved self-righteousness and malevolence of the tinker, who is linked with both Culla and Rinthy as a third wanderer in the purgatorial dream (229).

Outer Dark is also a road narrative, or more precisely two or even three or four interwoven road narratives, governed by dream logic while retaining a loose chronology and approximate verisimilitude to lived experience. As a road narrative, it has obvious structural affinities with some of McCarthy's later books, especially *Blood Meridian*, *The Crossing*, and *The Road*. Even more insistently than these novels, though, *Outer Dark's* road narrative is recursive, the linearity of the road broken by seemingly haphazard but fateful intersections of characters' paths, by repetition, and by circling. And even more than is usual in a picaresque tale, the road narratives of *Outer Dark* are fragmented. The focus shifts abruptly from Culla's experience to Rinthy's and back, with briefer digressions to other characters such as the triune or, especially at the moments of their deaths, to Squire Salter, the snakehunter, and the tinker. Culla and Rinthy's alternating scenes, which emphasize their isolation from one another and from any sense of community, occur with striking discontinuity, often after substantial intervals of weeks or seasons, and sometimes achronologically. The passages' seasonal references suggest that even some of the Holmes' similar experiences such as their perceptions of maddened horses or calling mockingbirds are not synchronous, yet within the temporal and spatial dislocation characteristic of the novel, such repetition reinforces the feeling that the pair are always tracking adjacent to one another in a long series of near misses. A kind of narrative isolation also governs the representation of the triune in the first sections of the novel. Until they intersect with Culla himself, the three dark figures are narrated only in italicized interchapters as if on one level they remain figments of his dreams, projections of his inner dark, forecasting or representing his own dark impulses and deeds but existing on a different plane from the events of the novel proper. As the narrative progresses, however, they impinge ever more directly on the experience of Culla and the other characters, fatefully intersecting with them in a variation on the convergences of Rattner with Sylder (*The Orchard Keeper*) or the judge with the kid (*Blood Meridian*) or Chigurh with Moss (*No Country for Old Men*). Thus the novel's structure raises questions of the triune's nature and identity that cannot be resolved on a literal level but that reinforce the novel's philosophical grounding in gnostic myth and symbol.

Almost from the beginnings of McCarthy scholarship, a debate has evolved around the nature of the metaphysical grounding of *Outer Dark*. The earliest treatment, by William J. Schafer, gives the book a Christian reading, identifying a source of its title in Matthew 8:9–12, in which "outer darkness" is a spiritual state of pale belief or unconviction.[1] Despite his claim that McCarthy demonstrates an "antimetaphysical bias" (2), Bell also recognizes *Outer Dark*'s metaphysical concerns, relating the opposition between Rinthy and Culla to the blind man's dualism of "word and flesh" (*OD* 240). He suggests that the blind man's theology "seems less Christian than Manichaean, for the separation of word and flesh in *Outer Dark* is complete; and the word is, moreover, decidedly unmanifest, an alien idea" and characterizes the novel's world as a realm where "some demented and unapproachable God invisibly presides" (*Achievement* 35, 38). But he argues that McCarthy's vision is essentially nihilistic, that *Outer Dark* is "as brutally nihilistic as any serious novel written in this century in this unnihilistic country" (*Achievement* 34). Although John Grammer concurs with Bell when he observes that the novel offers "not the faintest hint of providential guidance," he nevertheless finds it "positively turgid with moral import" (38, 36). In "Naming, Knowing and Nothingness: McCarthy's Moral Parables," Arnold explicitly counters Bell's assessment of McCarthy as nihilistic and seconds Schafer's approach; he stresses Culla's self-persecuting sense of hounded guilt and his persistent unknowing, connecting his experience not only to biblical passages in Matthew, Corinthians, and Revelations but also to those of the condemned in the outer circle of hell in Dante, souls who will forever remain beyond grace. More recently Christopher Metress has attempted to reconcile Christian and nihilist readings by approaching the novel in light of the negative theology of medieval mystics in "*Via Negativa:* The Way of Unknowing in Cormac McCarthy's *Outer Dark*." Picking up on Arnold's query, "who is to say, finally, that the swamp even awaits the blind man?" ("Naming, Knowing" 54), Metress argues that the blind man's experience of life as a realm of "obscure metaphysical abundance" is counterposed to Culla's outer dark in that it suggests a mystical alternative through acceptance of the darkness of unknowing, acceptance that God is unknowable and that He may thus best be apprehended through acknowledgment of his Unknowable nature (152).[2]

Most of these readings of the novel's metaphysics have been productive in their own ways, and all—even Bell's nihilist reading—have recognized the metaphysical allegory at the heart of the novel. There is clearly a pattern of nothingness in *Outer Dark* that any reading must accommodate, as even Arnold's and Metress's do. At the same time, the pattern of biblical and Dantean references in this novel and in McCarthy's other works is significant. Many readers have noticed the Christian imagery in McCarthy's work, and Jason Ambrosiano, in "Blood in the Tracks: Catholic Postmodernism in *The Crossing*," has discussed McCarthy's reflection of his specifically Roman Catholic heritage. But McCarthy's moral and spiritual parables seem to me to be highly syncretic, blending and transcending his reading in a variety of theological and philosophical works, especially their mythic elements. *Child of God*, for instance, makes allegorical use of Platonic mythology complicated with gnostic overtones as it charts Lester Ballard's progressive spiritual blindness and descent into the mere materialism of human flesh. In "McCarthy and the Sacred," Arnold has recently demonstrated the relevance to *The Crossing* of the work of the mystic Jacob Boehme, whom McCarthy quotes in an epigraph to *Blood Meridian*; and Metress briefly comments on Boehme as a theologian whose thought is compatible with the apophatic approach of the *via negativa* (149). J. Douglas Canfield discusses the relevance of Heidegger's existentialism in his "Crossing from the Wasteland into the Exotic in McCarthy's Border Trilogy," and various scholars such as Frank Shelton, William Prather, and David Holloway have examined the echoes of French existentialists in McCarthy's work, especially in *Suttree*.

McCarthy directly refers to "gnostic workmen" in *Suttree* (464), and in "*Suttree* and *L'Etranger*: The Hounds of Gnosticism" Dale Cosper and Ethan Cary challenge earlier readings of the Knoxville novel as absurdist, arguing that it is more gnostic than Camus's *The Stranger*, despite their many similarities of plot, character and theme. *Blood Meridian*, as Leo Daugherty has shown in "Gravers False and True: *Blood Meridian* as Gnostic Tragedy," explicitly invokes gnostic thought in its references to archons, the planet Anareta, and the ogdoad, as well as its depiction of the Seeker who strikes fire out of the rock in the epilogue. Harold Bloom, himself a longtime student of gnosticism, appropriately warns against a reductive reading of that novel as a "Gnostic fable," yet he acknowledges that "even though McCarthy deliberately cuts off any traditional explanations of a negative transcendence, such as a Gnostic explanation or a Manichaean explanation or an Orphic explanation, still, the intimations reverberate" (Josyph 210, 213). Although it too stops short of representing the transcendence that gnosticism yearned toward, *Outer Dark*, also, it seems to me, should be read partly through its intimations of gnostic and related Mandaean and Manichaean myths and symbols. In fact the gnostic revaluation or deconstruction of what has come to be mainstream Christian teaching and especially the Judaic tradition that lies underneath it, may comprise the

most prevalent (but not the only) pattern of metaphysical intimations informing the novel. Gnostic images and ideas also recur in *Child of God* and even
more strikingly in *Suttree,* the Knoxville novel on which McCarthy was actively
working from the onset of his writing career, including the time in which *Outer
Dark* was composed. The gnostic aspect of *Outer Dark* is one of the most significant markers of its doubling by *Blood Meridian:* both works ambiguously
play out elements of the gnostic tragedy of the fleshbound human spirit, one
set against a proto-southern dreamscape, the other against a bloody Southwest,
surreal in its very naturalism. In both, McCarthy foregrounds humankind's
tragic condition within cosmos rather than transcendence; certainly none of
his major characters achieves it. Yet the potential for transcendence is, I think,
strongly implied, not only in the late appearance of counterpointing characters
who seem to possess a spiritual direction noticeably lacking in the main characters but also in the narrative emphasis on the spiritual void or alienation of
the main characters themselves, which posits for the reader their great spiritual
need. These implications redeem the vision of the novels from nihilism, just as
gnosticism itself is not properly classified as a nihilist philosophy even though
it exhibits some nihilist elements.

Gnostic thought and writing was considered heretical and was systemati-
cally suppressed by the early Christian church, and thus it was known through
the nineteenth century via a handful of extant documents and via the antignos-
tic writings of such early church fathers as Irenaeus, the late-second-century
Bishop of Lyons. However, the discoveries in 1902 of a trove of Manichaean
manuscripts at Turfan in Chinese Turkestan (Grimstad 15) and in 1945 of the
Nag Hammadi gnostic manuscripts in Egypt created great excitement among
scholars of religion and antiquity by adding substantially to the archive of
gnostic and related thought. Because of a variety of problems of ownership and
competition among scholars, the Nag Hammadi documents were not fully translated from Coptic and published in English until 1977 (Pagels xiii, xxiv–xxix),
but the worldwide anticipation of their publication brought new attention to
the ancient gnostics during the years when McCarthy was working on *Outer
Dark, Child of God,* and *Suttree.* The most likely source of his understanding of
gnosticism before the completion of *Outer Dark* is Hans Jonas's seminal *The
Gnostic Religion: The Message of the Alien God and the Beginnings of Christianity,*
published in English in 1958 and again in 1963—the year in which McCarthy
likely began writing *Outer Dark*—with an additional chapter on the Nag Hammadi manuscripts and an epilogue exploring the philosophical affinities of
gnosticism, existentialism, and nihilism. Other sources in English available to
McCarthy early on include *Fragments of a Faith Forgotten* (1900) by G. R. S.
Mead, whose works did much to popularize gnosticism and whose Theosophical Society influenced W. B. Yeats and other modernist writers in Europe

(Grimstad 19–20); Jessie Weston's widely-known *From Ritual to Romance* (1920)—influenced by Mead's *Thrice-Greatest Hermes* (1906), and which in turn influenced T. S. Eliot's *The Waste Land;* and *Primitive Christianity in its Contemporary Setting* (1956) by Rudolf Bultmann, under whom Jonas studied as a graduate student (Grimstad 16). Gnosticism, especially in its emphasis on self-knowledge as a form of redemption, was also a profound influence on Carl Jung, evidence of which is found in his autobiography *Memories, Dreams, Reflections;* his neo-gnostic myth "Seven Sermons to the Dead"; his essay "Gnostic Symbols of the Self"; and his *Answer to Job* (see Grimstad 48–55).

Jonas quotes extensively from a variety of gnostic manuscripts, and before his work on *Outer Dark* McCarthy could also have found translations in editions such as Robert M. Grant's *Gnosticism: A Source Book of Heretical Writings from the Early Christian Period* (1961). He might have read in *The Nag Hammadi Library* (1973–77) as he worked on his big Knoxville novel. He probably could not have read Elaine Pagels's *The Gnostic Gospels* (1979), an exposition of the theological, political, and ideological differences between the early Roman Catholic Church and the gnostic thinkers, before completing *Suttree,* but he might well have known it by the time he completed *Blood Meridian* (1985).

In his study of *Blood Meridian,* Leo Daugherty concludes that McCarthy draws primarily from Manichaean versions of gnosticism in that novel. Hans Jonas traces commonalities between the Hellenistic and later, eastern schools of gnostic thought, the Mandaean and the Manichaean, to argue that they represent various manifestations of a unified religion. At the same time, he distinguishes two primary branches of gnosticism, the Iranian (which includes the Manichaean), which postulated an original precosmic Darkness that entrapped elements of the Light in the darkness of cosmos, and the Syrian-Egyptian, which traced the derivation of the world's darkness from a failure in the Divine itself (Jonas, *Gnostic Religion* 130, 174). Jonas devotes separate chapters to the variations of the gnostic myth found in the diverse documents, but he also derives a central, definitive gnostic vision or myth that unifies all these "heretical" sources that early church fathers found inimical to Christianity as they defined it. He shows that certain symbols and mythic elements recur in the gnostic writings, often the same images found in the Bible and in Christian teaching or in Hellenistic tradition, but with different valuation or implications. One of the most significant emphases of Jonas's book is that "there is an indissoluble mythological core to gnostic thought as such. Far remote from the rarefied atmosphere of philosophical reasoning, it moves in the denser medium of imagery and personification" (Jonas, *Gnostic Religion* 46–47).

Outer Dark's allusiveness to gnosticism, too, functions primarily on the levels of myth and metaphor and ranges freely among the various manifestations described by Jonas. McCarthy's lack of narrative interest in tracing the failure in the Divine would seem to support Daugherty's claim that the author drew more from the Manichaean version of gnosticism than the Valentinian (Syrian-Egyptian); the Manichaean idea of an original principle of darkness, an oppositional force to the Light of the Unknown God seems more consistent with McCarthy's treatment of evil in his novels. Nevertheless, in *Outer Dark* his evocation of gnostic symbols and mythic elements follows Jonas in echoing these ancient documents from an amalgamated perspective without attempting a consistent reflection of one system in preference to another. In exploring McCarthy's deployment of gnosticism in his Tennessee novels, I use the term *gnosticism* in the inclusive sense that Jonas does, to refer to all those ancient writers, the Christian gnostics and the Iranean and the Syrian-Egyptian sects, who share the underlying mythos that Jonas defines. When I refer to *Outer Dark* as "gnostic," I do not mean to imply that it constitutes a modern gnostic myth, such as the self-conscious adaptations of Carl Jung in "Seven Sermons to the Dead" or of Thomas Mann in the prologue to his *Joseph* tetralogy (see Grimstad 49, 29) but that it reflects McCarthy's awareness of gnostic symbols, character types, and anticosmic attitudes and his extensive borrowing from or alluding to them in creating his own parable of spiritual alienation in the cosmic realm.

The key tenets of gnosticism, according to Jonas, begin with the "radical dualism" of its theology. The True Deity is not conceived as the Hebraic Creator God; rather, He is utterly transmundane and alien to the cosmos: "To the divine realm of light, self-contained and remote, the cosmos is opposed as the realm of darkness." The power(s) that created the world, whether archons or the demiurge, are themselves alien to the Unknown Father" and ignorant both of Him and of their own subordinate status. Similarly, "The transcendent God Himself is hidden from all creatures and is unknowable by natural concepts. Knowledge of Him requires supranatural revelation and illumination and even then can hardly be expressed otherwise than in negative terms" (Jonas, *Gnostic Religion* 42–43). (This approach to the Divine through negative theology links gnosticism with the much later medieval *via negativa* discussed by Metress.)

As a salvation religion, the gnostic system is strikingly anticosmic, far more than either Christianity or Platonism. Cosmos is the "domain of the Archons," "a vast prison whose innermost dungeon is the earth, the scene of man's life." Separating humanity from the Unknown God are the enclosing spheres of planets and stars, associated with the archons and often personified as active demonic forces: "Thus the vastness and multiplicity of the cosmic system express the degree to which man is removed from God. . . . The Archons collectively rule over the world, and each individually in his sphere is a warder of the cosmic prison," even barring the soul's attempt to return after death to its original home in God (Jonas, *Gnostic Religion* 43).

The anticosmic dualism of gnosticism led to its "contempt for nature" (Jonas, "Epilogue" 337) and informs its notion of human nature as well. The human's transmundane spirit or pneuma is "a portion of the divine substance from beyond which has fallen into the world; and the Archons created man for the express purpose of keeping it captive there." The archons fashioned two components of man's nature to imprison the spark of the divine: body, and "soul"[3] or psyche—the "appetites and passions of natural man," created in the image of the archons' own psychic nature: "In its unredeemed state the pneuma thus immersed in soul and flesh is unconscious of itself, benumbed, asleep, or intoxicated by the poison of the world: in brief, it is 'ignorant.' Its awakening and liberation is effected through 'knowledge.' . . . The goal of gnostic striving is the release of the 'inner man' from the bonds of the world and his return to his native realm of light. The necessary condition for this is that he *knows* about the transmundane God and about himself, that is, about his divine origin as well as his present situation, and accordingly also about the nature of the world" (Jonas, *Gnostic Religion* 44). However, because God is alien to cosmos, humans cannot know of Him through natural means. Therefore an agent of revelation is required. The Alien Man (Jesus, in Christian gnostic systems) who bears this illumination "is a messenger from the world of light who penetrates the barriers of the spheres, outwits the Archons, awakens the spirit from its earthly slumber, and imparts to it the saving knowledge 'from without.' . . . The knowledge thus revealed . . . comprises the whole content of the gnostic myth, with everything it has to teach about God, man, and world" (Jonas, *Gnostic Religion* 45). More particularly, however, the *gnosis* imparted is the "knowledge of the way": the spirit's way out of the world and beyond the imprisoning spheres to the realm of light. The gnostic myth of the spirit's ascent emphasizes its journey through successive spheres, during which it divests itself of layers of the psyche until, stripped of all earthly admixture, it is reunified with the divine, contributing its mite to the ultimate restoration of divine wholeness (Jonas, *Gnostic Religion* 45).

Before examining the specific ways in which McCarthy's novel resonates with ancient gnostic myth, I think it wise to clarify that Grammer's discussion of the southern pastoral in McCarthy as "gnostic" is quite different from my undertaking here. Grammer's understanding of the word is borrowed from Eric Voegelin by way of Lewis Simpson's *The Dispossessed Garden*. Simpson writes,

> Gnosticism—the record of which is ancient but the major development
> of which comes with its seemingly irresistible realization in modern sci-
> ence, industrialism, and technology, and in the economic systems these
> have generated . . . —is the belief that knowledge available to men

(gnosis) can be used to change the very constitution of being. . . . In eliminating from a world picture the undesirable elements, the gnostic mind
. . . makes a highly selective evaluation of the past. In extreme gnosticism
the past, I suppose, may just be eliminated as a dimension of existence. In
any case the gnostic mind concludes . . . that all history is known to it, up
to and including the final culmination which will in some manner be constituted of perfected men in a perfected society. (76–77)

Grammer applies Simpson's claim that "America is one of the most alluring
fantasies of a new world the gnostic imagination has conceived" (77) to the
utopian projects of the old South's pastoralism and the new South's urban
development and to the utopian denial of history that he finds at their core. But
it is important to recognize that in Grammer we are at four removes, at least,
from ancient gnostic philosophy. Since several scholars have now discussed or
merely labeled McCarthy's work as gnostic, and since some, such as Guillemin,
have begun to accept Simpson and Grammer's definitions, it seems worthwhile
to stress how far their definitions stray from theological gnosticism (*Pastoral
Vision* 55).

In *Gnostic Return to Modernity*, religion scholar Cyril O'Regan comments on
the vagueness of much use of the term *gnosticism*, lamenting that "the words
Gnostic or *Gnosticism* [sometimes] simply function as a longhand [*sic*] for a particular state of mind regarding the world, most often an agitation with respect
to its polymorphous out-of-jointness. Certainly, quite often the terms have
more rhetorical than propositional force" (25). He identifies Eric Voegelin as a
prime offender: Voegelin is "the thinker who has most annoyed the specialists
in Gnosticism, for he is often cited for illegitimate extension of the concept . . .
beyond the Hellenistic field" (244n5). "In Voegelin," O'Regan writes, "the term
Gnostic covers a dizzying array of religious, political, philosophical, and psychological discourses that amounts to an indictment of the whole of modernity . . .
from Machiavelli and Locke to the present" (28). O'Regan has Voegelin's ap-
propriation of the term in mind when he asserts that such writers make of
gnosticism "ciphers of decline at best, violation at worst, with classical and/or
Christian culture as their favored object" (25).

My focus is on the ways that *Outer Dark* engages the ancient religion, as
translated and interpreted only by scholars of gnosticism whom McCarthy
might have read, primarily Hans Jonas. My comments on gnosticism will thus
strike readers as very different from, even incompatible with, those of Grammer and others who follow Grammer's lead. The discrepancy can be resolved
by recognizing that Simpson and Grammer use the term *gnosticism* in a special
way adapted by Voegelin. It may be well to comment here on the specific dis-
crepancies I see between Grammer's use of the term and my own. Ancient

gnostics certainly evolved a myth of human life that discounted cosmic history: as O'Regan puts it, gnosticism does not exhibit "friendliness to time and history" (67). The only history of genuine, which is to say spiritual, concern to the ancient gnostics was the transmundane history of the fall of the Divine substance and the ongoing attempt to redeem the fragmented spirit through gnosis of its origin. Cosmic life was predetermined in all its essential characteristics from the point of its creation by the false god(s), the world-rulers. Thus the profoundly anticosmic gnostics embraced no utopian or progressive projects on the earthly stage, since all cosmic "order," whether natural or cultural, partook of the overriding disorder and darkness. Grimstad writes that the gnostic anticosmic orientation "fuels a spirit of revolt against the kingdoms of the world that cannot be redeemed by politics or the progress of history" (9). Such revolt, then, was not political or social. Pagels points out that gnostics "pursued an essentially solitary path . . . derive[d] from [their] insistence on the primacy of immediate experience" (145). If their religion was utopian, it was only so in its valorizing of the suppressed human spiritual element and the envisioning of a reunification with the Divine and the resulting end of—and liberation from— cosmic history. The gnostics might rebel against world-rule through either withdrawal or deliberate transgression of moral and civil law, but they devised no societal, communal projects to alter the experience of being *on earth*, unless their writing and teaching might be construed as such. Their use of gnosis to "change the very constitution of being" —as Simpson puts it—was a matter of the transcendent spirit, seeking an ontological state rather than a sociological or political one.

Thus Grammer's extension of the term (following Simpson and Voegelin) moves it even farther from its ancient origin when he defines as "gnostic" the impulse to "impose stability, order and reason upon . . . fluid reality" (34). Ancient gnostics were highly skeptical of both worldly "order" and reason. Grammer finds the "gnostic" impulse at work in *Outer Dark*'s community, which he claims has attempted to deny the power of time, and he attributes to this the "near-total estrangement" of the community, "presumably once unified and solid" (37). Consistent with my understanding of the ancient gnostics' perspective, I argue that the communities of the novel are neither declining nor progressing: in their estrangement they manifest and have always manifested the changeless outer dark that ancient gnostics sought to transcend.

In McCarthy's work, outer dark is a spiritual state, but it is also conceived as a physical reality. Gnosticism, Platonism, and Dante come together here in their similar notions of embedded worlds and in their conceptions of earthly life as a spiritual condition expressed in topographical metaphor. In gnosticism the notion is quite literal: cosmos, not Hades or hell, is the realm of darkness: it is literally the outer dark, alien to the Light and to man's divine spirit but also imprisoning, enclosing, mingling, and clothing the spirit in materiality. In Platonic myths the story of the soul's progress through successive purgations and earthly incarnations makes of earthly life, with its opportunities either for oblivion or for transcendent insight, a metaphor for the purgatory of Hades. And Dante's vision, his dream in a dark wood of the circles of the inferno, purgatorio, and paradiso, each characterizing the soul's spiritual state and its corresponding fate in the afterlife, makes concrete too his own spiritual progress through cosmic realms. The narrator Dante's dream of the journey is embedded in his cosmic life and effects its transformations there. The extended metaphor of earthly life as a spiritual/spatial journey in outer dark or purgatory or hell profoundly informs all of McCarthy's novels from *Outer Dark* through *Blood Meridian* and recurs in *The Road*, although his deployment of imagery from Plato, gnostics, and Dante (as well as the Bible and other classical mythology) differs in proportion and emphasis in each.

In gnostic thought, outer dark is the realm of the cosmos, removed from the Unknown Father, the "King of Light" whose realm is absolute light unmingled with darkness (Jonas, *Gnostic Religion* 57). The *Pistis Sophia* describes earth as "outer darkness" (quoted in Jonas, *Gnostic Religion* 116), a phrase that Jonas himself uses as a synonym for the world in his discussion of the Valentinian speculation (Jonas, *Gnostic Religion* 187). This oppositional "world of darkness" is described in one of the Mandaean texts as "utterly full of evil, . . . full of devouring fire . . . full of falsehood and deceit. . . . A world of turbulence without steadfastness, a world of darkness without light . . . a world of death without eternal life, a world in which the good things perish and plans come to naught" (quoted in Jonas, *Gnostic Religion* 57). Darkness functions throughout gnostic writings as a metaphor for the death of the spirit, its oblivion in the material realm, its imprisonment in cosmos. Thus in the cosmos, light from astral bodies is also darkness, emanating from the spheres of the archontic powers (the powers of the archons, or world rulers)—not an avenue to or metaphor for spiritual illumination as in Plato. Jonas writes, "In the Hermetic Corpus we find the exhortation, 'Turn ye away from the dark light' . . . , where the paradoxical combination drives home the point that even the light so called in this world is in truth darkness" (Jonas, *Gnostic Religion* 58). McCarthy's imagery of darkness and light, sun and shadows establishes the dreamscape in which the triune, Culla, and the tinker move and pursue their lives as a world of the dead, as a death-in-life. Rinthy's world, too, is a gnostic cosmos, but crucial differences mark her lesser entanglement with the dark. Culla, the dreamer, knowing nothing, is paradoxically most "aware" of the gnostic cosmos: most entangled in the tangible experience of its darkness. But the truly gnostic awareness is the narrator's. Enclosed within his nightmare, imprisoned in cosmos, Culla achieves no gnosis or other spiritual vision; he merely lives out the terrifying cosmic nightmare formulated by the gnostics but with none of their understanding of its origin and import.

Although the novel includes many daylight scenes, it is nocturnal in emphasis. Culla is literally encased in darkness in many of the most crucial scenes of the novel: his abandonment of the child, who is born at twilight; his ordeal on the turbulent river, where the men on the ferry "seemed to hang in some great depth of darkness like spiders in a well" (164); both his encounters with the triune; and of course his acquiescence in the murder of the child. The tinker's first day with the found chap takes him into darkest night as he travels late to return to his sister; his refusal to restore the child to Rinthy occurs at night; and the triune murder the tinker after darkness has fallen (229). Rinthy is often depicted in daylight, but she travels at night as well, and several of her scenes that are decisive either in terms of plot or imagery occur at night: her evening with the family who offer her food and shelter, when all are illuminated by the lamplight that minimally "set[s] back the darkness inside" (59); her repudiation by the tinker in the shadowy firelight of the dark cabin; and her departure from the "dead black foyer," the "maw of the dead and loveless house" she shares with a male companion, for the "outer dark," where she resumes her search for her child (211). In gnostic symbolism the cosmos itself is the dark house or dwelling, and Rinthy's choice takes her from the outer dark of the farmhouse to the outer dark beyond, leaving her in essentially the same condition. Finally she waits long and long as night falls in the glade where her baby and the tinker have been murdered. The triune, of course, are almost always described either in evening twilight (as if they personify the very falling of darkness) or in the shadowy dark of night, *"which suited them very well"* (3). Together with their daylight avatars, they are, of course, the "darksome ways afoot in this world" about whom the blind man warns an uncomprehending Culla (241).

As the dreamer of this nightmare, Culla manifests the gnostic notion that the spirit, in its cosmic life, is in a state of oblivion, asleep or intoxicated. When Rinthy rouses him from his dream of the "black sun," he wakes "from dark to dark," marking the continuation of his "dream" of darkness (5). Jonas points out that the various gnostic images of cosmic oblivion reinscribe earlier depictions of the dead in the underworld and that "in gnostic thought the world takes the place of the traditional underworld and is itself already the realm of the dead, that is, of those who have to be raised to life again" (*Gnostic Religion* 68). Indeed Culla traverses a "world of the dead" (131), and his path leads him to a "faintly smoking garden of the dead that tended away to the earth's curve," where he wonders numbly "why a road should come to such a place" (242). Throughout the novel, his perceptions often seem deadened. Although he is agile of mind and hand when he delivers his infant son, quick to perceive any threat of retribution, and, as Arnold points out, exquisitely sensitive to reminders of his guilt ("Naming, Knowing" 47–48), nevertheless he is slow to catch others' jokes and irony, slow to defend himself when treated with rudeness or injustice, almost laughably stupid in the lies and evasions he invents to fend off his tormenters, and beaten into a stupor by the relentless sun that dogs his steps. "Don't fall asleep there, you'll tip over and hurt yourself," the wagoneer taunts Culla, who suffers from sunstroke and is capable only of blinking dumbly in reply. When Culla turns slowly away, the man calls him back to ask, "You ain't drunk are ye?" (136). Culla's obliviousness speaks more to his suppressed spirit than to his intellect. His dullness is emblematic of his deep entanglement in darkness.

The tinker is subject to comparable oblivion as he travels in harness to his cart that "bobbled drunkenly" and leans against its drag, "looking at nothing other than the road beneath him," so that when Rinthy speaks to him, he "started in his traces like one wrenched from a trance" (184). As if his oblivion were contagious, Rinthy follows him in her own trance with downcast eyes, unaware that he is outpacing her. Once she sees that she is being left behind, she follows his cart "as if tethered to it," but not as if more fully aware. Rather, she is "like some creature rapt and besourced by witches' music, demon piping" (187). Her trances derive from her obsession with her child, and when she leaves the farmer to search for the baby, she rises in the middle of the night "half tranced," as if "some dream had moved her so" (211). But her oblivion is not entirely a result of her deepening grief over her son. Even before Rinthy leaves the cabin where she gives birth, she is described, as Nell Sullivan points out ("Evolution" 69), in a series of doll metaphors suggesting her lack of inner vision and animation (see *OD* 24, 32, 53). The doll or marionette image links her surprisingly with her nemesis the tinker, who before the fire in the deserted cabin looks "like an effigy in rags hung by strings from an indifferent hand" (189), an allusion to the inept artificer god.

In Manichaean myth, the "unconsciousness" of man in the cosmos derives from his being bitten by the "Sons of Darkness," often compared to serpents or rabid dogs, and mankind's oblivion is thus "a veritable infection by the poison of darkness" (Jonas, *Gnostic Religion* 69). In "The Hymn of the Pearl," the poison of oblivion is taken in as food and drink as a necessary consequence of bodily life: "They mixed me drink with their cunning and gave me to taste of their meat. I forgot that I was a king's son, and served their king. I forgot the Pearl [the transcendent spirit] for which my parents had sent me. Through the heaviness of their nourishment I sank into deep slumber" (quoted in Jonas, *Gnostic Religion* 69). The passage's voice belongs to the Son of Light, the transcendent Savior, but in drinking of cosmos He suffers the same infection as humankind and stands for us all. Thus the myth resonates with Culla's unknowing, as well as with his unappeased hunger throughout the novel, with his thirst for the beehiver's alcohol, with the scene of inverted communion in which he eats of the triune's charred meat mindlessly but with choking distaste. It also informs Rinthy's parallel "communion" scene in which she eats of the "hard and sandy and tasteless" cornbread offered by the tinker who bars her from her child (190). All these images suggest their poisoning by darkness. In their outer dark, Culla, the tinker, and to some extent Rinthy, too, are in a realm of spiritual oblivion and death, the all-too-tangible cosmic underworld of gnostic myth that McCarthy compares explicitly to purgatory: ironically, they are *"like those old exiles who divorced of corporeality and enjoined ingress of heaven or hell wander forever the middle warrens"* (229)—ironically, because Culla and Rinthy's incest and the tinker's mercantile enterprise, as well as his claim of their child and the very act of eating and drinking—all their corporeal acts—mark them as prisoners of the material world. While the allusion to purgatory hints at the Christian possibility of deliverance through atonement, the language of McCarthy's simile shuts down that potential, implying that without external intervention the three are *"forever"* locked in a closed system of outer dark.

The Cosmic Shadowland: *Culla*

As one might expect in a novel of outer/inner dark, images of light and dark prevail; especially significant are the shadows that dominate Culla's chapters. In Dante's *Divine Comedy*, shadows are a sign of corporeality, and frequently the "shades"—who themselves cast no shadow—are startled at the shadow thrown by the living Dante as he travels through their realms. Shadows are more prevalent images in *Outer Dark* than in gnostic myths of cosmic existence, but in one of the Nag Hammadi texts, *The Origin of the World*, Shadow is prior even to Chaos and Darkness and is associated with them in a line of descent: "Since everybody, the gods of the world and men, contend that nothing existed before the Chaos, I will prove that they all are mistaken, for they never knew the origin of Chaos, nor its root. . . . The Chaos originated from a Shadow and was called 'Darkness'; and the Shadow in turn originated from a work [a divine failing through the agency of the *Pistis Sophia*] that exists since the beginning" (quoted in Jonas, "Epilogue" 298). From this Shadow, Envy, "devoid of spirit," was conceived and aborted, and of this abortion, Matter is the afterbirth (quoted in Jonas, "Epilogue" 304). In Valentinian texts dealing with the precosmic failing of the Sophia (Wisdom), her fall into "ignorance and formlessness . . . 'brought into being the Void-of-Knowledge, which is the Shadow . . . of the Name.'" That is, Jonas explains, the Shadow was produced when she blocked the light of the Name, the Unknown Light (Jonas, "Epilogue" 300). Thus shadow is darkness, associated with all the dark characteristics of the gnostic cosmos, especially matter, psyche, and unknowing. *Outer Dark* synthesizes these implications of Dantean and gnostic shadow imagery and amplifies them.

Culla not only walks in the shadows of the world he inhabits, he is also insistently described as standing in his own shadow. His cast shadow is a repetitious reminder even to Culla not only of his fleshly existence but also of his earthly "stain": "The man's shadow pooled at his feet, a dark stain in which he stood. In which he moved" (13). The stain is of his incestuous relations with his sister. Culla's shadow, the stain of incest, and the child itself all function as gnostic symbols of the spirit's fleshly entanglement. They prompt, at varying levels of consciousness, Culla's very un-gnostic sense of personal responsibility and guilt for his corporeal nature and deeds. In the "deep gloom" that settles into the cabin as Rinthy gives birth, Culla notices that "his arms were stained with gore," and he fetches water to cleanse the child (14). Later he sees dried blood sifting from his palms and rouses himself "to wash his hands and his arms, slowly and with care" (15). His cleansing conveys the Lady Macbeth–like implication: his impulse is to erase the stain of his incestuous deed, whether by washing his hands, cleansing the bloodstained baby, or putting it away from him.

As the fleshly stain, the shadow expresses the earthly body in which man is imprisoned. In one of several theatrical images that suggest the world as the surreal arena on which the archontic powers stage their grand cosmic illusion, Culla stands isolated in a deserted town square illuminated only by moonlight, "turning, an amphitheatrical figure in that moonwrought waste manacled to a shadow that struggled grossly in the dust" (131). Like the tinker's clanging traps, with which he is willingly burdened and harnessed, the human's very body constitutes the cosmic trap. With nice ambiguity, then, the novel's shadow imagery sometimes negates the more obvious dualism of body and shadow and identifies the shadow with body, flesh, the entrapped earthly being, suggesting paradoxically that the embodied being is some alter self embedded within and divorced from the doings of its dark shadow, the spirit or a separate self at least partly alienated from the agency and will of the shadow. There is a trace of this when the tinker and his sister carry the Holme infant through the moonlight, their shadows "so foreshortened they seemed sprung and frenzied with a violence in which their creators moved with dreamy disconcern" (23). However, the image carries a pregnant gnostic ambiguity: as those who cast the shadows, the pair are, at some level of being, aloof from the frenzied violence; yet as shadow themselves, handiwork of the gnostic artificers of the world, they are also helplessly involved in the cosmic violence that is observed with "dreamy disconcern" by their oblivious archontic creators.

Shadows most emphatically have agency or reflect some essential aspect of the cosmic self in this novel. That is, they are not *mere* illusion, as we might find in Platonic myth. Rather, they seem a literal manifestation of Jung's concept of the shadow, that archetypal dark side of the self deriving from the collective unconscious that complements yet is not acknowledged by the ego.

Jung articulated this idea in *Aion: Researches into the Phenomenology of the Self* (1951), a work in which he explicitly acknowledged gnosticism's influence. Jung wrote, "The shadow is a moral problem that challenges the whole ego-personality, for no one can become conscious of the shadow without considerable moral effort. To become conscious of it involves recognizing the dark aspects of the personality as present and real. . . . The [moral] inferiorities constituting the shadow . . . have an *emotional* nature, a kind of autonomy, and accordingly an obsessive or, better, possessive quality" (8). Culla, who most obviously engages in the enterprise of denying his Jungian shadow and who never acknowledges it as a real presence in his life, is thus most helplessly possessed by his shadow. Projected into the narrative's dream world as a literal shadow, it assaults the Squire hours before the triune murder him (47), suggesting that Culla's shadow is also *their* shadow or even that they constitute his shadow, as I discuss more fully below. The scene is prefigured when Culla finds Rinthy digging up the false grave of their child, and "his long shadow overrode her"—a passage that also reflects his original sin of sexual assault against her (32). Rinthy is nineteen in the present time of the novel, which suggests she may have been only eighteen at the time of the incestuous act—barely a woman (126). Had she been any younger, the act would have constituted statutory rape on Culla's part, whether it was violent or merely coercive. But if we recognize this passage at the false gravesite as a shadow of that prior act, it suggests that he has indeed assaulted her with violence: his shadow, associated on one level with body and will and in another compatible sense with the Jungian shadow aspect of the self, "overrode her," and she screams as she finds herself (again) "against his chest" (32). In the scene when Culla paints the barn roof and pauses, in spite of his desire to repudiate his fleshly stain, to ogle the breasts of a girl hanging laundry, we are told that "his shadow moiled cant and baneful over the lot below him," enacting once more the moiling turbulence of gnostic outer dark and the emotional turmoil of the Jungian shadow (91). When Culla flees the deserted town square of Preston Flats as if to escape the amphitheatrical vision of his shadow struggling in dust, his shadow, too, flees "nimbly over the roofs," a comment on both his will to evade his hounded condition and his state of possession (131). And as Culla nears the culmination of his endless journey, the narrator comments via his shadow on his continuing entrapment: "He went on, . . . shambling, gracelorn, . . . before him under the high afternoon sun his shadow be-wandered in a dark parody of his progress" (241–42).

In the fire-lit cabin where Rinthy has followed the tinker, the agency of the shadow and the shadow as self are again suggested, but with less emphasis on the shadow as an aspect of the unconscious. As Rinthy urgently negotiates with the tinker for the return of her child, their shadow-selves sway "like dancing cranes" in closely mirrored move and countermove (191). When their mock courtship dance fails, the tinker grasps the lamp and "their shadows wheeled wildly from each other and froze on opposite walls," plunging both into deeper turmoil and sealing them in unresolved conflict over the child (194).

In the amphitheatrical image, the dark cosmos in which Culla's shadow struggles in the dust is a "moonwrought waste." More often it is the sun, as the primary agent creating shadows, that is personified as a relentless and inimical force. Seldom if ever is the sun presented unambiguously as a metaphor for spiritual vision or divine illumination.[4] It is as if McCarthy, through the image of the sun's casting a person's shadow, metaphorically extends the gnostic idea that "life has been cast (thrown) into the world and into the body" by the archontic powers associated with the stars (Jonas, *Gnostic Religion* 63). The sun is introduced as a hostile agent in the first sentence of the novel, where it is linked with the dark triune, who move "*with something of its own implacability*" (3). Complicating the hint of an oppressive cosmic order in the sun's implacability, Culla later notices the shadow of a weed in the beehiver's mouth rapidly rotating on his face "like a sundial's hand beneath a sun berserk" (79). The paradox implied in McCarthy's image of a berserk sun is central to gnostic thought: the order of the cosmic realm is indeed an order, albeit one of oppressive law and necessity, yet from the transcendent point of view cosmic order (*harmonia*) is actually turbulence and chaos. Gnostics personified astrological bodies, associating them with the archons. Explicit personification of the sun occurs in *Outer Dark* when the exhumed corpses are displayed in the town square: "The sun stood directly over them. It seemed hung there in glaring immobility, as if perhaps arrested with surprise to see above the earth again these odds of morkin once commended there" (87). Any benign quality in the sun's surprise is countered here with its looming and glaring attention, again suggesting its implacability. Culla's sense that "someone should have cared more" than to expose the dead "beneath these eyes and such a sun"—literally the eyes of the townspeople, but by extension also the eyes of the sun—reinforces the sun's malevolent supervision as well as hinting that all exposed to its relentless glare are themselves among the dead, hounded by their own shadows (88). And its oppression is evident in another town, where people attempt to escape into shade but find no relief, "moving beneath the blinding heat like toilers in a dream stunned and without purpose"—suggesting once more the plague of unconsciousness (shadow, sleep, dream) enforced by the archontic sun (134–35). (And of course these gnostic associations of the sun with malevolent cosmic forces dominate the solar imagery of McCarthy's desert novel, *Blood Meridian*, as well.)

This is also the "black sun" of Culla's framing dream, which ambiguously darkens with will and agency, signaled by diction implying action and animation: it "*would darken* and all these souls would be cured of their afflictions before it *appeared* again . . . and the sun [*began*] *to blacken*. . . . The sun *paused*. . . . Then the sun *buckled* and dark fell *like a shout*. The last wirethin rim was *crept away*. . . . The sun *did not return* (5–6; emphasis added). Linking this passage with the tinker's complaint that he has seen so much evil in the world that he doesn't know "why God ain't put out the sun and gone away" (192), most readers have seen the darkening sun as the face of the Judeo-Christian god, the light of whose countenance shines blessings on mankind but who commands obedience to his moral laws. The blind traveler at the end of the novel tells a story that reiterates and glosses Culla's dream. He suggests that the man whose affliction was not obvious—Culla himself—has not caused the preacher, who after all may be "no true preacher," to go away (241) but rather that the agency may be that of the "darksome ways afoot in this world." Since in Culla's dream, an expression of his deep sense of transgression, he is blamed for causing the sun itself to go away, by extension we may understand that the blind seer is exonerating Culla of that guilt. However, in gnostic myth, the True God is always alien and unknown. He has never been a presence in cosmos to be forfeited. Thus His remoteness is not a sign of human guilt or original sin but of mankind's tragic, pitiable condition in the world. Further, the sun and planets are associated with the false creator(s) or artificer(s) of the world. Culla's dream, then, can be read through gnostic myth in two ways. One is that the falling of darkness is a shadowing or an eclipse of the true Unknown Light through the agency of darkness; the other is that the black sun Culla witnesses has never been the true Light at all but rather a false sun whose very presence marks the ascendancy of dark powers in the cosmos.

Without gnosis Culla—Everyman—needs the release offered by the novel's blind traveler or messenger because in his unameliorated shame over his incest, he takes on the blame for the darkness of the universe itself—a blame and responsibility that in gnostic deconstruction of the concept of original sin belongs only to the ignorant creator(s) of the cosmos, who entangled innocent spirit in matter, never to be released until each spirit is "cured" of its cosmic blindness and affliction and returned to the true Unknown God. This, gnostics believed, would take eons, which to them implied vast stretches of time and cosmic space. The terror that this "cosmic exile" under the dark sun inspired in the gnostics was often expressed in the plaint, "I wandered through worlds and generations" (Jonas, *Gnostic Religion* 54, 53). Thus the benighted people in Culla's dream wait so long under the dark sun that "the stars of another season" light the sky above them, still imprisoning them in the darkness from which they turn on Culla (6).

Amnion of Light: *Rinthy*

In pointing out that Culla and Rinthy in some senses each create his or her own world, Bell has demonstrated that Rinthy is more associated with light than is Culla, especially in the earlier sections of the novel, and he notes that increasingly Rinthy travels (travails) in an "agony of sunlight" toward her tragic ending in an ironic "grail of jade and windy light" (*OD* 97, 237; *Achievement* 47–52). But these two images of light are actually opposed in their mythic associations if one recognizes the gnostic valuation at work in the image of an agonizing sun—literally a sun that is implicated in Rinthy's *struggle* to connect with her child. In contrast the word *grail* carries more beneficent Christian connotations. Yet it too quietly reinforces the allusion to Rinthy's struggle, her agonizing quest. Further, the light here is "windy"; in *Outer Dark* wind always implies the turmoil of cosmos, as when Culla raises his hands in supplication or threat to the "mute and windy heavens" or even when his road leads him to the final swamp of rank or dead vegetation and "stale wind" (33, 242). The agonizing gnostic sun's death-dealing nature is further hinted in the closing image of Rinthy's "sundrained cerements" (237). The light imagery associated with Rinthy is indeed ambiguous, as Bell has recognized without distinguishing between the sun imagery and other figures of light. In her sections the sun often retains its status as a hostile cosmic power. For example, when Rinthy speaks to the lawyer on the street, the midday sun "rode darkly" above them, evoking the black sun of Culla's dream (148).

Yet Rinthy is also associated with light in its more usual senses: benediction, grace, insight, and a force in opposition to darkness. Her pale blond hair suggests a halo, and she is described as "mantled" in light in ironic tension with the opening description of the triune, who are haloed in "*spurious sanctity*" (76, 3). But the light surrounding Rinthy is not characteristic of the world of this novel, nor even of Rinthy's wider sphere of action. The narrator tells us that even when she has become "half deranged" she moves in an "amnion of propriety," and this amniotic image of her childlike innocence and protected status is subtly echoed in the bubble of light that seems to set back or ward off the dark even though she is ultimately subject to it (151). If, as Bell points out (37–38), Culla travels in a soundless void, Rinthy moves in an amnion of light that seems frail and circumscribed but just sufficient to shield her from outer dark: a "thin yellow flame that kept her from the night" (62). Others, like Luther's callow son, who assumes Rinthy is a widow and thus sexually available, may attempt to transgress her "ring of light," but with no success (63). Jonas identifies as an important Mandaean concept that of the *Sh'kina*, or habitation, typically charged "with the connotation of glory as the light-aura surrounding . . . beings [of Light] like a dwelling" (*Gnostic Religion* 98). Rinthy's amnion of light, then, links her with gnostic Uthras, comparable to the angels of the Judeo-Christian tradition. However, Rinthy is not an angel but a very mortal human, entangled like Culla in the cosmic realm. Still this light suggests her potential escape from darkness. She illustrates the gnostic conception of humankind as essentially "the potentially knowing in the midst of the unknowing, of light in the midst of darkness" (Jonas, "Epilogue" 328). In her night with Luther's family, Rinthy is repeatedly enclosed in lamplight thus. She carries the lamp "votively before her" like an "acolyte," her "face seized in the light she bore" (62–63). The image suggests that she is a devotee of the light, a bearer of light, and possessed ("seized") more by light than by darkness; yet it does not imply that darkness is entirely vanquished from her world but only tentatively held at bay: she has entered the family's cabin out of "untenanted night" and the lantern "set[s] back the darkness inside" in only a limited fashion (58–59). Later when Rinthy enters the cabin with the tinker who will deny her her child, she moves to stand in a "fading patch of light like one seeking warmth of it or grace" (188). The invocation of grace makes this fading light an explicit precursor of the glade in which her search ends, with the miniaturized image of the glade's "grail" of light suggesting its constricted domain as well as its pricelessness—yet ominously echoing too the pinpoint of light in a "glozed cup" that has lured Culla to the triune (168). The glade is an amnion of light, but darkness in all its cosmic qualities has penetrated this glade, where Rinthy finally slumbers at night.

Another source of ambiguity in the light imagery of the novel derives from the gnostic idea that like food, sexuality, and the beauty of nature, the "light" of the cosmos is an aspect of its lure that entraps the spirit in matter. This might be true even of light in the more beneficent sense that we see associated with Rinthy. "In Mani's speculation," Jonas writes, "a divine likeness as a bait [was] used . . . by the archons to lure and entrap divine substance [spirit]" in cosmos (*Gnostic Religion* 164). Thus, though Culla's conscience is sometimes stabbed with reminders of the stain/shadow in which he stands, he is also attracted to the light and warmth of the sun or fire (another paradoxical gnostic symbol of darkness; see Jonas, *Gnostic Religion* 156). Arrested and made to march barefoot to the justice of the peace, he advances "upon his lean and dancing shadow with feet that winced in the cold sand," but he also feels the sun rising on his back, "and it felt good" (198). He is twice lured to the campfires of the triune like a moth to flame. In their first encounter, Culla is more frightened of his experience on the flooded river than he is of the three indistinctly silhouetted figures, even though he hears one of them ask, "You want me to shoot him?" He pauses in indecision until the ferry begins to spin him rushing away from the bank. Then he throws them the line, comes ashore, and "mak[es] his way through the woods toward the light" (169). In the second meeting, Culla is even more explicitly drawn to the light: "Holme came limping out of the woods and crossed a small field toward the light. . . . When he entered the glade he could see men seated there about the fire and he hobbled on, one hand raised, into the firelight. When he saw what figures warmed there he was already among them and it was too late" (231).

Despite her amnion of protective light, Rinthy is helplessly involved in darkness as well. Late in the novel, when she stands on the threshold between the farmer's house where she has been living and the outer dark, she chooses the outer dark. Yet as she sets out again in her fruitless but love-driven search with the sunrise behind her, she is compared to a "deranged refugee from its occurrence" (211). Her shunning the rising sun is a striking reversal of Culla's relishing the sunrise on his back, as well as of the action in Culla's dream, where all yearn for the return of the sun that has turned its face away. But the paradox implied in Rinthy's directional "choice" between the sun at her back and the outer dark into which she journeys, two gnostic symbols of cosmos, suggests both an aspect of cosmic necessity and an internal tension in Rinthy's being: she would avoid the gnostic sun with its associations with cosmic necessity, yet to seek her son she must travel in outer dark.

Culla is lured by sun and fire, but it is Rinthy who is more explicitly associated with moths. As a bearer of light, she is "moth-besieged" (64). Even more than Culla, she herself is drawn to light. She wishes for clean windows in the cabin she shares with her brother, a wish for clear vision that Culla repudiates: "I ain't warshin no winders" (28). But in either sibling's association with moths lies a hint that attraction to cosmic light is fatal for the spirit. When Rinthy wakes after her delivery and asks for her baby, the lamp Culla carries "held her eyes," an image of trance-like captivity; the response Culla offers is not the truth, but a message of death: "It died, he said" (25). The threat of ensnaring and destruction in light is hinted again when Rinthy stands backlit by the windows of a country store, "trapped in fans of dusty light, a small black figure burning" (57). The most pregnant of these images occurs when Rinthy sits with Luther's family, "the lamp just at her elbow belabored by a moth whose dark shape cast upon her face appeared captive within the delicate skull, the thin and roselit bone, like something kept in a china mask"—a striking figure of spirit imprisoned in matter suggesting that for all her grace, Rinthy shares in the cosmic entrapment (59). Ironically the moth as physical creature casts a shadow, a "dark shape," yet the visual illusion of this dark moth as captive spirit suggests the pneuma benighted in matter. At the same time, the explicit association of Rinthy with the moth is another detail that marks her spiritual ascendency, especially since the image of the captive moth is conjoined with images suggesting the fragility of the material body in which it is housed. The passage at Luther's table prepares for the recurrence of the moth when Rinthy pulls away from the farmer she has been living with. As the man sits tired and brooding alone at his kitchen table, a moth "floundered at the lamp chimney with great eyed wings" and falls "prostrate and quivering on the greasy oilcloth table-cover," whereupon the man crushes it with his fist (211). In this context the moth unknowingly attracted to light, only to be burned and then killed, suggests that Rinthy's attempt to live with this man has somehow resulted in the death of her spirit. It is not that he seems especially brutal or mean-spirited, despite his crushing the moth in frustration; there is nothing to suggest that he has acted abusively to Rinthy but rather that she has shut him out: she closes down any communication, and they sleep in separate rooms. It seems that her transient attraction to a home and domestic life with this farmer has temporarily lured her from her quest for her child, which proves the stronger lure even though it too is a displacement of the spiritual quest—a counterfeit light to which she is drawn.

Flood, Mud, and Swamp: *Turbid Water*

Like the sun, which gnostic myths assign a metaphorical import different from either Platonic or Christian implications, water imagery undergoes a partial revaluation in gnostic speculation. Jonas writes that the Mandaeans placed great emphasis on the use of "living" or flowing water in their rituals and may have adopted the concept of living water from the Old Testament. They settled by rivers to be close to living water, which was of sublime origin (*Gnostic Religion* 97–98). Gnostics also developed the opposing metaphor of "turbid water" or "troubled water," the "'water of the Abyss [or Chaos]': the original matter of the world of darkness with which the living water mingled" (*Gnostic Religion* 99; interpolation in original). Turbid water was associated with the noise and turmoil of the cosmos: "Man drawn into the whirlpool and made oblivious of his true being is to be made one of the children of this world." And to drink of turbid water was to taste the archons' "wine of ignorance" (Jonas, *Gnostic Religion* 71)—an idea compatible with the Platonic notion of Lethe, even though the mythic contexts diverge.

As both realistic and mythic elements, flooded rivers are prominent in all of McCarthy's novels from the Tennessee period. Moreover, in *Outer Dark* and *Child of God*, turbulent rivers impinge directly on the fates of the oblivious male protagonists Culla and Lester, both lost in the outer dark of matter. The gnostic turbid waters cited by Jonas are almost entirely such disturbed, turbulent rivers or seas associated with chaos. But in *Outer Dark* McCarthy also deploys the primary meaning of "turbid" water as muddied or stagnant, extending an image pattern that begins in the slimy pool of the pesticide pit in *The Orchard Keeper* and that receives striking new expression in the sewage-laden river and the seeping cesspipe of *Suttree*. Perhaps McCarthy's imagination was sparked by the Valentinian gnostics' idea that water and earth together are the "nether" elements that comprise the cosmos, earth being identified with matter and water with darkness (Jonas, *Gnostic Religion* 205, 204).[5] But he does not borrow directly from gnostic symbolism in his imagery of swamps and mire in *Outer Dark*. Rather, McCarthy extends the implications of gnostic turbid water images, synthesizing with them Platonic and Dantean implications, to present not only turbulent but also stagnant water as images of spiritual death.

In his mad whirlwind of flight, Culla Holme repeatedly is thrown into creeks or swamps, capturing the gnostic idea that man's spirit is "cast onto the worthless earth" or into the "stinking body"—thrown into the outer dark of cosmos (see Jonas, *Gnostic Religion* 59, 88). This occurs first in the night scene in which he abandons his baby, when he is "confused in a swampy forest, floundering through sucking quagmires." As he circles sightlessly, he stumbles into the creek, "splash[ing] into it thigh and crotch before he knew it was there" (16–17). The genital imagery is significant here, linking Culla's obsession with and denial of his sexual crime with humanity's tragically mingled components of body, psyche, and spirit.[6] In addition, the shock of finding himself crotch-deep in this almost motionless creek "before he knew it was there" foreshadows his plunge into the circle of light cast by the triune's campfire and seeing "too late" who keeps watch (231). Culla's is the inner/outer turmoil of man locked in cosmos, his paranoia an obscure terror of his position in the gnostic world, with no gnostic assurance of salvation and deliverance. Sometimes his headlong flight results in a parallel shock at his cosmic position on land as well. Fleeing pursuers, he wades a shallow creek and "plunged into a canebrake. . . . He crashed on blindly. When he emerged from the brake he was in a road, appearing suddenly in a final and violent collapse of stalks like someone fallen through a prop inadvertently onstage, looking about in terror of the open land . . . before turning and lurching back into the brake" (89–90). The stage trope again suggests the artifice of the gnostic cosmos, but here it also emphasizes the terror of exposure experienced by man cast into this alien and artificial world. Lunging on, Culla falls again, skidding a few feet in pine straw; then he tries to jump a creek but loses his footing and tumbles "face down in the water" (94). When he drinks from the shallow stream, he chokes and vomits. Later he will choke on the parched corn he tries to eat, and he will choke on the mummified meat fed him by the triune. All these instances of Culla's choking suggest his intuitive repudiation of the world's wine of oblivion, his repudiation of the conditions of earthly life even as, driven by his body, he constantly seeks food and drink. After Culla vomits, the narrator tells us laconically, "he drank again" (94). "When he [Adam: man] eats and drinks," the dark powers boast in one of the gnostic speculations, "we will entrap the world" (quoted in Jonas, *Gnostic Religion* 72). Culla's drinking again comments obliquely and ironically on his disavowal of his sexual stain as well. After a brief time away from Rinthy and his child, Culla lusts after a young woman again, and this lust immediately precedes his panicky flight from the punitive men, as if the lust or guilt has summoned them. His flight is thus an attempt to escape the cosmic condition of inner drives and guilt he can never evade. (The gnostics' answer to this onto-logical problem was to repudiate the very concept of sin.)

As denser versions of turbid water, *Outer Dark*'s mud and mire also connote humankind's earthly stain and the spirit's cosmic plight. At least one gnostic document hints at this when the Messenger calls Adam to awaken and "put off thy stinking body, thy garment of clay" (quoted in Jonas, *Gnostic Religion* 85), and the association of clay (or dust) with flesh is common in Judeo-Christian writing as well. On the first night after Culla leaves home, rain falls through "such darkness he did not trust his balance": a gnostic image of darkness (water) intensified in combination with darkness itself. The rain mingles with clay to create the muddy medium through which Culla travels the next day. He enters town with "mud slathered to his knees, wading through a thick mire" (37). Later, running from his scene of renewed lust, Culla crosses a hoglot where a boar (the first of several hogs in Culla's scenes, all of them avatars of human nature) rises up out of the wallow. Like the darkness and the stain of shadow through which Culla moves, such mire reflects Culla's spiritual state, the tragically mingled nature of his being. "Everybody's subject to get in a ditch sometime," Culla tells a teamster, and his cliche resonates with the gnostic nightmare of the novel: Culla's earthly life is essentially confined to the stag-nant ditch—as is the life of every body, human as much as porcine.

The primary and culminating image of stagnant water is the swamp to which Culla's road leads him, a "garden of the dead" or "landscape of the damned" in which a "stale wind" blows through vegetation that "clashed softly like things chained." This appalling swamp, then, is the cosmos itself, depicted in imagery that is Dantean with a gnostic overlay: the cosmic underworld, stag-nant water and wind, imprisoned beings. The sexual paranoia of the scene links it even more explicitly with the gnostic vision. When Culla tests his footing in the mire, "it rose in a vulvate welt claggy and sucking" threatening him again with his sexual nature, which both tempts and shames him. He retreats from the vulvate swamp, but this escape is yet another denial and delusion. It is Culla's own cosmic road that has "come to such a place," and the serene pres-ence of the blind prophet implies, as Arnold and Metress have suggested, that the seer's road, cartographically identical to Culla's, will take him no such place (242, 152).[7]

In gnostic myth, as the spirit awakens, it "calls the Great Life to account for the existence of the world as such and for its own exile there: that is, it asks the great 'Why?' which, far from being appeased by the awakening and the re-minder of its origin, is powerfully stirred up by them and becomes a main con-cern of the gnosis just initiated. This query is . . . called 'the lawsuit concerning the world'" (Jonas, *Gnostic Religion* 88). Though Culla wonders why his road brings him to the swamp, he does not acquire the gnosis to ask the profound, central gnostic question of why man is cast into outer darkness. Rather, he remains the imprisoned spirit, clothed in clay and oblivion. In the gnostic "Poimandres" of Hermes Trismegistus, the whirling of the heavenly spheres begets the elements and then the creatures of the cosmos, which are by nature imbued with whirling turbulence: the demiurge "set his creations circling in endless revolution, for it begins where it ends" (Jonas, *Gnostic Religion* 150). As Arnold has noted, the endlessly circling Culla too begins where he ends and ends where he begins: in the cosmic swamp, in outer dark ("Naming, Knowing" 47, 53). Nor does turning back from the swamp take him to a different road with a different end. He avoids the blind Messenger who might set him on another path and continues his benighted wandering.

The wild river that swamps the ferry is the most authentically gnostic image of turbid water in *Outer Dark*. The scene recalls the disastrous, apocalyptic river-crossing of the Bundren family in William Faulkner's *As I Lay Dying* (echoed again in *Child of God*) as well as T. S. Eliot's poems "The Hollow Men" and "The Waste Land," which informed Faulkner's vision. But Culla's river-crossing in "total dark" that delivers him into the presence of the triune, carries also some peculiarly gnostic implications (165). Like the antagonistic sun, a hypostasis of the demiurge, the turbulent river is a hostile agent. This raging river is foreshadowed when Culla carries his baby along the Chicken River with its "swollen waters coming in a bloodcolored spume from about the wooden stanchions . . . with a constant and vicious hissing," as if in commentary on his murderous endeavor (15). The rising river he tries to cross on the ferry hisses too, associating it not only with Dante's Acheron but also with the Judeo-Christian and some gnostics' conception of the serpent as a principle of evil: "The river hissing blackly past the landing seemed endowed with heavy reptilian life." The turbid waters rush "raging" and "howling" until the ferry is wrenched free of its cable; then "the wall of water receded" as if the river's objective is fulfilled, leaving Culla in a stagnant "windless calm" and utter darkness. Still, he can hear it "seething . . . beneath him." When he offers the boot of the dead ferryman, it sinks "instantly as if a hand in the river had claimed it." And the river continues to watch him with its "seething face" (160–68).

In further personification of the river as an agent of darkness, Culla perceives it as mouthed, a devouring and murmuring presence. The maddened horse, prefiguring the hogs and doubling Culla and all cosmic creatures, casts itself into the river and is "swallowed" by the turbid waters of darkness. The river continues to threaten Culla, "mouth[ing] the hull gently," and he hears it "whisper" to him "as if it were looking for him." He can "see the pale teeth of a rip in the river . . . and he could hear it like the stammerings of the cloistered mad."

Then he sees the glimmer of a light on shore, "a pin-flicker set in a glozed cup," offering him false reprieve from the terrifying river. He must choose between the dark-faced river and the faceless, depthless figures ashore, between the dark and the light that is also darkness (166–68). Either way, he is thrall to the agents of darkness that hound him.[8]

The will of the river is linked with the triune, especially with the speechless, nameless one who seems to have arranged the convergence of the four and who smiles at Culla's approach (169). The bearded leader claims that the mute is responsible for their presence there: "He's the one set the skiff adrift this mornin. . . . Even if it just drifted off he still done it. I knowed they's a reason. We waited all day and half the night" (178). That is, the mute has apparently stranded the triune by freeing a rowboat that might have taken them across the river, keeping them there (even though they are bound by "nothin") until Culla's late-night arrival, for which they have kept a signal fire. Here the leader claims to less knowledge than the mute, and he is surprised and interested to learn that Culla is not the ferryman, raising again the association with Charon and the Dantean underworld. But despite these hints, this ferryman is mortal, and this killing river is not the marshy/turbid water between Purgatory and Hades but the turbulent/turbid water of the gnostic cosmos. Culla has not crossed with great difficulty from one sphere of the underworld to another, although the triune may appropriately enough be seen as demonic. In fact, as he whirls downriver Culla becomes disoriented, and it is impossible for the reader to discern whether he leaves the river on the opposite bank or spirals back to the one he started from. He tells the triune, "We never made it," suggesting that he may perceive he has not successfully crossed (170). But whether or not a crossing is achieved matters little for a reading of the gnostic implications of the book. As in each of Culla's experiences—his stranding on the dark waters, his interrogation by the triune, all his houndedness and the repetitious thwarting of his neediness—Culla's progress is illusory, and each of his chapters comprises a different poetic, dreamlike representation of the same cosmic condition. Like so many counterfeit apparitions in the novel, the river crossing is no true crossing, and Culla's meetings with the triune mark no change of destiny. His subjection to them has been his destiny all along.

Bound by Nothin: *Outlaws and Archons*

Gnostic rebellion often involved repudiating the Hebrew God of laws and commandments, whom gnostics identified with the demiurge or world artificer rather than the true Unknown God. The triune are subtly linked with the world artificers when Culla surrenders his boots to its leader, who "seized them and examined them, . . . turning them in his hands like some barbaric cobbler inspecting the work of another world" (179).[9] More relevant, however, is the

conception of the demiurge or archons as enforcers of cosmic laws in ignorance of the True God. The world-rulers functioned in absolute isolation from
that Alien God, imagining that there was no power beyond themselves. Thus
they were at once punitive ministers of law and necessity in relation to their
human creations and free agents in relation to the Unknown God, unbound by
any higher allegiance or responsibility because ignorant of His existence. They
formed a repressive cosmic law unto themselves. "Where are you bound?"
Culla asks the bearded leader. The answer: "I ain't. . . . By nothin" (233). It is
these qualities of the dark powers McCarthy stresses when he conceives the triune who watch Culla with "predacious curiosity" (170) as a grim parody of the
Christian trinity roaming the earth in the guise of outlaws. William C. Spencer glosses the three as unholy inversions of the Father (the leader), the Son
(Harmon), and the Holy Spirit (the mute, whom he also associates with the
Freudian principle of the id): "The three marauders . . . comprise a triple allegory of evil, with the bearded leader symbolizing lawless authority and destruction, Harmon representing violence, and the idiot corresponding to ignorance"
("Cormac McCarthy's Unholy Trinity" 91). But in fact all three are associated
with lawless authority (as well as cosmic law), violence, and ignorance, with reference to the gnostic conception of the world artificer(s) and governor(s). By
differentiating the three, McCarthy achieves a more dynamic mythical representation of the various attributes of the rulers of the gnostic world than he
might embody in a single figure so economically drawn (although in a different fictional context, he accomplishes a similar feat stunningly in the mono-
lithic figure of Judge Holden), but I read the three in their trinity associations
as truly "consubstantial": various manifestations of a unified and rich conception of the demiurge and its world-ruling *heimarmene.*

Outer Dark rings various changes on the concept of the trinity in another
instance of the repetitions that pattern the novel. There are several triads com-
prised of the Holmes in various combinations: the broken mother/father/child
family structure of Rinthy, Culla, and the baby; the trinity of consciousness (to
modify a phrase from Faulkner) of Culla, Rinthy, and the tinker; the three feral
father-figures: Culla, the tinker, and the leader of the triune; the triangle of
Rinthy, the tinker, and the contested child; the doubling of both Culla and his
son in the mute, and the trinity of consciousness in Culla, Rinthy, and the blind
man. In addition, the novel includes other triads not involving the Holmes: the
three hanged men; the three mother-figures Rinthy meets in her travels; the
three farmers; the three agents of community law; the three "preachers" associated with the three versions of Culla's dream of the eclipse. Such insistent
repetitions of triad structures reinforce the perverse Trinity association of the
triune and hint at the incarnation of the triune's essential characteristics in the
cosmic make-up of all humans.

Jonas points to the "Christian-gnostic triad of pneumatics, psychics, and sarkics ('fleshly men')" based on the relative ascendency of the three components of humanity (*Gnostic Religion* 232). But in terms of gnostic challenges to or variations of Christian teaching, Jonas identifies no particular emphasis on the number three, and the archontic powers were not presented as tripartite ones.[10] In fact, like the seven figures of the hog drovers and parson, who watch Culla floating downriver from the bluff above him, the archons are usually numbered at seven corresponding to the seven planetary spheres, a gnostic borrowing from the planetary gods of Babylonian theology (Jonas, *Gnostic Religion* 43). *Outer Dark*'s archontic trinity, then, is on one level a neo-heretical reinscription of the Christian trinity as gnostic archons, emphasizing the profound differences between Christian and gnostic conceptions of the creator and between Christian and gnostic experiences of the created world.

Jonas writes, "The Archons collectively rule over the world, and each individually in his sphere is a warder of the cosmic prison. Their tyrannical world-rule is called *heimarmene*, universal Fate, a concept taken over from astrology but now tinged with the gnostic anticosmic spirit. In its physical aspect this rule is the law of nature; in its psychical aspect, which includes for instance the institution and enforcement of the Mosaic Law, it aims at the enslavement of man" (*Gnostic Religion* 43). Jonas shows that the "Poimandres" of Hermes Trismegistus links the concepts of *heimarmene* and *harmonia*, and he quotes its passage asserting that man embodies "in himself the nature of the harmony [*harmonia*] of the Seven [the archons]." Jonas concludes that in this and some other gnostic texts "*harmonia* stands for a totality of forces (the Governors) denoted by its unifying characteristic (the form of their collective government)" in relation to mankind. That is, for these gnostics the Greek concept of *harmonia*, an expression of their cosmos piety, is reinterpreted as the equivalent of *heimarmene:* the essential power system of the gnostic cosmos in its "'psychological' aspect" as well as its physical one (*Gnostic Religion* 151n8). *Outer Dark*'s ominous, smiling enforcer-figure armed with a rifle and ironically named "Harmon" thus semantically connects the triune with the gnostic concept of *heimarmene*. The *heimarmene* revealed by the world "is unenlightened and therefore malignant force, proceeding from the spirit of self-assertive power, from the will to rule and coerce. The mindlessness of this will is the spirit of the world, which bears no relation to understanding and love. The laws of the universe are the laws of this rule, and not of divine wisdom" (Jonas, "Epilogue" 327). *Outer Dark* develops the malignant, mindless, coercive triune as *heimarmene* in both aspects of natural law, the physical and the psychological, linking the triune with want and death and with moral law, judgment, and guilt.

"Never . . . had nothin, never was nothin," the leader taunts Culla, reminding him of his extreme poverty (233). The Holmes are so poor that Culla has never had the means to take up smoking and Rinthy has never tasted store-bought white bread. The triune preside gleefully over Culla's further loss of what little he has, the clothes on his back. "Looks like you about out of a shirt," the leader comments complacently as Culla's wet and threadbare garment splits (171); further enforcing his poverty, they rob him of his fine stolen boots and give him the worst of their own. The triune's continuing effect on his life is suggested by his walking barefoot by the end of the novel. In relation to Culla's poverty, the triune manifest both the physical and psychological aspects of *heimarmene*. Like his sexual drive, Culla's economic poverty provokes power-ful emotional responses, fueling a resentful sense of entitlement that impels him to steal and maybe also to assault Rinthy. His only inheritance is his father's rifle, an emblem of male potency, which he sells to finance his escape from erotic attraction to Rinthy and his consequent sense of guilt. As he repairs the rifle, he addresses it in anger: "Now damn ye, slip if ye can," and Rinthy, accus-tomed to Culla's displacement of his shame onto her, reacts as if he refers to their incest (30). Culla rids himself of the rifle, but it resurfaces in the hands of Harmon as the triune confront Culla with his guilt.[11]

The three are obviously and consistently associated with literal death or the threat of death. Like ghouls, they dress in the garments of the exhumed dead, anticipating the necrophilic material of *Child of God*. And in the exchange of boots, they foist on Culla the fetid garments of death. When they execute Squire Salter, they arm themselves with scythes and brushhooks, and though the narrator explicitly presents them in imagery of proletarian uprising, hint-ing their enactment of the downtrodden Culla's wish, they are simultaneously figures of the Grim Reaper in his inevitable mowing of human lives (35). Gram-mer reads them as "figures of *time*," and they are (35). But more than that, they are the "*grim triune*," three-in-one hypostasis of death and darkness "*in consub-stantial monstrosity*"—an inversion of the Christian trinity's association with eternal life (129). As many have noted, the triune's spokesman is one of the false preachers of the book. But there is another implication in the snake-hunter's identifying the bearded leader in his stolen black suit as a "*Minister*" (129): as one of three agents of *heimarmene*, he is a minister of death to the snakehunter, as to the hanged millworkers whose lynching he incites, to the tinker, and to the unclaimed child—a minister of destiny to all. And although the triune's murders may punish those who treat the Holmes unkindly, death is meted out as well to those who merely cross Culla's path (Clark and the snakehunter) or who never interact with him or Rinthy (the millworkers) or to the innocent (their child). In their death manifestation, then, as in their asso-ciation with the relentless sun and the turbid waters of cosmos, these consub-stantial three embody an inimical yet impersonal force of natural law. Not only Culla is sunstruck and death-haunted in cosmos. The gnostic sun glares upon the just and the unjust, and the death-force is ubiquitous and eternal. The novel swells with references to those who have predeceased its opening pages, and if Rinthy merely sleeps at the end of the novel and, like Culla, will live to continue on her path, both will yet fulfill their mortal subjection to *heimarmene*, as their child has. The triune's spokesman addresses this aspect of necessity as well as the fated experiences of sexual desire and poverty that torment Culla when he tells him: "You ain't no different from the rest. From any man borned and raised and have his own and die. They ain't one man in three got even a black suit to die in" (235).

The child's murder marks Culla's complicity in his son's death, his literally taking the baby's fate into his own hands for a second time when he submits him to the triune. In doing so, Culla implicitly rejects the leader's suggestion that he could pretend to avoid complicity by allowing *heimarmene* or fate to deliver the child to death: "Unless you'd rather for Harmon to" (235). There is a strong implication, then, that Culla willingly yields his son to death rather than abandoning him again to the world and the chance that he will resurface, or in the language of the triune's spokesman, rather than naming and claiming this sign of his guilt as his own. As Ann Fisher-Wirth observes, the triune are "corollary to, implicit in, Culla's hard dream of mastery," his need to efface the child as "the best, inadmissible evidence of the body's desire and vulnerability" (136). But the child's consumption in gross parody of the Christian rite of communion also gestures at the gnostic idea that the Savior's consumption by the cosmic powers might be a salvific act. Just as humans' eating and drinking were thought to be acts of ingesting the poison of outer dark, and thus to be minimized according to ascetic gnostics, some gnostic myths envisioned the substance of the Alien Man, sent to gather the pneuma out of cosmos, as poison to the archontic powers.[12] In the "The Hymn of the Pearl," the Savior, son of the King of Light, paradoxically clothes himself in the terrestrial garment (flesh) "in order to exhaust the powers of the world" (Jonas, *Gnostic Religion* 119). He confronts the Serpent or Leviathan, the "earth-circling dragon of the original chaos, the ruler or evil principle of this world" (Jonas, *Gnostic Religion* 116) and puts him to sleep. That is, with poetic justice He subjects the Serpent to the same oblivion to which the powers of darkness subject humankind. In other gnostic texts this feat is accomplished explicitly through the Savior's submission to being devoured by the personification of Darkness because "the Light is as much poison to the Darkness as the Darkness is to the Light. Thus in Manichaean cosmogony the Primal Man, seeing his impending defeat in the encounter with the forces of Darkness, 'gave himself and his five sons as food to the five sons of Darkness, as a man who has an enemy mixes a deadly poison in a cake and gives it to him'" (Jonas, *Gnostic Religion* 120).

In reading *Blood Meridian* as a gnostic novel, it is possible to view the kid's fate in the jakes as his submission to the judge's cannibalistic consumption in this salvific sense. Such a gnostic reading involves a new irony, though: the kid's self-sacrificial act does not vanquish the judge from the cosmos, suggesting that the kid is not Primal Man but just "the man." After his triumph in the jakes, the judge dances with energy and joy, boasting that "he will never die" (*BM* 335). Neither does the cannibalizing of Culla and Rinthy's child seem to accomplish the vanquishing of Darkness from within, despite enacting one version of the gnostic salvation myth. This is the triune's last deadly act, and unlike Judge Holden they make no further bodily appearance in the novel. But even if we imagine their power to be temporarily soothed with the child's consumption, their agency is still manifest in the world. Rinthy's ambiguous final sleep suggests rest from her driven search and yet her continuing entrapment in cosmic oblivion.[13] And Culla wanders dully on, condemned never to awaken from his gnostic nightmare. The mute child, with his visible dualism of scorched and unblemished halves, with one eye socket empty and the other blinking owl-like in a hint of the potential for gnosis, is dualistic man himself, pneuma tragically mingled in matter. He passively suffers what the Alien Man will voluntarily undergo in order to free spirit from matter, but the child's sacrifice in this novel is human suffering without liberation, the pneuma in him too isolated and alienated a portion of Light to effect cosmic redemption. Devoured by Darkness that keeps him trapped in cosmos and subject to *heimarmene* even after death, the child is abject in the pre-Kristevan sense of the word. He is also, as Fisher-Wirth writes, "pure outcast, pure victim . . . forever not called forth into the protection of the Father"—a Kristevan perspective that resonates strangely with the gnostic conception of humankind as cast helplessly into darkness, unprotected from cosmos, and deaf to the call of the true Father (135).

The Dark Necessity of Psyche

Jonas rarely cites references to dreaming in the gnostic texts. However, he quotes one passage from the Valentian "Gospel of Truth" (*Evangelium Veritatis*) that seems highly pertinent to *Outer Dark* as a gnostic nightmare. In this work the narrator asks what the "great Life" would have humankind understand about its condition in the world and then supplies this answer: "I am as the shadows and phantoms of the Night." Jonas continues:

> When the light of dawn appears, then this man understands that the
> Terror which had seized upon him, was nothing. . . . As long as Ignorance
> inspired them with terror and confusion, and left them unstable, torn and
> divided, there were many illusions by which they were haunted, and empty
> fictions, as if they were sunk in sleep and as if they found themselves a

prey to troubled dreams. Either they are fleeing somewhere, or are driven ineffectually to pursue others; or they find themselves involved in brawls, giving blows or receiving blows; or they are falling from great heights . . . until the moment when those who are passing through all these things, wake up. Then, those who have been experiencing all these confusions, suddenly see nothing. For they are nothing—namely phantasmagoria of this kind. (quoted in Jonas, *Gnostic Religion* 70)

However, for Culla and the other cripples in his framing dream, the light of dawn never appears, neither in that dream nor in the dream of life that encloses it. Certainly the idea of life as a dream is widespread in western philosophy and literature, and this gnostic passage dovetails in some ways with Dante's dream-vision in *The Divine Comedy*. Where gnostic literature and *Outer Dark* depart from Dante and much Christian visionary literature, however, is their suggestion that unknowing man is trapped in the troubled dream of life which of itself can offer him no salvific vision: an inferno/purgatorio with no recognition of a paradiso. We might look to Yeats's play *Purgatory* for a modern parallel, a purgatorial nightmare that is prominently structured through a "dream's redundancy" and that comprises a closed circuit dooming the characters to endless repetition (*OD* 231). In "'Go to sleep': Dreams and Visions in the Border Trilogy," Arnold rightly argues that in McCarthy's works dreams function in a Jungian more than a Freudian fashion, offering visions, avenues to truths not readily accessed in other ways; however, he says little about how this emerges in *Outer Dark* or *Child of God*, acknowledging that Culla Holme and Lester Ballard are "harder cases" and commenting of Culla only that his "opening nightmare . . . tells *us* all we need to know of his suppressed guilt" (42, emphasis added). Culla's nightmare does not provide him with new vision. The difference between *Outer Dark* and McCarthy's works in which dreams offer insight to the characters themselves derives from the nature of this novel's dreamer and particularly to the gnostic aura of his dream. While Arnold comments insightfully on the kid's dream of the coldforger in *Blood Meridian*, he does not consider either of McCarthy's gnostic novels as dream-narratives as a whole. Doing so leads us to see that a different dream experience characterizes some of McCarthy's work: the nightmare as the cosmic prison that is life. Arnold stresses the dream as vision: as a way of transcending the limits of consciousness and empirical knowledge. In *Outer Dark* and *Blood Meridian*, the life experiences of the male protagonists are largely presented as gnostic or purgatorial nightmares with no readily apparent way out of the oblivious mundane self. In these works the primary access to a radically different vision comes via those who are alien and immune to the nightmare: the blind man of *Outer Dark*, the seeker of *Blood Meridian*'s epilogue.

We might consider here the gnostic conception of the unconscious or the psyche, the aspect of self that since Freud and Jung we have considered the font of dreams. Gnostic thinkers saw psyche as far from a transcendent or benign or even neutral aspect of self. As a creation of the world-artificer(s), psyche joined with body to keep the spirit trapped and alienated in cosmos. Rather than an avenue to spiritual insight, psyche was by nature and origin antithetical to spirit. Like mortal flesh, psyche was an aspect of *heimarmene* or cosmic law: shaped in the image of the ignorant, presumptuous, and selfish world-powers, it encompassed all aspects of what we call human nature except the luminous or spiritual.[14] Jonas writes that in gnosticism, "the *psychical* envelopments too are considered impairments and fetters of the transmundane spirit. . . . In their sum they are the empirical character of man, comprising all the faculties and propensities by which man relates himself to the world of nature and society" (*Gnostic Religion* 158).

The implication, then, is that humans carry within their own psychological nature the cosmic darkness that alienates them from their source in the Divine: "As the 'terrestrial envelopment of the pneuma,' the 'soul' [psyche] is the exponent of the world within man—the world is *in* the soul. A profound distrust, therefore, of one's own inwardness, the suspicion of demonic trickery, the fear of being betrayed into bondage inspire gnostic psychology. The alienating forces are located in man himself" (Jonas, *Gnostic Religion* 269). A man "can know his heart, but he dont want to," says the hermit to *Blood Meridian*'s kid. "Best not to look in there" (19). "*The murengers have walled the pale . . . , but lo the thing's inside,*" says the world-sick narrator of *Suttree* (4). In gnostic teaching the inwardness of man becomes the arena in which is staged the contest between cosmos and Spirit, between darkness and the Light, that has little to do with our contemporary conception of psychology; and the contest is grossly uneven since the spark of the Divine slumbers deeply, wrapped in its cosmic envelopment until awakened by intervention from the divine Messenger. In the gnostic view spirit is the repressed. It is worthwhile to let Jonas sum up at length, for the resonance of his words with *Outer Dark:*

> If the soul [psyche] represents the cosmos in the inwardness of man . . .
> then man's inwardness is the natural scene for demonic activity and his
> self is exposed to the play of forces which it does not control. These forces
> may be considered as acting from outside, but they can act so because they
> have their counterpart in the human constitution itself, ready to receive
> their influence. . . . Therefore it is the natural condition of man to be a
> prey of the alien forces which are yet so much of himself. . . . This is the
> interiorized aspect of cosmic destiny, denoting the power of the world as
> a moral principle: in this sense heimarmene is that government which

the cosmic rulers exercise over us through our selves, and its manifestation is human vice of any kind, whose common principle is nothing but the abandonment of the self to the world. Thus inner-worldly existence is essentially a state of being *possessed* by the world, in the literal, i.e., demonological, sense of the term. . . . The terrified gnostic glance views the inner life as an abyss from which dark powers rise to govern our being, not controlled by our will, since this will itself is instrument and executor of those powers. (*Gnostic Religion* 281–83)

This *heimarmene*, invested in humans' own psyches, ruling and hounding them paradoxically both from without and from within, functions in much the way the dark triune do in their relationships to Culla and to the tinker. From this perspective, they are archontic, yet not quite hypostases of archons. Figments of Culla's framing nightmare, "endowed with a dream's redundancy," they are his doubles and his Jungian shadow—as Spencer says, "the incarnation of man's own inner darkness" ("Unholy" 91); yet they are also the darksome forces literally afoot in the world who meet him face to face, "like revenants that reoccur in lands laid waste with fever: spectral, palpable as stone" (231). Their palpable enactment of Culla's impulses, their tormenting him without yet killing him, and their associations with judgment reinforce such a gnostic reading of them as psychological yet also physical manifestations of archontic *heimarmene:* of the whole gnostic nightmare.

The Jungian perspective is useful in reconciling these seemingly incompatible aspects of the triune. In a passage from *Aion* that might serve as a psychological gloss on the gnostic loathing of cosmos and longing for the transcendent realm, Jung discusses the phenomenon of projection, which leads "to an auto-erotic or autistic condition in which one dreams a world whose reality remains forever unattainable. The resultant *sentiment d'incomplétude* and the still worse feeling of sterility are in their turn explained by projection as the malevolence of the environment, and by means of this vicious circle the isolation is intensified." In other words, "Projections change the world into the replica of one's own unknown face" (9). An image of the river, another avatar of archontic *heimarmene*, suggests this clearly. Gazing into the water, Culla sees the river's face "in sullen and threatful replication" (167). The replication in this Narcissus-image can only be of Culla's own face, and the river mirrors his sullenness, his threatfulness, in this scene just as it mirrors the triune he soon will meet, and as the triune mirror his own psyche and deeds. If the triune are Culla's dream-projections, they are himself. They are his projected (because repudiated) shadow. Culla's denial of his incestuous and murderous impulses— aspects of psychological *heimarmene* that he disavows—brings them forth in a projected reality that is tangible indeed. Jung writes that the ego-consciousness "is able, by means of a considerable expenditure of energy, to repress the shadow, at least temporarily. But if for any reason the unconscious gains the upper hand, then the valency of the shadow . . . increases proportionately. . . . What lay furthest away from waking consciousness and seemed unconscious assumes, as it were, a threatening shape" (28). That is, "the psychological rule says that when an inner situation is not made conscious, it happens outside, as fate" (71).

Much like the jailed kid's meeting with the judge who accuses him in *Blood Meridian*, a confrontation that may well be the kid's own nightmare (*BM* 305–9), Culla's direct encounters with the triune may be read as his inward experience. Both as dream-figures and as agents of psychical *heimarmene*, then, the triune may be seen as outward projections of Culla's unconscious and as introjections of cosmic rule or the shadow within him. In this sense, too, Arnold is right when he claims that "the unnamed companion has, just by *being*, directed Culla to [the triune] to confront his guilt" ("Naming, Knowing" 50). One of the triune's prominent roles is to challenge or trick him to acknowledge his crimes. Simply by being, they confront him with the moral challenge that Jung ascribes to the shadow. Except in Culla's dream of the eclipsed sun, his sense of guilt is nowhere more evident than in his arraignment by these three, which is in fact, like the framing dream, a self-arraignment.

The triune's tormenting of Culla is sometimes accomplished through direct accusations, sometimes guilt-raising insinuations. The leader's words function rather like the stain of shadow in which Culla moves, painfully reinforcing his sense of guilt under cosmic moral law. As he sits with the three at the campfire before the first interrogation, he "rubbed his hands together" (171), an unconscious gesture suggesting not only his anticipation of a much-needed meal but also the hand-washing ritual of guilt: manifestations of both physical and psychological *heimarmene* at work in him. Interestingly the triune's interrogation does not begin until Culla has accepted their meat, chewing "in a hopeless circular motion" a mass with "the consistency of whang" and the taste of sulphur (172). The leader begins his insinuated allegations by referring to Culla's veal boots, which we know he has stolen from Squire Salter, then jumps to the unexpected challenge: "What did ye do with the horse?" The implied connection between the two is that Culla has stolen both, or at least coveted the horse as he once has the boots: "More horse than you could handle was it?" the leader asks, "Or maybe you was afraid to take it. That makes sense" (173). As the arraignment continues, the triune accuse Culla through innuendo of yet more sins and crimes, only some of which we have seen him commit: coveting the ferryman's shirt (176), killing him and the rider, driving Rinthy away (178), neglecting his family (181). Since there is an element of truth to some of these charges, the interview has the effect of ambiguously reinforcing other hints that Culla is responsible for the crimes that occur in his wake and of which he is suspected—even those we see committed by the triune. But as a self-interrogation, its primary effect is to establish that Culla's pervasive sense of guilt exists in tension with his terrible need to deny his acts and urges. Indeed Culla's shame and guilt are what compel him to commit further acts of evil and ignorance, culminating in his delivering his child up to death in order to hide the incest behind his delivering him into life. "I wasn't ashamed," says Rinthy, and in the gnostic world of this novel, that moral serenity denotes her greater affinity with the Light (156).

In the second encounter with the triune, Culla's steadfast denial begins to crack, and he gives himself away in spite of his desperate need to repress his guilt. When he sees the tinker's cart and the child, he tacitly concludes that the maimed boy is his own repudiated son, and he moves toward acknowledging the boy when he sullenly challenges the triune to explain "what happent to his eye," voicing the natural law that "he ort to have two" (232). The tables in this ironic dialogue between self and psyche are momentarily turned, as the triune pretend innocence and ignorance of the child's ill fate and deflect Culla's accusation. Moments later Culla looks from the cart to the child and asks where his sister is, again implicitly staking a claim that he will not fully embrace. When the leader says that the tinker was "that'n you used to trade with," Culla hears yet another accusation in these bland words and responds defensively. But in spite of himself, his truthful defense that "I never give him no chap. . . . I just told her that," betrays him into admitting another transgression: his lying to Rinthy. The leader's culminating and most direct accusation, "I figure you got this thing here in her belly your own self and then laid it off on that tinker," elicits only a partial denial from Culla, "I never laid nothin off on no tinker"— which is the truth (233). But if Culla is attempting to defend himself from his overpowering sense of guilt, he denies the wrong half of the charge, in effect obliquely admitting to the incest that he has tried all along to repress psychologically and literally.

Having come this close to facing the truth, Culla turns morose with the triune, revealing his repressed anger at his poverty: "I never give nobody nothin. I never had nothin" (233). Then he asks the entirely pertinent question, "What are you?" first beneath his breath, then aloud, "sullenly." But he receives no reply. The answer, of course, cannot be put into words within the novel's narrative logic. But Culla's next assertion, "You aint nothin to me" (234), is another denial that suggests just the opposite—not merely in its double negative but also in light of the implications that the triune are a manifestation of Culla's psyche, a status that is hinted early in the novel when the tinker finds Culla's tracks converging from separate directions, "as if their maker had met in this forest some dark other self in chemistry with whom he had been fused traceless from the earth" (20). Culla's queries about the triune's identity send us back to the bearded one's mysterious remark when Culla resists surrendering his boots: "I think maybe you are somebody else. Because you don't seem to understand me very much," a passage that hints that Culla is in fact not someone other than the spokesman, much as he would like safely to partition away from his conscious life what the triune represent (179). At the same time, the leader's words evoke the gnostic's sense that slumbering deep within man's being lies an alien self or spirit: "However profoundly man is determined by nature, of which he is part and parcel—and plumbing his own inwardness he discovers in layer after layer this dependence—there still remains an innermost center which is not of nature's realm and by which he is above all its promptings and necessities" (Jonas, *Gnostic Religion* 160). But this alien self in Culla is so deeply suppressed that it is hard to see his intermittent sulky resistance to the triune as anything like gnostic rebellion. (Bell comments that "Culla's passivity . . . seems like a resigned obedience to an inexplicable and unmanipulable destiny"; *Achievement* 38). In both interviews these transitory moments when Culla attempts to repudiate the triune mark his resentment of his pending and inevitable submission to necessity: just as he gives up the boots, he gives up his child. Both acts seem to result, as Arnold has argued in "Naming, Knowing, and Nothingness," from his refusal fully to own his guilt. Ironically, as Culla steps psychologically closer to acknowledging his repressed child, he both repeats and denies his murderous intentions toward it.

However, in the gnostic view, such guilt is foisted on man by his psychical *heimarmene*, by his very informing with the "shalt nots" of the false god, the ignorant world-artificer. In a gnostic reading, the point is not so much that Culla should acknowledge his sin and seek redemption, as Christian readings would have it, but that his earthly deeds have nothing to do with the True God and nothing to do with his spirit, the alien captive within his worldly being. In this sense Culla unconsciously speaks a gnostic truth when he tells the triune they are nothing to him, to his "innermost center which is not of nature's realm and by which he is above all its promptings and necessities" [Jonas, *Gnostic Religion* 160]. But in Culla the innermost center, the spiritual component, is submerged much deeper than it is in Rinthy, and as agents of physical and psychical *heimarmene*, the triune are very far from nothing to him. Jonas points out that "the gnostic concept of salvation has nothing to do with the remission of sin ('sin' itself having no place in gnostic doctrine, which puts 'ignorance' in its place)" (*Gnostic Religion* 127). Further he notes that one aspect of gnostic "antagonism toward the Old Testament religion and toward its God, the reality of whom is by no means denied" is the recurring "assertion that . . . the Mosaic Law issued from [the] world-ruling angels, among whom the Jewish god is prominent." As gnostics developed this aspect of their myth, they assigned the four names of the Jewish god to four of the seven planetary archons identified with the world artificers. Gradually a "polemically drawn likeness emerged with increasing preeminence from their number as an unmistakeable caricature of the biblical God—not venerable indeed, but none the less formidable" (*Gnostic Religion* 133–34). So rather than owning and atoning for transgressions against the Hebrew God's commandments, against cosmic law in its moral aspect, the gnostic spirit attempts to make itself "invisible to the archons who would block [its] way [its transcendence], and especially to their prince, who in the role of judge would make it answerable for its deeds under his law. Since the gist of this law is 'justice,' the Gnostic's intended escape from its sanctions is part of the general antinomian attitude and expresses the repudiation of the Old Testament God in its moral aspect" (Jonas, *Gnostic Religion* 135–36).[15] Lacking gnosis, and not aware enough of his cultural/religious heritage to know what a Jew is, Culla knowingly repudiates neither the Old Testament god nor the Mosaic laws he violates, and his very sense of sin leads him deeper into the realm of transgression in exemplification of the psychological truism that what one resists persists (215). Thus as an essential condition of his existence, he is interminably hounded by the law, by his own guilt, by human and surreal agents of judgment. This is one reason why the many human agents of law and judgment without justice in *Outer Dark*—the squires and constables and the morally righteous—seem so often to be avatars of the triune or of one another: all who inhabit cosmos are both subject to and manifestations of cosmic *heimarmene*. Their ubiquity in the world is one of its nightmare qualities.

Paradoxically, in his hostile challenges and hints about knowing and not knowing, the bearded leader himself unwittingly suggests the importance of spiritual gnosis and hints of the potential for knowledge that lies repressed in humankind, rather like our contemporary understanding of the unconscious: "He might know somethin and him and me neither one know about it," the leader says of the mute, and his words might just as well apply to Culla (175). His idea is anticipated and subtly extended by the snakehunter, who claims, "I know things I ain't never studied. I know things I ain't never even thought of" and "the more I study a thing the more I get it backards" (125). This claim of knowledge prior to thought or study, knowledge that is truer because it is not based in worldly experience, hints at a different kind of cognition than the psychologically repressed, however, since such repression implies a denial of something experienced. In gnostic epistemology, this right knowledge stemmed not from the suspect psyche—as any conception springing from psyche would likely not be true knowledge—but from the submerged spirit. The snakehunter and leader's comments, then, comprise hints to Culla of the suppressed spirit within him, hints that arise despite the triune's association with archontic *heimarmene*. Thus embedded within this dialogue of self and soul or psyche, one can faintly detect a small voice of spiritual intimation arising out of Culla's own being and asking to be heard despite his fleshly and psychological entanglements. But there is no indication that Culla, in his amnion of silence, can hear any such thing. Jonas suggests the paradoxical way in which this spiritual intimation is itself repressed according to gnostic myths: "It is only the awakening from the state of unconsciousness ('ignorance'), effected from without, that reveals to man his situation . . . and causes an outburst of dread and despair; yet in some way these must have been at work already in the preceding state of ignorance, in that life shows a tendency . . . to resist the awakening" (*Gnostic Religion* 68–69).

Rinthy, Tinker, Culla, Seer: *Gnosis and Nothingness*

Bell, Arnold, and Metress, among others, have discussed the pattern of the characters' unknowing in *Outer Dark* from various metaphysical perspectives. It seems appropriate to add to the mix further consideration of unknowing in the context of gnosticism, a religion that was centrally concerned with the problem of unknowing, that holds affinities with the later *via negativa* and nihilism, and that deconstructed biblical and Platonic traditions. Not knowing characterizes not only Culla but also Rinthy, the tinker and the triune, and several minor characters. Surely most of the characters in the novel are illiterate and thus ignorant in that sense, yet most are skilled in some trade or craft. The issue of knowledge that is of central import in *Outer Dark* is not the characters' possession or lack of cognitive training or skills, of course, but their lack of spiritual gnosis. In some instances the unknowing is explicitly spiritual. Rinthy does not know whether she is saved (109). The judgmental tinker does not know why God has not "put out the sun and gone away" (192). And Culla does not know whether he can be cured (5). But any pragmatic ignorance in the novel also hints at the more crucial obliviousness underlying the human condition. This metaphorical implication seems most evident in the parable of the arrogant Squire Salter, whose reliance on his black servant and on hired laborers like Culla has made him unfit for life, contributing to his self-deluded and simmering animosity against those he judges more shiftless than himself. He claims that he has "never knowed nothin but hard work" and that "what I got I earned"; yet he sits paralyzed, raging and fumbling with his harness, waiting for the servant to hitch his horse to the buggy rather than do this task himself (47). His big white house with its columns (a hint of antebellum splendor based on slave labor) is peeling in shabby decline. The squire's tools have not been maintained either, the axe dull, the saw broken. And the fallen tree seems to have lain in the squire's yard pending the fortuitous arrival of a hand who could "swing a axe" (42). These hints of the squire's lack of skill, conjoined with his roles as Culla's judge and persecutor and as the black man's subjugator, link him with cosmic *heimarmene* and suggest that the repressive and judgmental aspects of social and racial hierarchies are yet more instances of the darkness afoot in the world. The illiteracy of the novel's other squire, the justice of the peace who judges Culla guilty of "trespass," carries similar implications (201). Transcending all the novel's instances of pragmatic unknowing is the characters' shared oblivion in the gnostic sense of being drunken with cosmos, asleep, alienated from the true God and from the Divine in themselves.

In gnostic systems salvation was not the personal issue of faith or moral behavior that it is for mainstream Christians. The world was not divided into the sinful and the saintly or elect, but into the ignorant and the gnostic (the "knowing ones"). Although gnosis was seen as not only a means to spiritual salvation but also a form of cosmic salvation for the individual (Jonas, *Gnostic Religion* 32), ultimately salvation was a matter of the reunification of the Divine on a transcendent scale and a transmundane level—a reunification that must gather in all individuals because all share the alienated spirit. In light of this gnostic perspective, when the snake-hating crone offers Rinthy the self-righteous Christian's challenge, "I don't believe you been saved have ye?" and Rinthy declares with simple frankness that she does not know, she does not convict herself of agnosticism, as the crone seems to imply—"Ah, the old woman said, one of them"—but of the natural state of ignorance or agnosis (109). Indeed, despite her unknowing, Rinthy carries herself with something like uncomplicated faith, traveling in her amnion of light and sanctity. Physically she is not strong; Culla tells the triune, "She was sick. . . . She never was a real stout person" (177). It is as if her bodily frailty corresponds inversely to the comparative strength of the spiritual component in her. In contrast Culla, as the more spiritually mired of the two, claims he "ain't never been sick a day in my life savin the whoopincough one time" (138).[16] Nevertheless, Rinthy is still a victim of her cosmic being—her "halt corporeality" and her psychological compulsions (97). Like her brother, Rinthy doesn't always tell the truth, she steals food when she is hungry, and she abandons the man who has offered her a home and seems to want a caring relationship with her. Although she is chaste, she is desperate enough to offer sexual favors in return for her son if she must; this is the implication of her resolute turning to face the tinker, holding a flower to her breast like a bride, and telling him that she will do "whatever" to earn the baby's return (189, 186, 191). Despite such yielding to worldly necessity, despite her seeming to know nothing of God or salvation, until the tinker's shattering refusal to restore her child she displays all the personal serenity of an individual possessed of deep faith.

Unlike Culla, Rinthy pursues an abiding goal based in love, and Arnold's association of her given name with Paul's first letter to Corinthians and its emphasis on love is apt: "Love bears all things, believes all things, hopes all things, endures all things" (13:8; "Naming, Knowing" 48–49). If her name is short for "Corinthians," though, there is yet further ambiguity. Complicating the association of Rinthy with love is the fact that when Paul addressed Corinth, the thriving commercial center was considered a place of worldly corruption, and the epithet "Corinthian girl" to designate a prostitute was common across the Mediterranean region. "Corinth was famous . . . for its temple of Aphrodite where a thousand prostitutes reputedly served, contributing thereby to the city's general reputation for immorality." Paul's epistles to the newly formed Christian church in this city of "excessive self-indulgence" centrally focus on "the transcendence of material preoccupation" (Palmer 162). Thus Rinthy, as the spiritually more innocent partner in incest, is paradoxically associated with both transgression against Mosaic law and transcendence of sensual lust. Perhaps the paradox is resolved if we consider that it is Culla's transgression the novel foregrounds, his treatment of his sister as if she were a "Corinthian girl." Rinthy's innocent love and longing for her child seem to be the source of her steadfast "faith," which seems spiritual in nature if not religious in expression. Her love lies behind the "willingness to disbelief" that prompts her to reject Culla's false version of things: his lie that their baby is dead and his guilt- and death-haunted view of life (32).

However, in gnostic thinking reproduction was often seen as a strategy of the world-artificer(s) to keep the spirit in cosmos. Gnostics' injunction was usually against sexual lust, but some ascetic sects also repudiated marriage and family in their determination to make as little use of the world as possible and to do nothing that would advance the cause of the cosmic rulers. Jonas writes that for gnostics, "More than sexual love is involved in [the] role of *eros* as the principle of mortality. . . . The lust for the things of this world in general may take on many forms, and by all of them the soul [spirit] is turned away from its true goal and kept under the spell of its alien abode" (*Gnostic Religion* 73). Rinthy seems strangely untouched by her sexual experience, even "virginal," as Bell says. He notes somewhat paradoxically that she is "driven by an idealized love" (*Achievement* 35). But her longing for her child imprisons her, as any obsession would. The somatic expression of this is her constantly flowing (and chafing or chapping) breast milk, which marks her love for the things of the world even as it ironically associates her with Living Water. As Fisher-Wirth points out, her flowing milk "stains her with the sign of her need" (134). The milkstain carries connotations of the flesh and psyche, as does the stain of the shadow in Culla's sections.[17] But in the world of *Outer Dark*, Rinthy's capacity for devotion is also a mark of her relative beatitude even as it condemns her to maddening grief; hers is a "frail agony of grace" (237). The novel's sympathetic valorization of love, then, tempers the gnostic nightmare without undercutting it.[18] Rinthy too seems to exemplify the gnostic conception of the tragic "mingling" of spirit in cosmos. Her alien spirit, though less submerged in her than in Culla, is still subject to confusion, fear, and longing for reunification, "the frightened and nostalgic state of the soul [spirit] forlorn in the world" (Jonas, *Gnostic Religion* 65). Indeed her worldly longing to be reunited with her mortal child parallels and ironically displaces the longing of the spirit for reunification with the Divine. So it is apt that several readers associate her with the *mater dolorosa*, the grieving Virgin Mary, the Mother who symbolizes "suffering humanity" (Fisher-Wirth 134).

To emphasize human unknowing, gnostic mythology conceived of the spirit as a stranger in the cosmos. The spirit "suffers the lot of the stranger who is lonely, unprotected, uncomprehended, and uncomprehending in a situation full of danger. . . . The stranger who does not know the ways of the foreign land wanders about lost; if he learns its ways too well, he forgets that he is a stranger and gets lost in a different sense by succumbing to the lure of the alien world and becoming estranged from his own origin" (Jonas, *Gnostic Religion* 49). The designation "stranger" could apply to anyone in cosmos: the alien Messenger from the world of Light, the gnostic, or the alienated, unknowing spirit. Since all three possessed a spark of divinity distanced from the true God, their experiences in cosmos were analogous, and in the myths they often stand for one another metaphorically.[19] In McCarthy's novel, Rinthy is most forcefully identified as a stranger, although Culla too is sometimes addressed as "stranger"; for both the expression points to their lost wandering, uncomprehended and uncomprehending, in outer dark (206, 220). "They ain't a soul in this world but what is a stranger to me," Rinthy sighs (29). "Since I was one and kept to myself, I was a stranger to my fellow-dwellers in the inn [the cosmic dwelling]," says the alienated spirit in "The Hymn of the Pearl" (quoted in Jonas, *Gnostic Religion* 55–56). The action of *Outer Dark* expresses this metaphysical concept allegorically: once the Holmes leave one another, they meet no one they know in their separate sojourns, and the aborted relationship between Rinthy and the farmer suggests the impossibility of breaking through the barriers of estrangement that separate one spirit from another in cosmos or escaping what Gerhard Hoffmann calls "the ultimate solitude and unhumanness of the universe" (224).

Rinthy's position as an essentially innocent woman-child entrapped in "this world" of the flesh is echoed in the child-whore Magdalena kept in sexual slavery in *Cities of the Plain*, of whom the blind piano-player says, "My belief is that she is at best a visitor. At best. She does not belong here. Among us" (81). ("The alien," writes Jonas, "is that which stems from elsewhere and does not belong here"; *Gnostic Religion* 49). The innocent held captive in a brothel stands as a gnostic metaphor for the alien spirit imprisoned in cosmos: Bishop Irenaeus recorded the gnostic conception that the Sophia (wisdom), imprisoned by the world-powers, transmigrates from body to body, suffering repeated indignities and finally becoming a prostitute in a brothel (Mead 169). And we can back-read the metaphor from *Cities of the Plain* to see its application to Rinthy as well, trapped in a world of sexual assault and harassment, harsh judgment and stunted love. Despite her serenity and courage, Rinthy too experiences the fear of the alien spirit endangered in cosmos. In phrasing that emphasizes her own frightful isolation in the world, Rinthy asks the crone, "Ain't you scared by yourself?" When the old woman asks the same of her, Rinthy responds, "Yes mam. I always was scared. Even when they wasn't nobody bein murdered nowheres" (116). Her candid reply establishes her fear as an ontological condition—the essential terror of the human position in the world. Though Culla is most clearly the one "lost" in cosmos in the second sense Jonas describes, that of "succumbing to the lure of the alien world and becoming estranged from his own origin" (*Gnostic* 49), and Rinthy seems less thoroughly alienated, she shares in Culla's lostness as well: "Yes, I'm lost" (58), she affirms to the family who shelter her from the darkness and in whose house at night she is acutely aware of her status as stranger: "She listened for a bird or for a cricket. Something she might *know* in all that *dark*" (65, emphasis added).

Notwithstanding her spatial wandering, in the time frame of the novel Rinthy traces a very definite narrative arc. In contrast to the circling and repetition that characterize her brother's "progress," she moves from losing her chap, through searching for him, following with blind faith the faintest of clues and encountering numerous obstacles, to painful resolution in her discovery of the whitened ribcage that is the child's material remains. However, her faithful but displaced searching that ends in bones resonates with terrible irony against the tradition of Christian allegories of the seeking soul's progress.[20] The "end" of her search may well function as a modernist resolution for the reader alone, because for all her gentleness, faith, and love, Rinthy is neither a Christian pilgrim nor a gnostic Seeker on a mission to recover the Light. Rather, she is perhaps the least dire case of the unknowing ones who sojourn through a gnostic world, the misguided seeker in whom spirit is not completely estranged and who is most fit to receive the gnostic message. Irenaeus, the Bishop of Lyons who critiqued gnosticism in the late second century, paraphrased the concept of the gnostics' immunity to the trammeling of the cosmos: "As gold sunk in filth will not lose its beauty but preserve its own nature, and the filth will be unable to impair the gold, so nothing can injure them, even if their deeds immerse them in matter, and nothing can change their spiritual essence" (quoted in Jonas, *Gnostic Religion* 271). This seems almost the case with the unknowing Rinthy, yet she is still tragically mingled in cosmos. She reflects humanity's cosmic situation "as that of the potentially knowing in the midst of the unknowing, of light in the midst of darkness"—a condition that prompted the gnostics' compassion (Jonas, "Epilogue" 328).

The culminating image of the baby's ribcage, doubled in the tinker's pendulous brisket that weathers to a "bone birdcage," is a memento of the human body as a cage for the spirit, yet Rinthy's search that leads to such bone cages also implies that her very longing for her son comprises her never-ending shackles, her psychological *heimarmene* (238).[21] She does "not know what to make of" the scene of destruction she finds at the triune's campsite. Her unknowing here tends ominously toward denial, both psychological and spiritual, and the narrator twice tells us, "She waited . . . but no one returned." Indeed, "She waited all through the blue twilight and into the dark" (237). This long waiting in darkness, which has been Rinthy's condition all along, reinscribes the essential circumstances of Culla's opening dream of the eclipse; the novel leaves Rinthy in the dark night of the cosmos, still grieving, asleep. But the pathos of her unreprieved longing is a crucial counterpoint to the comparatively disengaged sympathy the reader is likely to experience when confronted with Culla's "gracelorn" ignorance and his failure in compassion for his kin or his fellow humankind—even though we may also pity him for his sufferings as a cosmic pawn and scapegoat (241). The Holme siblings together evoke the dualistic gnostic attitude: contempt for the ignorant principle in humankind and in the world, deep pity for the captive Divine spark in humanity.

The tinker, as one of three foregrounded purgatorial figures in the novel, is also strongly associated with the outer dark of unknowing. He relates to others primarily through his mercantilism, and dragging his vendor's cart he recalls Bertolt Brecht's eponymous old Mother Courage (1939), who follows warring armies across Europe for decades, drawing in a laborious stoop her supply cart hung with wares, and whose devotion to trade above all else costs the lives of her two sons and her mute daughter. And still stage directions indicate that she "*harness[es] herself to the cart*" (scene 12) and "*trudges on alone*" (scene 11). The "harness" of material trade the tinker has "devised for himself," stoops him as well: unharnessed, he remains "still bowed in his posture of drayage" (184, 188).[22] He is described as "gnomic," a "stage dwarf," "malformed," as if to suggest the spiritual stunting at his core (6, 19, 188). Indeed his bowed body reflects the Valentinian conception of the archons' creation of man out of water (darkness), earth (matter), wind (counterspirit), and fire (desire): "This is the tomb of the body with which man was clothed so that it be [for him] the fetter of Matter" (quoted in Jonas, *Gnostic Religion* 204; interpolation Jonas's). (The opening dream links Culla too with cripples, but unlike them Culla does not exhibit any outward manifestation of his maiming, which hints that his deformity exists on a deeper level.) "*Stooped and hounded*" by his traps, the tinker travels amid the "clatter of his wagon and the endless tympanic collision of his wares," an image that invokes the gnostic conception of the noise and turmoil of the world (229, 21).[23] And in its moribund stillness, the image of his face "hung" in the cabin's firelight, "a mask of morbid tranquillity like the faces of the drowned," both foreshadows his death by hanging and links him with the cosmic oblivion of turbid water, a death-in-life (191).

The tinker's dealing in pornography reinforces his stultifying involvement with matter. Like Culla he is implicated in matters of the flesh yet harshly judges what he perceives as sexual or moral transgression. Like Rumpelstiltskin and the Pied Piper, fairy-tale figures with whom he is linked, the tinker traffics in flesh in a rather literal way, too, appropriating the child of others. Since love forms no part of his makeup, this *"cheerless vendor"* seems to want the Holme baby only as a possession, claimed perhaps out of his sense of self-pitying entitlement in compensation for the difficulty of his life, as Bell suggests (229; *Achievement* 51). But he takes no better care of the child than Culla does—or than Mother Courage does of her three children. Before the boy is a year old, he has been terribly burned and half-blinded, placing him too among the ranks of the maimed, and the tinker plays his part in delivering the child to the triune and to death. Thus it is ironic and unjust that the tinker decides Rinthy "ain't fit to have" her son. When Rinthy claims, "That ain't for you to judge," he counters, "I've done judged" (192). He repeats Culla's act of willfully separating Rinthy and the child, like him bringing to bear the harshest of judgment for the transgression of Mosaic law in incest, simultaneously denying the incest yet affirming it in his final angry words to her: "Bitch. . . . Goddamn lyin bitch" (194). His confused mixture of material motives and psychological judgment identifies him as another lost cosmic wanderer. However, unlike Culla, who clearly directs judgment inwardly in his self-interrogation in the triune/camp-fire scenes, the tinker's unknowing is most obviously manifested in his arrogant assumption that he does know, that he can judge others; in enacting his judg-ments against Rinthy, he functions as an avatar of cosmic *heimarmene*. At the same time, he is himself subject to *heimarmene*. When the triune appear to him in the glade, they *"might have risen from the ground. The tinker could not account for them,"* suggesting that they arise like his own inner urges, repeating the role they play in their dealings with Culla (229). This surfacing from the abyss is the only hint we have that the triune may function as psychological *heimarmene* for the tinker; we are privileged to see only the result of their role as physical *heimarmene* in the tinker's hanged body. But if we recognize this scene as a dou-ble for Culla's two confrontations with the triune, we might wonder if the tin-ker's encounter too is belated self-judgment, his death self-imposed.

Culla's unknowing is manifested in a variety of practical and more meta-physical ways. He has little sense of the day of the week or even the time of day, suggesting that he is lost in time as well as in space (26, 46, 162). He doesn't know whether turbid creek water is fit to drink, whether Johnson County is a mean place, the name of the triune's leader, nor where Rinthy is (82, 85,

174–75, 182). His opening dream makes it clear that he does not know if he can be cured, and the blind man implies that Culla really does not know what has caused the sun to go away. Culla even claims not to know where he got his veal boots, and such claims of ignorance joined with his other psychological evasions provoke the bearded leader to challenge him, "You don't know much, do ye?" (176, 178). Culla often asserts that he doesn't need anything, and he rarely asks for anything but work. His reluctance to ask for food arouses Squire Salter's animosity and suspicion, and his later inquiry about how long he might work for the J. P. for nothing but food elicits a cold response. Yet Culla is so poor in everything that his neediness is one of his defining qualities. Although he intermittently acknowledges only his material needs while being unconsciously but relentlessly driven by his psychological ones, his spiritual poverty (ignorance) is his most essential burden. Arnold's invocation of Revelation 3:17 is relevant here: "For you say, I am rich, I have prospered, and I need nothing; not knowing that you are wretched, pitiable, poor, blind, and naked" ("Naming, Knowing" 53). Culla knows he is poor in material wealth, but he does not acknowledge the kind of poverty Jesus means. When the blind man asks if there is anything he needs, Culla can scarcely understand the question because he associates this gentle old man who is selling nothing with the tinker who has asked similarly, "You all need anything?" (7). So Culla smiles at the man in one of the very few times he smiles in the novel—all of them marking his own lack of understanding. He smiles because he can't see that this blind traveler has anything to offer (240). Culla's earlier denials of his worldly drives and needs prepare for this scene in which he denies his need for spiritual awakening. When the old man intuits Culla's deep lack and offers a gnostic reinterpretation of his dream and his life, Culla's nervous response is "I got to get on"—a refusal of this benediction (241). Thus his deepest ignorance, resulting from his oblivion in cosmos, is that he needs spiritual enlightenment.

This quality of Culla's unknowing is most apparent in his responses to aggressive queries about his destination. According to Jonas, "The discovery of [the] transcendent inner principle in man and the supreme concern about its destiny is the very center of gnostic religion" (*Gnostic Religion* 124). Culla's destination functions as a metaphor for this more essential destiny. He does not know where he is going, as he confesses reluctantly to the beehiver and the triune. And the bearded leader pointedly mocks him, saying Culla is "from nowheres nowhere bound" (233). This dual ignorance on Culla's part about his literal/spiritual origin and destiny compresses and reverses Theodotus' definition of liberating gnosis as "knowledge of who we were, what we became; where we were, whereinto we have been thrown; whereto we speed, wherefrom we are redeemed" (quoted from Clement of Alexandria's *Excerpta ex Theodoto* in Jonas, *Gnostic Religion* 45). It marks him as a man lacking in gnosis, for the "Gospel of

Truth" asserts, "He who . . . possesses the Gnose [gnosis], knows whence he is come and where he is going" (quoted in Jonas, *Gnostic Religion* 89).[24] In *Outer Dark*, to ask where one is from or where one is headed is implicitly and innocently to pose a gnostic question, a question to which Culla has no answers. Nothing gives Culla transcendental direction because, as the bearded leader of the triune implies, he is entirely "bound" by cosmic *heimarmene*.[25]

Culla's lack of a sense of ultimate destination is emphasized in his counterpointed conversations with the triune, who keep him bound, and the blind old man, who offers him new insight. The blind man remarks that every day he sees "people goin up and down in the world like dogs. As if they wasn't a home nowheres" (240). He is describing Culla Holme, of course, and the status of the siblings' last name as a homophone of *home* (noted in Bell, *Achievement* 40) works as an unheard reminder throughout Culla's travels, an unheeded because guilt-inducing incantation calling him to reunite with his sister and son. Even more crucially, the repetition of his name may suggest the Call of the Alien spirit within and without to refocus his path toward his Home with the Unknown Father. (The only father whom Culla acknowledges is "dead"; 207.) Indeed his full name is a homophone of the "Call of Home."

The metaphor of the transcendent Home versus the cosmic dwelling or inn comes in for some emphasis from Jonas. In the Turfan fragment, the messenger from the transmundane sphere greets man, saying, "Power and prosperity of the Living/unto thee from thy home!" (quoted in Jonas, *Gnostic Religion* 83). Jonas employs the metaphor himself, in the context of the spirit's sense of alienation in cosmos: "The alien is that which stems from elsewhere and does not belong here. To those who do belong here it [the transcendent Home] is thus the strange, the unfamiliar and incomprehensible; but their world . . . is just as incomprehensible to the alien that comes to dwell here, and like a foreign land where it is far from home" (*Gnostic Religion* 49). And the concept of home received special weight in Manichaean asceticism, which literalized the gnostics' "not feeling at home in [the] world" by frowning on the building of houses (*Gnostic Religion* 231). McCarthy's characters' contradictory longing for home and flight from it, explored by Witek, is evidence of their alienation from the world in this gnostic sense. Witek echoes gnostic imagery when she concludes that McCarthy's domestic spaces—hovels, campfires, caves—"teach us that no place in the world is home . . . that every boy must be the frontiersman of what will turn out to be a grave-sized chunk of earth" ("Reeds" 142). Culla himself does nothing to create or maintain a home in the world. After he leaves the cabin in which he and Rinthy have squatted for four months, his only attempt at creating a domestic space for himself is in his act of "trespass" in an old cabin, but neither his trespass nor his homelessness is an act of rebellion based in the gnostic recognition that permanent homes bring, to import Witek's gnostically apt language again, "not freedom but alienation" ("Reeds" 141). Rather, his troubled relation to "home" is an ontological given. The grieving mother Rinthy shares in this. Even though she feels she has been "run off from" (101), she is the first to leave Culla, and she admits that she has never lived anywhere much (156). But as Witek points out, "When Rinthy leaves, she is trying to trade her brother's house for her son's" ("Reeds" 140). When she leaves the farmer she is attempting again to find a home in her child. Whether we are contemplating physical domestic spaces or earthly love here, all the real and potential homes that Rinthy flees or seeks are counterfeit homes, displacements of the transcendent home. On the other hand, the traveling blind man's apparent homelessness may very well constitute a deliberate act of ascetic revolt against cosmos or a sign of his recognition of the world as a counterfeit home.

The triune's reaction to Culla's name further hints the gnostic import of "home." The people Culla meets on the road often falter with his name, calling attention to it, but usually it is his given name (perhaps a shortening of "McCullough") that they do not recognize. Only the triune's leader balks at his surname, Holme: "The word seemed to feel bad in his mouth" (174). As an agent of cosmic destiny, he unconsciously finds distasteful any suggestion of the spiritual home that the cosmos is designed to bar the alienated spirit from reaching. As an expression of Culla's own psychological being, the leader's reaction against the naming of home suggests the depth of Culla's spiritual alienation and the soundness of his slumber in cosmos.

The idea that Culla is bound to the cosmic path he treads is implied also in the insightful blind man's query, "What needs a man to see his way when he's sent there anyhow?" (241). But the blind traveler's passive syntax leaves the identity of the sender ambiguous, and that ambiguity is entirely relevant from a gnostic perspective. A Judeo-Christian reading would locate in his words a message of God's providence at work in human life and an admonishment to submit to God's will and plan. But such a message is so wildly at odds with Culla's experience of the world that it may seem glib and even foolish—indeed, blind—which is another reason Culla ignores the old man. As befits the Christian culture of the novel's setting, the blind man uses the language of Christianity—"sin," "prayer," "word," and "flesh"—as much or more than the language of gnostic myth. But in this novel, Christian implications are almost always subject to the gnostic revaluation as well. Indeed once gnosticism is invoked at all, it implies a revaluation of the Judeo-Christian and Hellenistic traditions. Thus a gnostic reading hears in the man's multivocal question reminders of the transcendent Messenger who is "sent" to call spirit out of the world, of a human's "thrownness" (or "sentness") into the dark cosmos of the world rulers, and of the ineffectuality of all natural means of sight or insight to assist him in finding his way within the world or out of it: ideas much more in keeping with

Culla's dark nightmare. When he contrasts the gnostic and existentialist implications of the idea of "thrownness," Jonas asks, "What is the throw without the thrower, and without a beyond whence it started?" ("Epilogue" 339). Gnosticism's postulation of the thrower, the Sender, and the beyond aligns it more with Christianity than with modern existentialism's "dualism without metaphysics" (Jonas, "Epilogue" 340), but the two ancient religions part ways in their differing conceptions of the nature and identity of the Sender(s)—for the Christian system the Creator and Supreme God who sends humanity into the world and who sends His son after; for gnosticism the counterfeit god, the world-creator who throws humankind into cosmos, on the one hand, and the very distinct Unknown God who sends the Messenger to retrieve humanity from darkness on the other.

As an attempt to remedy Culla's unknowing, the traveler's query implies a gnostic repudiation of both the world and any human attempt to master it, instead hinting of the Way or Path of gnosis that leads the spirit out of the cosmic path onto which he has been thrown. His point that "It's all plain enough. Word and flesh," while couched in Christian terminology, yet points to the gnostic dualism of spirit and cosmos as well (240). And the old man's reference to the "way" is an explicit reference to the transcendent Messenger (or Traveler or Stranger), who is "sent" to bring gnostic understanding and teaches "'knowledge of the way,' namely, of the soul's way out of the world" (Jonas, *Gnostic Religion* 45). Arnold's and Metress's arguments that the blind man is actually on a different path from Culla's are relevant to such a gnostic interpretation: even more than the love- and grief-bound Rinthy, this ragged old man is the affirmative figure in the novel, traveling with serene assurance and his "blind smile," asking the strangers he meets if they need anything (242). As a gnostic traveler, he is relatively free of cosmic destiny or *heimarmene* (Jonas, *Gnostic Religion* 160n14), and his destination is not the claggy turbid water of cosmos but the spirit's true home in Light. What he has to offer is a new Way. Culla needs not to see his way with his eyes but to harken to the call of the Messenger. But Culla is still too oblivious to listen—as he has been from the beginning, "not listening, never listening" (9).[26] This is why he is often depicted in a void of silence. When the Messenger pointedly questions why a man needs to see his way, Culla responds evasively, "I got to get on" (as he will again when the blind man explicates his dream of the eclipse), confirming his oblivious commitment to the cosmic road on which he has been traveling (241). He imagines that the old man is more lost than he: "Someone should tell a blind man before setting him out that way" (242). Culla, of course, is the truly blind or deaf man who needs telling, but when he encounters the Messenger, he deflects the call to his transcendent home.

Bell finds evidence of nihilism in *Outer Dark* in the fact that its characters seem to inhabit "an obscure, existential void," a world that, whether dream or reality, constitutes an "existential nightmare" orchestrated by some deranged and inaccessible Power (*Achievement* 33, 39). And he sees—rightly, I think— that the light-attended Rinthy "remains in her maze . . . ; and her child, rather than being proof against the world, is proof of it" (*Achievement* 34). He identi- fies the blind man's theology as Manichaean and finds it inadequate to counter the darkness of the novel's action, commenting that the "word" the blind man invokes is "decidedly unmanifest, an alien idea" (*Achievement* 35). Thus he identifies nihilistic aspects of the novel that characterize gnosticism as much as modern existentialism, and if McCarthy's novel engages Jonas's *Gnostic Religion* in as thoroughgoing a fashion as I have been arguing, McCarthy himself would have been entirely aware of the philosophical congruence—and essential dif- ferences—between the two.

In "Gnosticism, Existentialism, and Nihilism," the epilogue Jonas added to the second edition of his book (1963), he discusses the surprising similarities that he (as a former student of Martin Heidegger) finds between the modern nihilist philosophy of the Western world, with its roots in Pascal and the sci- entific revolution, and the ancient gnostic religion of the first three centuries A.D., when the vast machinery of the Roman Empire provoked a revaluation of Hellenic cosmos piety and the corollary virtue of playing one's part in the whole and for the good of the whole. Both eras, for different reasons, produced a zeit- geist of "cosmic nihilism": "an estrangement between man and the world, with the loss of the idea of a kindred *cosmos*" ("Epilogue" 325, emphasis in original). Gnosticism involved a profound sense of homelessness and alienation in the world, with the celestial spheres personifying the hostile world-powers separat- ing humankind from the true God. In existentialism the homelessness of man in the universe is accentuated in his sense that in the vastness of the universe revealed by modern science there is only indifference; nothing in the celestial sphere recognizes the human, and it turns on him or her a cold and impersonal gaze. And nothing exists in a transcendent world that corresponds to the indi- vidual's own impulse to value and care about his or her life and being; existen- tialism lacks the great affirmation of gnosticism that tempers its pessimism about the world. However, existentialism and gnosticism share a painful aware- ness that god is not manifest in the world, "not revealed or even indicated" by it ("Epilogue" 327). Such a "hidden God," Jonas says, "is a nihilist conception: no *nomos* emanates from him, no law for nature and thus none for human action as a part of the natural order" ("Epilogue" 332); and Jonas finds affinity between the ground of gnostic antinomianism and that of Jean Paul Sartre. Further, he remarks the common imagery of "thrownness" that originates in gnostic myth and recurs in Pascal's conception of man as "cast into the infinite immensity of spaces" (quoted in "Epilogue" 334) and in Heidegger's *Geworfenheit*, from *Sein und Zeit:* the quality of "'having been thrown,' which to him is a fundamental character of the *Dasein*, of the self-experience of existence" (334).

But Jonas does not equate gnosticism with modern nihilism. Both philosophies exhibit a dualism between man and the world, a separation between man and god, but unlike the perception of Nietzsche and later existentialists that God is dead, Jonas shows that gnosticism's "extreme dualism is of itself the very opposite of an abandonment of transcendence. The transmundane God represents it in the most radical form. In him the absolute beyond beckons across the enclosing cosmic shells. But this transcendence . . . does not stand in any positive relation to the sensible world" ("Epilogue" 332). Later he writes, "In the gnostic formula it is understood that, though thrown into temporality, we had an origin in eternity, and so also have an aim in eternity. This places the innercosmic nihilism of the Gnosis against a metaphysical background which is entirely absent from its modern counterpart" ("Epilogue" 335). It seems to me that this distinction goes to the heart of the critical disagreement over the metaphysics of *Outer Dark*. Glimmers of transcendence are faint indeed in the vividly realized cosmic nightmare derived from Culla's experience and entangling all other characters except the blind seer, who appears on the scene late in the day. But this is entirely consonant with the gnostic orientation of the novel. If the potential for transcendence were "all plain enough" (240)—as it is to the blind man—that very gnosis would radically temper and even dissipate the cosmic nightmare (as it finally does for Suttree). As *Outer Dark* suggests, it might alter the world as experienced, as it certainly has for the blind Seer and as it comes closer to doing for Rinthy than for her brother. The nihilism of the novel is of this gnostic kind, manifest indeed and yet contained within the closed system of the cosmos; Bell is right to recognize it and to argue that the blind man's message is ineffective in terms of altering Culla's experience. But Arnold is also right when he points to the novel's negative methods of suggesting spiritual alternatives to Culla's experience. Its Christian allusions suggest a transcendence not yet grasped by the Holmes, and its gnostic ones do so even more emphatically. "The world is a wild place in McCarthy's fiction," Arnold wrote in 1994, a few years after his seminal comments on *Outer Dark* in "Naming, Knowing, and Nothingness," "and its God a . . . mostly unknowable God, but a God whose presence constantly beckons" ("Blood" 14).

This is a novel of outer dark; its very title posits an opposing realm of inner light. The book's presentation as a dream-narrative denotes it as not necessarily representative of the world we may inhabit. Readers may find in it greater or lesser congruence with the experiential world depending on their own philosophical orientations. But its gnostic vision does not establish that McCarthy himself is either a nihilist or a neo-gnostic. Rather, his engagement with gnostic myth here and in later novels, together with his manifest knowledge of Plato, Christianity, Dante, Boehme, Emerson and Thoreau, William James, the Book of Mormon, modern existentialism, and other religions and philosophies, including science and complexity theory, demonstrates that he is profoundly interested in the problematic human position in the universe and in possibilities for transcendence.

The Wilderness Nightmare: *Gnostic "Ecology"*

The gnostic perspective profoundly affects the depiction of the natural world as nightmare in *Outer Dark*, which appears to diverge from the ecological vision of *The Orchard Keeper* but is finally no retreat from it. In the gnostic view, humanity shared with other natural creatures an origin in darkness and subjection to physical *heimarmene*, yet this common nature did not ameliorate the fact that both humankind and the natural world, subject to necessity, were agents of oppression to one another—with the emphasis on nature's oppression of humanity. When Jonas outlines the differences between modern nihilism and gnosticism, he addresses their conceptions of nature: "Gnostic man is thrown into an antagonistic, antidivine, and therefore antihuman nature, modern man into an indifferent one. Only the latter case represents the absolute vacuum, the really bottomless pit. In the gnostic conception the hostile, the demonic, is still anthropomorphic, familiar even in its foreignness, and the contrast itself gives direction to existence—a negative direction, to be sure, but one that has behind it the sanction of the negative transcendence to which the positivity of the world is the qualitative counterpart. Not even this antagonistic quality is granted to the indifferent nature of modern science, and from that nature no direction at all can be elicited" ("Epilogue" 338–39). Culla's flight from an actively hostile nature marks *Outer Dark* as more gnostic than existential, but both views of nature are opposed to the ecological understanding of human and natural interdependence that usually characterizes McCarthy's writing.

In the anticosmic gnostic nightmare the realms of nature were all wilderness. There was none of the pastoral impulse described by Leo Marx in *The Machine in the Garden* or by Annette Kolodny in *The Lay of the Land*, no sense that mediating between society and wild nature might lead to anything positive or that resting on the bosom of nature might lead to a primal harmony. The gnostic view of wild land was in some ways compatible with longstanding orthodox Christian traditions that portray it as a realm outside of the providential garden, a realm of evil—conceptions that influenced some early American responses to wilderness, as Roderick Nash postulates in *Wilderness and the American Mind* (1967). The pious Christian's metaphor of earthly life as a wilderness condition (Nash 3), seen in the writings of American Puritans, also expresses the gnostic's alienation in all of nature. Nash traces the derivation of the word "wilderness" to its root in "will": wilderness is that which, having a will of its own, opposes the will of man (1). For the Christian it often referred to the places on earth where god is not or the places humankind has been unable to transform into a garden. For the gnostic, however, all of cosmos was the anti-human, antispiritual realm, and the wilderness condition invested all of nature both external to humanity and internal. In this sense, for the dualistic gnostic there was no pastoral middle ground, no harmonious blending of nature and civilization. Nor was there any analogue to the Puritan aspiration to construct a city upon a hill, that might, as Nash says, redeem "the world from its 'wilderness state'" (35). Civilization, too, was wilderness—an idea that anticipates, but with different root causes, the late-nineteenth-century development of the metaphor of the urban wilderness. The gnostic shared none of the orthodox Christian's sense of God's providence working through nature or through His people. As many readers of *Outer Dark* have noticed, God is not a presence in this world. Neither, as Witek observes, is the earth perceived as a nurturing Mother ("Reeds" 142). Nor, as Hoffmann points out, is nature the "retreat" or "consolation" represented in *The Orchard Keeper;* rather, "Nature . . . seems to join the machinations of evil" represented by the triune (224, 226).

In the nightmare of *Outer Dark*, gnostic contempt for and fear of nature are manifested in the perceived antagonism of the sun, turbid rivers, and swamps and in the novel's depictions of animal and plant life as part of the world's oppression of the spirit. Bell observes that "Culla is repeatedly required to negotiate or fend off thick vegetation, weeds, waist-high grass, encroaching stands of trees" (*Achievement* 37). This clinging, entangling, lowering vegetation—the "dense cover" that Nash identifies as "classic wilderness"—is the stuff of grim fairy tales and wilderness nightmares, and it augments the novel's other gnostic imagery of cosmic entrapment ("Preface" xv). But the novel's garden imagery offers little relief, suggesting that human attempts to tame or collaborate with nature result in similar entanglement. The garden of the grandmother is "well-tended," yet its "pretty" flowerbeds are "rank growths of beebalm and phlox" (98). Beebalm (*monarda*), a perennial that bears a showy but spidery flower and loves damp soil, is invasive and resistant to human restraint, a plant known in gardening lore as a "thug." Thus it is an apt gnostic image of nature's allure and snare, and the rank fecundity of this garden tempers the sentimental portrait of pastoral and domestic contentment that Rinthy perceives in the woman who nurtures her plants and her grandbaby. When Rinthy rests for a season with the farmer, she tries to create a similar garden, duplicating the grandmother's expression of love for some of the things of the world. But in Rinthy's furled flowers "poisoned by dark" planted around her "dead and loveless house," we may see not only a realistic description of the twilight folding of flowers but also a gnostic warning against involvement in the world, a reflection of the human inhabitants of cosmos infected by the poison of its darkness (209, 211). Rinthy's flowers prefigure the *"poisoned grass"* on which the triune have slept, an image that identifies the archontic powers as causative agents that are poisoning the natural world (229). The association of the garden with poison is reinforced when Culla drinks from the well behind the snakehunter's cabin; he sees in close juxtaposition a "small garden grubbed out of the loamy soil and beyond that an impenetrable wall of poison ivy," implying both the puniness of mankind's attempts to tame nature and the overwhelmingly poisonous character of the natural world (118). This poison, then, does not characterize only the realm of uncultivated wilderness; in this novel gardens share in the rank, poisonous quality of all nature, and the pastoral realm is barely distinguishable from wilderness. All cosmos where humankind wanders alienated from an Unknown God is a "garden of the dead," all a gnostic wilderness (242).

In the gnostic view to garden or to farm, as to eat of the world, is to invite the poison of darkness in. All plants are weeds, all animals varmints. The pastoral or frontier professions of so many of the novel's characters thus imply their entanglement with the world of nature that may seem benign but that, as a manifestation of cosmos, is antithetical to the human spirit. In this sense, the nightmare vision of *Outer Dark* is profoundly antipastoral, as Guillemin observes, and just as profoundly antiwilderness because anticosmic (68).

In his treatment of Old World ideas of wilderness imported to America, Nash discusses the typical opposition of the garden and wilderness: "If paradise was early man's greatest good, wilderness, as its antipode, was his greatest evil" (9). In *Outer Dark* such opposition is moot. Rinthy's farmer, who may strive to make a pastoral garden of his land, achieves no restoration of an Eden; rather, he is like the expelled Adam condemned to endless and spirit-numbing labor. Jonas explains that in the "bold allegorizing of the biblical text" of the story of Eden favored by some gnostics, the knowledge that the snake imparts is spiritual gnosis, and it is the jealous and judgmental world artificers and rulers who expel Adam and Eve into their life of oppression. In this remythologizing, the serpent's gift of knowledge "is the first success of the transcendent principle against the principle of the world, which is vitally interested in preventing knowledge in man as the inner-worldly hostage . . . : the serpent's action marks the beginning of all *gnosis* on earth which thus by its very origin is stamped as . . . a form of rebellion" (Jonas, *Gnostic Religion* 93).[27] Rinthy's nameless farmer, however, is an unredeemed, unenlightened, unrebellious Adam figure. Like the tinker, the farmer is "stooped" by the machinery of his repetitious work; he and the mule harnessed with him both pass "like shades" (209). He gazes "dumbly" at the simple cold supper Rinthy places before him and eats it "listlessly like a man in sorrow. . . . He'd see all night again tonight the mule's hasped hoofs wristing up before him and the cool earth passing and passing, canting dark and moldy" (210). He longs for companionship in his dark and oblivion-inducing garden, but Rinthy, no Eve, is "mute," remote, gone (210).

Rinthy's strange fear and loathing of "varmints" reinforces the novel's gnostic nightmare of a hostile natural world. The noseless grandmother peers into the forest where Rinthy dreads to see wild animals "as if she held camera with something that paced them in the black pine woods beyond"—a passage that links natural predators with the triune themselves (67).[28] Despite Rinthy's Disney-esque association with birds and butterflies, she is not at home in the natural world (98). Her fear does not appear to have the realistic grounding of Arthur Ownby's. Despite the menacing aura of the world, no large predatory beasts roam the landscape of *Outer Dark*. The greatest threats of injury from animals are those posed by the terrified horse on the loose ferry or the panicked hogs that sweep Vernon over the bluff. These hogs are joined by other malevolent pigs: the domestic boar that rises up out of the wallow (like nature itself welling up in the human psyche) when Culla flees his human hunters and the crone's sow, who watches her and Rinthy with "hostile cunning" (93, 114). Such imagery inverts young Ownby's yeoman's valuation of his pigs over the vengeful panther, and in *Outer Dark*, humans, horses, and pigs are linked as natural creatures in a gnostic world—domestic yet wild by their very nature. Not only are there no panthers prowling the outer dark, but the rattlesnakes that the crone fears and detests have been curbed by the likes of the snake-hunter, so that now the vigilance of the old woman is largely a displaced reflex, and the "snakes" she fends with her hoe are nothing but tree roots (109). Rinthy and the crone's terror of varmints, then, is not realistic, based in experience of a literal, ecological wilderness, but a metaphor for an ontological given, a dread of the world as gnostic wilderness. Rinthy shuns unnamed and unseen "varmints" as the ancient gnostic avoided the world-powers patrolling cosmos.

Even the small creatures of this novel, while they do not present much realistic threat to man's physical well-being, are sometimes presented as subtle reminders and avatars of the cosmic powers that monitor and harass humankind. As Culla drinks the beehiver's whiskey, a hawk wheels slowly above him as if keeping watch over his progress in oblivion (81). From the door of the cabin where the tinker has led her, Rinthy sees "dark little birds" fly over the fields toward the sunset "like heralds of some coming dread" (188). When she closes the door, she finds hanging behind it "a coat cocooned in spiderweb like some enormous prey"—a gnostic image of the human spirit, cloaked in flesh, preyed upon and entrapped in the natural world (189). The parson joins the hog drovers, "fending flies" (221). Early in the novel as Culla walks toward the store, a "horsefly followed behind his head as if towed there on a string," again suggesting his houndedness by the world of nature; however, the echo of Warn Pulliam's buzzard on a tether, also hints that the tormenting is mutual. The snakehunter roots in his beard for the "small life" infesting it, and he routs it as well (26, 124).[29]

The wilderness and frontier aspects of the world of *The Orchard Keeper* have a realistic ground. In contrast the gothic "wilderness" of *Outer Dark* is a mythic manifestation of its gnostic cosmos.[30] When Rinthy voices her fear of varmints, she is riding in the wagon with Luther's family from their upland dwelling through both forest and canebrake to a town only a half-day's wagon ride away. In terms of the generalized topography both in Leo Marx's schema in *The Machine in the Garden* and in the westward migration of American settlements, this "wilderness" has no business occupying a spatial middle ground between Luther's farm and the town (although of course the historical westering of the frontier did leave such wilderness pockets, "islands in a growing sea of civiliza-tion," especially in mountainous regions such as East Tennessee (Nash 248). But wilderness landscape in *Outer Dark* recurrently materializes out of place to be stumbled into unexpectedly, as if all its characters live on some strange fron-tier between the familiar and the alien. The ubiquity of wilderness hints that all nature is wild and that man's attempts to cultivate or domesticate the natu-ral world arise from his ignorance of its cosmic alienness and of his transcen-dent spirit lost in it. All three of Marx's emblematic environments—the town, the pastoral countryside, and wilderness—are nominally represented in *Outer Dark*, but there is no essential difference among them. In this gnostic world humans may hope to escape the wilderness of nature or of human nature, but their ontological position in all environments is the same.

The novel's topographical dislocations are ecological as well as cultural, with swamps abutting uplands, pasturelands adjacent to deep forests. The triune cross a cultivated field and immediately enter a wood traversed by a road, where they kill Squire Salter (51). Culla runs from the main street of Cheatham into a field, then woods, then a canebrake, out of which he falls into a road, then plunges back into cane and deep woods, all before collapsing breathlessly—within less than an hour, perhaps (88–90). Rinthy leaves the turnip farm on foot around noon and soon walks out of the "cleared land" and into "a deep and marshy wood" where she walks for miles through uninhabited land before coming on the "slattern shack" of the old woman late in the afternoon (108). In the next chapter Culla traces a similar path—perhaps the same path—walking "down out of the kept land and into a sunless wood where the road curved dark and cool, overlaid with immense ferns, trees hung with gray moss like hag's hair"; on this deserted road he arrives at the cabin of the snakehunter (117). It is as if McCarthy has envisioned in *Outer Dark* a mythic place in which many ecological systems of the American South, from the high river bluffs of the

Appalachian foothills to the swampy canebrakes along the rivers to the west and farther south, are coterminous.[31]

The novel's wilderness environments, always dark and threatening, are contiguous to cultivated lands and towns—to say nothing of the several cabins nestled into clearings in the forest in European fairy-tale fashion, and wilderness is ever at hand to engulf the characters without warning, like the dreaded inwardness of gnostic psychology.[32] Indeed the characters' parallel, repetitious abruptions into clearings and glades or into the only slightly less claustrophobic roads, towns, and farms, cleared spaces where all the human interactions occur, suggest that the tangled wilderness condition is the essential one in this novel and that human clearings represent not the Puritan idea of "island[s] of spiritual light in the surrounding darkness" but counterfeit and illusory amnions of light in the uniform darkness of the world (Nash 35). Fisher-Wirth reads the novel's glades as "vengeful" and threatening womb-images (131). I see the glades as wombs or amnions as well, but ones that offer the illusion of protection from the encroaching threat of cosmos as wilderness. That is, it is not the clearing itself that threatens but the cosmic wildness both investing and surrounding it. Sometimes, in their light-filtering, grail-like qualities, the clearings are presented in ironic temple imagery, as in Stephen Crane's *The Red Badge of Courage*—especially when a character is there alone. Consider the "green serenity" of the space where Culla rests from his second flight in the woods, "kneeling like something broken or penitent among the corrugate columns" of trees with "the light falling long and plumb through the forest" (90). In such passages wilderness clearings offer illusory sanctuary from the persecuting human realm. But as wombs or as sanctuaries, these glades only appear to hold back the hostile natural or human world that threatens from the perimeter or that rises up from within the psyche. The triune's campfires are a particularly clear illustration of this, as if McCarthy uses them to interrogate primitive man's use of fire to create, as Nash writes, a "magic circle of light" to comfort and protect him from the "darkness beyond" ("Preface" xvi). As arenas for encounters with the triune, such clearings and campfires are themselves invested with darkness. And the larger clearings of human space within the natural world—towns and farms—prove equally threatening, especially to Culla, suggesting that for the man who is most subject to outer dark, even the realms of human "dominance" over nature remain under the thrall of hostile cosmic rule.

Clearly certain natural images are selected for their metaphorical or mythical import rather than their realistic or naturalistic impression, although in his other work McCarthy typically combines the two features seamlessly. Thus mandrake, a European plant, spontaneously springs up below the dead tinker, "as it will where the seed of the hanged falls" (238). And the millhands are hanged in a blackhaw, the rather small *viburnum prunifolium*, which grows to only about fifteen feet and thus seems an unlikely hanging tree, but which carries such a resonant common name and bears metaphorically apt blue-black fruit (95). When specific birds are identified rather than the nameless "small and anonymous birds" that often populate the novel's terrain (198), they too are chosen for their connotations, as with the hawk that hovers over Culla in predatory circling, the bats that "*hunt the glade*" where the tinker and the baby will die, "*like little voiceless souls*," and the dawn mockingbird Culla hears at the triune's dying campfire or the twilight one in Rinthy's dooryard who tells "what he knows of the night" as if in ironic, mocking commentary on their choices (229, 183, 209). Nevertheless, McCarthy has not turned his regard entirely away from the empirical reality of the natural world, and gnostic dread of nature coexists in dialogic tension with an understated ecological perspective, which surfaces surprisingly in this dark novel. (Indeed McCarthy's techniques of depicting his wilderness nightmare depend for their effects on a full understanding of nature and ecology.) The novel's imagery of animal life often conjoins the gnostic view of the creature under cosmic oppression and the modern ecologist's awareness of biotic communities and of humanity's implication in the destruction of wildlife. A mysterious incident in the town where Rinthy consults the doctor hints at this: Rinthy notices a woman in the street carrying "a feedbag in which something alive struggled mutely." This might be any small being—a puppy, a piglet, a snake, an infant, although the "feedbag" hints that this hapless creature is to be eaten. The ambiguity makes this creature an image of both human and animal trapped in cosmos and subject to alien powers who, like the woman in control of the feedbag, regard the life around them with an "empty look" even as they oppress it (147). The unknown creature's muteness links it with the child who suffers in abject silence but also with the mindless mute, one aspect of the triune. Both animal and human, the image suggests, are thrown into the world without a voice, where they struggle unheard. Yet in the gnostic view both, in their mute struggles, are tragically implicated in the darkness and ignorance that imprison them not only from without but also from within, and the feedbag is not only the world but the bodily envelope. As a purely ecocentric emblem, the image posits the silenced natural world at the mercy of indifferent humanity; the gnostic context enlarges this implication to include humankind as victims of a hostile cosmic power and also suggests that anthropocentrism is one aspect of cosmic *heimarmene* with which other natural creatures must contend.

Naturalistic images of the silencing of animal life merge an explicitly ecological vision with the gnostic one. Culla's journey in an amnion of eerie silence not only suggests his deafness to the gnostic message but also the human's disruption of animal life when he intrudes upon it, the silencing of the voice of nature in humankind's unsympathetic presence: "Swamp peepers hushed constantly before him and commenced behind as if he moved in a void claustral to sound" (131). Such silence also takes on the gnostic implications of humankind's hostility to nature in a way that meshes poignantly with contemporary ecocentrism: "Night fell long and cool through the woods about him and a spectral quietude set in. As if something were about that crickets and nightbirds held in dread" (16). The antagonistic presence is the triune, to be sure, but it is also Culla himself. And Rinthy, who early in the novel is described in terms of romantic harmony with nature—"butterflies attended her and birds dusting in the road did not fly up when she passed"—later has the same effect on wildlife as Culla does: as she walks through the swampy land that leads to the old woman's shack, "sunning turtles tilted from stones and logs at her approach" (98, 108).

There are many images of dead or maimed creatures in *Outer Dark*, some subjected to death as an aspect of physical necessity, others crushed by human will or blind human technology, as in *The Orchard Keeper*. Rinthy's farmer smashes a moth beneath his fist, enacting in the most dramatic way Adam's dominion over animals, and a store clerk "dementedly" follows the flight of a "huge melonstriped fly" with his eyes and then "flattened [it] against a cracker-jar" (84). The images of the "wheelcrushed toad" and the "*burst lizard who dragged his small blue bowels*" (82, 51) in the squire's wagon track recall the electrocuted owl and injured sparrow hawk of the first novel and prefigure the jackrabbits, owl, and hawk struck by motor vehicles in *Cities of the Plain* (21–22, 34) and *No Country for Old Men* (44–45). However, in the context of the triune's murder of Salter, the image of the ruptured lizard draws a parallel between the triune, as mythic personifications of harsh cosmic necessity responsible for the death of the squire, and humanity itself as blind agents of *heimarmene* in the destruction of wildlife.

In *Outer Dark*, we confront imagery of natural predation, though not as foregrounded as in *The Orchard Keeper*, and the emphasis on the human waste of animal life remains, but some of the imagery of entrapment undergoes a significant modification: here we encounter animals contained unto death within the human domicile. Thus in close juxtaposition to the coat wrapped in a cocoon of spiderweb, Rinthy finds lying on the floor of the cabin a dead bird "spooned to a shell, faintly soursmelling." When she turns the carcass with her toe, "a small white grub writhed in the damp spot it left" (189). Together the cocooned coat and the lifeless bird, presumably trapped in the cabin until its death of exhaustion, are reciprocal images of human and animal captivity in cosmos and suffering under one another's influence. The image is echoed in the next chapter, when Culla enters a deserted cabin and finds on a bed "a dead cat leering with eyeless grimace, a caved and maggoty shape that gave off a faint dry putrescence." When he drags the mattress outside, "long bright red beetles" scatter from under the cat (196). Since the cat seems to have chosen the isolated bed as its place to die of natural causes, the image suggests less obviously the entrapment of natural creatures within human structures and gives more weight to the reciprocal invasion of the human realm by nature, like the woodrat who lives in the crone's shabby cottage (114). In addition to the cat, Culla discovers dead beetles, mouse droppings, and a live "deermouse" in the cabin, worms in the mealbin, and swifts in the chimney (196–97). The animal imagery associated with Culla's very provisional settling in parallels Lester Ballard's struggle to expel nature from his squatter's cabin, first the blacksnake and then, with increasing frustration, the fox and hounds that race through his meager dwelling (*Child of God* 16, 23–24). But in *Outer Dark*, in addition to the implication of nature's inroads on a barely defended human realm, the images of dead animals in both cabins suggest their entombment in human constructs, human space cleared to expel wilderness, even when their deaths are of natural causes.

In *The Orchard Keeper*, too, we find images of containment, but there human responsibility for the entrapment of nature is not presented so fully as an aspect of cosmic necessity. That novel's main characters, especially John Wesley Rattner and Arthur Ownby, learn to value nature for itself and stand opposed to the officers of soulless, mechanized culture who ignore its plight. For the characters of *Outer Dark*, there seems no option for an ecologically enlightened view of nature or humble recognition of humankind's interdependent position within complexly ordered biotic communities. The gnostic sense of human and other natural creatures' subjection to a dark cosmic order that predestines their mutual animosity overshadows this centerpiece of the ecologist's value structure. The novel's contemporary ecological vision comes in hints from the narrator alone, intruded from without the cosmic nightmare in a subtle critique of gnostic and pioneer horror of wilderness. Such hints arise in the novel's images of the small creatures tortured even by such rudimentary human technology as exists in the premodern setting of the novel. They become even more pronounced in the imagery of the hunt.

Culla's conversation with the snakehunter and, to a lesser extent, Rinthy's parallel conversation with the androgynous crone, herself a snakehunter, interrogate the traditional utilitarian view of wilderness described by environmentalist writers. The pioneer-style wastefulness of these two hunters (ambiguously suggested to be one and the same) establishes that in the world of *Outer Dark* there is at work no scarcity theory of the value of nature such as Nash finds evolving in the United States once civilization became the norm and wilderness was pushed to the fringes. Neither do they experience any guilt over the destruction of the land as Mother, such as Kolodny finds a frequent corollary to the American pastoral impulse. The old woman has stockpiled so much fire-wood that her very living space is severely diminished. But she also values trees for the shade and cooling they provide, so she won't allow any wood to be cut near her shanty. Her greed for the resources of nature is selfish and willful—parallel to her expulsion of her husband Earl's hunting dogs and his father, and perhaps Earl himself, of whom she bluntly says, "Earl died" (110); ironically, this primitive yet avaricious soul functions as an emblem of the American willingness to exhaust nature in an uncurtailed drive for material comfort and accumulation, hypocritically coexisting with the desire to keep our own back-yards free of blight.

The male snakehunter's wastefulness is more similar to the kind we find re-pudiated in *The Orchard Keeper*. Like the first novel's minor characters who abuse the natural world, the old man's attitude about his hunting is one of "demented enthusiasm" (124). He gleefully tells Culla how he used to kill up to a dozen geese with one blast of his shotgun before goose hunting was outlawed—and perhaps afterward as well, since he is worried that Culla might be a game war-den. He appears to be a frontiersman of sorts since there is no livestock near his cabin, only two hounds (117). However, he seems to have hunted not for food but rather for profit. He has pursued a livelihood as a hunter, selling geese for fifty cents each, and has killed so many over his lifetime that he claims, "I'd be a rich man today if I'd not blowed it in on whores and whiskey," revealing the profane commodities for which he has exchanged the birds' lives (123). He began his snakehunting because a man offered to pay him one dollar per lin-ear foot of snake. His collection of rattles recalls the dead snake Ownby and Scout find on the mountain with its rattles cut away, an image that connects this scene to the bounty hunting repudiated in the first novel. The man who has set the old man hunting asked if he could capture snakes alive, perhaps imagining that he could kill them later in such a way as to keep their hides undamaged, since it is the skin of the giant rattler tacked on the old man's wall that has caught his attention.[33] However, the snakehunter's jars of rattles con-firm that he has not captured the snakes alive but has killed a great many for bounty, keeping their rattles as souvenirs or to give away as trinkets to enhance the sound of guitars or banjos. This old man, who seems genial enough in his treatment of Culla, is gradually revealed as an offensive agent of the mindless commodification of nature, and the old woman's miserly storing up of firewood links her with his mindset. And just as her judgmental attitudes about the "common habits" of her husband's family (ironically coexisting with her pride that her father-in-law was a squire) reinforce our perception of her corollary biotic arrogance, so the snakehunter's racist attitudes also reinforce our per-ception of his egocentrism and anthropocentrism in his relation to the natural world (121).

The garrulous snakehunter becomes the novel's primary spokesman for the utilitarian view of nature, much as Squire Salter is the spokesman for the utilitarian relation of employer to employee as he sizes up Culla, "looking him over with those hard little eyes as he would anything for sale" (42). "You know snakes is supposed to be bad luck," the snakehunter tells Culla, "but they must have some good in em on account of them old geechee snake doctors uses em all the time for medicines. . . . Even a snake ain't all bad. They's put here for some purpose. I believe they's purpose to everthing" (124). The old man presents himself as an apologist for snakes, expecting to gain Culla's approval, and underlying his position are the Judeo-Christian concepts of providence and man's divinely ordained dominion over animals. His egotism in the face of nature derives from the "concept of man as superior to other living things by virtue of being made in the image of the Creator" (Nash 193). According to this tradition, nature is created not for itself but for humanity's use; thus no responsibility, respect, or humility is required of humankind in relation to other life. This is the historical western view of nature that John Muir questioned philosophically in *Our National Parks* (1902) when he answered the question, "What are rattlesnakes good for?" by exposing its underlying arrogance—"As if nothing that does not obviously make for the benefit of man had any right to exist; as if our ways were God's ways"—and by asserting that rattlesnakes are "good for themselves, and we need not begrudge them their share of life" (57, 58). Ecologist Aldo Leopold also challenged the utilitarian view scientifically and ethically when he affirmed in his foreword to *A Sand County Almanac* that the natural environment is a community, not a commodity (xviii). Nash quotes a claim from Leopold's lecture notes that is especially relevant to McCarthy's meditation on snake hunting: "when we attempt to say that an animal is 'useful,' 'ugly,' or 'cruel' we are failing to see it as part of the land" (Nash 196).[34]

If we consider the gnostic re-mythologizing of the serpent as a principle of gnosis rather than as an aspect of evil or wilderness, this further undercuts the snakehunters' enterprise, but from an entirely different perspective. To hate or to kill snakes as both these old people do signifies their opposition to gnosis. When the crone associates snakes with hounds and loose women, reflecting the traditional Judeo-Christian coding of snakes as evil, and when the snakehunter speculates about the purpose or utility of snakes, they reveal their blindness and lack of spiritual understanding. Thus the pervasive gnostic context of the novel calls into question the mainline Christian one that comes more readily to mind in the snakehunting scenes. The Christian bias against snakes is of a piece with the Christian bias against wilderness: both represent evil in that tradition. McCarthy's implications that our "natural" repugnance to snakes is in fact cultural and that other cultural valuations are possible (such as the gnostic mythologizing of snakes as symbols of gnosis, invoked here, or the native

American respect for all natural creatures or the Australian aboriginal myth of the dream-serpent) not only undermine the varmint-hating characters of *Outer Dark*, but qualify its wilderness paranoia.

This novel's themes of varmints and bounty hunting are entirely consistent with McCarthy's treatment of them in his other novels, and though they coexist with its gnostic wilderness nightmare, they comment on that nightmare and temper it considerably. The gnostic context suggests that as the byproduct of traditional Judeo-Christian attitudes, bounty hunting and killing creatures are part of the demiurge's oppression, built into the cosmic system in physical and psychological *heimarmene*. The Old Testament God's curse for the disobedience of Adam and Eve is the curse of the jealous demiurge: as the serpent forever bites man's heel, mankind forever bruises its head (Genesis 3:15). And human psychology makes for judgmental designation of weeds and varmints, the useless, both in the biological realm and the human. (Another implication of Culla's name is that he is a "cull"—one of the community's outcasts or scapegoats.) Although some gnostics reinscribed the role of the serpent in the myth of Eden, they did not repudiate the biblical tradition of an adversarial relation between nature outside the garden and mankind. Indeed they exacerbated it, seeing all of nature as wilderness unredeemed by any principle of providence. But McCarthy's ambiguous, dialogic juxtaposition of the two religious traditions with each other and with ecocentric alternatives suggests finally his interrogation of both the orthodox Christian and gnostic attitudes toward nature, both the providential/utilitarian and the anticosmic, and signals the novel's implicit affinity with the views of Muir and Leopold. This is discernible in the sober contemplation the narrator directs to both ancient traditions that feed the western nightmare of humanity's biotic arrogance and in the understated ecocentrism of its many images of creatures suffering in their shared environments with humans.

Current Ferries, Rural Squires, and Hog Drives: *Realistic Underpinnings*

Guillemin argues that "*Outer Dark* is structured as a book-length allegory working with pseudo-realistic conceits" (*Pastoral Vision* 68). And indeed, unlike *The Orchard Keeper, Child of God*, and *Suttree, Outer Dark* does not map a specific locale in East Tennessee. However, McCarthy imaginatively draws upon specific features of the East Tennessee culture to detail particular events of *Outer Dark* while subsuming them to its overarching parabolic dream-structure. As Matthew Guinn observes, in this novel McCarthy employs "the working materials of regionalism to fashion prose that might be termed 'postmodern local color,' creating an uneasy mixture of mountain folkways set against . . . a blighted landscape" (98). Recognizing the realism in McCarthy's allusions to these phenomena does not obviate allegorical readings but rather allows us to perceive more clearly the nature and purposes of his surrealistic distortions and thus to read more perceptively those scenes depicting situations that are "surreal" or paradoxical in reality. Three such manifestations are particularly interesting because they inform critical nodes in Culla Holme's ceaseless wandering—all involving his being accused of one crime or another and his denial of guilt. These are the current-driven cable ferries that characterized the deep river valleys of East Tennessee, the great hog drives along the French Broad River, and the Justice of the Peace (or squire) system for adjudication of petty crimes in Tennessee that began to be reevaluated in the 1890s because of the problem of white-capping (vigilantism) in Sevier County and that came under further scrutiny in the 1930s.

Culla and Rinthy make several river crossings, most of them by bridge. But late in the novel, just before he first meets the sinister triune at their campsite, Culla walks down a bluff to a rude landing, and together with a horse and rider, boards a ferry of clever design. It is a flatboat rigged with ropes and an over-head cable stretching from one bank to the other, and it is propelled by the river's current when the ferryman angles the boat properly. The ferryman explains that he controls the movement of the ferry by loosening or tightening the lines on either end of the craft: "Just change them lines is all they is to it. If you was to set em both the same you wouldn't go nowheres." "Might bust the cable," the ferryman continues prophetically (162), and that is exactly what occurs in midriver for reasons that remain mysterious enough to implicate not so much the hapless ferryman but the triune who pull Culla from the water, if not Culla himself.

Such current-driven ferries were quite common in nineteenth-century America; according to John Perry in his *American Ferryboats* (1957), many remained in operation into the twentieth century (50). Perry claims that the cable ferry "is a tool which has been invented over and over again, at many times and many places, the product of need, of situation and of chance observation" wherever there was "a river too deep to ford, too narrow for sailboats, and too swift for oarsmen" (45–46). Of course the river must be narrow enough that a rope or cable can stretch across without sagging into the water (47, 54). Perry argues that any ferryman who devised a craft to be pulled across a river on ropes, either with oars or hand over hand, would soon discover by chance that when a boat is angled thirty degrees to the current, it "would gently and smoothly drift across the stream without help" (46, 44). However, when Culla asks the ferryman if his father invented the current ferry, he answers, "Naw. Folks say he done but he never. He seen one like it somewheres" (162).

One place current ferries could be seen was on the deep rivers of East Tennessee, which "offered limited fords" and thus mandated heavy reliance on ferries (Holmes 3). About 60 percent of the ferries in use in Tennessee during the

Civil War were in the eastern third of the state. Many privately owned ferries were destroyed in the war but reestablished later, and the number peaked between 1900 and 1930 (Holmes 4). Older residents of the neighborhood where the McCarthy family first lived when they moved to Knoxville recall ferries where Sequoyah Hills bounded the Tennessee River banks. Sam Fowler, born in 1928, lived with his parents on the same street as the McCarthys (Cherokee Drive then, since renamed Noelton). He recalls that when he was a "very small kid" he rode on Blow's Ferry, "an old wooden boat between cables that stretched across the river. On the far side was Peter Blow's mansion" (Berwick 52–53). Another resident, Bill Schriver, born in 1931, remembers not only Blow's Ferry but also a smaller one that crossed to Looney's Island in the middle of the river. The island was submerged when the TVA dammed the river in 1943; presumably both ferries discontinued service then, if not earlier (Berwick 78).

Around 1870 F. G. de Fontaine visited such a ferry on the French Broad River and wrote this description:

> The ferry itself was antique and innocent of any but the rudest invention. It was cheap in construction, and the perfection of . . . simplicity. . . .
>
> A rope extending to some convenient tree on either bank; a flat-bottomed boat and a stout negro—that was the machinery. You drove down, whooped, received an answering yell, possessed your soul in patience until the return of the crazy craft, and entered cautiously. The cable passed through a guide-post attached to the gunwale, and the ferryman, seizing it with a peculiar wooden key, gave it a twist, and commenced the process of pulling his freight to the other side. If any thing gave way, as was not unfrequently the case during a freshet, you drifted helplessly down the current, with the chance of being poled ashore in some out-of-the-way spot, or of a cold bath in the river. (quoted in Perry 45)

De Fontaine's description is somewhat ambiguous, and Harry Fenn's illustration for it in William Cullen Bryant's *Picturesque America* (1872; reprinted in Perry 46) "somehow missed the point," according to Perry. Fenn's ferry appears to be pulled across the river by hand, but Perry thinks that De Fontaine had actually seen a current-driven ferry on the French Broad (45). Donald Davidson's river history, *The Tennessee*, which mentions the locations of many ferries along its course, prints an illustration by Theresa Sherrer Davidson that seems a better model of the flatboat ferries with cable rigging described by De Fontaine and McCarthy, except that the overhead bank-to-bank apparatus for the cable is not evident.[35] Her illustration includes three figures: the ferryman, wearing a cap that matches McCarthy's description of "a strange sort of hat that appeared vaguely nautical" (159); a man who seems to be a waiting passenger; and a third man approaching on horseback (Davidson 2:146)—the three figures in McCarthy's ferry scene.

De Fontaine stresses the risk of a broken cable. Perry writes that when wire cable became available in the early nineteenth century, the risk decreased; but earlier, rope "exposed to the elements, subjected to greater strain than its makers intended, and kept in service much too long, often broke. It snapped, usually, when the strain was heavy; as in spring freshets when the current was strong and the water turbulent" (47). However, neither of these conditions would seem to explain the ferry accident Culla experiences. The ferry runs on cable rather than rope. Nevertheless, when they encounter some difficulty and the rings that house the cable screech "in a demented fiddlenote," they hear "a loud explosion and something [i.e., the broken cable] passed above their heads screaming and then there was silence" (164–65). It is winter, "the season for high water and swift movement on the Tennessee" and perhaps on this unnamed river (Davidson 1:153). But the ferryman has recently made an uneventful crossing to Culla's side, and though he comments without much concern that the river is rising, there is no rain until later in the night—and then only a light drizzle. No flash flood or torrential downpour creates the extraordinary stress on the cable. All the same, the river becomes turbulent soon after they embark, and the ferryman inexplicably allows the ferry to square up broadside to the current, so that they "seemed to be in high wind and water was blowing over the deck. The river was breaking violently on the canted flank of the boat, a perpetual concussion of black surf that rode higher until it began to override the rail and fall aboard with great slapping sounds" (164–65). The ferryman dashes from end to end of the vessel, anxiously watching the cable overhead and virtually "dancing among his ropes" (164). But despite his efforts, the boat goes "careening through the night wildly" and seems "to be racing sideways upriver against the current." When the cable breaks, the boat lurches, and suddenly Culla is "drifting in windless calm and total dark" (165). The ferry runs on cable, there are no floods, the night is calm, and the ferryman is experienced, having grown up learning the occupation. The wreck of this realistically drawn ferry, then, is a mystery that compels the reader to ponder what force has disturbed the river and moved the ferry broadside to the current, creating the illusion of high wind, breaking the cable as the ferryman has predicted, killing him and the rider, panicking the horse, and subjecting Culla to a whirling night-journey before delivering him to the campsite of the triune, where he is accused of causing this mayhem.

In Culla's very next scene, he is discovered sleeping in an abandoned cabin, and its owner marches him barefoot and at gunpoint to the local squire, where he is charged with "trespass"—a term that carries both legal and moral implications. Like so many scenes in *Outer Dark*, the arraignment veers toward the surreal, this time as the question of Culla's guilt is negotiated in terms of a choice between two foreordained punishments:

> I don't figure I done nothin wrong, Holme said.
> Well if you want to plead not guilty I'll have to take you over to Harmsworth and bind ye over in custody until court day.
> When is that?
> The squire looked up at him. About three weeks, he said. If they don't postpone ye. If you get postponed it'll be another six weeks after that. And if you get . . .
> I'll take the guilty, Holme said. (201–2)

Ironically, when Culla pleads guilty and is sentenced to work out his fine on the squire's farm for ten days at the rate of fifty cents a day plus room and meals, he receives what he desperately requires—work, food, and shelter—the basic needs that have been deferred or interrupted throughout the narrative. This odd double-reversal of justice is not lost on the plaintiff, John, who complains that he himself receives no benefit from the squire's decision. But the squire—an absurd version of the archontic forces of law and judgment—insists, "Don't make no difference about fair or not fair, it's against the law. You ain't authorized to work no prisoners. . . . You done right bringin him in like ye done. But you cain't ast me to break the law and turn him back over to ye" (205).

The scene extends the novel's exploration of guilt, false and true judgment, and expiation, but its surrealism is closer to historical reality than one might suppose. Indeed the scene illustrates with great economy the flaws of the Justice of the Peace system in Tennessee, which was based on the English system for swiftly administering justice in cases of minor statutory offenses and misdemeanors in a rural society, and in which the potential for abuse was rife. As the son of a TVA attorney, McCarthy may have heard at home all he needed to know about the outdated Tennessee JP system, which was still in effect in the 1930s when his family moved to Knoxville. But given what we know of his diligent research habits, it seems likely that McCarthy also knew articles by Robert S. Keebler and T. L. Howard published in the *Tennessee Law Review* in the 1930s outlining the problems with the system and calling for reforms such as those already implemented in Mississippi, Virginia, and other states.

Keebler points out that "the reason for the existence of justice courts is to have local courts always at hand ready for the issuance of criminal warrants, the fixing of bail bonds, the binding over of offenders, and the [trial] of petty causes, without awaiting the action of a court of record, which meets perhaps only once or twice a year" (9). But in the JP system established in many American states, there was no accountability, and conflicts of interest were permitted.

Abuses stemmed from the very nature of the system, as described by Howard: "The justice is an elective official. He is typically unsalaried, depending upon the fees of litigants in his court for his livelihood. He rarely has any education or qualifications, other than political, for the job. There is ordinarily a great over-supply of justice courts, which leads to unwholesome competition among the justices for business" (19).

Culla Holme's hearing before the squire is nearly a textbook illustration of the flaws in the JP system. Since the justice was elected by the citizens of his civil district, he tended to be landed and well known, with political aspirations; but, especially in a rural area, he might have no knowledge or experience of the law or even be illiterate. Culla's squire pretends knowledge of the law, and he certainly understands what the law allows him to get away with, but when Culla's case is to be recorded, the squire calls his wife Ethel to do the writing and instructs her to guess at the spelling of Culla's name—suggesting that, like Culla, the squire can do neither.

This squire also makes a pretense of accountability. The JP court was not required to make a transcript of its proceedings, so many of the accused would skip appearing before the justice to plead not guilty, preferring instead to appeal their convictions before the county courts, where the evidence was presented anew (Keebler 15; Howard 25). The Tennessee Code of Laws did require the justice to keep a docket in a "well bound book," regularly recording each case and "showing the name of the offender, the time of the trial, the description and date of the offense, on whom the offense was committed, the judgment rendered, and the execution thereof" (quoted in Howard 36). When plaintiff John challenges the justice, "I guess you goin to pay back the county his wages, or fine, or whatever," the squire claims, "Well now . . . you know my books is open to anybody" (204). But in fact he produces no books—neither docket nor account book—and he instructs his wife to record Culla's case on a loose form. She inscribes his name and his plea of "Guilty of trespass" (202). Then the squire chides her, "You ain't forgot the date have ye? Like you done on some of them last'ns," which tells us not only that he habitually hands over this task to her but also that their record-keeping has been none too consistent (203). No description of Culla's offense or notation of the plaintiff in the case is recorded. And the wife finishes her writing before the squire hands down his sentence, so Culla's fine and his obligation to work off the fine on the squire's land also go unrecorded. Howard's vetting of justices' dockets showed that many of the justices in Tennessee "appear never to have heard of this provision" for documentation in the code of laws, and his examiners found numerous irregularities, some of which adumbrate those of McCarthy's squire. Howard cites one JP who kept no docket, so the examiners gathered data from his warrants instead, some of which indicated payment of fines, but with the amount unrecorded. Another kept a docket, but half the cases were undated. "There were 77 cases in which fines had been assessed but there was no way of determining whether the fines were paid or not. The record of a large number of [his] cases was kept on separate sheets of paper and not in his docket" (36). Indeed Howard's field work was done partly to determine to what extent the facts might substantiate Keebler's various charges against the JP system. Five years before Howard's article, Keebler had complained that "there is no check or supervision of our justices of the peace." The irony behind McCarthy's squire's claim that his books are open to anyone is that under the JP system, as Keebler writes, "No auditor checks their books. No supervisor see [*sic*] that cases are properly docketed and records preserved. Who among us knows what fees any justice of the peace receives, or what fines he collects? To be sure, all fines are supposed to be reported quarterly to the Chairman of the County Court; but it is left largely, if not entirely, to the integrity of the justice of the peace to make a proper accounting" (16).

Since justices received no salary and were compensated only when a defendant was found guilty, cynics often said that JP stood for "judgement for plaintiff" (Keebler 11). In his impassioned indictment of the system, Keebler writes that under the fee system, the "judge must favor his friends who bring him the business. Justice must give hostages to fortune." In the worst cases, constables were sent out to round up business, and because he could not afford to hire a lawyer, it was often "the ignorant day laborer carrying a half pint on his hip must pay the toll. Unless the defendant pleads guilty, the justice of the peace must bind the defendant over to await the action of the grand jury. . . . [The justice] must get his fees out of the defendant or not at all; and so by all the arts and refinements of coaxing and coercion, brow-beating and persuasion, the poor fellow is led into pleading guilty and taking a small fine . . . rather than hire a lawyer, pay a bondsman, and await the uncertainties and delays of a criminal trial" (14). Howard concurs that one of the chief evils of the system was the extortion that resulted from the small offense law, "under which a person charged with a misdemeanor has the choice of pleading guilty before a Justice and paying a fine and costs, or of pleading not guilty and being bound over to the grand jury for indictment" (Howard 37). Thus Culla, who believes he hasn't done anything wrong, naturally finds pleading guilty preferable to being held for trial in three weeks, or nine, or more. The ironies are not only that this rather specious accusation and corrupt hearing provide the only situation in which Culla is finally willing to admit to any trespass but also that this wanderer with no acknowledged responsibilities pleads guilty to avoid delay in his aimless travels. The scene repeats and inverts Culla's two arraignments by the triune, which sandwich it, where he steadfastly denies both guilt and responsibility and sacrifices the life of his son.

In Culla's last episode before he meets the triune and his repudiated son for the final time, he encounters a vast river of hogs being driven to market, witnesses their stampede like the Gadarene swine (Matthew 8:28–32; Mark 5:1–20; Luke 8:26–32) over the bluff and into the river, and is accused of inciting the stampede that kills one of the drovers. While the biblical import of this scene is just as obvious as the classical underworld associations of the ferry-crossing scene, the chapter also provides the most explicit connection of the world of *Outer Dark* to nineteenth-century East Tennessee, since the French Broad River marked the route of the great livestock drives from the "hog and hominy" state of Tennessee over the mountains to the cotton-growing regions of South Carolina and Georgia. Indeed the drovers of *Outer Dark* are headed for "Charlestown" (Charleston), South Carolina, one of the main hog markets for nineteenth-century Tennessee farmers. The road for these hog drives ran parallel to the French Broad River from Sevier County into North Carolina, and it was kept in remarkably good repair until about 1885, when railroad transport replaced the great overland livestock drives.

The hog drives are documented in several histories of East Tennessee and western North Carolina, but it seems most likely that McCarthy read of them in Wilma Dykeman's popular river history, *The French Broad* (1955), which devotes a whole chapter to the phenomenon, and in one of her sources, an historical and anecdotal article by Edmund Cody Burnett, "Hog Raising and Hog Driving in the Region of the French Broad River" (1946). Both accounts agree on the basics, but Burnett's article includes firsthand reports, since his family operated a ferry where many of the droves would cross the river. In describing the fluid motion of the herd, both sources consistently establish the image of a river of hogs flowing parallel to the actual French Broad River, but in the reverse direction. Employing the gnostic imagery of turbid water that is so prominent in other contexts in the novel, McCarthy describes the hogs approaching the river road as a "howling polychrome tide" or as a "weltering sea" that "flowed" through the valley and drifted up the slopes "in ragged shoals"; the drivers move among them "like crossers in a ford," and when they stampede, Culla escapes to a rock "like one threatened with flood" (213–18).

Each source offers relevant details that the other does not. Dykeman includes a probably apocryphal story of a station owner on the French Broad who disguised himself as a "negro" to rob the drovers as they returned home carrying the cash proceeds of their livestock sales (150)—a story that may inform Judge Holden's tale of the harnessmaker in *Blood Meridian*.[36] Burnett's article twice makes the connection between Tennessee hogs and the Gadarene swine, a mythical implication that McCarthy amplifies in *Outer Dark*. Burnett recounts that when transporting hogs, the ferryman installed movable railings around the perimeter of the ferry to keep them penned (a detail that matches the description of the current ferry in McCarthy's novel). But once in a while "a hog, who had not been wholly subdued by his fattening-lot schooling or who was not sufficiently restrained by the load of fat he carried, would plunge over or through the railing into the river"; sometimes such hogs drowned despite all human efforts at rescue: "At such a time I would be reminded of the story in the Bible about the herd of swine that rushed headlong into the sea. 'If,' I reflected, 'Satan should decide to go the whole hog and enter into that whole ferryboat full of hogs, there would be as big a drowning as the Bible tells about.' But my sympathies were all with the hogs, not with Satan" (91). However, Burnett's childhood sympathies depended on context. When the hogs would break into his father's cornfields, little Edmund was charged with chasing them out. "Then I began to dislike hogs," he recalled. "If Satan would enter into all of them and make them rush headlong into the creek and get drowned, I was on the side of Satan in that job. There were, indeed, many times and occasions when the voluntary—or instinctive—conduct of the hogs would induce in either man or boy moods in which no pious thought could thrive" (95). Such musings may lie behind the fated drover Vernon's conversation with Culla, during which he ponders hog nature; but unlike Burnett, who asserts that "one can learn a lot of hog psychology by associating with hogs" (95), Vernon has concluded that "hogs is a mystery by theyselves. . . . I've run with hogs since I was just a shirttail and I ain't never come to no real understandin of em" (216). In this novel the mystery extends to both hogs and humans.[37]

Both Burnett and Dykeman distinguish between the terms "driver"—those hired to handle the hogs—and "drover"—the owner or manager, who might ride ahead of the herd on horseback (Burnett 102; Dykeman 141). McCarthy ignores this distinction, consistently referring to Vernon and the others as "the drovers." Indeed, when he vetted a draft of my article on him for the *Dictionary of Literary Biography* in 1979, McCarthy queried my use of the term "drivers," in response to which I adopted his usage, "drovers" (and continue that practice here). Perhaps "drivers" had twentieth-century connotations he wished to avoid. And it is always possible that McCarthy also had other sources for his understanding of the hog drives. Davis identifies "drivers" as those who "specialized in simply driving livestock on foot or horseback from one destination to the next" and "drovers" as "herdsmen who raised hogs and cattle for the sole purpose of taking them to distant markets," as opposed to the yeoman farmers who raised livestock for their own use but who might sell some to "passing drivers or drovers" (131). At any rate, the novel makes clear that the hogs are the drovers' "charges" but actually belong to someone named Greene (218, 223).

If McCarthy follows the historical sources, the reader can estimate the number of hogs in this massive drove from the number of drovers. Burnett notes that "it seems to have been an almost invariable rule to assign one driver to each hundred hogs" (100). When Culla watches the drovers and the preacher backlighted on the bluff above him as he is carried by the river current, he sees that there are seven figures (227). Subtracting the preacher and adding back the dead Vernon leaves the original number of drovers at seven. Thus the hogs would number approximately seven hundred, not an unrealistic number. Burnett's hog drover friend Jesse Stokely, who supplied a fair amount of his first-hand material, told him that the usual drove was about five hundred hogs, "sometimes as low as 300, but occasionally as high as 1,000" (100). In *Outer Dark*, two hundred of Greene's hogs fling themselves over the bluff and into the river, a substantial loss out of a total of about seven hundred.

As realistic as the depiction of the hog drive is in some of its features, there are two other historical details from these sources that McCarthy does not follow. Burnett (90) and Dykeman (142) depict the drivers using whips to control the movement of the hogs. McCarthy's drovers, on the other hand, carry staves, which reinforces their association with false shepherds—"no true swineherds"—and agents of darkness (218).[38] His other departure from his sources hints that this hog drive is no true hog drive either, despite its basis in the history of the French Broad. According to Burnett, "The hogs were started to market only after they had consumed the grower's surplus corn and had been fattened sufficiently to be butchered. The fattening began as soon as the corn was sufficiently mature to feed, which was about the middle of August, and reached the finishing stage in late October or early November, or at the latest in the beginning of December. Accordingly, the driving season was concentrated mainly in November" (88).

In *Outer Dark*, however, Culla comes upon the hogs "on a good spring day"—when no right drover would be herding stock to market (213). Thus even when the novel is most indebted for its texture to the history and lore of East Tennessee, McCarthy's handling of these details establishes his landscape as the spiritual realm of outer dark or the inner dark of dream, a place in which the realistic details that may appear have, finally, no true "valence to anything in the shapen world" (227). Or, as in McCarthy's master-narratives, they are the stuff of which dreams are made: threads from which he weaves a dream-world.

Chapter Three

The Cave of Oblivion   *Child of God* (1974)

Child of God, McCarthy's story of the stunted life of a lonely necrophile—from the loss of his family farm, a version of the pastoral expulsion, to his spiraling descent through ever more essential losses, to his death and dissection at the hands of the state—is fairly simple in structure but highly complex in tone and narrative stance. Brilliantly synthesizing such varied influences as Platonic and gnostic myths, Faulkner's *As I Lay Dying* and "A Rose for Emily," Melville's *Moby-Dick*, John Fowles's *The Collector*, the various versions of *Psycho*, locally and nationally known multiple murders, case studies of necrophilia and Sevier County history and topography, *Child of God* can be read as gothic horror and allegory, as an indictment of America's materialism, as a naturalistic story of society's creation of its own scapegrace villains, as a rumination on the mystery of evil, and as a metaphysical meditation on the theme of fate versus will.

One of the notable achievements of *Child of God* is its compassionate portrayal of one of the most offensive criminals in all of serious literature—a man whose acts challenge the limits of our optimistic definitions of humanity. Many of the details of Lester's motives and behavior relating to necrophilia are drawn from the studies of necrophiles in R. E. L. Masters and Eduard Lea's curious 1963 compendium *Sex Crimes in History*, a survey of sexual deviancy that draws on literary and historical accounts as well as psychological profiles, mostly European, but includes few modern clinical case studies. According to Masters and Lea, the necrophile who murders to obtain corpses is rare, and he seldom manifests the psychology of the more common necrophile. They distinguish between the "true necrophile" and the necro-sadist, who might murder and then sexually assault his victim: "The sex act [the necro-sadist] performs is usually only an extension of his violation of his victim. The necrophile, on the other hand, is often quite incapable of making an effective sexual approach, and especially a sadistic one, to a living person" (116). In *Child of God*, McCarthy conflates both profiles, inventing in Lester a true necrophile who also murders to collect corpses. The opportunism of Lester's first necrophilic experience identifies him as a genuine necrophile, and his later turn to murder is prompted by a complex mixture of his despair of making human contact, his distrust of others, his recognition of his role as pariah, his conflicted sense of attraction to and disapproval of his sexually tempting victims, and his pent-up rage. Except for his attempted murder of Greer, Lester kills as a means to a practical, sexual end, and he is not primarily motivated by the desire to mutilate and destroy, as the necro-sadist is. Nevertheless, Lester's passionate behavior with his first body may have been partially suggested to McCarthy by a detail from the classic case of necro-sadist Sergeant Bertrand, who described his first sexual experience with an exhumed body: "All the joy procured by possession of a living woman was as nothing in comparison with the pleasure I felt. I showered kisses upon all parts of her body, pressed her to my heart with a madman's frenzy. I overwhelmed her with the most passionate caresses" (Masters and Lea 121–22). However, Lester's scenes of passion are strangely reverent; far from mutilating bodies, as Bertrand always did, he tries against all odds and time to preserve them. He manifests some of the behaviors of the true necrophile Giuseppe Alessandro, who was witnessed passionately kissing a corpse "dressed in an elaborate silken gown with a strand of pearls about its neck" and who had "disinterred her body and with superhuman strength transported her coffin over the mountains" (Masters and Lea 222).[1]

The experiences that lead to Lester's necrophilia resemble those of the true necrophiles reported by Masters and Lea, many of whom had lost parents to death when they were young, for whom the corpse represented the lost mother. The case of Victor Ardisson, particularly, may inform the dynamics of Lester's relationships with the dumpkeeper's daughters and the scantily dressed woman he finds asleep on the road: Ardisson "proposed marriage to the girls of the place, but was ridiculed by them. It is not proved that he ever thereupon tried to rape a girl. As a substitute, he would follow the girls when they went to urinate, and masturbate at the same time" (124). Lester's voyeurism, his confusion in the face of death, and his humiliating or enraging encounters with women—all factors contributing to his necrophilia—ground his bizarre behavior in realism.

Even before Richard Woodward's assertion in his 1992 interview with McCarthy that Lester Ballard is "based on newspaper reports of such a figure in Sevier County, Tenn.," rumor had it that *Child of God* was based on an actual murder case (31). However, contemporary articles about McCarthy in the Knoxville newspapers and subsequent commentary on his work by East Tennessee natives have neither identified nor acknowledged such a Sevier County case. Nor has my own search through likely years of the Knoxville *News-Sentinel* led to the discovery of a murderer from the immediate Knoxville environs who might be the inspiration for McCarthy's study of necrophilic homicide. Indeed, in a letter of August 16, 2000, Sevier County historian Beulah Linn wrote me,

"I am 88 years old and I do not recall this murder case," adding, "The surname Ballard is a very old and respected Sevier County family." Such a Sevier County case may yet be identified, but this seems increasingly unlikely. However, two murder cases at a further remove do seem to inform McCarthy's portrait of Lester Ballard: the James Blevins case in north Georgia, near Chattanooga, Tennessee, which came to light in April of 1963, and the earlier Ed Gein case in Plainfield, Wisconsin, which broke in November 1957. Gein was the model for Norman Bates in Robert Bloch's 1959 novel *Psycho* and in Alfred Hitchcock's 1960 film based on the novel.

Both cases were covered in news media available to McCarthy in Knoxville in the late 1950s and early '60s. McCarthy was very likely living in Sevier County, the setting of *Child of God*, at the time of Blevins's arrest, preliminary hearing, and the first of his two trials—from April 1963 to May 1964. We know that McCarthy was in Sevierville when his sister Maryellen married on June 10 ("Miss McCarthy" 6). However, after McCarthy and Lee Holleman separated (the precise date is unknown, but it must have occurred between June of 1963, when they attended Maryellen's wedding together, and spring of 1965), he spent some time in Asheville and in New Orleans, working on *Outer Dark* and *Suttree* ("Author Lives in Blount"; Woodward 31); in June of 1965, after *The Orchard Keeper* was published, he shipped for Europe, remaining there until December 1967 (Fields, "Knox Native"). Thus McCarthy may not have been within range of the news reports concerning all of the second Blevins trial in spring of 1965 but likely was in the Knoxville area for some of that time; he was out of the country during all of the activity subsequent to Blevins's acquittal and later release from further legal proceedings in November 1966. However, since the idea for *Child of God*, given its affinities with the various treatments of the Ed Gein story, may predate the Blevins case by several years, it seems likely that McCarthy followed the second case with special interest in it as raw material for a novel of murder and necrophilia, and it is possible that friends or family sent McCarthy clippings and kept him informed of developments in the Blevins case during his periods of absence or that he researched the outcome of the case when he returned from Europe.

Though drafting did not begin until about 1970, McCarthy's original concept for the novel may date from as early as December 1957, with the exposure of Gein's murders in national newspapers and *Time* and *Life* magazines. McCarthy had returned from the Air Force in Alaska and enrolled at the University of Tennessee by the spring term of 1957—a season of floods in Knox and Sevier counties. By the summer of 1959, the year he began writing *The Orchard Keeper*, thus committing himself to a writing career, interest in the Gein case was revived with the publication of Robert Bloch's novel *Psycho*. Although the book was not well received by highbrow literary critics, it was reviewed in the

New York Times Book Review (in the "Criminals at Large" column) and the New York *Herald Tribune*, receiving praise as an effective thriller, and it would eventually win an Edgar Award from the Mystery Writers of America. In its initial popularity, Bloch's *Psycho* quickly went through its first hardcover printing of ten thousand copies and nine paperback reprintings by Fawcett (Rebello 11–12, 188). In 1961 and '62, McCarthy lived in Chicago, where he would have had easy access to the accounts of the Gein murders in the *Milwaukee Journal* and the *Chicago Tribune* (Fields, "Knoxville Author").

In the summer of 1960, the Gein case received additional exposure through Hitchcock's extensive publicity campaign for *Psycho*. As early as May 4, Hitchcock had made a prerelease press announcement that his new film was about "metaphysical sex" (Rebello 145). Concerned that the shocking subject of his film would not go over with critics and intent on preserving the full effect of the surprise ending for audiences, Hitchcock broke with customary practice by refusing any advance screenings for reviewers and by inaugurating an advertising blitz to warn that patrons would not be admitted after the start of the film. He made the punctuality policy a contractual requirement for any theater showing the film (Rebello 148–49). Though tame by today's standards, publicity photos for *Psycho* showing Janet Leigh clad in a bra and half-slip or John Gavin nude to the waist were the first such suggestive photos used to promote a mainstream American film, and they contributed to its notoriety (Rebello 152).

Perhaps because Hitchcock had alienated the critics, when *Psycho* opened in New York on June 16, 1960, it received "middling-to-hostile" reviews, and the Roman Catholic Hitchcock became distressed when the Legion of Decency of the Catholic Church awarded the film a "B" rating, which designated it "morally objectionable in part for all" (Rebello 160). Nevertheless, the film generated popular response on a scale that surprised both the director and Paramount Pictures, earning fifteen million dollars in the United States in its first year (Rebello 181). Hitchcock responded by personally undertaking a worldwide publicity tour, and the film was such a widely acknowledged cultural phenomenon that it generated continued post-release interest in Hitchcock interviews and in his career as a director. Indeed, according to Stephen Rebello it dramatically turned around his reputation: "No matter how Hitchcock assessed his own work, slowly but surely after *Psycho*, the moviemaking and journalistic worlds would begin *telling* him just how good he was. Hitchcock career retrospectives at major museums throughout the world became commonplace" (175).

At the height of this commotion over Hitchcock's *Psycho*, McCarthy left the University of Tennessee after the summer term of 1960[2] with the intention of pursuing a writing career and with two novels, *The Orchard Keeper* and *Suttree*, already under way. McCarthy may first have taken an interest in Ed Gein in 1957, or perhaps the reaction to *Psycho* in 1960 sent him back to the journalistic reports of the Gein case; either way, the *Psycho* phenomenon seems to have been important to the genesis of this novel. It may be that McCarthy's remove to Chicago was prompted by his desire for easy access to the newspapers that had reported the case and that he returned to Sevier County to do further research for the book. Though of secondary influence, the later Blevins case, which McCarthy could research at home in Tennessee, reinforced McCarthy's conception of his voyeuristic necrophile in significant ways.

James Blevins, Lookout Mountain Voyeur

Though a complex legal story, the Blevins case is simpler in its influence on *Child of God* than is the Gein case. Known as the "Lula Lake murders," this north Georgia case was reported briefly in the Knoxville *News-Sentinel* and extensively in the *Chattanooga Daily Times*, with full accounts of trial testimony, in the period between April 1963 and November 1966. It is plausible to assume that it was also covered on nightly television news broadcasts from Knoxville and Chattanooga. The case seems to have suggested some of the particular voyeuristic practices that characterize Lester Ballard, who starts his progressive perversion as a peeping Tom, furtively watching the sexual encounters of couples parked on the Frog Mountain turnaround. It specifically informs the episode of Lester's penultimate murder on Frog Mountain, when Sheriff Turner and his deputy search for an engaged couple reported missing and find only their car pushed down the mountainside, as well as Lester's bungled final double-murder attempt on the turnaround (145–53). As a sensational murder case that occurred fairly close to home, the Blevins case also may have influenced McCarthy's brooding on the relationship between outlaw and community, a concern that informs each of his works of the Tennessee period, and on the ambivalent response of "good citizens" to unspeakable acts—as the Ed Gein case and the White Cap history of Sevier County did as well.[3]

On the afternoon of Sunday, April 14, 1963, James Melvin Blevins, a twenty-seven-year-old carpenter and father of three from Catoosa County in north Georgia, left his family after Easter dinner at his parents' house, donned a camouflage suit, and drove to the eastern slope of Lookout Mountain to hunt for couples parked there. He said later that he had done this frequently, hoping to see someone having sex: "I was there to watch people" (Wilkerson, "Spied" 1). The same afternoon, sixteen-year-old high school student Carolyn Newell and her fiancé, nineteen-year-old Orville Steele, known as "Pete," left her family's house in Happy Valley near Chickamauga to go for a drive. They ended up at Lookout Mountain, where they were seen by several people, including James Blevins. When he spotted them sitting on the fender of the car, he said, he "'got off the side of the road and sat down' to watch" (Wilkerson, "Spied" 2).

The young couple never returned to Carolyn's house, but Pete's car, the air let out of its right front tire, was found on the abandoned rail bed where they had last been seen; several days later, after an intensive canvassing of Lookout Mountain and dragging of Lula Lake, attended by speculation that the pair had eloped, like the deputy's hypothesis that a missing couple has "run off" in *Child of God*, searchers found their bodies a hundred and fifty yards down the slope from their car (147). Both had their hands tied behind their backs with binder's twine, and Pete was tied to a tree. Both had been strangled. Carolyn had suffered head wounds inflicted by a blunt instrument. She was disrobed from the waist down, her clothing was shredded, and the coroner would find that she had been "repeatedly raped" prior to her death (Wilkerson, "Spied" 2).

Blevins's behavior was normal in the days immediately following the murders, according to his ex-wife, Patricia Ann Blevins, who testified as a defense witness in Blevins's trial even though she had divorced him by then. However, a few days after Easter he told her he was troubled by newspaper stories about the missing couple because he had seen them on Lookout Mountain on that Sunday, and he asked her to go there with him to look for them. Frightened, she refused. At the time of the dragging operation in Lula Lake, Blevins told her that the rescue workers were "wasting their time; they're on the side of the mountain; they might still be alive." When a television news bulletin reported that the bodies had been found, she testified, Blevins became anxious: "He said that whoever did that might have seen him up there and they might be after him. . . . He said he was afraid to go to the sheriff and tell him because he might implicate himself." After that, he began sleeping with a rifle next to the bed (Lewis, "Ex-Wife" 1, 37). Blevins himself testified, "I knew I'd been up there walking around in that camouflage suit . . . and that I would be a No. 1 prospect. I asked my daddy-in-law if he would go to the law with me to tell what little bit I knew about it, but he didn't know what to do either" (Lewis, "Jury" 9).

Apparently based on the statements of several individuals who had seen both Blevins and the murdered couple on the rail bed, Blevins was picked up for questioning on April 23. Two other material witnesses were also to be questioned, but Walker County Sheriff W. F. Harmon would not reveal any names "because of the feeling of the people and because we don't want to harm any innocent person in any way" ("Three Men" 5). Col. Frank M. Gleason, the attorney who would defend Blevins, soon declared to the press that his client was innocent: "They've got the wrong pig by the ear" ("Little Progress" 1). Even before he was charged in the slayings, Blevins was moved from the Walker County jail for his own safety "because of the high passions of angered community residents" ("Slain Girl" 3). Sheriff Ralph Jones, who as deputy sheriff in 1963 was the chief Walker County investigator of the crime, testified in 1965 that on the day after Blevins's arrest a material witness warrant was taken out against him, but this could not be found by the time of his second trial. Blevins underwent extensive questioning for hours, interrogation that he and his attorney would later characterize as intimidation. Blevins declared that this grilling made him "a nervous wreck" and that he was never informed of his rights (Lewis, "Blevins on Witness" 1, 9). He was given a series of lie detector tests by Georgia Bureau of Investigation (GBI) agents, perhaps at his own request. One agent testified that the test he administered revealed that Blevins "had guilty knowledge" of the murders; but another, who administered a second test immediately afterwards, "decided that the suspect was 'too emotionally disturbed' for conclusive results" (Lewis, "Blevins Defense" 11).

On May 7, two weeks after Blevins had first been picked up as a material witness, Carolyn Newell's parents swore out a murder warrant against him. The parents of Pete Steele followed suit on the next day. Despite the outrage in the community over the killings, articles in the Knoxville *News-Sentinel* and the *Chattanooga Daily Times* on May 8 identified Blevins by name ("Father" 1; Wilkerson, "Girl's" 1, 9), ran photographs of him, and revealed that he was being held in the Floyd County jail in Rome, Georgia. In the preliminary hearing held on May 22, Blevins admitted spying on the couple but denied killing them. He was bound over for trial without bond and was indicted by the Walker County grand jury on two counts of first-degree murder on August 22. In his argument against the indictment, Gleason conceded that his client was "a 'weakling,' a 'sex degenerate' and 'peeping Tom'" but claimed that he was innocent of the murders ("Suspect" 35). He moved for a change of venue, citing the impassioned feelings about the case in Walker County and the "adverse newspaper, radio and television publicity." He argued that if it was unsafe for Blevins to be held in the Walker County jail, then it was not possible for him to receive a fair trial in that community either ("Blevins to Await" 9). However, the change of venue motion was denied, and that decision was upheld by the Georgia Court of Appeals and the Georgia Supreme Court, in appeals that delayed Blevins's trial for almost a year.

The first trial for the murder of Carolyn Newell began in the Walker County Superior Court on April 27, 1964. Laying the groundwork for a subsequent appeal, Gleason moved for abatements on the grounds that neither the grand jury that indicted Blevins nor the current panels of prospective jurors had been drawn in open court but rather in the clerk's office. These pleas were denied, and the trial proceeded. A prosecution witness, V. D. Stewart, sheriff of Catoosa County, testified that during the two weeks of questioning Blevins admitted he had let the air out of Pete Steele's tire, hoping that Pete would go for help and leave Carolyn behind, so that he could then rape her. In cross-examination Gleason challenged Stewart's testimony, querying why he had not brought forth this information in the preliminary hearing. But GBI agent Jack

Knott asserted that Blevins, after first omitting any mention of letting the air out of the tire because he was ashamed of his peeping Tom activities, had told him the same story. Other GBI agents and Sheriff Harmon confirmed the testimony of Stewart and Knott. Knott also recalled that Blevins said to him at one point: "Reckon I could have killed them and don't remember it? I don't believe I could have done that." On a drive back from Atlanta, where Blevins had been taken briefly for questioning, according to Knott, Blevins commented, "Y'all are happy and I'm sitting in hell" (Lewis, "Hairs" 11).

After Patricia Ann Blevins testified for the defense, James's parents took the stand. His father testified that he and his son had hunted and fished together since James was six, and that James still walked around in the woods frequently, adding "He's kind of a lonely man." Blevins's mother stated, "I know he was up on that mountain doing sinful things, but he didn't murder anyone" (Lewis, "Ex-Wife" 37). Blevins testified that he had seen convicted murderer Roy Jeffery in his black pickup truck in the Lula Lake vicinity on the afternoon of the murders, but during rebuttal, witnesses swore that Jeffery had been with them all day and that his truck had not been in working order. Blevins also testified that Newell and Steele left their car and walked off into the woods and that he followed them, not within sight but hearing their voices, until he heard "something like somebody had pulled a limb off the side of a tree"; then he went back toward their car. Approaching it, he heard the air escaping from the tire and jiggled the valve. "But it didn't stop," he said (Lewis, "Jury" 9). In his closing statement, Gleason said, "We all believe it's a horrible crime, I'm not trying to say otherwise. . . . I'm not going to try to uphold the character of that degenerate over there but he isn't being tried for having contemptible habits, he is being tried for murder" (Lewis, "Blevins Is Found" 2).

On May 5, 1964, after ten hours of deliberation, the jury found Blevins guilty without recommendation of mercy in the murder of Carolyn Newell. Under Georgia law, this meant a mandatory death penalty. But Blevins's sentence of electrocution was stayed when Gleason moved for a retrial on the grounds that the jurors had not been drawn publicly in open court. The Walker County judge overruled this motion, but his judgment was reversed by the Georgia Supreme Court ("Blevins v. The State" 141 S.E. 2nd 426). The retrial began May 10, 1965, as McCarthy was preparing for his trip to Europe. By this time Blevins had been a prisoner for over two years: "'I've just quit counting the days any more,' the trim, 29-year-old young man said softly. 'It's been a long time. There's not much to do. I do a few crossword puzzles now and then and I guess I read a lot'" ("Blevins Has Quit" 11).

On the day before the second trial opened, the *Chattanooga Daily Times* rather disingenuously remarked, "The case has undoubtedly caused more comment, publicity and public sentiment than any case in the North Georgia area during many years previously" (Lewis, "Blevins' Trial" 71). Indeed rumors had been reported in the *Times* from the day the young couple was reported missing. When their bodies were found, spectators mobbed the crime scene. The flesh of Carolyn Newell's leg had been partially eaten by animals and this fueled a rumor that the murderer had mutilated the bodies. A reward fund for information leading to the arrest and conviction of the murderer was established, and it quickly grew to over two thousand dollars. A crowd of 550 people turned out for Blevins's preliminary hearing, and state troopers were brought in to assist county officers "to maintain order and guard against any demonstrations" (Wilkerson, "Spied" 1). Such a combination of horror, fascination, and voyeurism exhibited in this tiny community relatively innocent of crime yet quick to rush to judgment and even potentially violent—characteristic enough of smalltown America—is reflected in Sevier County residents' attempt to lynch Lester Ballard and their refusal to see him as much like themselves despite their salacious interest in and intuition about his crimes: "What did you want with them dead ladies? . . . Was you fuckin em?" one asks him (182). It is also reflected in the citizens of *Outer Dark*, on which McCarthy was working in May 1965 in preparation for his transatlantic trip.

Interestingly, however, the simmering impulse to violence in Walker County seems to have cooled at least intermittently as the trial process dragged on and as images of James Blevins reached the public. Timid, ashamed, soft of voice, and small of frame, the James Blevins who emerges gradually from the reports of the *Chattanooga Daily Times* is not unlike like the final image of the similarly named Jimmy Blevins in *All the Pretty Horses* when John Grady watches his "small ragged figure" limping off barefoot into the trees with his assassins and thinks, "There seemed insufficient substance to him to be the object of men's wrath. There seemed nothing about him sufficient to fuel any enterprise at all" (177). John Grady's perception is adumbrated in that of the Sevier County mob who abduct Lester but who look for his clothes to replace his hospital gown because even to their outraged eyes, "he didn't look like much" (178). The narrator evokes that perception yet more sharply in the reader when Lester, dressed at the men's insistence in outsized overalls, his empty sleeve tucked down the bib, is marched off barefoot to his place of threatened execution by his tormenters, and it is reinforced when Lester presents himself back at the hospital, "a weedshaped onearmed human swaddled up in outsized overalls and covered all over with red mud" (180–81, 192).[4] Even James Blevins's sexual propensities came to seem more childish and pathetic than monstrous as he testified that on that Easter afternoon "I was enjoying the country and looking for couples to watch" and that he had begun doing this "around the age of 15" but had all but quit by 1963 (Gallant 40). Blevins was reluctant to come forth with what he knew about the missing couple, he said, because "I knew that if I got in this, the fact I was a Peeping Tom would come out. I was ashamed of it. . . . I had a guilt complex about being a Peeping Tom" (Gallant 40). Patricia Ann, who had married James when she was fourteen, he nineteen, revealed that "we didn't have a marriage, we were just staying in the same house together" (Lewis, "Blevins Upheld" 13). Thus citizens' outrage at the alleged murderer dissipated over time. The *Chattanooga Daily Times* observed that during the first trial "interested spectators frequently packed the large courtroom to hear the array of witnesses testify against the defendant," but in the subsequent proceedings, except for the first days when the court was crowded with prospective jurors, "it has been rare when more than 50 persons at one time have been present for simply observing the trial" (Lewis, "Trial" 3).

In the second trial, new witnesses for the defense testified that they had seen three men, one wearing a camouflage suit like Blevins's, standing by the roadside about three quarters of a mile from the murder site.[5] Gleason reprised his argument that there was simply not enough time for Blevins to have committed the murders. In his summation the prosecuting attorney, Earl Self, asserted, "Sex has destroyed his mind and sex has caused this killing," but the jury disagreed (Lewis, "Blevins Case" 26). After deliberating three and a half hours on May 21, 1965, they found Blevins not guilty of the murder of Carolyn Newell. The verdict was announced to a courtroom holding only forty spectators. Blevins received the verdict quietly, but tears filled his eyes; as several well-wishers congratulated him, he said, "Thank you for your prayers" (Lewis, "Blevins Cleared" 1, 5). The newspapers reported no public outcry, no violent demonstrations.

Blevins was still under indictment for the murder of Pete Steele, but he was awarded a bond in the amount of seventy-five hundred dollars and was freed. Gleason pushed for a speedy trial and won a ruling from the Georgia Supreme Court that Blevins should either be tried for the Steele murder in the August 1966 term (which would end November 1) or released (Bowles, "Blevins Awaits" 7). The trial was scheduled for October 3. In the weeks after the trial date was set, Gleason claimed, he "received 10 telephone calls 'threatening to hang [Blevins] or shoot him.'" Like Lester Ballard, who returns to the sanctuary of the hospital after escaping his tormenters and his imprisonment in the cave, Blevins asked to be put back in jail because, he said, "It was safer down there than walking the streets." Finally the trial was cancelled a week before it was to have begun, and after twenty-eight months, Blevins was released on November 3. He indicated his intention to move to Huntsville, Alabama, since he had lost his friends and reputation in his home town of Rossville, Georgia, and if he stayed he "would still fear for my life from certain people. . . . Perhaps I would fear as much from the law as the people. . . . There are certain law officials that wouldn't hesitate to do me harm—I've found that out from experience." As a free man, Blevins declared his determination "to go out in the world and make a good citizen. . . . I'm going to try to build back again. . . . It's hard to do after all I've lost through this—work and health. But I believe I'm man enough to do it" (Bowles, "Blevins, Now" 1, 4).

Although it ends on a more hopeful note than does McCarthy's novel, Blevins's history as reported in the newspapers suggested a modus operandi for Lester Ballard's crimes, one that was compatible with the setting in rural East Tennessee, and it hinted a plausible progression from voyeurism to murder. In Blevins's generalized sense of guilt and the suggestions of his oppression by agents of the law and by judgmental citizens, his story also resonates interestingly with gnostic images of humankind's hounded state in cosmos, which are so central to McCarthy's conception of *Outer Dark*. But for the metaphor of necrophilia that so predominates in *Child of God*, McCarthy seems to have drawn on another murder case farther away from home.

Ed Gein, Plainfield Necrophile

The Plainfield, Wisconsin, case of multiple murderer Ed Gein was more sensational and much more infamous than that of James Blevins.[6] Like Blevins, the fifty-one-year-old bachelor Gein was a slight, quiet man, "mild-looking, mild-spoken," and it horrified his neighbors to learn that he was a murderer of an unthinkable kind ("Portrait" 39). According to psychiatrists who reviewed his case, Gein was the son of a repressive, domineering mother who insisted that women his age were sinful and vice-ridden, and many of his victims bore a resemblance to his mother. It is not entirely clear whether Gein practiced necrophilia in the literal sense that Lester Ballard does. He robbed the graves of recently deceased women, stealing body parts or whole corpses and hoarding them. In his rather isolated farmhouse where he lived alone after the deaths of his mother and brother, horrified investigators found human heads, skulls, ten masks made from human faces (some adorned with lipstick), and articles made from human skin (Leonard 1). But in its absence of specificity the press's frequent use of the terms "body parts" or "other parts" prompts the inference that Gein may also have collected sexual organs from his victims. The earliest newspaper reports of Gein's psychological evaluations, citing his transvestitism, fetishism, schizophrenia, ambivalence toward women, and voyeurism, labeled him a "sexual psychopath" but did not use the term "necrophile" ("Doctor" 1). It was reported, however, that Gein would undergo further tests of his "sexual attitudes" (Kienitz, "Gein" 16). Gein's psychosis led him to commit both murder and mutilation. In his summer kitchen, investigators discovered the headless, eviscerated carcass of matronly Bernice Worden hanging by the heels like a dressed-out deer. Gein admitted to killing her and another middle-aged woman, Mary Hogan, who had been missing for three years, but the other heads, *Time* reported, "Gein insisted he had got by opening fresh graves in nearby cemeteries (he watched the obituaries for prospects). Usually he took only the head and some other parts of the body; only once, he said, an entire female corpse. By no coincidence, one of the graves adjoined his mother's." The article cited the opinions of psychiatrists that Gein's "development had somehow been arrested so that he continued, childlike, to perceive people as mere objects" and that his mutilating women who "reminded him of mother ... and preserving parts of them satisfied two contradictory urges: to bring her back to life and have her with him always, and to destroy her as the cause of his frustration"; it concluded that "apparently Gein practiced neither cannibalism nor necrophilia, but preserved the remains just to look at" ("Portrait" 40). But the even more sensational photo-spread published in *Life* asserted that "psychiatrists, studying his actions, believe he is a schizophrenic or split personality, torn between love and hate for women—and perhaps also suffering from a savage form of necrophilia, or love of the dead" ("House of Horror" 27).

Contradictory and oversimplified as these journalistic assessments are, their depictions of Gein's necrophilic tendencies align with the case studies of necrosadism in Masters and Lea's *Sex Crimes in History.* That Lester Ballard murders like the sado-necrophile but does not mutilate may be attributable to the joint influence of the Gein story and of Masters and Lea's study. Even more alienated than the odd little "ghoul-slayer" Ed Gein, Lester seems motivated by the terrible longing for human contact and fear of rejection that are characteristic of the true necrophile, but his abandonment by his perhaps unvirtuous mother also seems to fuel a latent rage that flares increasingly as his experiences of loss accumulate ("Graves Probe" 3).

The *Milwaukee Journal* stories about the Gein case chronicle both community reaction to the disclosures and the descent of sightseers on the small town of Plainfield. As in *Child of God*, Gein's neighbors engaged in myth-making from hindsight, recalling, accumulating, and transforming memories of odd interactions with the loner: folks' sudden memory of his strange tendency to admit guilt whenever someone teased him about having something to do with people's disappearances, children's stories that Gein kept shrunken heads in his house, one woman's assertion that she had caught him peeping through her window, an acquaintance's claim that Gein had patted a man's stomach and commented that it was just about right for "roasting." Some declared candidly that they had had no inkling that Gein was capable of his crimes. Others discredited his claim that he had obtained most of his corpses by grave-robbing, partly because they didn't judge him physically capable of it and partly because they suspected he might be covering up other murders than the two to which he had confessed.

From almost the beginning, it was apparent that Gein was the victim of severe mental illness that might make him incapable of standing trial, and he was eventually found legally insane. So the local reaction to Gein was not characterized by the pronounced anger and tendency to vigilantism McCarthy attributes to his fictional Sevierville. Within the first week of Gein's arrest, Methodist minister Kenneth Engelman visited him in the Wautoma County jail to pray with him. As Engelman entered the cell, commenting kindly that "it was a difficult day for the prisoner," Gein began to cry. In explaining his visit to the press, the Reverend Engelman said that he went to see Gein "because he felt Gein needed spiritual counsel." He remarked, "I'm a Christian minister and Mr. Gein is a *child of God. . . .* God may be nearer to Mr. Gein than the rest of us because God comes closer to people in dealings with life and death. Mr. Gein is closer to such things than the rest of us" ("Mental" 3, emphasis added). Engelman's compassion for a man whose behavior seems beyond all human potential (or so we would like to think) is echoed in McCarthy's title and in his treatment of the warped Lester Ballard as a damaged child and a painfully lost soul, but Lester's designation as a "child of God" also resonates dialogically with the gnostic conception of human nature as created by the counterfeit god to suppress spirit in psyche and matter.

Voyeur, Necrophile, Psycho: *Novel, Script, and Film*

In the much-transformed story of Norman Bates that Robert Bloch loosely based on Ed Gein in his novel *Psycho* (1959), necrophilia remains foregrounded. But Bloch and, later, scriptwriter Joseph Stefano and director Alfred Hitchcock all underplay the necro-sadism that was so prominent in the reports of Gein's murders and mutilations, splitting out Norman's necrophilic obsession with his mother and "Norma's" murderous vengeance as they build entire plot and thematic structures on Norman's split personality. More than the actual manifestations Gein exhibited, Bloch and Hitchcock's images of necrophilia echo William Faulkner's in "A Rose for Emily," in which Emily Grierson, proscribed from love by father, cousins, and unsympathetic community, apparently murders her uncommitted beau Homer Barron to keep him forever by her side. The Jefferson townspeople who investigate after Emily's death find a decayed corpse companionably laid out beside the impression of a second body and, we presume, one of Miss Emily's own iron-gray hairs on the pillow (130). Similarly Lila Crane, investigating the disappearance of her sister, finds the imprint of a body in the bed of Norman's mother, and later finds her actual corpse in the fruit cellar (Bloch 203–4, 207–8; Stefano 120, 125). McCarthy forgoes the horrific effects of such climactic revelations, but he emphasizes the thwarting of a natural impulse toward love and acceptance that Faulkner's story had explored sympathetically and that the stories of Ed Gein and of Norman Bates had employed more as a hindsight explanation of gruesome psychotic behavior.

One manifestation of Gein's necrophilia passes in a traceable line of descent through Bloch's novel and Hitchcock's film to *Child of God*. The early *Life* article reports that Gein had embalmed nine of the heads found at his farm, and in his home, authorities found "books on embalming, a syringe and formaldehyde" ("House of Horror" 30). But though there was embalming fluid in some of the body parts discovered in Ed Gein's farmhouse, investigators were cautious about assuming that Gein had tried to preserve them himself, recognizing that he may have exhumed embalmed corpses—which ultimately proved to be the case with at least some of them. Nevertheless, Gein's taxidermy implements and his early desire to be a doctor (Kienitz, "Robbed" 2) suggest obsessions with the material body that are rather common in case studies of necrophilia (see, for example, Masters and Lea 127–29). And he told his questioners that he had preserved his face masks by "rubbing them with oil and keeping them as cold as possible" ("Ghoulish" 1). In Bloch's *Psycho*, Norman too is interested in taxidermy. Mary Crane notices a stuffed squirrel in the back room of the motel office, and Norman says, "Cute little fellow, isn't he? I've often wished I had a live one around that I could tame for a pet," articulating the necrophile's psychosis in a displaced version (45). Searching his house, Lila finds his taxidermy tools, though she does not recognize them for what they are (206). By the end of the novel, the psychiatrist, Dr. Steiner, has learned that Norman tried to give his mother's corpse the illusion of life by using his taxidermist's art (216). In the filmscript the stuffed squirrel is translated to several birds—one of Hitchcock's trademarks. Norman tells Marion that his mother is as "harmless as . . . one of these stuffed birds," and she appears finally as a "stuffed, ill-preserved cadaver" in the cellar of the Bates home (Stefano 48, 125). Lester Ballard knows nothing of the taxidermist's art, but he shares the impulse. A trace of the stuffed birds of Stefano and Hitchcock's *Psycho* appears in *Child of God* when Lester brings a nearly frozen robin to the idiot boy, who chews its legs off because, Lester projects, "He wanted it to where it couldn't run off"—echoing the sentiment of Bloch's Norman Bates and revealing an underlying motive for his own murders (79).

McCarthy's novel foregrounds manifest sexual necrophilia, while it was apparently only latent in Gein's murders or thinly suppressed in the popular accounts. Bloch, Stefano, and Hitchcock shied away from depicting it: Norman resurrects only Mother's body, effectively protected by the incest taboo, while in fidelity to Mother he suppresses the tempting body of Mary/Marion Crane, sinking her and her car in the swamp.[7] But paradoxically McCarthy unflinchingly holds Lester's sexual perversion before us, even as he rejects the sensational treatment in which all accounts of Ed Gein or Norman Bates indulged. He handles his shocking subject with restraint and delicacy, treating it as an extended metaphor of man's spiritual blindness, his confusion by materialism.

Yet as *Child of God* is also a critique of voyeurism, McCarthy risks titillating his readers; as does Hitchcock in *Psycho*, he implicates us all. Significantly there is very little in the accounts of Ed Gein's crimes to convict him of voyeurism except the charge that he kept parts of human bodies to look at them. But voyeurism surfaces unmistakably in the journalism relating to the Gein case. Most egregious is the *Life* article, with photographs of Gein, his house interior and exterior, his victims, his town, his neighbors, occupying more space on the page than the accompanying text—typical of *Life*'s approach to its stories. Included are an oblique shot of victim Bernice Worden in her open coffin (her head restored) for the necrophilic or merely prurient among us and, like a mirror cynically held up to the reader, a photo from the interior of Gein's house of a man and woman outside peering "through dirty, tattered curtains and past the cluttered sill into the kitchen." The caption reads, "Looking into Gein's world" and it notes, "All week Plainfield's people came to see the house they had long ignored" ("House of Horror" 25).

Interestingly, the articles in the *Milwaukee Journal*, which are the most restrained of the contemporary accounts, attribute voyeurism less to Wisconsin locals than to the mob of journalists, photographers, and other outsiders brought to Plainfield by the news of Gein's crimes. Officials had to guard Gein's house to keep curiosity-seekers away. The weekend after the crimes were discovered, the *Journal* reported, "Thousands of sightseers jammed this otherwise quiet central Wisconsin community . . . and went out to take peeks at the farm where the slayer lived. An estimated 3,000 to 4,000 cars with entire families—children included—cruised through town, stopping occasionally so the occupans [*sic*] could ask townsfolk directions to the Gein farm" ("Gein's Story" 8). The following spring, when Gein's farm was to be auctioned off, "Plainfield area residents . . . feared that the 'open house' [scheduled for a Sunday and the auction to follow on the next weekend] would be turned into spectacles." Before the open house could take place, Gein's farmhouse burned down. Officials suspected arson, the only hint of vigilantism in the Plainfield murder case. The *Journal* reported that "the fire eased some of [the local people's fears of a spectacle], although most area residents say they did not condone arson." But the fire itself may have contributed to bringing another stream of the curious to the farm on the day of the open house. One radio estimate of twenty thousand spectators was discredited by the guardian of Gein's estate, who admitted that over two thousand cars were parked at the farm that day. Many people "drove past the farm and then into Plainfield, seven miles away, to see the Worden hardware store, where Gein murdered Mrs. Bernice Worden" ("Crowd" 8). The next week, a crowd of two thousand again convened at the Gein farm, although only a few meant to bid on the property ("All That Gein" 2). Despite the comparative restraint of its reporting and its sympathy for the Plainfield community, the *Milwaukee Journal* indulged in its own voyeuristic photography, printing numerous photos of Gein, his victims, his farmhouse exterior and interior (including the parlor Gein had closed off since the death of his mother), two chairs that "may or may not be ones which were reported fitted with seats made of human skin," and aerial shots of the cemetery where law officers had attempted discreetly to dig up two graves adjacent to Gein's mother's to verify his claim that he had robbed them ("Gein Confesses" 1; Kienitz, "Find Two" 1; Kienitz, "Gein's Ghoul" 2).

In his novel *Psycho*, Robert Bloch follows the *Milwaukee Journal* in portraying smalltown life as predominantly cooperative and supportive of its citizens. The local sheriff is reluctant to investigate Norman's connection to Mary Crane's disappearance, and Sam explains to Lila that in a small town "everybody knows everybody else, nobody wants to stir up trouble or cause unnecessary hard feeling. . . . There's nothing to make anyone suspect Bates. [The sheriff has] known him all his life" (164–65). Bloch does not implicate the community until the murders are uncovered, and then he depicts the media circus and rumor mill the discovery unleashes. Bloch makes voyeurism primarily a feature of Norman's psychosis, then, but also links it with a mirror motif and the underlying theme of mutual guilt: the guilty awareness of watching and the guilty sense of being watched that plague Norman Bates and Mary Crane, respectively. Hitchcock's film emphasizes mirrors; he instructed the set decorator George Milo to provide shiny fixtures in the bathroom where Norman kills Marion, and he would tell him, "Let's have lots of mirrors, old boy" (Rebello 70). And he makes even more of the guilty watching, employing camera angles and tracking to place the viewer in complicity with the camera's eye, inviting us to peep into Sam and Marion's hotel room window in the very first scene, quite independent of Norman's viewpoint, and then to peer through the peephole into Marion's room at the Bates Hotel to watch with Norman as she undresses. He reinforces this effect with images of watching eyes, blank eyes, reflective eyeglasses, even shower drains as eyeballs. Indeed Hitchcock shot most of the film through fifty-millimeter lenses on thirty-five-millimeter cameras to create the nearest possible approximation of human eyesight. As script supervisor Marshal Schlom recalled, "He wanted the camera, being the eyes of the audience all the time, to let them [view the action] as if they were seeing it with their own eyes" (Rebello 93). Scriptwriter Stefano remembered, too, that Hitchcock wanted to use sound as well as visual imagery to implicate the audience in Norman's voyeurism. At Hitchcock's direction he added the following to the scene in which Norman peeps at Marion: "The SOUNDS come louder, as if we too had our ears pressed against the wall" (Rebello 48; Stefano 50). And like Bloch's novel, the script and the film emphasize the swarm of newspaper and television reporters gathered outside the courthouse when Norman is being tried, their ranks swelled by "the curious and the concerned and the morbid" (Stefano 126).

Child of God opens with Lester Ballard not quite covertly watching the "carnival folk" who have gathered to witness the auction of his homestead. As in Plainfield, they are drawn there partly out of prurient curiosity. Like Hitchcock, McCarthy invites us to look over Lester's shoulder through his cabin window at the dead girl who lies naked and seductively arranged on the hearth and then, Lester-like ourselves, to watch as he makes love to her (92, 103). He inveigles us into forgetting she is a corpse or into seeing her simultaneously as corpse and woman as Lester does, referring to her with feminine pronouns and counterpointing her puppet-like movement with active verb forms as if she were still capable of volition, as when Lester hauls her up the ladder with a plowline: "*She rose* slumpshouldered from the floor with her hair all down and *began to bump* slowly up the ladder. Halfway up *she paused*, dangling. Then *she began to rise* again" (95, emphasis added). Or in the parallel scene at the end of the novel, when state officials raise the corpses from Lester's cave: "The rope drew taut and the first of the dead *sat up* on the cave floor, the hands that hauled the rope above sorting the shadows like puppeteers. Gray soapy clots of matter fell from the cadaver's chin. *She ascended* dangling" (196, emphasis added). He challenges us to acknowledge our voyeurism and our related ambivalence about the dark deeds of our fellows—to *see* Lester as he struggles in the flooded creek: "See him. You could say that he's sustained by his fellow men, like you. Has peopled the shore with them calling to him. A race that gives suck to the maimed and the crazed, that wants their wrong blood in its history and will have it. But they want this man's life" (156). He reminds us of the voyeurism in our history, describing the carnival atmosphere of an 1899 public hanging of two Sevier County White Caps who had turned from vigilantism to murder for hire. This reminiscence resonates with the auction of Ballard's property and the attempt to lynch him (166–67).

Finally, McCarthy implicates our voyeurism as it tends to separate us from others in negative judgment, extending the theme that so predominates in *Outer Dark*, with its implications of cosmic oppression. McCarthy unmasks as received opinion the pretense of "objectivity" in the newspaper and magazine accounts of Gein—the hypocritical perspective of the respectable community joined in aghast judgment of the outlaw. This is reflected in the chapters of *Child of God* in which Lester's neighbors casually apply hindsight to his life, futilely attempting to account for his behavior or pretending foreknowledge they could not have had. (One section of the *Life* spread, headlined "Neighbors Recall Gein's Talk of Women, Murder—and Embalming," is devoted entirely to such hindsight; see "House of Horror" 28–29. Bloch's novel devotes a summary paragraph to it; 210–11.) Not only does McCarthy counter the oral histories of his Sevier Countians with chapters that foreground Lester's criminal experience from a privileged viewpoint, but he almost never employs the perspective of Lester's victims, as do all texts of *Psycho*. (Faulkner too avoids this in "A Rose for Emily," as do Dostoevsky in his intimate portrait of a murderer in *Crime and Punishment* and Camus in *The Stranger*.) And McCarthy especially rejects the psychoanalytic explanations appended to each version of the Gein/Bates story, which invariably feel inadequate and muddled, as in the magazine articles in *Life* and *Time*, or pretentious and oversimplified, as in *Psycho* novel, script, and film.[8] The contrast between the titles *Child of God* and *Psycho* is a telling one. Always McCarthy insists on the mystery and the humanity of Lester Ballard—on the mystery of humans' dark capabilities and muffled spirituality. The most prevalent point of view in *Child of God* (aside from the narrator's own) is Lester's, though it seldom achieves interiority and is focused primarily on his sensory experience; the effect of this is to evoke our recognition of commonality with him even if our deeds are not as beyond the pale, while also maintaining provocative distance. By looking dispassionately at Ballard's life, McCarthy invites us to see him compassionately. Filmmaker Richard Pearce recognized in this a "'Negative Capability' of a very high order" ("Foreword" [v]), and it was *Child of God* more than any other of McCarthy's works that prompted Pearce to ask McCarthy to write the screenplay for *The Gardener's Son*—another work that challenges the community's view of its "ghost villains" and finds a certain "nobility" in a man who has committed a murder (Pearce, Research newsletter received April 7, 1975: 8; "Gardner's [*sic*] Son" G7).

  Child of God ends with a sequence of scenes that parallel scenes in the film *Psycho*, as if McCarthy is paying homage to the film that influenced his conception of his finally very different novel. The first of these is the scene in which Lester, wearing a "frightwig and skirts," rushes Greer with murderous intent (172). As several critics have suggested, Lester's cross-dressing in their clothing and hair implies his "introjection of and identification with his female victims," his desire "to seize the very identity of his victims" (Jarrett 51; Ciuba 97). More specifically, his attack on Greer is a planted trace both of Ed Gein, with his obsession with scalps and face masks, and of Norman as Mother, especially when "she" assaults Marion Crane in the shower.[9] Indeed one effect of this scene is to put us, for the only time in the novel, into the perspective of Lester's victim, as Greer, like Marion Crane, looks up to find this grotesque parody of feminine wrath bearing down on him: "an apparition created whole out of nothing and set upon him with such dire intent" (173). Lester has taken to watching Greer, stoking his anger, and while it seems quasi-logical that he would eventually turn to murdering for hate as well as for "love," it is rather jarring to find him cross-dressing in the clothing and scalp of one of his victims. McCarthy prepares his reader for this scene when he writes that Lester had "long been wearing the underclothes of his female victims but now he took to appearing in their outerwear as well. A gothic doll in illfit clothes, its carmine mouth floating detached and bright in the white landscape" (140). But the scalp is startling. Far from mutilating the dead as Gein did, Lester has previously taken great pains to preserve them, placing his shots laterally through the neck or at the base of the skull so as to maintain their beauty and the illusion of life. But Lester's enactment of a key scene from *Psycho* hints that on another level the murders have been committed and the scalp taken in acts of Gein-like sadism directed against the faithless Mother who, like his female victims, seems to Lester of questionable virtue. Further, although there is little in the novel to support a reading of Lester as schizophrenic in the sense that Norman Bates is—certainly nothing to corroborate the notion that he has introjected the personality of the mother who abandoned him—yet his attack in the guise of an avenging "mother" on the man who has taken possession of the Ballards' domestic space suggests symbolic wish-fulfillment on the part of this neglected and bereft "child." Lester does share Gein and Bates's ambivalence about women. His attraction to them is equally balanced with his anger, which we can trace to his mother's abandonment, his being falsely accused of rape by the "old whore" he finds by the roadside (52)—in whom he may perceive an avatar of his mother—and his rejection by taunting or scornful girls.

Like Norman Bates, Lester is committed to an insane asylum instead of prison. Unlike Norman, who ends completely absorbed into the personality of Mother, giving reader and filmgoer a final thrill of horror at his psychosis, Lester never dissociates himself from his own deeds. Like Mother Bates, however, he does disclaim insanity, declining to speak with his neighbor in the asylum, "a demented gentleman who used to open folks' skulls and eat the brains inside with a spoon," since Lester "had nothing to say" to a man he judges "crazy" (193). Remaining much like us, Lester defines himself as normal.

Bloch's novel ends with the scene of Norman/Mother in the asylum. Interestingly Hitchcock's film makes this the penultimate scene and ends instead with the image of Marion Crane's car, in which lie her body and the money she has stolen, rising from the swamp where Norman has submerged it. Similarly, in final salute to the film, McCarthy's novel ends, after Lester's death, with the image of his corpses rising from the cave in which he had hidden them, another return of the repressed that only incites the community to renewed efforts to deny any kindred impulse.

Child of God engages Hitchcock's film so significantly as to suggest that McCarthy's very idea to write a novel exploring man's darkest impulses—and his tendency to repress and deny them—through the story of a murderous voyeur/necrophile originated at least partly in his encounter with *Psycho*. Hitch-cock's experimentation with cinematic techniques to heighten the audience's awareness of the ways in which viewers are implicated in Norman's voyeurism is answered in *Child of God* by McCarthy's narrative strategies toward the same end. But McCarthy's decision to write a study of a child of God rather than of a psycho may stem from his philosophical and artistic dissatisfaction with Hitchcock's (and scriptwriter Stefano's and novelist Bloch's) psychoanalysis of Norman Bates, a structurally after-the-fact analysis which in seeking to explain merely explains away, separates Norman from the experiences of the normal human, and finally fails to illuminate in any essential way the universal mystery of the human heart or spirit. Instead, McCarthy's third novel extends the medi-tation on gnostic psychology begun in *Outer Dark* with that novel's exploration of another child of the gnostic world-artificer whose drives and denials lead to incest and infanticide. At the same time, given the ways in which *Child of God* resonates with details peculiar to Bloch's *Psycho* or to the *Time*, *Life*, and *Milwaukee Journal* articles about Ed Gein, it seems plausible that McCarthy sought out these earlier treatments as well as the film. It may be that when James Blevins was accused of murder in 1963, elements of that case meshed so well with the thinking and research McCarthy had already done for *Child of God* that he followed its progress with special interest. But all of these sources are completely absorbed into McCarthy's vision for his novel. It is a measure of McCarthy's success that despite his planting a sequence of rather obvious traces of *Psycho* near the end of *Child of God*, readers failed to notice them for over twenty years.

McCarthy in Sevier County

In the flood year of 1963, ten years before the publication of *Child of God* and two years before the publication of his first novel, McCarthy and his first wife, Lee Holleman McCarthy, were living in Sevier County, Tennessee ("Miss McCarthy" 6). McCarthy's second wife, Anne DeLisle, recalls that McCarthy later took her to see a little clapboard cabin in the Waldens Creek area, where he had lived for a time. There, she told journalist Mike Gibson, he introduced her to "a rugged cast of woodsmen and moonshiners and rocker-bound Sevier County old-timers" with whom they drank "clear mountain whiskey from a mayonnaise jar, its rim still haloed by creamy white paste. . . . 'Cormac taught me these people were the real salt of the earth, the *real* people of Tennessee. "Do anything fer ya' if they like ya', and anything to ya' if they don't."'" Per-haps on DeLisle's authority, Gibson asserts that *Child of God* is set in Waldens Creek (30), and this seems plausible. The location of Waldens Creek between Sevierville nine miles to the northeast and Blount County over the mountains to the west fits the situation of Lester's unnamed environs (see *CoG* 96, 127), and the name is ironically apt. Further, there was a Fox's Store at Waldens Creek, to which the novel refers (99, 124–26). A photograph of Fox's Store is included in a reminiscence by Hazel Brewer, a Waldens Creek native, in *Sevier County, Tennessee and Its Heritage* (119); as recently as 1982 the store was identified on a map of the Sevierville area in a tourist's pamphlet (Williams, *101 Places* 45).

With a population of only 2,890 in 1960, Sevierville itself was then a little-known county seat situated in the Great Valley of East Tennessee on the flood-plain between the east and west forks of the Little Pigeon River ("Sevierville" Table I; 8). Like much Tennessee limestone country, Sevier County is home to various sinks and caves. The largest and best known are the Forbidden Caverns east of Sevierville, not "discovered" until 1964 (*Sevier County* 131). The prominent topographical features of Sevier County—mountains and coves, flood-prone rivers and little-known caves—together with its most striking architectural feature, the splendid county courthouse built in the Beaux Arts style just before the 1896 White Caps trial of Pleas Wynn and Catlett Tipton—all figure significantly in *Child of God* (Jones 59–62).

As occurs in the spring of Lester's twenty-seventh year (126), Sevierville flooded at intervals until the TVA widened, straightened, and rechanneled the Little Pigeon River in 1967, effectively eliminating flooding until 1994. The floods occurred between mid-December and mid-April, most typically in the spring because of intensive intervals of precipitation and very high runoff when vegetation was dormant. The TVA's Douglas Reservoir on the French Broad River at the northern edge of Sevier County, finished in 1943, accommodated only about four or five inches of this runoff, leaving Sevierville vulnerable to floods. Because all 381 square miles of the Little Pigeon River watershed lie entirely within Sevier County, about two-thirds of the county is affected when flooding occurs (*Sevier County* 130–31; Cooper 5, 32). And because the Little Pigeon River's branches sandwich Sevierville, the overflow of flood waters is channeled into the nearby business district and the courthouse square (Fox A5). Floods of fourteen to eighteen feet were recorded in 1867, 1875, 1896 (the year of the White Cap trials), 1920, 1928, 1957 (the most likely date for the main action of *Child of God*), two times only six days apart in spring 1963 when McCarthy himself was living in Sevier County, 1965, 1966—and yet again in 1994 and 2002, despite the TVA's flood protection program (*Sevier County* 130). A 1984 article about "Sevierville's Last Great Flood" of 1965 reprints several press photos of the inundated town, including one of motor boats docked in the town square and one of a flooded street on the courthouse square, with a caption reading: "Flood almost topped meters at Court and Commerce" (Fox A5). In *Child of God*, Sheriff Turner gazes at the flood water "stretching in quiet canals up the streets and alleys, the tops of the parking meters just visible," and Deputy Cotton jokes that he had to give Bill Scruggs a ticket because he "caught him goin up Bruce Street speedin in a motorboat" (160–61). Equally relevant is a photo from the 1963 flood, reprinted in the *Tennessee Conservation-ist* in 1979, of four men in a motorboat traveling past drug and dry goods stores down one of the streets on the town square, a shot taken from the courthouse—an image that suggests Sheriff Turner, Deputy Cotton and Mr. Wade in their rowboat (Barksdale 22).[10]

Because time markers other than seasonal imagery are rare in *Child of God*, the flood reference helps us tentatively to date the action of the novel. Mr. Wade, the old man who tells the deputy about the White Caps, says he was born in the flood year of 1885 (166)—not a flood year listed in the county his-tory, which suggests that McCarthy drew on his own experience of the floods of 1963 and contemporaneous news reports of the 1957 and 1963 floods more than on historical accounts of earlier floods on the Little Pigeon. Lester dies in April 1965, and although the text is not explicit, it seems he has spent sig-nificant time in the state mental hospital before his death (193–94). The flood that forces him to move his possessions from one cave to another on higher ground occurs in late winter (154); the actual flood of 1957, a flood caused by extended heavy rains that affected both Knoxville and Sevierville, peaked on February 1, earlier than the more typical spring floods recorded in March and April (*Sevier County* 130). A photo taken in Sevierville and published February 1, after only twelve days of rain, shows two men maneuvering a rowboat over the flood waters (*News-Sentinel* 1). A news report of that day said that the Ten-nessee Valley, devastated by the worst floods it had experienced in years, was to get more rain and that Sevierville residents had fled their homes in flash flood-ing the night before ("Smoky Streams" 1). A Knoxville *News-Sentinel* story on February 5 noted that it had rained for sixteen of the previous seventeen days, with still more predicted; by that time the water level at Douglas Reservoir had risen fifty-four feet and thus was twenty-seven feet above flood level ("More Rain" 10). In *Child of God*, a rain-soaked Lester observes the flooded creek and fields from his vantage point on the mountain, and the narrator comments that "it had been raining for three days"; it continues to rain as Lester struggles to move his belongings, and it is drizzling when the sheriff and Cotton patrol the flooded town in their rowboat (154, 161).

If we conceive the action of the novel to take place, as its details suggest, in the flood year of 1957 (the year of Gein's arrest), that would make old Mr. Wade seventy-two, and it would mean that Lester is incarcerated for seven years before he dies; it would place Lester's birth in 1930 and make his life in Sevier County flood-free until the year of his arrest at twenty-seven, which might help explain his naïve wonder at even the disorder of the winter woods. It would also make his first experience of these turbid waters of darkness coincide with his year of necrophilic oblivion. It would make him too young to serve in

World War II: there is no reference to his having done military service. Further, this would place in the Depression years both his mother's abandonment of the family and his father's selling off of the timber. K. Wesley Berry writes, "We know that the timber on the land being auctioned in the opening scene was cut about fifteen to twenty years ago (5), and that Lester's father hanged himself about seventeen or eighteen years ago. Perhaps Ballard senior sold the timber off his property as a last desperate means of support" (64). If so, then Lester's father killed himself in 1939, before American involvement in the war and near the end of the Depression.

The Cave as Leviathan

Like other topographical features of *Child of God*, the caves underlying Sevier County that form a locus for much of the novel's action are grounded in reality. Thomas Barr's 1961 geological survey *Caves of Tennessee* describes virtually every feature of the cave formations and the animal life in Lester's underground world, and conversely McCarthy weaves into his novel each creature Barr has documented inhabiting the caves of East Tennessee. Through his father's TVA associations, McCarthy may also have known Berlen Moneymaker, chief geologist for the TVA, or his unpublished thesis on East Tennessee caves, which Barr consulted in the writing of *Caves of Tennessee*. Larry E. Matthews updates Barr's descriptions of specific caves to reflect more recent discoveries in his *Descriptions of Tennessee Caves* (Nashville: State of Tennessee, Division of Geology, 1971). However, no cave described in any of these works exhibits all the characteristics of either of Lester's cave dwellings: neither the large central room with an opening to the sky, the red clay floor, the dripping stalactites, the narrow corridors leading to other rooms, the columns and basins, the underground stream, the tunnel and chimney, the higher room with ledges for his collection, the "ancient ossuary," the bottomless drop, the small cell-like room with a tiny opening to the surface of his primary cave, where he hides his corpses and where he later eludes his captors only to lose himself in unknown sections of the cave system; nor the entrance through a sinkhole and down a corridor to a domed room with "myriad fissures" to the upper world of his second cave dwelling, where he takes refuge during the flood (107, 133–35, 157–58, 188). While it seems clear that McCarthy read Barr's *Caves of Tennessee* for his work on *Child of God* (and *Suttree*), drawing on its catalogue of various cave features, and that he may also have been influenced by the discovery of Forbidden Caverns east of Sevierville in 1964, Lester's caves are finally places of McCarthy's imagination.

The cave system that Lester inhabits—more extensive and labyrinthine than any described by Barr or Matthews—is a spiritual underworld corresponding to Lester's lost, blind, and constricted state of soul. Its stalactites are "dripping limestone teeth" and its wet walls "with their softlooking convolutions, slavered over as they were with wet and bloodred mud, had an organic look to them, like the innards of some great beast" (133, 135). Confined in his monstrous cave, Lester is like Jonah in the belly of Leviathan, but unable without the agency of "some brute midwife" to deliver himself from that physical and spiritual captivity (189). Indeed Lester's three-day imprisonment in the cave, ending with a grotesque earthly resurrection, is an ironic reflection of Christ's prophecy that "as Jonah was three days and three nights in the belly of the whale, so will the Son of man be three days and three nights in the heart of the earth" (Matthew 12:40). As such, it ambiguously suggests Lester's potential, as a son of God like the Jews and the Ninevites, for receiving a merciful resurrection of the spirit, but the whale imagery also suggests Lester's spiritual oblivion as a child of the demiurge imprisoned in the Leviathan of cosmos. Further, it resonates with Father Mapples's sermon on Jonah in *Moby-Dick*, where he stresses Jonah's guilty flight from God, which makes him an outcast to all mankind. "So disordered, self-condemning is his look, that had there been policemen in those days, Jonah, on the mere suspicion of something wrong, had been arrested ere he touched a deck. How plainly he's a fugitive!" says Mapples, and one thinks not only of the guilt-driven Culla Holme in *Outer Dark* and the abashed James Blevins of north Georgia but also of Lester's persecution by others of his community (*Moby-Dick* 46). In the sermon Jonah, shown to his stateroom in the ship, finds it a low-ceilinged cell or tomb, like Lester's tiny cave-prison, and Mapples remarks, "Then, in that contracted hole, sunk, too, beneath the ship's water line, Jonah feels the heralding presentiment of that stifling hour, when the whale shall hold him in the smallest of his bowel's wards" (47). For the puritan Mapples, the lesson to be drawn from Jonah's story is that of true repentance, which relies on God for deliverance. Jonah proves worthy because he "does not weep and wail for direct deliverance. He feels that his dreadful punishment is just. He leaves all his deliverance to God" (49). But while picturing his own death and wishing for a "brute midwife" to deliver him, Lester offers neither prayer nor repentance, focused as he is on the literal and material problems of his existence; instead he relies on persistent digging to free himself from his stony cell yet remains imprisoned in his pathology (189). For some gnostics, Mead writes, "The Jonah-myth was a type of the initiate, who, after being three days and three nights in the 'belly of Sheol' or Hades, preached to those in Nineveh, the Jerusalem Below, that is to say, this world" (447). But Lester, released and returned to Sevierville, though an initiate to the prison-house of materialism, brings no enlightening message to his neighbors similarly trapped in cosmos. Lester's caves resonate strongly with both gnostic and Platonic mythologies as emblems of spiritual blindness. For both, earthly life itself is figured as the cave.

Platonic Intimations: *The Descent into Materialism*

Despite its elements of realism, *Child of God* is finally neither a tale of local color nor a detective story, though there are qualities of each in its makeup. Much of the novel's power comes from McCarthy's adapting these realistic elements to exploit their mythical or allegorical import. As in many of his works, McCarthy's strategy in *Child of God* is to employ mythic images and patterns to transcend the material body of the referential world, inviting allegorical readings and guiding the reader to ponder metaphysical issues. In *Child of God*, metaphysical concerns extend the gnostic implications of *Outer Dark* and cluster more consistently around analogues to Platonic myth than around the orthodox Christian mythology consonant with either Lester's culture or McCarthy's Roman Catholic heritage.

The influence of Plato on McCarthy's thought was documented biographically by Garry Wallace in 1992. With his companion Betty Carey, Wallace traveled to El Paso in 1989 to meet with her friend Cormac McCarthy for advice about a book she hoped to write. There they also met book dealer and professor of philosophy Irving Brown, who spoke with McCarthy regularly and who told Wallace that "in his opinion McCarthy had over-read Plato" (135). McCarthy clearly engages Platonic philosophy in many of his works from *Outer Dark* (1968) on, beginning with Culla Holme's dream of being told by a prophet that he might be among the souls who will be "cured" (5). In Plato's *Gorgias* myth, the myth of the day of judgment, only those souls who after death are judged capable of cure are subject to purification in "the prison-house of just retribution, which men call Tartarus" and subsequent incarnation as humans (Stewart 134). After *The Orchard Keeper*, McCarthy's novels in which his seeking or drifting protagonists are depicted in terms of quests or anti-quests explore with varying degrees of realistic grounding his great underlying concern with mankind's struggle toward (or blundering away from) the spiritual insight or gnosis of which they are capable (although he rarely invokes the theological concept of spirit directly). With some crucial differences, this is also the burden of Plato's myths relating to the soul's progress (or lack thereof) back toward the Truth or the Light to which it was exposed at its creation, a process involving sequential incarnations of the soul, intervening purifications in the cave of Tartarus, the soul's choice of the circumstances of its next life in accord with the wisdom achieved in Tartarus, its subjection to forgetfulness through imbibing the waters of Lethe, and then its incarnation in "the cave of this world"—"a cave of forgetfulness" or oblivion, a metaphor later adapted by some gnostics in their conception that the world is a labyrinthine prison and earth its "innermost dungeon" (Jonas, *Gnostic Religion* 43). Elements of Platonic philosophy were blended with eastern religious philosophies in the gnostic synthesis (Jonas, *Gnostic Religion* 24).[11] Common to both, among other ideas, is the belief in a transcendental truth and the sense that materialism threatens to obscure such light or gnosis.

In his 1904 translation and commentary, *The Myths of Plato*, revised and reissued in 1960, just as McCarthy was beginning to write his Tennessee novels, J. A. Stewart shows that while the individual myths embedded in Plato's dialogues are shaped to advance specific arguments, together they form a rather cohesive whole illustrating Plato's cosmology, ontology, and epistemology. Further, Plato's myths profoundly inform Dante's cosmology and his emphasis on the soul's progress in *The Divine Comedy*. Stewart writes that the "theological doctrine of Purgatory, to which Dante gives such noble imaginative expression, is alien to the Hebrew spirit, and came to the Church mainly from the Platonic doctrine of purification" (145). McCarthy understands this resonance between Plato and Dante and employs it in his fiction; that phenomenon, together with his uses of various Platonic and neo-Platonic myths discussed by Stewart, suggests that Stewart's study may be a source of McCarthy's knowledge of Plato.

While McCarthy's philosophy is no clone of Plato's, as his concurrent affinities with gnosticism and existentialism make clear, he shares the emphasis of all three philosophies on the importance of the search for value and meaning, and in several works (most notably *Outer Dark*, *Child of God*, *Suttree*, *Blood Meridian*, and *The Sunset Limited*, but also to some degree in the Border Trilogy) he evokes the Platonic or gnostic conception of earthly life as a purgatorial experience or a netherworld. Rarely, however, does McCarthy directly invoke optimistic notions of an afterlife, a cycle of reincarnation, or a transmundane reunification with the divine. When John Grady dreams of the murdered Jimmy Blevins, the boy tells him that being dead is "like nothing at all" (*APH* 225). In *The Sunset Limited*, the traditional Christian idea of heaven is raised, and Black, the man of faith, seems to embrace it, but White, the man of intellect, emphatically rejects it as distasteful—as does Suttree. Only in *The Road* is the idea that one may accompany one's loved ones into an afterlife given a positive valuation by a major character and without narrative undercutting— but also without narrative endorsement. McCarthy's novels typically remain grounded in the life one experiences in this world, even while he explores humankind's sense of being not wholly of this world. He honors the naturalistic world and the world of human culture for good or ill far more than the gnostics, who repudiated cosmos entirely, and more than Plato, who despite his Hellenistic cosmos piety, tends to dismiss the material world as illusion at worst or to value selected elements of it as symbols of the Ideal world at best. Indeed, in their love for the world, specifically the natural world, some of McCarthy's sympathetic characters have more in common with the transcendentalist Thoreau or the existentialist Camus than with the gnostics or even

Plato. Nevertheless, in *Child of God* particularly, McCarthy employs elements of Platonic myth to define the metaphysical dimensions of Lester Ballard's trials and crimes, exploring this aspect of his experience more fully than the psychological dimension. Though we cannot equate McCarthy's philosophy with Plato's any more than we can label him a gnostic, it is fruitful to accept McCarthy's implicit invitation to contemplate Lester Ballard through Plato's myths and symbols, and through their reuse or revaluation in gnostic mythology.

Failure of Vision and the Love of Material Bodies

As Lester Ballard's scuttling in darkness through caves suggests, McCarthy's analogies to Plato's myths largely cluster around problems of vision, and the Cave Parable is most obviously invoked. When Lester is confined in the hospital, his physical position echoes that of Plato's cave dwellers, prevented by the circumstances of their existence from direct perception of the light: "A room scarce wider than the bed. There was a small window behind him but he could not see out without craning his neck and it pained him to do so" (175). Moreover, throughout much of the novel, Lester literally dwells and is imprisoned in caves. The narrator evokes images of fire casting a "shadowshow" against cave walls or comparable backdrops (159, 183). He associates Lester's cave with Tartarus through allusions to Hades or to "stygian mist" and through Lester's impression that its stream "ran down through the cavern to empty it may be in unknown seas at the center of the earth" (141, 158, 170). But even before Lester's descent into the caves, the voyeurism and carnality that characterize his approaches to women and lead to overt necrophilia evoke the Platonic idea that if the visual sense is rightly an avenue to Truth and apperception of Ideals, evil results from humanity's blindness and materialism. As we have seen, gnosticism shares the concern with human blindness and oblivion, but it parts ways with Platonism and orthodox Christianity in absolving humankind of the responsibility for its "evil" nature, which results from the mingling of spirit (light) in the dark oblivion of matter. Such alternate implications are not absent in *Child of God*, as in the narrator's description of Lester as a "drowsing captive [who] looked so inculpate in the fastness of his hollow stone you might have said he was half right who thought himself so grievous a case against the gods" (189).

In the "Discourse of Diotima" from the *Symposium*, Plato tells the myth of Eros, describing progressive initiation into the love of beauty. This progress culminates when the lover's object is no longer transient material bodies but the ideal of eternal Beauty. The true lover—or philosopher—is a seeker or a lover of wisdom rather than one who already possesses it, and his search begins with the love of one, then two, then all beautiful earthly bodies, growing to the love of beautiful customs, then doctrines, and finally eternal Beauty or True

Virtue (Stewart 370–77). The narrator Diotima says that as Love is the desire to possess Good always, Love aims at immortality. But Lester's necrophilia is a dreadfully perverted version of aiming at immortality in love. Bell writes that it derives from his "unprotected exposure to raw time and his conditioned belief that what is living—his mother, his father, and his home—is what is lost" (*Achievement* 64). Similarly Grammer notes that Lester's hobby of collecting corpses constitutes a "mad protest against history itself, against the passing of time." But it is difficult to agree with Grammer's implication that Lester actually achieves with his corpses his desired end: "a timeless order, immunity to change" (40). There is no Platonic transcendence here. Lester's bodies, pursued and treasured, are the very image of mortality. No less than the living are they subject to fire and flood. And, as Ciuba notes, "*Child of God* never overlooks the sheer onslaught made upon the body by death; rather, it . . . records the corpse's wooden rigor, downward drag, and final putrefaction" (96). Though Lester pursues the illusion of immortality, he can ignore but not evade time's decay. The blatant failure in necrophilic love of Lester Ballard, this novel's everyman, to transcend the corruptible material body constitutes an extreme and obvious emblem of his failure of vision and wisdom, of his oblivion, and this suggests that McCarthy employs the figure of the necrophile almost playfully, as a grotesque parody of Plato's Diotima myth in this novel in which no one in Lester's materialistic culture achieves the ideal progress she describes.

Lester's deep involvement in love of matter seems a gnostic warning against love of the world, in which sexual love itself is represented as a kind of necrophilia. Jonas writes that for the gnostic, the principle of *eros* was not one of "striving for immortality," as it was for Plato; rather, through love of all things of this world, the spirit "is turned away from its true goal and kept under the spell of its alien abode" (73). The *Corpus Hermeticum* cautions that "he who has cherished the body issued from the error of love, he remains in the darkness erring, suffering in his senses the dispensations of death" (quoted in Jonas 73). Thus the novel's indictment of this grasping and materialistic culture is quite insistent, and it extends the meditation on materialism from the gnostic perspective found in *Outer Dark* by giving it even more prominence in the allegory of necrophilia and voyeurism.

Lester is emblematic of the society from which he arises. His collection of corpses has its parallels in the dumpkeeper's "levees of junk and garbage" presided over by the upturned remains of two dead cars "like wrecked sentinels," and in the rubble tip of the nearby quarry where he searches for cast-off goods (26, 38–39). While far from middle-class America, the novel's Sevier (significantly pronounced "Severe") County is a mountain valley of ashes set within the beauty and terror of the natural world—a valley whose inhabitants hoard material remains or dead and deadening material; Lester's sifting the ashes of his burned cabin for the remains of his first beloved (like Legwater's sifting the ashes of Kenneth Rattner) reflects the materialistic orientation of his culture.[12] The ruthless opportunism of Lester's near-neighbors, who legally cheat him of material goods in the auction of his farm or in the barter of watches, is implicated in the formation of Lester's necrophilia (129–32).[13] From this society in which the weak are dispossessed, Lester learns to take possession of others forcibly. Moreover, his feat at the shooting gallery parodies the worker's endeavor in a capitalist society: he converts his time and skill into prizes or rewards until he becomes burdened down by these goods, the giant stuffed tiger and bears with which he peoples his cabin (67). Lester's shooting and hoarding his human victims is an extension of the same impulse: he expends his talents and efforts in amassing material goods—much like ourselves, perhaps.[14] The quarry and the dump with their dead machinery are merely less covert versions of Lester's boneyard. The flood scene in which the hardware storekeeper salvages his goods immediately follows and pointedly parallels that of Lester's carrying his own "chattel" to higher ground (162–63, 154–58). It is apt that when Lester meditates his assault on Greer, he spies on his bespectacled alter ego as he sits (in the most recognizably middle-class image of the novel) in Lester's repossessed farmhouse, engaged in the purchase of seeds, living goods, from a catalogue (109). Philip L. Simpson says of the serial killer Quentin in Joyce Carol Oates's *Zombie* that his "'asocial' point of view is constructed in part from specific ideological positions. One of those positions is the privileged status of patriarchal science and consumer culture in the United States, which . . . fails to realize or acknowledge its manipulation or destruction of others"; so too with Lester (170). From this perspective, Lester's necrophilia functions as a metaphor not only for the materialism Plato and the gnostics rejected but also specifically for American consumerism, which McCarthy critiques through the dual lenses of these ancient philosophies.[15]

Necrophilia shocks because of the practitioner's failure to see that his beloved is mere material. Indeed the necrophile loves the corpse precisely because she is an illusion. Masters and Lea point out that although the necrophile is usually acutely uncomfortable in encounters with a living being whose will may oppose his own, his necrophilia depends upon the human likeness of the corpse and its "aura of consciousness" (112). That is, most necrophiles do not love or find arousing death itself or all dead creatures but only the human dead. This is because it is human connection, human "warmth," they desire: "It is at bottom the body as a person, not the body as mere felicitously arranged and compounded substance, or even as decaying matter, which [the necrophile] requires for his gratification; . . . he insists upon a subject that has become an object, but in some sense remains a subject also" (112–13). Lester's first "lover," with whom we see him most actively engaged, is the unresisting receptacle of all his thwarted love and desire: "He poured into that waxen ear everything he'd ever thought of saying to a woman. Who could say she did not hear him?" (88–89). Later he dresses her in lingerie, poses her seductively before the fire so that he can go outside his cabin to gaze at her through the window to become aroused (the most pathetic of the many scenes of Lester's window-gazing) and tells her without contradiction that she wants sex with him (103). When the temperature falls and she becomes a "frozen bitch" or when his enjoyment of a later victim is delayed until he finds her "cold and wooden with death" and he "howled curses until he was choking," the extremity of his rage derives only in part from his free-floating anger at the will of all who have previously abandoned or rejected him (102, 152). It is prompted at least as much by his frustration at the intrusion of cold reality on his comforting illusion. Lester's is a willed blindness, willfully maintained.

Thus as a pursuit of illusion, Lester's very literal progress from the love of one *body* to many subverts and perverts the progress Diotima outlines and constitutes a descent into materialism rather than the transcendence she describes. As Jarrett observes, "His error is in perceiving not merely the female but the whole world as objective spectacle, with himself its collector" (53). His blindness is progressive. His initial approach to the woman abandoned by the roadside (another double of Lester himself) is not devoid of empathy or recognition of her humanity: "Ain't you cold?" he asks her (42). (The men who threaten to lynch Lester will ask him the same question and similarly demonstrate the transience of their charity.) However, foreshadowing his necrophilia, Lester's compassion is more easily prompted when he thinks this woman is dead, or at least sleeping. Nell Sullivan rightly observes that "as long as the woman is sleeping and de-animated, she receives the approbative term *lady*, but waking, she becomes 'a goddamned [old] whore'" (74; *CoG* 41, 52; emphasis Sullivan's). Lester may see his faithless mother in her, and she too seems drunkenly to confuse him with someone else when she says, "I knowed you'd do me thisaway" (42). While Lester usually fumbles awkwardly around desirable women, once this "lady" assaults him with a rock he exhibits no fear of verbally or physically confronting her. Her behaviors certainly reinforce the lesson that dead women are quieter, safer, less likely to put the law on him: in all ways preferable to the living. But before she assaults him, it does not occur to him to shoot her, even though he carries his rifle. (Nevertheless, his spiteful ripping away her gown as a trophy foreshadows the more extreme behavior soon to come.) Even after his enraging wrongful arrest for assaulting this woman, he is attracted to the innocence of a young girl who watches fireworks with wonder and who, for the narrator, presents a vision of timeless loveliness. But here as later the narrative voice encompasses a vision that Lester does not fully achieve; something in his gaze frightens the girl, breaks the spell and provokes her narcissistic self-consciousness: "She saw the man with the bears watching her and she edged closer to the girl by her side and brushed her hair with two fingers quickly" (65). In later embracing the illusion offered by necrophilia, Lester commits himself to progressive blindness rather than progressive illumination, becoming the antithesis of both the Platonic philosopher and the gnostic seeker. By the middle of the novel, he squats over the ashes of his burned cabin, looking with "eyes dark and huge and vacant" for remains of his first necrophilic love (107). Lester's necrophilia, manifesting a self-willed blindness to the decay and materiality of the flesh, both echoes and mocks or complicates the Platonic idea that love (philosophy) aims at immortality and perhaps implies that in aiming at transcendence through an appreciation of natural beauty, Plato's system takes inadequate account of the stubborn materiality of the world and its occupants, who face first of all the problem of how to live in it.

Just as Lester's response to the beauty of women becomes perverted as he collects ever more decaying bodies, his response to the beauty of the natural world is numbed in all but a few scenes, and he fails to access what is for Plato its redemptive potential to evoke recollection of Eternal Beauty and hence of Justice, Knowledge, and Temperance—a concept Plato explores not only in the "Discourse of Diotima" but also in the *Phaedrus* myth. As a squatter in the ramshackle cabin of his kindly neighbor Waldrop in Waldens Creek, Lester's circumstances roughly parallel Thoreau's at Walden Pond. But Lester derives neither Thoreauvian nor Camusian sustenance from the natural world.[16] Even when the narrator presents the world as a radiant vision, Lester often is oblivious. In winter, approaching the nadir of his moral/spiritual descent, Lester begins to stalk Greer, who has bought the Ballard homestead. Walking to his old place, Lester sees this landscape: "It was almost noon and the sun was very bright on the snow and the snow shone with a myriad crystal incandescence. The shrouded road wound off before him almost lost among the trees and a stream ran beside the road, dark under bowers of ice, small glass-fanged caverns beneath tree roots where the water sucked unseen. In the frozen roadside weeds were coiled white ribbons of frost, you'd never figure how they came to be. Ballard ate one as he went" (128). McCarthy performs one of his marvels here, placing us simultaneously within Lester's perspective and outside of it (as indeed the novel as a whole accomplishes). The crystalline images of winter light and snow and ice are dazzling, but Lester's perception is captured in the metaphors of the lost and shrouded road, the threatening glass-fanged caverns (recalling the "dripping limestone teeth" of his cave), and the sucking, invisible water—images that derive more from gnostic world-dread than from Platonic cosmos piety. Though in one sense Lester sees the ribbons of frost, the wonder derives from the narrator alone. To Lester, the ice ribbons are to be consumed materially, and his eating one parallels his sexual consumption of the material

bodies of his "lovers."[17] Similarly Lester fails to understand the behavior of a
pair of hawks he sees joined in air (they couple on the wing and they are said
to mate for life) because he "did not know how hawks mated but he knew that
all things fought" (169). Earlier he pauses to watch as hounds harry a boar and
it fights back viciously: "Ballard watched this ballet tilt and swirl and churn
mud up through the snow and watched the lovely blood welter there in its
holograph of battle, spray burst from a ruptured lung, the dark heart's blood,
pinwheel and pirouette, until shots rang and all was done" (69). Lester recognizes beauty only in sexually objectified women or in the whirling, chaotic violence of the gnostic vision of cosmos, the mingling of purity (snow) in matter
(mud and blood). Bell argues that Lester is "oblivious to beauty" and that "he
is not an observer. He is innocent of, and uninterested in, the nature of the
materials of the world and of how processes and procedures produce specific
results" (*Achievement* 64). One crucial exception, of course, is Lester's interest
in the material of and fashion in which his girlfriends' bodies are made. And he
is fascinated by the feral "ballet" staged by the hounds and the boar they pursue and may even watch it with a perverted aesthetic appreciation, as is suggested by his pausing to observe, in his natural amphitheater, the "lovely blood"
weltering in the snow. On the other hand, the recognition of the scene's specifically balletic quality is quite likely the narrator's alone, another aesthetic image
that marks the narrator's perception as qualitatively different from those of Lester or his neighbors. Lester's typical lack of susceptibility to the world's beauty
marks him as a man devoid of Platonic vision, but neither does he possess any
compensating gnostic awareness of natural beauty as a snare for the spirit.

Voyeurism, Narcissism, and the Opportunity for Self-Recognition

Almost as prevalent as images of Lester's voyeurism, particularly his surveil-
lance of his victims through the windows of cars or houses, are instances of his
seeing his own reflection in water, windows, or other people. The primary import of these images of Lester as Narcissus derives neither from the popular
interpretation of the Narcissus myth as a warning against self-love nor especially from the psychological interpretation of it as a warning against dependence on others for one's self-image—although this phenomenon is at work in
McCarthy's subtle delineation of Ballard's psychology. (Abandoned in one way
or another by both parents, he has not had the loving parental gaze mirroring
back his own face, thus to establish a strong sense of his own worth and being;
later he lives up to and exceeds the negative expectations of the people around
him, which are given voice most explicitly by the aptly named Sheriff Fate
Turner, whose prediction that "murder is next on the list" of his mean acts
Lester soon fulfills; see 56.) Rather, the Narcissus references in *Child of God* go
beyond Hitchcock's use of mirror imagery to suggest the Platonic idea of the

role of vision in achieving wisdom, particularly as presented in Plotinus' allegorical, neo-Platonic interpretation of the Narcissus myth, which Stewart cites: "Seeing . . . those beauties which appear in bodies, he must not run after them, but knowing them to be images and vestiges and shadows, he must flee to that of which they are the images. And if any one should pursue them, wishing to take them as real, they would be like a fair image borne on water, and when he desires to seize it . . . plunging to the bottom of the stream, he disappears. In the same way, he who grasps beautiful bodies and will not let them go, is submerged not only in body but in soul, within the dark depth hateful to his own mind, where, remaining blind in Hades, he dwells among shadows, there as here" (Stewart 231–32). Lester's voyeurism and necrophilia are repetitions of Narcissus' fateful error—a mistaken application of vision and erotic attraction resulting in his drowning in materialism. The gnostic "Poimandres" similarly sees the things of the world as a distracting mirror of the divine, attracting humankind's love away from its proper object (Jonas, *Gnostic Religion* 161). The self-destructiveness of Lester's path, implied in the Narcissus references, is given overt expression when he attempts to ford the flooded creek with his possessions: "Anyone watching him could have seen he would not turn back if the creek swallowed him under" (155).[18] The scene links the Platonic implications of the Narcissus myth with the gnostic implications of turbid water, suggesting that Lester's self-destructive oblivion is his commitment to matter and to cosmos in its devouring aspects. Holloway makes the related points that Lester's necrophilia becomes finally a pursuit of his own inertia and destruction, and that his descent into the bowels of the earth represents "the existential bad faith of his desire to merge with the very soil of the land" (131–32, 150–51). Lester's final pneumonia, his sickness of spirit, or pneuma, is itself a death-by-drowning, implying that his trading the prison of the Platonic or gnostic cave for the existentialist prison of the State is no true deliverance for this persistently blind and troubled soul.

Plotinus explicitly relates the Narcissus myth to Plato's myths of the soul's drinking forgetfulness from Lethe before incarnation. Stewart summarizes in language that invokes gnostic symbols as well as Platonic ones: "Souls . . . descending, at their appointed times, come to the water which is the Mirror of Dionysus [which Plotinus identifies with Lethe], and enamoured of their own images reflected therein—that is, of their mortal bodies—plunge into the water. This water is the water of oblivion, and they that drink of it go down into the cave of this world" (232). All souls drink of the waters of oblivion, but the wisest drink the least. Plotinus's interpretation thus relates the Narcissus myth to Plato's explanation of the individual's prenatal choosing of the circumstances of his life in accordance with the wisdom he has achieved. In light of these myths, the life of the cave and oblivious materialism is the apparently hapless and fated Lester's chosen world—an environment reflecting the character-defining choice he made before birth and symbolizing his lack of spiritual insight, as the cramped and mean-spirited lives of his self-righteous neighbors symbolize theirs. At the same time, if we view his oblivion through the gnostic lens, spiritual blindness is again suggested, but with less personal responsibility since such oblivion is the ontological given of the human spirit thrown into and mired in cosmos as a child of the artificer god.

Stewart cites also Ficino's neo-Platonist interpretation of Narcissus as "a thoughtless and untried man, [who] does not see his own face. He turns his regard by no means to his proper substance and worth, but pursues his reflection in water and tries to embrace it. That is to say, he admires beauty in a perishable body, like moving water, which is the shadow of his own rational soul" (233). Indeed Lester's Narcissus-like moments are all near misses, lost opportunities to see his own face truly—as when his voyeurism is turned back on him and he is mirrored and confronted by the dead girl he sees through the car window—"Out of the disarray of clothes and the contorted limbs another's eyes watched sightlessly from a bland white face"—or by the retarded boy who watches him set his house afire—"the last thing he saw through the smoke was the idiot child. It sat watching him, berryeyed filthy and frightless among the painted flames" (86, 120).

The clearest reference to the myth of Narcissus in *Child of God*, occurring just before Lester's vision of the ice fangs and sucking water, implies that he approaches vision or understanding yet shies away from it. Lester comes to a mountain spring: "Kneeling in the snow . . . Ballard leaned his face to the green water and drank and studied his dishing visage in the pool. He halfway put his hand to the water as if he would touch the face that watched there but then he rose and wiped his mouth and went on" (127). The scene ambiguously suggests both his near-recognition of his "proper substance and worth" and his pursuit of shadows or illusions. Similarly, late in the novel, in another of the scenes of reversed voyeurism which always offer the potential for recognition, Ballard sees a boy watching him from the window of a church bus: "He was trying to fix in his mind where he'd seen the boy when it came to him that the boy looked like himself. This gave him the fidgets and though he tried to shake the image of the face in the glass it would not go" (191). This is as close to epiphany as Ballard comes, yet he refuses it.[19] Nonetheless, such scenes play off of the Platonic idea that the opportunity for insight always lies before a man because, even though he has imbibed the waters of forgetfulness at his birth, knowledge of Truth inheres from his creation. And with their emphasis on the alien spiritual component imprisoned within body and psyche, this of course was an idea the gnostics shared, but with more pessimistic emphasis on the obstacles to insight.

A less philosophically loaded image that contributes to the Narcissus pattern occurs when Lester visits the dumpkeeper's house in hopes of seeing his favorite of Reubel's daughters, perhaps intending her for his second object of necrophilia: "Behind the house stood the remains of several cars and from the rear glass of one of them a turkey watched him" (110). In its mirroring of the novel's other images of reversed voyeurism, and especially in its foreshadowing of the little boy who seems to watch Lester from the window of the church bus, this image is parodic, yet it hints of an opportunity for Lester to recognize his material, animal impulses, and it reinforces the psychological pattern of self-consciousness that characterizes Lester as much as it does Norman Bates and Marion Crane—his obsession not only with watching but with being watched. Such self-consciousness also punctuates his furtive encounter with the first dead couple: in Lester's perception, the dead man winks at him complicitly ("he lay staring up with one eye open and one half shut") and watches what he does to the dead girl; even the girl's breasts appear to be "peeking" at him "from her open blouse" (88). He does not close the eyes of the man whose place he has taken, but he does close the girl's—perhaps not only to further the illusion that she is alive and sleeping but also to avoid her gaze (87–88).

The function of such images is modified again in the case of the man with the shotgun who squats in the truckbed watching Lester through the rear window of the truck while his companions prepare to lynch the small necrophile (181). The scene echoes those of Lester himself peering at his potential victims through car windows, and significantly, here the Narcissus figure is not Lester but the man, a representative of the community, who fails to see his own face in that of Ballard.[20] In terms of the Platonic myths, the man with the shotgun fails to recognize that his own and all men's positions in the world are similar to Lester's: condemned to imperfect wisdom by the conditions of existence and offered sequential chances for correction through seeking insight. As in *Outer Dark*, the judgmental community consistently tries to explain Lester's acts in such a way as to prove his constitutional difference from them. The consensus is that Lester "never was right": that his necrophilia places him outside the pale (21). They neither recognize Lester's potential for a different kind of life nor acknowledge their essential kinship with him. (As Lang observes, on the other hand, the novel as whole is designed to create an uneasy balance in the reader between shock at Lester's crimes and "a simultaneous awareness of Ballard's potential for other roles, other identities"; 109). Missing among Lester's peers is the gnostic's compassion for humankind's tragic position within the world, alienated from God and from his or her own spirit. The juxtaposition of the dissection of Lester's body with the exhuming and bagging of his corpses as "Property of the State of Tennessee" (196) at novel's end suggests a parallel between Lester's descent into the materialism of necrophilia, a kind of inquiry into the human body (he inspects one victim's "body carefully, as if he would see how she were made"; 91–92), and that of the socially and legally approved forensic, medical, and undertaker's professions. But this is a commonality to which his community is blind.

McCarthy's deft manipulation of narrative stance in *Child of God* positions the reader to recognize Lester as a being much like him or herself—making the novel itself a Narcissan mirror for the reader. While McCarthy's novel is not typical of the American serial killer fiction and films that became prominent in the decades after *Psycho*, Philip Simpson's observation that such works can fruitfully be read as cultural criticism holds true for *Child of God* as well. The serial killer is "never as Other as might be supposed at first glance," Simpson writes. Such fiction "compels thoughtful observers to acknowledge their own murderous impulses" and invites us to recognize that "serial killers literalize spiritual and nationalistic ideals that most of their fellow Americans share" (24). Grammer points out that "An armed man [such as Lester Ballard], prepared to defend the country and his own liberty and property, was for our ancestors the ideal republican citizen, the foundation of stable order" (39). And Holloway suggests that the commodification of the female body and of his own sexual desire is one of the American traits Lester literalizes (128). Other American characteristics and values we might recognize in Lester include his improvisation (albeit clumsy), his resilience as the underdog, his rage to control the natural world. Or, as Bell eloquently observes, "McCarthy has conceived pathetic Lester as a berserk version of fundamental aspects of ourselves—of our fear of time, our programmed infatuation with death, our loneliness, our threatening appetites, our narcissistic isolation from the world and the reality of other people" (*Achievement* 55).

Celestial Intimations and the Oracles of Dreams

In the intervals between his egregious offenses, Ballard's narrative is punctuated with opportunities for insight—glimmerings and intimations. His sightings of stars ambiguously invoke not only the hostile stars associated with gnosticism's cosmic rulers but also, dialogically, the creation myth in Plato's *Timaeus*, which tells that in making human souls, God divided a mixture of the elements into as many souls as there are stars, "and to each star he assigned a Soul, and caused each Soul to go up into her star as into a chariot, and showed unto her the nature of the All, and declared the laws thereof which are fixed and shall not be moved" (Stewart 261). In Plato this is the original source of the soul's wisdom forgotten at birth. The gnostics would later reinscribe the world-artificer of *Timaeus* as the demiurge bent on obscuring the spirit's understanding (Jonas, *Gnostic Religion* 43–44), but in Plato, God gave humans vision "to the end that, having observed the Circuits of Intelligence in the Heaven, we might use them for the revolutions of Thought in ourselves, which are kin, albeit perturbed, unto those unperturbed celestial courses; and having throughly [*sic*] learnt and become partakers in the truth of the reasonings which are according to nature, might, by means of our imitation of the Circuits of God which are without error altogether, compose into order the circuits in ourselves which have erred" (Stewart 266). Thus Plato stresses that the natural order man perceives in the movement of heavenly bodies should both remind him of his inherent understanding of the Truth and inspire him to imitate that order in his life. But when Lester looks at the stars, his vision is more consonant with the gnostic revaluation of Plato's cosmos piety, in which the stars are "the personified exponents of the rigid and hostile law of the universe. . . . The starry sky—to the Greeks since Pythagoras the purest embodiment of reason in the sensible universe, and the guarantor of its harmony—now stared man in the face with the fixed glare of alien power and necessity" (Jonas, "Epilogue" 328). Lester sees the stars as voyeurs like himself, watching him with "lidless" fixity, "remote" and alien even when they prompt questioning, as when he witnesses the awakening of bats in a "false spring" and sees them "ascend . . . like souls rising from hades" to depart through a hole in the roof of his cave: "When they were gone he watched the hordes of cold stars sprawled across the smokehole and wondered what stuff they were made of, or himself" (133, 141).

Although he no more possesses gnosis of a hostile cosmos alien to the human spirit and to the Good God than he has imbibed Platonic insight, Lester cannot perceive a positive order in the world, inferring only the principle that "all things fought,", a principle that both McCarthy and Plato acknowledge, but that both would view as a half-truth or worse (169). (One thinks of the profound exemplars of love countering the hostility of the world in *Outer Dark*'s Rinthy, in the many characters who extend charity to Billy in the Border Trilogy, in Black—Everyman as Jesus—in *The Sunset Limited*, and even more affirmatively in the father and son of *The Road*.) Like many of McCarthy's protagonists who perceive no transcendental order either in cosmos or in a transmundane world, Lester wishes to arrogate to himself the prerogative of the creator: "Coming up the mountain through the blue winter twilight . . . he wondered at such upheaval. Disorder in the woods, trees down, new paths needed. Given charge Ballard would have made things more orderly in the woods and in men's souls" (136). Lester perceives a need for more order—less wildness—in both nature and psyche. But from a gnostic perspective, as Jonas emphasizes, "Far from being chaos, the creation of the demiurge, unenlightened as it is, is still a system of law . . . [:] *heimarmene*, oppressive cosmic fate" ("Epilogue" 328). Because Lester is himself composed of nature and psyche, in which his enveloped pneuma sleeps in oblivion, his will to impose order on cosmos partakes of archontic imposition. "It is his own chaotic life," as Jarrett writes, "that Ballard wills to order through a violence projected on others" (41). Alternatively and dialogically, from a Platonic perspective Lester's very longing for order may derive from the immortal part of his soul. His inability to perceive an acceptable order in cosmos (for Plato the transcendental order, for McCarthy the order that results from the synthesis of the life of the body in a real world and the life of the inner spirit—from lucid perception of one's place within "the world itself") marks the ascendance of the mortal or appetitive part of his soul.[21] This "appetitive" soul, Plato says in *Timaeus*, "hath in itself passions terrible, of necessity inherent—first, Pleasure, evil's best bait, then Pains that banish good things, also Confidence and Fear, two heedless counsellors, and Wrath hard to entreat, and Hope easily led astray. These did they [the lesser gods to whom God delegated the responsibility to mould and guide the mortal part of man] mix with Sense that lacketh Reason, and Love that dareth all, and so builded the mortal kind of Soul" (Stewart, 268).

This passage—anticipating the gnostic conception of the world in human nature—virtually catalogues the passions wracking Lester, which are only occasionally calmed by his immortal soul or his suppressed spirit. After his day and night of desperate removal from his flooded cave to one on higher ground, during which he nearly drowns, loses many of his possessions, and soils all, Lester emerges exhausted from his new cave to survey a "dead and fabled waste. . . . He had not stopped cursing. Whatever voice spoke him was no demon but some old shed self that came yet from time to time in the name of sanity, a hand to gentle him back from the rim of his disastrous wrath" (158). Regarded in light of Plato, despite his manifest rage, this old shed self, kin to the "old foreboding" that has earlier stayed Lester's hand from senselessly killing a bluebird, may be the immortal soul, or the conscience-like daimon assigned to guide the soul through life (25). In designating the voice that speaks through Lester as not-demon, McCarthy perhaps alludes to another way in which both gnostics and orthodox Christians deconstructed a Platonic concept. Jonas writes that to comprehend the great difference between the late gnostic idea that "each man . . . is from birth possessed by his demon . . . and the Greek position, one need only recall the Greek doctrine of 'the guardian daimon with us from our birth,' and generally compare the depraved concept of 'demon' in Gnosticism and Christianity with the classical one, which denoted a being superior to man in the divine hierarchy. The gap is as great as that between the two conceptions of the cosmos, of which the concept of 'demon' is the direct function" (*Gnostic Religion* 282–83). Lester's gentling not-demon is thus more akin to the Platonic daimon or the gnostic inherent spirit, both conceptions emphasizing humanity's potential for spiritual insight.

McCarthy's passage also reflects the story in *Timaeus* that the gods positioned the liver close to the appetitive soul, which resides in the breast, so that mirror-like, it can reflect the intelligence of the immortal part into the appetitive soul and might fill it "at one time, with fear, . . . at another time might make it mild and gentle, and give unto it a space of calm at night, wherein it should receive the Oracles of Dreams, meet for that which is without Reason and Understanding" (Stewart 269). These calming Oracles of Dreams, to which the immortal soul makes the appetitive soul receptive, are what later lead to Lester's transient recognition of the beauty of the natural world even as he reconfirms the fatality of his course in his dream of riding a mule through sunlit woods: "Each leaf that brushed his face deepened his sadness and dread. Each leaf he passed he'd never pass again. They rode over his face like veils, already some yellow, their veins like slender bones where the sun shone through them. He had resolved himself to ride on for he could not turn back and the world that day was as lovely as any day that ever was and he was riding to his death" (170–71). For Lester this dream offers yet another ungrasped opportunity for insight; in the next scene, dressed in skirt and scalp and presenting an image utterly at odds with Plato's notion of the man guided by his immortal part, Lester attempts to murder Greer and to enforce, White Cap–like, his own archontic conception of order and justice.

The Heedless Blacksmith and the Origin of Evil

Plato's myths concerning the limited wisdom manifested in humanity's earthly incarnations often correspond with his etiological myths of the soul's creation and its nature, and thus they explain man's potential for both good and evil. In Tartarus all souls may ultimately be cured of their forgetfulness and foolishness through their punishment and their witnessing of the warnings of other foolish souls (*Gorgias* myth, Stewart 134). When the soul finally achieves this wisdom, it ascends to the Plain of Truth or the star of its origin, no longer subject to correction and reincarnation. In Plato's mythology, human failings are sometimes explained by the partial or intermittent agency of God, who created the immortal part of the soul and exposed it to Truth, but who left the body and the mortal soul (analogous to the gnostic psyche) to the design of the young gods, as in the *Timaeus* myth (Stewart 262) or who created the world and then withdrew for a period, during which time men forgot their maker and governed themselves less well, surviving only because of such gifts of the gods as seeds, herbs, fire, and the mechanical arts of Hephaestos (agriculture and technology), as in the *Politicus* myth (Stewart 189).

Defending the *Politicus* myth's naive treatment of the problem of evil, Stewart describes the comparable myth of the Birth of Iron in the Finnish epic, the *Kalewala*. In accordance with Finnish belief that to overcome a difficulty one recites its origins, the Birth of Iron myth is an elaboration of a charm-formula that must be told by the magician-hero if he is to cure a wound. As an etiological myth, the Birth of Iron tells of the origin of evil in iron, as does McCarthy's own blacksmith's creation story introduced in *Child of God* when Lester takes an axe to be sharpened. Though the events of the two stories are not identical, they have interesting affinities where they touch on the problem of evil in iron, or in human beings.

The Birth of Iron myth partly explains the origin of evil as a lapse on the part of the blacksmith. He intends to create iron for good purposes only, and the myth tells of his care at each stage in the process. At one point, Iron, who fears Fire, begs the Smith to withdraw him; but the Smith answers, "If I take thee now out of the Fire, thou mightest grow up to be evil, and all too danger-ous; thou mightest murder thy nearest-of-kin," and he leaves Iron in the Fire until he swears never to do harm. (*Child of God* playfully inverts this detail of the myth when Lester angrily throws his frozen-up rifle into the fire, "but fetched it out again . . . before it had suffered more than a scorched forestock"— saving it to do further harm; 159.) Because Iron needs to be hardened, the Smith next prepares a bath, asking the bee to add its honey. But the evil Wasp overhears the Smith, and substitutes her venom for the "noble" honey, a ruse undetected by the Smith: "Without heed he cast the metal therein, when he had drawn it out of the Fire. . . . Then came it to pass that Iron was made hurt-ful." Significantly, however, the old man who hears this tale narrated by the wounded hero concludes that Iron alone—not his well-intentioned though momentarily heedless creator—is responsible for the evil he does: that no one coerces him to do evil (Stewart 199–204).

In McCarthy's similar parable of the creation of iron, the blacksmith describes the principles of his craft as he dresses Lester's axe, using language that establishes the analogy between the blacksmith and the creator of human-ity. Like the events in the Birth of Iron myth, the lecture of McCarthy's black-smith suggests that evil may be introduced by the creator's heedlessness: "Never leave steel in the fire for longer than it takes to heat. Some people will poke around at somethin else and leave the tool they're heatin to perdition but the proper thing is to fetch her out the minute she shows the color of grace. . . . It's like a lot of things, said the smith. Do the least part of it wrong and ye'd just as well to do it all wrong" (72–74). This set piece would seem to suggest that the careless creator bears responsibility for the evil in man. (In gnostic myths the artificer is sometimes inept; often he is an active principle of oppression or evil.) However, the analogous relationship of McCarthy's blacksmith parable to the Birth of Iron story and its context within a novel that invokes analogues to Platonic as well as gnostic myth temper that view. In Plato human suffering is finally and most consistently attributed to the lack of wisdom with which the soul approaches Lethe, succumbing to thirst on its release from Tartarus, drinking too deeply of forgetfulness, and thus choosing the circumstances of its earthly life foolishly (in the most extreme cases missing the opportunity to choose in such a way as to avoid doing unredeemable evil) and subsequently conducting its life without wisdom. In the "Myth of Er" in *The Republic*, Plato emphasizes that no one is constrained to choose an evil life: "Even for him whose turn cometh last, if he hath chosen with understanding, there is prepared a Life, which, if only a man bear himself manfully, is tolerable, not wretched" (Stewart 153). Thus, from Plato's perspective, the fate that Lester bemoans, feeling himself "so grievous a case against the gods," results from the soul's own first choice and remains his responsibility (189). If one perceives the world as a gnostic netherworld, Plato might say, that grim ontological perception is itself an out-picturing of one's own oblivion. Stewart's comments on the "Myth of Er" resonate in various ways with much of McCarthy's work: "the Soul, choosing the circumstances, or Life, chooses, or makes itself responsible for, its own character, as afterwards modified, and necessarily modified, by the circumstances, or Life. . . . To be free is to be a continuously existing, self-affirming, environment-choosing personality, manifesting itself in actions which proceed, according to necessary law, from itself as placed once for all in the environment which it has chosen[, . . .] the environment which is the counterpart of its own character. . . . The momentary prenatal act of choice . . . is the pattern of like acts which have to be performed in a man's natural life. Great decisions have to be made in life, which, once made, are irrevocable, and dominate the man's whole career and conduct afterwards" (176–78).[22]

Lester curses his fate and considers himself grave evidence against the creator; the novel implicates his community of similarly blinded men and women and delineates the purgatorial world of Sevier County (and America) as one in which humans participate in mutual torture and persecution, much as in McCarthy's gnostic nightmares *Outer Dark* and *Blood Meridian*. But the allusions to both Platonism and gnosticism (and the relationships between them) suggest that if there is an answer, it lies in resisting the draw of materialism and seeking a more transcendent way of being in the world.

Through its evocations of Jonah's whale, the gnostic leviathan, Hades, and Plato's cave, with its implications of the limits of human vision and of humanity's bondage to matter, Lester's descent into the caves implies that his life as experienced is an outward manifestation of his inner reality and thus reconfigures questions of fate and responsibility. Lester himself dimly recognizes the cave as metaphor for his whole existence when he imagines that after his death in the cave, mice will nest in the "lobed caverns where his brains had been"—although, characteristically, he conceives the evacuation of his fleshly brains rather than any transcendence of his spirit (189). Regarded through the lens of Platonic myth, Lester's retreat to the caves of Sevier County stands as the most metaphysically explicit element in the pattern of like acts that define his life and make him the community's scourge and scapegoat. In the light of both gnostic and Platonic myth, Lester's early life prefigures his cave life, and indeed the earthly cave of oblivion is Lester's environment throughout; his entombment in the cave after he eludes his persecutors is a parable of his whole life (as well as those of his neighbors); and his release from the underground cavern is a "rebirth" into the cave of this world—just as Rinthy's exodus from her dark house delivers her into outer dark, or Culla's escape from the turbid river places him in the hands of the triune, both symbols of the dark cosmos. Jonas comments on the labyrinthine quality of the cosmos suggested in gnostics' referring to it as multiple realms: "In the worlds the soul loses its way and wanders about, and wherever it seeks an escape it only passes from one world into another that is no less world" (52). After long searching for a way out of the cavern, Lester sees a shaft of sunlight: "It occurred to him only now that he might have passed other apertures to the upper world in the nighttime and not known it" (188). But Lester remains unenlightened, and his delivery from the cave is no resurrection but merely a transmigration from Tartarus to earth, or from one cosmic netherworld to another. When he gives himself up to the hospital, that revered human institution for the study and cure of the material body, Lester's eyes remain "caved and smoking" (192).

Chapter Four

Stranger in the Garden of Industry

The Gardener's Son (1977)

McCarthy's earliest dramatic effort, *The Gardener's Son*, was written in 1975 and 1976, while McCarthy was still engaged with the composition of *Suttree*. The film, directed by Richard Pearce, was first aired on public television in January 1977, but a script was not published for almost twenty years. (The published version is based on an earlier draft than the shooting script housed at the University of South Carolina.) Although the core of the film's story was to be a revaluation of the extant historical materials relating to the Gregg and McEvoy families, *The Gardener's Son* demonstrates marked continuity with the philosophical orientation of McCarthy's other works of the 1960s and '70s, carrying forward the gnostic aura of *Outer Dark* and *Child of God* and introducing the related existentialist perspective of *Suttree*.[1] Indeed, like *Suttree*, the screenplay may be read as a gnostic/existentialist allegory, revealing McCarthy's full awareness that gnosticism informs and is revivified in the thought of Heidegger, Camus, and other existentialists, in which post–Industrial Revolution dread of the urbanized and mechanized collective functions as a modern analogue of the ancient gnostic dread of cosmos.

Building on the work of Hans Jonas and other scholars of gnosticism in her study of the gnostic perspective in modern European writers, Josephine Donovan shows that existentialism and ancient gnosticism both derived from parallel foundational experiences of "the sense of alienation, the quest for authenticity, and the absence of God" (60). "Each was in its time a rebellion on behalf of the authenticity of the self against abstraction, rationalism, objectification: the one is directed against that of the modern scientific-industrial *Weltanschauung;* the other against the rationalism of the classical cosmos. . . . Both movements tend to hypostatize the systems they reject into mythic Enemies" (57). Existentialists often reinscribe the archons of ancient gnostic systems as "cosmic bureaucrats," an antinomian tendency we have seen already in McCarthy's depictions of governmental and judicial agents in his first three novels (16). Both philosophies emphasize humankind's "thrownness" into a world to which they feel alien: "The Gnostic vision of alienation," as revived in modern existentialism, "sees the human being as a prototypical stranger thrown into a hostile universe, under the rule of oppressive bureaucrats who have allies in the nonspiritual [men and women] of this earth, and separated by an infinite abyss from the Ground of being" (18). Each system of thought urges that humanity "be re-rooted in a sacred ground" (7). Thus each seeks a gnosis which is "fundamentally a call to truth, to the existential truth of being," a "resacralization of human life" (6, 58). "Each seeks to liberate the self from the false encumbrances of the world's reality that it may develop into a higher stage of ontological plenitude" (70–71). But in the desacralized modern world, the search for such truth has been de-mythologized: "What the ancients viewed as cosmological happenings, the moderns see as immanent experiences. Thus, what the [ancient] Gnostic described as the flight of the soul toward its heavenly home, the modern identifies as the authenticating trajectory of the self in its process of realization" (xiii). For the existentialist, the "gnosis may be seen . . . as a mystical revelation that is immanent and which opens the subject in to an intense existential reality which makes the outer world seem insubstantial and unreal by comparison" (28). Such existentialist gnosis constitutes a recognition of the "authentic self" (analogous to the gnostic pneuma) and simultaneously makes the individual acutely aware of his or her "fundamental alienation from the material reality of this world" (30). Existentialists "share a Gnostic faith that there is such a thing as a potentially *true* self" and "posit the existence of a potentially authentic core of acosmic reality which can be obscured or negated or thwarted by the 'outer' forces of this world, especially the public world of *das Man*," Heidegger's concept of humankind in the collective, alienated from authentic being (69). Thus in the context of the death or absence of God, in a desacralized world, "The modern Gnostic response . . . , like the ancient, centers about the problem of evil, the problem of alienation, of 'loss of place' and the quest for an authentic place or identity" (50).

Donovan traces one path of influence from ancient gnostic thought through Heidegger to Sartre (61). Another link between gnosticism and existentialism lies in Albert Camus's dissertation, "Entre Plotin et Saint Augustin" (University of Algiers, 1936; published in *Essais*, 1962), with its chapter on gnosticism focusing on "the problem of evil, redemption, the theory of intermediate beings (archons)" and the conception of an alien and ineffable God (Donovan 291). The dissertation also includes a chapter on Plotinus, and Donovan concludes that Camus's own thought represents a tempering of the gnostic with the neo-Platonic Plotinian, especially in Camus's affirming response to the natural world, which like McCarthy's rejects the ancient gnostics' repudiation of nature. Camus's modern reprisal of gnostic ideas is especially relevant to two of McCarthy's works from the late 1970s, *The Gardener's Son* and *Suttree*. Critics have long noted Camusian elements in *Suttree*. Thus it is no surprise that in the screenplay's attempt to find what McCarthy termed "a certain nobility" in the "natural rebel," the historical Robert McEvoy condemned for murder ("Gardner's" [*sic*]), and in its reinscription of the "official" documents of the custodians of history, *The Gardener's Son* blends some of the gnostic ideas and imagery we have seen in *Outer Dark* and *Child of God* with the neo-gnostic/existentialist perspective of Camus, especially as it is developed in *L'Etranger* (*The Stranger*).

The Weaver God and the Material Factory

In his research newsletter of April 7, 1975, the first of several sent to the Alicia Patterson Foundation in New York, director Richard Pearce quotes a gnostic passage from Melville's *Moby-Dick*, quite possibly with input from McCarthy, who may already have been collaborating with him: "Nay—the shuttle flies— the figures float from forth [*sic*] the loom; the freshet-rushing carpet forever slides away. The weaver-god, he weaves; and by that weaving is he deafened, that he hears no mortal voice; and by that humming, we too, who look on the loom are deafened; and only when we escape it shall we hear the thousand voices that speak through it. For even so it is in all material factories" (quoted in Pearce 8). If we accept the indirect invitation to read *The Gardener's Son* through this passage, as if it were an epigraph to the screenplay, we may recognize the Graniteville Mill as another of McCarthy's ontological place metaphors, like the dark swamps and lowering woods of *Outer Dark*, the caves of *Child of God*, the river and city of *Suttree*, the desert of *Blood Meridian*, the cramped subway tenement of *The Sunset Limited*, and the ash heap of *The Road*. The screenplay's gnostic cosmos is represented in the material factory, the bureaucratic and commodified world of the Industrial Revolution recently imposed on the pastoral landscape, a world in which a human is defined by his or her economic role within the collective structure and usefulness to the system's machinery, where one is likely deafened to his or her own voice, the inner call of the pneuma or authentic self, as well as to the voices of other mortals. The machinery of the loom—the cosmos—causes human deafness reflecting the deafness of the weaver god, the artificer demiurge who is oblivious to both the true, alien God and the pneumatic spark in humankind. Melville's lines pick up the gnostic emphasis on the alienating noise of the world: Jonas describes the noise of the world as one of the central images of ancient gnosticism (*Gnostic Religion* 73–74). This noise has a twofold effect: "Meant to deafen and confuse, it also frightens and causes Adam [humankind] to look toward the stranger, to strain his ears toward the other voice" (*Gnostic Religion* 74). Both Melville and ancient gnosticism lie behind McCarthy's emphasis on "the roar and clatter of [the mill's] machinery" (shooting script 4–5) and the silencing of the looms at the moment of Robert McEvoy's final shooting of James Gregg—"*The clatter of the machinery in the background suddenly comes to a halt. There is an immense silence"*—as if Robert's act of rebellion against the Greggs and their factory constitutes an existential escape from the deafening of cosmos and creates a hitch in its very machinery (*GS* 57).[2]

Consistent with the Edenic associations of its title, *The Gardener's Son* suggests that the material factory is a fallen world, no longer a garden but rather the regimented and bureaucratic modern world ushered in with the Industrial Revolution. The mill's founder, William Gregg, who historically bridged the agrarian and industrial eras, is moribund in the screenplay's opening and dies on the night when Robert loses his leg. Gregg has naively or self-deludedly envisioned creating a "garden of industry" in Graniteville, as Mrs. Gregg reminds her son (shooting script 50), but the screenplay demonstrates that his concept is oxymoronic. This is abundantly clear in the social class condescension of both James and Mrs. Gregg—the one open and cynical, the other covert and hypocritical. It is hinted even in the eulogy for William, when the speaker innocently praises Gregg for "what he has wrought" in constructing the mill town, with its homes, churches, schools, and gardens, but also and "not least" for his installation of "the massive factory structure with its beautiful and perfect machinery" (19). In this system where machinery is valorized, the millworkers are stultified, deafened, and deadened in the daily routine of the factory, monitored in their working life by the archontic Timekeeper Mr. Giles and in all their activities by the paternalistic mill owners.[3] By the time Robert returns to Graniteville after his mother's death, the company gardens have been let go in a final repudiation of the pastoral; where his father the gardener once worked, *"weeds grow by the greenhouse wall and a number of panes are stoved and broken. . . . Inside are withered pottings,"* and when an old man opens the door to investigate who is inside, *"the late sun throws shadows of dead weeds across"* Robert (39–40), a reprisal of the sun and shadow imagery that prevails in *Outer Dark*. Bereft of his role as gardener, Patrick has been assimilated in the automated factory life, a deadened existence against which Robert rebels. Patrick's conciliation of the system results in his final separation from the natural world, a separation he himself initiated when he moved his family from their farm to the mill. It was primarily the young girls and children who were employed by the textile factories, a historical reality reflected in the scene directions (*GS* 19), so Patrick's reduction to the status of millworker is a movement that Douglas Canfield rightly sees as a "diminution and humiliation—and castration" ("Oedipal" 19).

Many intimations of the factory and mill village's bureaucratic oppressiveness are embedded in the scene directions, to be conveyed through the film's visual or aural imagery rather than its dramatic action or dialogue. But one such direction carries a great deal of gnostic/existentialist import that is difficult to realize fully on film: the morning startup of the mill is described in present-tense metaphoric language that recalls Melville's description of the material factory, suggests ominously the awakening of some rough beast or leviathan, and invokes both gnostic imagery of the whirling cosmos and existentialist imagery of the bureaucratic cosmic machinery: "*The great wheel that turns the spindles stirs sluggishly, the belts slither and turn, the overhead shafts begin to revolve, the spindles turn. Young girls and children are taking their place at their machines*" (19). Shots of this impersonal machinery recur throughout the screenplay, almost always accompanied by deafening noise. The machine's clatter is paired with another aural pattern that suggests the regimented quality of mill life. When Robert returns from his self-elected exile and alights from the train, "*in the distance the mill bell tolls*" (33), as it does with pointed regularity, morning and evening, throughout the screenplay (19, 24, 31, 51), and as does the church bell on the morning of William Gregg's funeral in an understated linking of factory and church as kindred institutions (18). These relentlessly tolling bells are echoed when Mrs. Gregg and Martha McEvoy reach an impasse in their conversation about James and Robert, the dead son and the condemned brother. When Mrs. Gregg refuses to hear that her son has sexually preyed upon the young girls in his employ, refuses even to hear Martha's compassion and shared grief, refuses—like Melville's weaver god deafened by the noise of the loom—to hear Martha's "mortal voice" pleading mercy, she picks up the bell she wields as mistress of the house and of the mill village and "*rings it vigorously*" again and again to summon her maid Daphne to expel Martha, but also "*as if to drown out the pleas of the supplicant*" (76). Such reiteration of tolling bells suggests the enforced conformity not only in the villagers' workaday lives but in their spiritual lives as well, ringing the cosmic doom or *heimarmene* that broods over the souls in Graniteville. The penultimate bell—another church chime—"*strikes twelve*" at the hour of Robert's execution, implicating the church itself in cosmic injustice (84).[4] And the filmed version ends with the continued tolling of the bells over the final music.

Several of the screenplay's characters function as archontic figures in existentialist avatars, as cosmic bureaucrats or figures of conventional judgment such as those who oppress Meursault in *The Stranger*, and it is against the world of commodification and regimentation, presided over by such oblivious figures of power, that Robert McEvoy rebels. Like Meursault's, Robert's rebellion seems underdetermined and mysteriously motivated if one looks for conventional psychological explanations but seems entirely meaningful when regarded as a gnostic or existentialist revolt against archontic oppression. Among the archontic types are the imperious Mrs. Gregg, who oversees the amputation of Robert's gangrenous leg, imposing her will on his by pulling rank on his cowed parents and watching the procedure with "*a curious expression of concern touched with a morbid if not salacious curiosity*" (17). Another is the arrogant Dr. Perceval, who flaunts his classical education and who bullies and condescends to the McEvoys, insisting on the medical necessity of amputating Robert's leg and adding brutally, "I'm sorry to be so blunt but you people will not seem to understand" (14). (This condescending line was deleted in the shooting script.) The doctor dons a butcher's apron to perform the operation, and his massive, shadowy assistant forcibly administers anesthetic, placing Robert in the dark of ether. Dr. Perceval, who has amputated thousands of limbs in the Civil War, is reprised in the dream-figure of the bone-surgeon in *Suttree*, avatar of the archontic huntsman. His "cadaverous" presence presides dispassionately over both of Robert's framing experiences of loss—of limb and of life—suggesting how, as a resident of Graniteville, Robert is thrown under the control of powers indifferent or hostile to his existence (vii).[5] The mill's exacting Timekeeper, its owner/manager James Gregg, and nearly all the agents of the legal system function similarly as oppressive archontic presences.

According to Donovan, in many modern works of fiction that manifest a gnostic world view, a "basic confrontation obtains between the hero, on the one hand, whose values are ultimately those of the subjective 'existential' reality of the 'soul' and its truth, and, on the other hand, the outer 'objective' social order which . . . represents an authority whose values, insofar as they can be determined, are antithetical to those of the hero. Most fundamentally they represent an obstacle to the hero in his or her quest for authenticity. Their worldview is a lie that denies the truth of being. . . . At worst . . . they operate according to rules and values that the hero cannot know but which have the effect of condemning him to alienation or death" (126–27). Robert's alienation seems to originate in his gangrened limb and the enforced amputation. The metaphorical castration links him with his ineffectual father, yet this terrible loss initiates a new level of awareness, awakening Robert to his ontological position within the world and both revealing and exacerbating his alienation.[6] Against his and his family's subjective awareness of the amputation as a primal loss, an evil that cannot be accommodated, Mrs. Gregg and Dr. Perceval bring to bear the force of scientific reason and pressure to conform to reasonable behavior as socially defined. Like the farm boy in Robert Frost's "'Out, Out—'" who begs his sister not to let the doctor amputate his mangled hand because he "saw all spoiled" and whose surprising death under anesthesia seems from a Camusian perspective a misdirected act of rebellion against life and the world, Robert tells Mrs. Gregg that he would "rather to be dead" than submit to the operation.[7] Her pious approach to reconciling him to this rationally necessary evil—that God forbids suicide, that God loves even the imperfect flowers in his garden—illustrates the least satisfying aspect of the Christian philosophy from a gnostic or an existentialist perspective, the problem of reconciling the world's evil with the notion of a benevolent Creator (Donovan 97). Robert's rejoinder, "If God put the rot in it then let it rot off" is no patient submission to a providential higher power; rather it seems an angry gnostic repudiation of the world as created: of flesh, cosmic life, and the demented artificer god who has "put the rot in" the world (15). In another archontic tactic, Mrs. Gregg deploys guilt and conventional piety to induce Robert to submit: "Think of your parents," she chides (15), and one recalls Meursault's condemnation for insufficient filial piety in *The Stranger*. But she finally reduces Robert to impotence by forcing him to look at his rotted leg, a shattering act that confronts him with his helpless position within a corrupt cosmos. He has not wanted to see it. The scene directions tell us he "*is very much afraid*," and he shakes his head in desperate refusal; but despite his efforts, "*His legs lie revealed. The injured one is loosely swathed in bandage through which discolored stains have seeped and his whole lower leg and foot are perfectly black*" (16). The scene reinscribes or adumbrates the scene in *Suttree* when Leonard insists that his friend help him dispose of his long-dead father's body and "with sick loathing" Suttree sees the "strange brown stains seeping through the sheets" (*S* 250). The scene emphasizes Suttree's nausea at the mortal human condition, the soul's imprisonment in this "mawky worm-bent tabernacle" (*S* 130). Robert's similar confrontation jolts him into a new consciousness of the dark nature of the world. In the filmed version, this receives visual emphasis in the scene's final shot, a closeup of Robert's anguished face glaring with wide-open eyes focused no longer on the leg but on the cosmos behind the camera.

The Revolt

The first part of Camus's *The Stranger* chronicles Meursault's initial complaisance and somnolence within the bureaucratic world of Algiers. His sun-induced murder of the Arab initiates his revolt, and his confrontation with the chaplain in the final chapter reveals his awakening into an existential gnosis. In *The Gardener's Son* we do not see Robert's daily routine before his crippling, but it is clear that the trauma of the rotted and lost leg is a primal cause of his alienation—or of his recognition of it. Hired on to sweep the management offices at the mill, with unscaled eyes he witnesses James Gregg and his Timekeeper Mr. Giles roughly turn away a family of impoverished hill people who seek work; Gregg comments more truthfully than he knows that "some of God's seed has fallen on barren ground" (24). Robert's intimate exposure to the material factory intensifies his alienation as he becomes aware of the social class condescension and cynicism underlying its paternalistic system. His abandoning his job to explore the hollow ground underlying Graniteville and to run "crazy in the woods like an Indian," as his oblivious father puts it, signals his repudiation of the mill and the power structure of the mill village (28). It seems he has rejected the church as well, perhaps in reaction against Mrs. Gregg's Christian moralizing and her God of corruption, although Patrick recognizes that "He aint no heathen. He's just got a troubled heart and they dont nobody know why" (30–31). Finally Robert simply leaves the petrified world of Graniteville in a gnostic repudiation or an existentialist choice—a negation of that cosmos and the inauthentic life it stands for. However, this departure is more an escape than a conscious existentialist project. Unlike Suttree, who leaves the nether world of Knoxville after his life-changing vision in his typhoid dreams, Robert seems to have come to a gnostic recognition of his position within cosmos but not yet a transcendent or even compensatory sense of an authentic self. His is a repudiation without affirmation.

Donovan identifies a recurrent gnostic pattern in several of Camus's works, including *The Stranger:* something "occurs to 'arrest,' to dislocate the protagonist; something makes him or her aware of . . . alienation, of the hostile archons—and out of this intensification of alienation emerges the redemptive *gnosis*" (130). For Meursault the arresting event is his murder of the Arab under the relentless glare of the sun; this murder "fractures the indifferent world in which Meursault has been 'happy' and it makes for his fall into the hostile world of the bureaucratic archons of the French judicial system" (Donovan 132). Similarly Robert's provoked murder of the oppressive James Gregg constitutes a more significant rebellion than does his wandering life in which he achieves only a temporary escape from the material factory. But the killing subjects him to the hostile world of Graniteville and the bureaucratic archons of the American judicial system. Robert has been brought home by the death of his mother, an invention that does not appear in the historical accounts of the McEvoy family from which McCarthy worked. Robert's grief and his outrage over Patrick's plans to bury Mrs. McEvoy in Graniteville—"She dont belong to the mill," he insists—condition his violent rebellion against Gregg (35). Thus he parallels Meursault: the death of Meursault's mother and the arrogation of control over her funeral by the agents of the rest home where she has died condition his violence against the Arab, whom he associates with the hostile hypostasized sun that has glared down on his mother's funeral procession and that again glares down on the murder scene.[8]

Robert returns to Graniteville a figurative stranger, as he has become a stranger to the community and his family even before his departure. With different effect than in *Outer Dark*, where Culla is often called "stranger," the hospitable Pinky warmly invites Robert to drink, saying "Aint no need to be a stranger" (46). But his night of drinking does not reassimilate Robert into the community. McCarthy emphasizes Robert's estrangement not only in the young man's adamant assertion that his mother does not belong to the mill but also in his reiterations that no one in the mill village "knows" him—not even his sister—and that James Gregg does not know Robert's father (39, 53). Indeed Gregg has an entirely mistaken "recollection" that Robert was fired from the mill for stealing, a hostile assumption about the young man that Robert repudiates as a lie and that foreshadows the lies and misrepresentations that result in his execution (54).

The invented circumstances leading to McEvoy's killing James Gregg roughly parallel those leading to Meursault's murder of the Arab in ways that reinforce the gnostic and existentialist perspectives of *The Gardener's Son*. Both protagonists have been drinking before the killings, suggesting their subjection to metaphysical oblivion. Masson's wine exacerbates Meursault's sun-induced somnolence and disorientation. Even before the first encounter with the Arabs on the beach, he feels "half asleep" from "all that sunlight beating down on my bare head" (67). When he returns alone to the spring where he last confronted the Arabs, he feels he must strain "every nerve to fend off the sun and the dark befuddlement it was pouring into me" (73). Although he realizes that he could turn back, the murder seems fated, almost an act committed while sleepwalking. McCarthy too inscribes intimations of gnostic oblivion in his screenplay, but does not prominently deploy Camus's gnostic metaphor of the oppressive sun as he had already done in *Outer Dark*. (The hostility of the sun is invoked only once in the screenplay, when Robert emerges into the midday street after his session with the photographer and is subjected to the alienating covert gaze of the villagers and the glare of the sun in which he stands blinking; 79.) Instead, McCarthy invokes images of literal and metaphorical darkness. Before his confrontation with Gregg, Robert spends the night in the doggery drinking rotgut whiskey and then sleeping drunkenly in an abandoned shed. Later we see him "*reeling*" toward Graniteville in the night, "*wobbl[ing] on into the darkness*" with the "hounds of gnosticism" howling after him—such hounds as pursue Suttree and that he learns to fly (51).[9] Although Robert commits his murder in broad daylight, as does Meursault, the aura of gnostic darkness lingers over his act. Physically awakened by the monotonous mill bells yet still hung over, he responds to their summons in almost zombie-like fashion, as if in answer to a kind of cosmic necessity. (In the filmed version, his staggering toward the mill is pointedly intercut with images of the millworkers at their machines, automatons performing their repetitive labor.) Once in the mill boardroom, Robert fills a glass from the tapped beer keg that awaits the stockholders and drinks again as he sits defiantly in Gregg's office chair. His drunkenness is not so much a realistic extenuation of the murder as a metaphysical expression of his cosmic oblivion.

Finally, in Camus and McCarthy's works, the antagonists are all armed for a showdown, as if to suggest the intuitive, incipient rebellion of Meursault and Robert against the inimical and impersonal world-powers represented by the

Arab and Gregg. In Camus's posthumously published novel *A Happy Death* (written in 1936; published in French in 1971, in English in 1972), which adumbrates *The Stranger*, the protagonist Patrice Mersault murders the unarmed cripple Zagreus in a seemingly gratuitous act that parallels Raskolnikov's murder of the pawnbroker in *Crime and Punishment*. When Camus reconceived the murder that instigates the existentialist rebellion for *The Stranger*, he made the Arab a much more threatening metaphorical presence, linking him and his knife blade with the glaring archontic sun and all that oppresses Meursault ("the Arab drew his knife and held it up toward me, athwart the sunlight. A shaft of light shot upward from the steel, and I felt as if a long, thin blade transfixed my forehead"; 75). McCarthy similarly avoids any suggestion that Gregg is a harmless victim—departing from historical accounts such as the Broadus Mitchell biography of William Gregg. In his desk drawer Gregg keeps a pistol, which functions as one symbol of his hegemonic power over the people of the mill village, much as his mother's handbell functions as hers. And as the pawnbroker does for Raskolnikov in *Crime and Punishment*, James Gregg represents for Robert McEvoy the oppressive economic system and cosmic injustice under which he and his family struggle. James's contemptuous flipping of a gold piece onto his desk in a rude attempt to buy off Robert, who has asked for nothing but human respect, not only telegraphs James's insulting Martha and the other women under his power but captures the whole of the commodified relations between the Greggs and the millworkers. The gesture focuses Robert's rage into a hatred that becomes obvious to James, who scrabbles fearfully for his pistol. Thus the glint of the gold piece triggers the specific acts of aggression between the two men, as the glint of the Arab's blade does in *The Stranger*. Both suggest sudden flashes of oppressive ontological insight in the protagonists. In both works the "murders" are existential acts of self-defense; in both the rebels stand in the dock for others: Meursault for his friend Raymond, whose fight he has taken up, and Robert for his sister, his father, and all the oppressed millworkers of Graniteville.

The Trial and the Lie of the World

Delivered into the hands of the law, Robert undergoes an absurd trial that follows historical events but also is shaped to engage the ontological issues of Meursault's trial in *The Stranger*. Each man is imprisoned, enacting the gnostic metaphor for humanity's ontological position within cosmos. And each suffers under the impersonal and relentless machinery of the law. In *The Stranger* the regimentation of the court proceedings and the constrictions of Meursault's freedom in prison reinstate the stultifying routine of his workaday life. The witnesses for the prosecution speak from the perspective of convention and thus pose the "lie that denies [Meursault's] truth of being" (Donovan 127). And the restrictions imposed by judge and prosecutor make even Meursault's friends' testimonies serve that lie. In *The Gardener's Son*, the machinery of the material factory, with all its metaphorical import, reappears in another avatar in the legal machinery of the court, where the prosecution and the defense conspire to protect the Gregg family's name and interests. The defense attorneys prevent Robert's testifying on his own behalf and do nothing to challenge the Timekeeper Giles's damning testimony that Gregg was not armed when Robert first shot him; nor do they counter the testimony of Gregg's doctor, who enters into the legal record James's dying declaration that he did not provoke the shooting. Conventional piety sanctifies this lie, even though James's ulterior motive to ensure that his family receive life insurance benefits offers the defense an obvious point of refutation. Barred from telling his own story, Robert can only answer these lies with well-timed and expressive spitting.

Only the black Yankee defense attorney, W. J. Whipper, attempts to mount a genuine defense for Robert. Surprising his white colleague, Jordan, Whipper asks the office boy Stark Sims whether he was asked to carry messages from Gregg to the young women of the mill. When Whipper introduces this line of questioning, the prosecuting attorney directs a meaningful glance toward defense attorney Jordan, who has raised his own eyebrows in surprise (64). Both recognize that Whipper is violating an agreement they have made with Mrs. Gregg not to call female witnesses nor to introduce the subject of James's sexual predations. In exchange for this courtesy, Jordan tells Patrick McEvoy, "we have exacted every consideration from the [Gregg] family"—suggesting how fully the legal proceedings are under the hand of the Greggs and the power structure they represent (61). Similarly (and absurdly) Meursault's lawyer files no motions to challenge the verdict "as this was apt to prejudice the jury" (134). Both Meursault's attorney and Robert's accept a guilty verdict from the outset and hope to win a mitigated sentence through conciliation, a position that allegorizes orthodox Christian conceptions of original sin and humankind's need for atonement, ideas challenged by gnosticism.[10]

In his rebellious attempt to introduce an element of truth into the jury's consideration of Robert's motives, Whipper takes a calculated risk. But the plan backfires because he himself is an outsider. Unfamiliar with the social and economic realities of the mill village and perhaps blinded by his own experience of oppression, the black lawyer has not considered that Sims is illiterate and thus does not know the contents of the notes he has carried. Whipper's bungled cross-examination leads directly to the imposition of the death sentence when Mrs. Gregg reneges on her conditional agreement to extend "every consideration"—a decision she reaffirms in her conversation with Martha when the naive girl blunders into the same forbidden subject of James's sexual predation. Patrick visits Whipper's room in the night to beg him to let Robert testify, a courageous defiance of social norms prompted by his desperation to save his son. However, it becomes clear that Whipper has since been cowed by the other attorneys. "I tried," he says, perhaps implying that he has tried to convince the defense team to place the full story into testimony (66). But he speaks to Patrick from a position of inconsistent gnostic rebellion. On the one hand, Whipper acknowledges the archontic principle afoot in the world. He points out that humans are more interested in justice than is the creator God— "Everwhere I look I see men trying to set right the inequities that God's left them with"—but also that in the corrupt world of humankind the very notion of justice is co-opted by scoundrels (67). On the other hand, he reverts to conventional piety akin to Mrs. Gregg's when he consoles Patrick with the platitudes that "God sends no man a burden greater than what he can bear" and that others (perhaps he has in mind black Americans of the antebellum and Reconstruction eras) have a worse lot—false comfort, which the previously mild-tempered Patrick vehemently rejects (68).

According to Donovan, in the system of the alien authorities against which the human struggles in existentialist works, "the lie is made the governing principle of the universe" (127). The lie that denies Meursault's essential nature surfaces specifically in the prosecutor's muddling the issue of his guilt by associating his murder of the Arab first with his incorrect behaviors at his mother's funeral and then with the unrelated case of a parricide who is to be tried in the same court session: Meursault, "morally guilty of his mother's death," as the prosecutor tells the court, "is no less unfit to have a place in the community than that other man who did to death the father that begat him" (128). He asks the jury to consider Meursault guilty of parricide and consequently to impose the death penalty. And if the Arab is a hypostasis of the archontic powers of the world, the false creator god or "father" of cosmos, the prosecutor's accusing Meursault of parricide bears a kind of ironic gnostic truth, and the death sentence manifests cosmic *heimarmene*. However, as in the gnostic conception of the alien spirit imprisoned in the material cosmos, the judgment against Meursault reflects the world's ignorance of his essential nature: when the archontic prosecutor looks into the face of the accused, he sees only "a monster" (102). Indeed the prosecutor claims that Meursault "had no soul, there was nothing human about [him], not one of those moral qualities which normal men possess had any place in [his] mentality. 'No doubt,' he added, 'we should not reproach him with this. We cannot blame a man for lacking what it was never in his power to acquire. But in a criminal court the wholly passive ideal of tolerance must give place to a sterner, loftier ideal, that of justice'" (127). Thus the cosmic principles of moral convention and judgment are brought to bear against Meursault's alien and alienated essence, upholding the lie of the world, the lie of sin, against mankind.

The court similarly demonizes, judges, and condemns Robert. Martha recalls the prosecuting attorney's assertion that "the image of God was blotted out of [Robert's] face" (93). Again, there is a kind of gnostic truth to the lawyer's archontic perspective, in that Robert's rebellion against the Gregg family represents a larger revolt against the creator god of cosmos. But Robert's trial is an absurd construction of lies that deny his nature, and even by worldly standards his sentence is out of proportion to his crime. Like Meursault, Robert is a cosmic scapegoat who bears the punishment for the crimes of others, those of James Gregg and the community at large: the historical Robert McEvoy was sentenced to death partly as a political gesture meant symbolically to redress the recent injustice done to black murderers of white men in Graniteville, who had been tried and executed with sickening ruthlessness by a racist society and its biased judicial system.[11] Thus the issues of McEvoy's case were falsified when these unrelated murder cases were yoked together with his in the minds of the jury. In McCarthy's screenplay these implications are presented with typical understatement. The dialogue of the men in the doggery alludes briefly to the racial tensions in the area. But unlike in *The Stranger,* the invocation of other murder cases is not an explicit ploy marshalled by the prosecutor. Indeed the screenplay's most overt references to the historical case against the black men condemned and hanged for killing whites is visual: "*There are nine black and three white jurors,*" the scene directions tell us. Visually emphasizing the racial separation in this Reconstruction-era southern society, "*The blacks wear light-colored clothes, the whites dark-colored.*" The prosecution and the defense teams each include two black lawyers and one white, but it is the white lawyers who do most of the talking, and both the sheriff and the judge, the primary agents of the legal system, are white (59). The shooting script also plans for a visual reference to black prisoners in the cells Robert passes—presumably on death row—as he is escorted to his execution (126).

Public sentiment also contributes to the excessive judgment against Robert. The community knows he has threatened the men Patrick has hired to dig a grave in the Graniteville cemetery and that Robert has angrily expelled the mourners sitting with his mother's body at home.[12] And his briefly turning his pistol on his father before surrendering it to him—another offense against filial piety—is witnessed by much of the mill society. Community outrage at Robert and his family can only be exacerbated when Patrick fails to inter Mrs. McEvoy, and the neighbors begin to smell her decaying corpse. The family's grief for her is less apparent to the village than their violation of conventional expressions of respect, their "Christian duty" (62). Communal bias against Robert and his father is dramatized in the hostile or judgmental gaze turned on both in the streets (65, 79; shooting script 101, 118, 123–24). A subtext of the screenplay, then, suggests that Robert McEvoy, already a stranger to the mores of the community by virtue of his family's Roman Catholicism, receives no mercy from the jury or the court at least partly because of his apparent lapses in honoring his mother and father, lapses that exemplify his rebellion against the power systems of the world both as created and as socially constructed.[13]

Donovan discusses the alienating effect the language of the court has on Meursault, who "is finally moved to nausea before the spectacle of the great lie of this world" (139). Like Robert's, Meursault's advocate warns him, "You won't do your case any good by talking" (124). When the judge asks him to explain his motives, Meursault tries, but his truthful statement "that it was because of the sun" elicits laughter from the spectators and exasperation in his attorney, who insists on speaking for him, oddly in the first person, throughout the remainder of the trial (130). After telling Meursault in the "rigmarole" of the law that "'in the name of the French people' [he] was to be decapitated in some public place," the judge again asks Meursault if he has anything to say. He thinks about it for a moment, Meursault tells us, and behind that laconic statement lies all his comprehension of the trial's absurdity and of his position. Thus he says nothing (135). Even more than Meursault, Robert is silenced throughout the trial while the roar of the legal machinery and its lies deafen the jury. The relentless force of that machinery is suggested in the obfuscating language of the court's officers: the legal jargon of the charges read at length in the trial's opening and of the verdict pronounced at its end (59–60, 68–69). Asked why judgment should not be passed on him, Robert does as instructed and does not speak. His silence suggests in addition that he is confused by the judge's barrage of language—rather like the kid bombarded by Judge Holden's verbiage in *Blood Meridian*—or that like Meursault he recognizes the absurdity of his situation. More important, the legal question raises the ontological one for the audience and perhaps now for Robert himself: what can a man say in his defense to the archontic judge or gatekeeper who denies the truth of his very being, who upholds the lie of the world? "He saith nothing," Judge Maher intones for the record, then proceeds to pass the death sentence to which every human is condemned (69).

The Condemned Man and the Question of Gnosis

After their trials, both Meursault and Robert McEvoy recognize with increased lucidity their ontological positions as always already condemned men. Their jailing and pending executions literalize the gnostic/existentialist metaphor of earthly life as imprisonment within an alien cosmos which is to end, without appeal, in death. In *The Sunset Limited*, White's metaphor for life is very similar: "the world is basically a forced labor camp from which the workers—perfectly innocent—are led forth by lottery, a few each day, to be executed" (122). *The Stranger* establishes this more explicitly than does *The Gardener's Son*, as Camus's final section rings changes on the metaphor both in Meursault's private musings and in his confrontation with the chaplain, who attempts to impose on him a Christian interpretation of his life and his guilt. Like Suttree, who becomes terrified at the "mathematical certainty of death," Meursault cannot accept the "brutal certitude" of his sentence, "For really, when one came to think of it, there was a disproportion between the judgment on which it was based and the unalterable sequence of events" that will lead to his execution (295, 137). He refuses the blandishments of the chaplain and spends his remaining life urgently pondering whether "there have been cases of condemned prisoners' escaping from the implacable machinery of justice" (136). He has in mind the guillotine and the armed police who will officiate at his execution, but also more broadly the institutionalized system of judgment and fate, suggesting once again the gnostic conception of cosmic *heimarmene*. Recognizing that he is condemned, Meursault emerges from his earlier passive indifference into an affirmation of life and of the sustaining beauty of the natural world and a repudiation of the system that allows mankind no out: "What was wanted, to my mind, was to give the criminal a chance" (139). He attempts to face his death with lucidity and to steady himself with the logical conclusion that since a man must die, it makes little difference just how long he lives before dying. But the archontic chaplain, whose visits he finds "irksome," intrusively insists that Meursault repent of his sins and turn to God, which from a gnostic perspective would constitute an affirmation of his chains (149). The chaplain's "consolation" that all humans are condemned to die and his complacent certainty that Meursault's sin must be atoned goad the prisoner into an angry but necessary assertion of his essential innocence. Rather like McCarthy's heretic in *The Crossing*, who consciously positions himself under the impending dome of the ruined church at Huisiachepic and who warns the complacent priest to save *himself* (C 157), Meursault grabs the chaplain by his neckband and challenges his certainties: "Living as he [the chaplain] did, like a corpse, he couldn't even be sure of being alive. It might look as if my hands were empty. Actually, I was sure of myself, sure about everything, far surer than he; sure of my present life and of the death that was coming. . . . I'd been right, I was still right, I was always right. . . . What difference could they make to me, the deaths of others, or a mother's love, or his God; or the way a man decides to live, the fate he thinks he chooses, since one and the same fate was bound to 'choose' not only me but thousands of millions" (151–52). This final assertion constitutes Meursault's existentialist gnosis, the immanent state of clarity and authenticity that offers a solution or more genuine consolation for the problem of living alienated within a hostile world remote from God. In *The Stranger*, Camus does not depict Meursault's death as he had detailed Patrice Mersault's;

rather he ends the novel with Meursault's gnosis, which is of itself warrant that he dies a "happy" death, facing execution with eyes open.

Robert's case is more problematic because the state of mind in which he approaches his execution is not given voice to the degree that Meursault's is. Canfield finds it a pointless sacrifice. He considers Robert, like Melville's Billy Budd, an agent of justice but queries "why must the agent hang? Nothing seems to come of it" ("Oedipal" 20). But if we approach the screenplay from the gnostic/existentialist perspective, we may recognize hints of a movement toward greater clarity in Robert, an achievement that grants him the nobility in the face of shame and execution that McCarthy aimed for, an open-eyed courage that links him with the twentieth-century existentialist hero Meursault even more than with Billy Budd, to whom the language and the crucifixion imagery of the screenplay implicitly compare him. As in *The Stranger*, these hints come in the scenes after Robert's sentencing, as if the shock of the death sentence itself pushes him toward full cognizance of his position in the world and full philosophical rebellion against it—a repetition and intensification of the rebellion that began with the shock of his lost leg. Donovan's observation about existentialist heroes applies to Robert as well: "One has to be metamorphosed into the prison of alienation before one can be metamorphosed out" (225). Thus a kind of "double" gnosis occurs, first the pessimistic gnosis of alienation, and later the more optimistic gnosis that constitutes a "psychological transcendence"—"a sudden, erratic, redemptive flash or insight which opens to the recepient [*sic*] the riches of a world other than the profane everyday one" (225, 194, 193).

Donovan writes that existentialist protagonists "struggle to discover and to sustain an inner truth" against the lie of the world (127). If Robert is silent in court, he is not so when he meets his sister in the street after his conviction and her failed appeal to Mrs. Gregg. Here he speaks out against the lies arrayed against him and the sentence imposed. In the shooting script the emphasis on the lie is most forceful: "They lied to me. Lied, lied, damn lied" (shooting script 120), and in both drafts he expresses an existentialist plaint for his life cut short: "They all said I'd . . . I was never born to be hung. I could of been somebody" (*GS* 80). Robert echoes Camus's conqueror in *The Myth of Sisyphus*, who says that "man is his own end. And he is his only end. If he aims to be something, it is in this life" (88). "I caint stop thinking about it," Robert tells Martha, suggesting an intense awakening to his position in the world and to the truth of its nature and his own. When Martha tearfully claims that she would have "told em any kind of lie" in court to counter those purveyed about Robert, he responds by affirming her life, telling her to find the best man to marry, "And you have a good life. Little sister. The best that anybody ever had in this damned world" (81–82). His compassionate if conventional advice to Martha reverses his angry accusation that she doesn't know him, constituting an opening of his heart to those who love him, in pointed contrast to Culla Holme (39). Even more important, it validates life even while it recognizes that humans live in a world that is "damned," a life-affirming position that is more Camusian than ancient gnostic.

In concession to the McEvoys' Catholicism and to the community's Christian piety, a priest, Father Heidenkamp, is sent to Robert's cell on the day of his execution. McCarthy inscribes no dramatic confrontation between the two, but once again the scene directions suggest a dynamic similar to that in *The Stranger*. When the scene opens, Robert sits quietly holding an anomalous bouquet of flowers, perhaps brought to him by the priest in an ill-considered and even ludicrous gesture. Father Heidenkamp stands off in a corner, *"reading silently to himself"*—a detail of staging that hints that Robert has already repudiated any consolation the priest has tried to offer (82). (Even this understated stage business is deleted from the filmed version, although the priest is present in the scene.) And yet Robert conducts himself throughout the execution with a grace and composure that suggest neither defeat nor defiance but a self-possession having nothing to do with the platitudes of the church. Robert's calm as he faces execution, so unlike his struggle against the oblivion of chloroform in the amputation scene, is further highlighted by its dramatic contrast with the wild despair of his father when Patrick comes to the jail so *"addled with grief"* that the jailers accuse him of being drunk and deny him a final meeting with his son on grounds of propriety: "We caint have this here," they intone in their conventional piety. "This is a sacred time" (82–83).

When the sheriff comes to conduct Robert to his hanging, the condemned man rises immediately and affirms, "Yes. I'm ready," another hint that he has achieved, off-screen, a psychological transcendence consonant with his lucid awareness of the nature of the world. He is led to the gallows, supported by his crutch on one side and by the priest on the other, a laconic scene direction equating church and crutch and implying the wooden deadness of each. In a final gesture fraught with significance, Robert hands off his crutch to the priest. Before killing Robert, his jailers drape him in a white robe, *"McEvoy cooperating and serious, like a priest being dressed for a sacrament"* (84), but if Robert is similar to a priest, it is no orthodox religion he professes, and the image suggests ironically that he is sacrificed to the false, archontic orthodoxy that rules his society.

The sheriff asks Robert if he has any final words, and like Meursault before the judge in the courtroom, he remains mute. But with the noose around his neck, he clears his throat ambiguously, either in anticipation of the garroting rope or as if to speak—as if he might share whatever insight he has achieved with those gathered curiously to watch him die. But the hangman, Mr. Clements, is too quick; the shooting script specifies that he has "jumped the gun" (128) when he releases the trap, and "*the body of McEvoy hurtles down into the room*" below (*GS* 85). The scene direction's emphasis on Robert's body is reinforced in Doctor Perceval's stepping forward "*to take the dangling figure's pulse*" (85) and in the ambiguous whittler's furtive carving a mute wooden likeness of Robert to fix the man in the memory of the community, but also to replace the living man. This reduction of Robert McEvoy to *body* amplifies our perception of the loss of something essential—if not a transcendent spirit, then at least the gnosis or message that this awakened man, who sees the truth of the world in which he is thrown, might communicate to his fellows alike condemned. Yet, though Robert does not speak for himself as Meursault finally does, the screenplay, in achieving a "history of the inarticulate," more subtly delivers Robert's gnostic/existential message.[14]

Chapter Five

Prisoner in Babylon *Suttree* (1979)

Except for the Border Trilogy (1992–98), *Suttree* is McCarthy's most ambitious work to date, and it represents the culmination of the work of his Tennessee period. Focused on the stuttering spiritual progress of Cornelius Suttree, an intelligent and perceptive artist/philosopher-in-the-making, also an alcoholic and soul-wounded man alienated from family, church, and twentieth-century American culture, the book is McCarthy's only truly urban novel, set primarily in Knoxville in the early 1950s. Just as *The Orchard Keeper* drew on McCarthy's childhood environs and some of the people he knew in the semirural Vestal community, *Suttree* details the world of Knoxville from 1951 to 1955, the world of McCarthy's late adolescence and early college years. McCarthy completed his work at Catholic High School in 1951, attended the University of Tennessee in 1951 and 1952, and served a four-year tour of duty in the Air Force beginning in 1953 before returning to Knoxville and the university in 1957. In the novel, then, McCarthy works from his intimate personal knowledge of the city of Knoxville mostly before 1953: its flavor, its geography, its social and economic realities, its architecture, its modes of transportation, its nightlife, and some of its respectable citizens and more colorful local characters. Virtually every street name, business, and building mentioned in the novel actually existed in the 1940s and 1950s, and Suttree's movements roughly chart the Knoxville of those decades as those of Raskolnikov map St. Petersburg in *Crime and Punishment* and those of Dedalus and Bloom map Dublin in *Ulysses*—although fellow Knoxville novelist Richard Marius is right to point out that McCarthy does not describe or explain these references: "He makes us natives, and if we do not know the landmarks, he cares not; if we care enough, we can learn them"—a technique that characterizes McCarthy's use of historical materials as well (118). But many of the Knoxville buildings and landmarks had already disappeared from the cityscape by the time that *Suttree* was published (see Marius, "*Suttree* as Window into the Soul of Cormac McCarthy"; and Luce, "Suttree's Knoxville / McCarthy's Knoxville"). One of the structuring motifs of this intricately patterned book is Suttree's witnessing of the deaths of his old friends and the razing of Knoxville's old buildings and neighborhoods. Indeed, in Suttree's dream fairly early in the book as he lies in the hospital, he hears the message, "Uneasy sleeper you will live to see the city of your birth pulled down to the last stone" (188). Thus this urban novel extends the "myth, legend, dust" or *ubi sunt* theme of *The Orchard Keeper* and anticipates the similar concerns of the Border Trilogy. Anne DeLisle has suggested that McCarthy was interested in capturing this disappearing world of his childhood: "He delved into its heart, not just dwelling on the circumstance. And when his Knoxville, the *real* Knoxville, disappeared, he disappeared. It was no longer the place as he saw it" (Gibson 34, emphasis in original).

In *Suttree* McCarthy describes in some detail those buildings that we know were the loci of many of his own childhood experiences: the Church of the Immaculate Conception (still in use) on Summit Hill north of Knoxville's market and city center, the Market House (razed after a fire in 1960), the old Catholic High School in the Victorian Ashe house on Magnolia Avenue northeast of the business district (a new high school was built on the site in 1952, but the Ashe house was used for classes until it was torn down in 1961; see Chandler). And Marius identifies a number of businesses that read "in McCarthy's pages . . . like epitaphs, tombstones to dead times": Squiz Green's tuxedo rental shop, Comer's pool hall, Lane's drugstore, Bower's department store, the Ellis and Ernest drugstore, Walgreen's, the bus terminal on Gay Street (118–19).

The bridges at Gay Street and Henley Avenue still span the Tennessee River, bracketing the business district of downtown Knoxville, but the riverfront structures of Front Street, "the stinking slums that hung like a filthy skirt falling into the river down Knoxville's principal hill," have been entirely demolished, replaced by the new city-county building and Volunteer Landing and, as Marius writes, by "the broad throughway [Neyland Avenue] that sweeps traffic away from football games," transforming the riverbanks into "lifeless concrete, the river into something one only saw briefly in passing, not pretty, not ugly, and certainly not an artery of life" (126–27). By the time *Suttree* was published, First Creek, which "passed down under the great concrete arch of the Hill Street viaduct and excreted its refuse into the turbid Tennessee River" just above the Gay Street bridge had been largely sealed away in a concrete conduit, invisible from the street, but "whose gurgling far under the city streets you can hear on a quiet night if you are in the right place" (Marius 116, 126). Mostly gone, too was the McAnally Flats neighborhood and its little shotgun houses west of Knoxville's city center.[1]

In addition, several of the characters in McCarthy's novel are based to one degree or another on his acquaintances in Knoxville. Newspaperman Bert Vincent, who wrote a regular human interest column entitled "Strolling" from which McCarthy may well have drawn incidents to reshape for his novel, and

Dr. John Randolph Neal, the lawyer and law professor who had served as chief counsel for Scopes in the famous 1925 trial over teaching evolution in the schools, were living figures in Knoxville in the 1950s (*S* 220, 366–67; Deaderick 582–83). The itinerant goatman/preacher was well known throughout the South, and Marius remembers that he used to show up in East Tennessee "every few years in the 1940s and 1950s" (118). McCarthy does not name him, but the actual goatman, Ches McCartney, preached in forty-nine states from 1930 to 1987. He claimed be more than one hundred years old when interviewers spoke with him in the early 1990s—but may actually only have been in his eighties ("Goat Man's Son"). His life and visits to many communities are documented in Darryl Patton's *America's Goat Man (Mr. Ches McCartney)* (Birmingham: Little River P, 1994). Patton's compilation of reminiscences, news stories, and photographs include none from the Knoxville papers. But on June 2, 1968, *News-Sentinel* columnist Bert Vincent ran a photograph of McCartney and his goats in his "Strolling" column and reported that he was camping in nearby Rockwood. Like McCarthy's policeman who wants the goats off the post office lawn, Vincent complained that the goats were unsanitary and caused traffic hazards (Vincent F1). Jim (or J-Bone) Long, who shares Suttree's drunken sprees, and whose family houses him when he is ill or injured, was a real-life friend who attended church with young Charles (Cormac) McCarthy (Confirmation Register, Immaculate Conception Catholic Church). The Long family's phone number and address on Grand Avenue in the Fort Sanders neighborhood repeat reality (*Knoxville City Directory, 1951*, 203). Some of McCarthy's friends claim that the character Gene Harrogate, or at least his watermelon venture, was based in some way on John Sheddan, "scholar, schemer, hustler, melon paramour" (Gibson 23), whose own excerpt from a novel-in-progress, "The Man from Davis Hollow," appears in Jeanne McDonald's anthology of Knoxville writers, *Voices from the Valley* (Knoxville: Knoxville Writers' Guild, 1994). However, in a letter of response to Gibson's article, Knoxvillian Buzz Kelley writes that Sheddan was "probably [McCarthy's] best and most loyal friend from the Knoxville crowd," holder of two master's degrees, and not at all "a violator of vegetables nor one to fornicate with fruits." "Whatever resemblance he bore to Cormac's fictional creation is purely incidental," he adds, claiming "I believe I know who the 'real' Gene Harrogate is, but out of respect for the living, I will not mention his name in print" (Kelley). On firmer ground are articles by Wesley G. Morgan, researched through local newspapers and records, one of which reconstructs the history of violence involving Clarence Raby, Lonas Ray Caughorn, Kathryn Underwood, Kenneth "Worm" Hazelwood, and Sprout Young, referred to in *Suttree* ("Season of death"). In another Morgan outlines the tumultuous life of Billy Ray (Red) Callahan, who figures more prominently in the novel ("Red Callahan"). Marius recalls an unnamed bootlegger who kept a speakeasy on his houseboat on the river (117), who may suggest Abednego Jones. Even James Herndon or "Sweet Evenin Breeze," whom Trippin Through the Dew is happy to have seen perform, was a transvestite who actually lived in Lexington, Kentucky (Simmons 57).

A primary focus, then, of this episodic novel, with its richness of texture and incident, is Cornelius Suttree in his Knoxville context. However, although the Knoxville of *Suttree* is largely the city of McCarthy's objective experience, it is also a purgatory or gnostic netherworld like the outer dark of Culla and Rinthy Holme and the cavernous underworld of Lester Ballard. On the Tennessee River bank Suttree occupies a liminal world between subsistence and commercialism, wilderness and city, poverty and middle class, communion and isolation, aspiration and materialism. The river and the city are metaphors for Suttree's spiritual imprisonment, his struggles with despair, his intermittent efforts to find a vision that will free him from his own kind of drowning in materialism—the materialism of mortal flesh and the materialism of American culture. Suttree's complex path keeps him circling the environs of Knoxville like Culla Holme circling in his dark wood. At intervals Suttree leaves the city, tracing spoke-like trajectories outward to the funeral of his son in the Cumberlands, to the Smoky Mountains a year later (an anniversary reaction to the death of his child), to the French Broad River during his mussel-brailing partnership with Reese only half a year after that, on romantic excursions to Gatlinburg or Concord or Asheville with Joyce; but each of these expeditions evokes death or at least despair, and rather than breaking out of the vortex of Knoxville, Suttree is sucked back until he finally breaks free in the epilogue. Like Lester Ballard and Robert McEvoy, Suttree descends to the underworld of the caves beneath the city. He succeeds in rescuing the feckless Gene Harrogate from those depths, but his own experience in the novel charts a spiraling down into despair and escapism that is characterized first by his alcoholism and then his sexual relationships with Wanda and Joyce, all tainted with materialism.

Coexisting with these metaphorical, geometrical patterns of escape and return, centrifugal pull, and spiraling descent is the pattern of Suttree's sought and unsought visions—mind-states that chart his intermittent glimpses of healing insight or his spiritual or philosophical or artistic dead ends. Integral to these, as well as to his everyday lived experience, are many intricate patterns of incident and imagery that give the novel its poetic structure and its multilayered significance: the archontic huntsman and his hounds in all their real and dream avatars; the deep time of astronomy, archaeology, and cultural succession; the helix or vortex of mortality; the stilling eye of the camera; the granting or withholding of grace; graves and burials; stone and flesh; rain and soot; purgation of the flesh in vomiting or excrement; the salute to or communion with the other—or its failure; the search for family and the alienation from brothers, mothers, and fathers earthly and divine; preachers false and true; the maimed and the crippled; the machine in the garden and the garden in the city; the urban wasteland and human "trash." Nothing in the novel is undoubled; everything resonates in complex fashion with multiple other details, often with a fractal variation of scale. To read this book is to listen to its internal echoes, what Bell calls its "resonating subject rhymes," to harken to "that resonance which is the world" of the novel and which is the "world itself" (*Achievement* 99; *APH* 162). Suttree himself is doubled not only by his dead twin or by his "little buddy" Gene or by Hooper the ragpicker (who stands for all mortals) but by all. In this rich novel invoking the Platonic and Dantean idea of life as a purgatory in which we may learn from others' stories and examples, many characters function specifically as foils for Suttree: Daddy Watson, Harvey the junk man, Leonard, Reese, Joyce, Ab Jones, and others. As Matthew Guinn points out in *After Southern Modernism*, Suttree himself is cognizant of this: "Keenly aware of the absence of his replicated form [his twin], Suttree seeks out his own reflection throughout the novel" (105). This seeking is manifested both in his attention to his literal reflection and in his relations with others.

Gnostic/Existentialist *Suttree*

A number of scholars have written of the existentialist vision in *Suttree*. In one of the earliest essays devoted to the novel, John Lewis Longley comments on Suttree's "existential consciousness" (82). In "Suttree and Suicide," Frank Shelton provides a more extended treatment of the novel's existentialist philosophy, especially in light of Camus's *The Myth of Sisyphus*, arguing that Suttree represents the "existential man facing the absurd, alien in a universe without meaning," a man who overcomes his attraction to suicide as a "relief from the burdens and torments of consciousness" and who finally affirms "the human will to action" (74, 73, 83). Similarly Richard Marius finds Suttree to be the alienated stranger, like Camus's Meursault, and the world of the novel one in which "the promise of heavenly redemption has evaporated, death is final, and men and women exist between the choice to commit suicide or to preserve life by continuing it day by day, as Camus suggested in *L'Homme Révolté*" (121, 125). William Prather's "Absurd Reasoning in an Existential World," published in the same collection as Marius, builds on Shelton and reinterprets the novel in light of Camus. Prather points out that physical suicide is only one of the responses to the absurd universe that Camus discusses in *The Myth of Sisyphus:* the "indescribable universe where contradiction, antinomy, anguish, or impotence reigns," and he explores Camus's other options: metaphysical suicide (through nihilism or avoidance strategies such as religious faith, hope, or love and domesticity) or "perpetual revolt," the option Camus preferred (Camus, *Myth* 23;

Prather 147). He concludes that despite Suttree's "growing realization that the aspects of life that are of key importance tend to unite members of humankind rather than dividing or isolating them," finally "*Suttree* is not about commitment at all, that it is instead about rejection, dissatisfaction, and absence of hope. . . . As [Suttree] . . . prepares to hitch out of the city, he is empowered by many of the rewards of absurd existence discussed by Camus: lucidity, an enhanced power of consciousness, the freedom to act with responsibility, and a posture of perpetual defiance" (148–49). Recently David Holloway has discussed the novel through the combined perspectives of Marxist critical theory and Sartrean existentialism. He views "McCarthy's aesthetic as . . . an unfolding Sartrean 'project,' whose late modernist aim is the resurrection of language" (111). He argues that Suttree's own project is "an existential reaffirmation of the self as a powerful mediating influence within and upon the world of matter" (140n14).

In their extended comparison of *Suttree* and *The Stranger*, Dale Cosper and Ethan Cary dispute the tendency to read *Suttree* as strictly existentialist or absurdist, arguing that the book does not fit Camus's criteria for the absurd novel and that employing *The Myth of Sisyphus* or other existentialist essays to explicate fictional works—either *Suttree* or *The Stranger*—is problematic, as Sartre pointed out in his "Explication of *The Stranger*" (Cosper and Cary 176, 156). Instead, they maintain, "McCarthy's strange narrator casts a pall of Gnosticism over the novel before the protagonist even appears, and is there at the end waiting for Suttree as he learns the lessons the entire novel is constructed to teach him" (175). By the end of the novel, they believe, Suttree "has become a Gnostic" (168) in the sense of one who shares in "a category of thought which posits a cosmic principle or daemon of evil pitted against goodness and innocence" (155n1). They find particular evidence of this in the omnipresent images of the huntsman and his avatars, who "represent a nightmarish, even goulish, force of evil at war in the world with forces of good" (167). I believe that Cosper and Cary are on the right track to recognize the gnostic influence in the novel, even though they create something of an either/or dilemma in their reluctance to reconcile its gnosticism with existentialism (169). As Hans Jonas and literary scholars such as Josephine Donovan and Kirsten Grimstad have shown, gnostic sensibility and imagery recur in existentialist works of the twentieth century. McCarthy blends the two philosophies in *The Gardener's Son* and again in *Suttree*.

In "The Dawning of the Age of Aquarius: Abjection, Identity, and the Carnivalesque in Cormac McCarthy's *Suttree*," J. Douglas Canfield suggests a synthesis of gnostic, existentialist and Christian readings. He concurs that the hunter and hounds pursuing Suttree "can represent some Manichaean prince of darkness," yet he seems to reject this gnostic reading (unnecessarily) when he observes, accurately, that "such monsters are, as Suttree fears, not outside but inside." At the same time, he also allows that "the monster is the capitalist system that both produces and contemns its underclass . . . [as well as] the virtually absent superego, represented by Suttree's absent patrician father, who sees meaning only in the institutions . . . that run the system, that enforce its divisive privileges," the bureaucracies that plague Camus's characters (675–76). Canfield's comments are more consistent with gnosticism than perhaps he recognizes, since gnostic dread of cosmos involved both resistance to worldly orders and authorities and painful recognition of the introjection of cosmos in the human psyche. Canfield's Kristevan reading of the abject in *Suttree*, like Ann Fisher-Wirth's treatment of *Outer Dark*, resonates in interesting ways with gnostic repudiation of cosmos. Finally, however, Canfield concludes that McCarthy is a "Catholic existentialist" with a long-term fascination with gnosticism and theosophy. He argues that Suttree recovers "a paradoxical definition of self that holds the abject at bay once more." For Canfield, the waterbearer who offers Suttree grace in the novel's epilogue is Aquarius, associated with Ganymede, the cupbearer to the gods, and who in New Age syncretism is a Christ figure (683). And in a footnote, he briefly discusses the gnostic roots of the New Age syncretism of the 1970s and '80s (683n5).

Other critics' comments demonstrate the prevalence in *Suttree* of gnostic intimations even for readers who are not aware of their ancient gnostic contexts. Many of these readers conclude that Suttree overcomes a dread of the world and achieves an acceptance of it that involves love of his fellows who share his pain. For example, Bell notes the novel's "odd dualism" (*Achievement* 83). He describes Suttree's progress as an effort to transcend death, which is both "animate and pervasive," and to arrive at a "reconciliation to the world itself," which wields such "disinterested authority over individual being" (*Achievement* 69, 76, 90). For Suttree, Bell writes, "Faith is a real task . . . , for it involves accommodating one's ideas to the world as it is" (*Achievement* 78). Suttree's "reluctant allegiance" to the world is thus "his only recourse," since God is absent from it (*Achievement* 77–78). Bell most often writes of the novel in terms of the existentialist search; for example he describes its characters as an "odd little band of ragtag existential heroes, each defining life in his own exclusive terms and each finding his own symbolic leverage against necessity" (*Achievement* 81). But his analysis is also compatible with the idea that Suttree achieves a limited transcendence of the gnostic dread of cosmos that paralyzes Culla Holme (76). Thomas D. Young Jr. arrives at similar conclusions via a different path. He notes "Suttree's disaffection from society [which] runs both more deeply and more dangerously than does Harrogate's"—a disaffection that I would argue derives as much from gnostic perspective as from the related existentialist view. With Young's focus on Suttree's awareness of humankind as a product of evolution—his search for "evidence of the primal forces out of which both the human animal and his culture were originally organized"—he concludes that Suttree makes no spiritual progress but remarks that instead, his perception of his evolutionary origin "as opposed to genealogical or theological models, restores the wonder of his life and validates the sacramental communion with pure experience as one's highest priority. . . . His spiritual hunger . . . can be satisfied by the things of this world. . . . The assertion of the ultimate integrity and sufficiency of the self and of the value of a human community based on an affiliation of such selves is what Suttree . . . comes to affirm" (113, 120). D. S. Butterworth follows Young's lead in focusing on McCarthy's "geological view of humankind," but he argues that Suttree achieves little in the novel and that McCarthy achieves no "rehumanization" of mankind (131). He observes of the novel's marginalized characters that they are "always already doomed, . . . never to be able to rise above the materiality of their circumstances" (132). However, Butterworth takes a more sociological approach than a metaphysical one, and does not read the characters' situation, mired in materiality, as emblematic of humanity's essential condition in cosmos, as I tend to. Nor does he quite recognize the gnostic image of the spirit's entrapment in matter and cosmos in the many depictions of Suttree in contexts of "containments and imprisonments," nor in the image of the mussel, "outer shell, inner meat, and, rarely, its innermost pearl"—although he certainly makes a negative approach to it when he observes that McCarthy "plays upon the paradigm of container and contained as it applies to notions of body as the container of the soul in order to affirm a quasi-nihilistic void in the body as material object" (133, 136).

Gerhard Hoffmann too notes the "adversity of the [novel's] world and the brutality of the authorities," and writes that in *Suttree*, "Behind the feeling of alienation looms the metaphysical void, God's presence in absence" (231, 234). Like Cosper and Cary, he argues that Suttree's reconciliation comes with the recognition that Christianity is not "the authentic bearer of the metaphysical dimension" (237). However, he concurs with Bell and Young—appropriately, I think—that Suttree's movement in the novel is toward "reconciliation with the world," achieved through his articulation of the "humanistic values of care and solidarity" (230, 238). James R. Giles follows Bell and other early critics in asserting that the world of Suttree offers "only the possibility of existential choice" (92). He also observes the "intensely concrete and deterministic" qualities of the novel's world, although he connects them with the novel's naturalism rather than with the gnostics' dread of materialism and their concept of cosmos as an inescapable aspect of human nature (93). He glosses the novel's threatful "unknown thing" as "essentially human impermanence—death as the irrevocable and astonishingly unjust pronouncement of an insane god who has withdrawn his grace from the human world," echoing the judgmental aspect of the demiurge and the absence from cosmos of a god of grace that were characteristic of gnostic thought (87). He recognizes the prevalence among the novel's characters of various "voices of a vindictive divinity" and the corollary that "all of McCarthy's people . . . [have] been judged with a harshness that exceeds [their] capacity for sin" (91, 92). Like Bell and Hoffmann, Giles argues that to achieve even a limited transcendence, Suttree must "realize that there are no permanent answers in a universe abandoned by god and then accept the fellowship that comes through bonding with those around him" (93).

For the most part, these interpretations conflict more in labels than in essentials. What I hope to do in the reading that follows, among other things, is to demonstrate the ways in which McCarthy synthesizes Platonic, gnostic, Christian, and existentialist images and concepts to inform Suttree's anguished alienation from the world and his final transcendence through freeing himself both from the guilt and life-denial inculcated by the Roman Catholic Church and from his gnostic obsessions with the mortal captivity in matter, arriving at his affirmations of an uncomplicated love for the natural world, of a true ministry in communion with his brothers and sisters in the streets, and of his own voice as an emerging artist and Messenger.

The Dream-Frame: *Suttree as Narrator*

The prologue to *Suttree*, with its salutation, "*Dear friend,*" establishes a narrative stance roughly analogous to those of *Child of God*, where the narrator occasionally addresses the reader directly, suggesting that Lester Ballard is "much like yourself, perhaps" and invoking us to "see him"; and *Blood Meridian*, where we are exhorted to "see the child" (*S* 3; *CoG* 4, 156; *BM* 3). The novels that bookend *Suttree* in order of publication may be seen as demonstrations and warnings to the reader of the violence and alienation at the core of human history and experience, but the big Knoxville book is more explicitly framed as such. The narrator of the prologue, guide and usher, leads us through the streets of Knoxville to an "*encampment of the damned,*" to the "*world within the world . . . that the righteous see from carriage and car*" and where "*another life dreams,*" then invites us to observe from the elevation of Knoxville's Gay Street bridge, figured as a nightmare theater where "*a curtain is rising on the western world*" (3, 4, 5). This world within the world is the life of the riverfront and the lower reaches of the city: the underworld of Suttree and his friends, a world not just of poverty and constriction, but of the dead. What's more, though we readers may number ourselves among the righteous who pass by this world at a pampered distance, snug in carriage or car, this is yet our very world, "*the western world,*" inside the ramparts yet beyond the pale, a world where players and audience alike are bones, "*webbed in dust*" (5). The prologue's narrator presents the action of the novel proper for our enlightenment, for our awakening, perhaps for our revivification; his literary antecedents include Dante's Virgil, the speakers of Shakespeare's prologues, Eliot's Prufrock, and even Dickens's ghosts of Christmas past, present, and future.

If the prologue is the opening half of a frame, it is in some respects a rather different one from those in *The Orchard Keeper, The Gardener's Son*, and McCarthy's story "Wake for Susan," all of which clearly position character/ "narrators" within a narrative present and establish their encounters with historical artifacts that evoke their constructions of the past. Yet in other ways *Suttree* manifests an extension and adaptation of the frame technique of these works of historical recovery. The time setting of the prologue and the identity of its narrator remain ambiguous, open to a number of possibilities, especially on first reading; there is no corresponding italicized section at novel's end that explicitly returns to the situation of this prologue. However, the italicized opening functions as prologue not only to the book as a whole but also more specifically to the first section of the novel proper (7–29), which does culminate in the situation of the prologue, with Suttree, drunk and sorrowful, standing in the rain on the Gay Street bridge as he closes out the day on which he has witnessed the raising of the suicide's corpse from the river. Both scenes echo and counterbalance the prologue.

The epilogue repeats imagery from the prologue with significant modifications that comment on the changed nature of Suttree's experience. The prologue is a night journey down through the warrens of the city to the abode of the dead, where the ramparts wall the enemy (death, despair) inside; this enemy is also the gnostic demiurge or weaver god invoked in *The Gardener's Son*, the "*thing*" that weaves with "*bloody shuttle shot through a timewarp,*" the "*carder of souls,*" the "*hunter with hounds*" (*S* 4–5)—recalling too the triune of *Outer Dark*. The prologue's water imagery is of the fecal mire of the river bearing the ruined artifacts of domestic life and the wastes of the western world to southern seas, and later—after the warning not to invite the enemy in—the benediction of light night rain that falls into the river's "*grail of quietude*" (5). In contrast the epilogue—presented without italics as if simply the next episode in Suttree's novel-long journey—depicts his sun-shot departure or escape from the city, attended by the blond waterbearer who offers a grail of water "all bright and dripping" both to the workers in "the pit" who raise their hands in "parched supplication" and to Suttree himself, standing unbeseeching in the heat and dust (470). In yet another benediction in the epilogue, Suttree in his new clothing is offered a ride that speeds him "out across the land"—clearly a transcendence of his past life (471). In this respect the narrative frame offers before-and-after pictures of Suttree's experience that echo some of the resolution achieved by Wes, John Wesley, and William Chaffee in their framed narratives as they walk away from the artifacts that prompted their reveries and insights or, in Chaffee's case, as he gazes out Martha McEvoy's hospital room window to the world beyond (*GS* shooting script 140). From the car window Suttree sees a "lank hound" following his scent from the river, and this segues into the novel's final words, which explicitly echo the prologue. The prologue's narrator speculates that the thing inside the walled city that threatens the human spirit is a "*hunter with hounds*" and warns us: "*Dear friend he is not to be dwelt upon for it is by just suchwise that he's invited in*" (5). The warning recurs in the epilogue's powerful last paragraph: "Somewhere in the gray wood by the river is the huntsman and in the brooming corn and in the castellated press of cities. His work lies all wheres and his hounds tire not. I have seen them in a dream, slaverous and wild and their eyes crazed with ravening for souls in this world. Fly them" (471). In retrospect the epilogue identifies the italicized prologue itself as one of several visions of the huntsman and his slaverous hounds, marking the prologue's dark night-journey as a visionary or dream narrative and by extension identifying the theatrical presentation of the novel's action as, on one level, a dream within a dream or a dream of a dream, harking back to *Outer Dark* and anticipating the complex epilogue of *Cities of the Plain*. In *Suttree* the epilogue's warning "Fly them" resumes the direct address to the reader that we find in the prologue, linking the narrative perspectives of the two, even though the situational presentations of the prologue and epilogue so markedly differ. One is reminded of the opening and closing of Culla's story in *Outer Dark*, where the nightmare he dreams in the cabin a few days before Rinthy gives birth is echoed in the words of the blind man he encounters in the last chapter. In both novels the lines between waking life and dreaming life are blurred, and experience as dreamed and as lived seem finally to have a pregnant continuity that reinforces the notion of life as a Platonic or gnostic or Dantean spiritual journey, both waking and sleeping.

While the links between the prologue and the epilogue suggest that the two are to be read as emanating from the same narrative voice, the "I" of the epilogue's last paragraph is ambiguous and may be read as both Suttree and the omniscient narrator. Throughout the novel, narrative point of view exhibits a fluidity between the frequent free indirect discourse representing Suttree's or sometimes Harrogate's experience ("To steal upon them where they lay, his hand on their warm ripe shapes, his pocketknife open"; 32); first person narrative clearly Suttree's ("Wrap me in the weathers of the earth, I will be hard and hard. My face will turn rain like the stones"; 29) or occasionally that of a minor character, such as the man in brogans who shoots Harrogate ("Could I call back that skeltering lead"; 35); and commentary that seems to come from a removed, but not objective, "authorial" narrator ("In the act is wedded the interior man and the man as seen"; 375), such as that we only rarely find in *Child of God* ("she let [Ballard] in, more's the fool"; 116) or in *Outer Dark*'s italicized inter-chapters ("they moved in shadow altogether which suited them very well"; 3) and more frequently in *Blood Meridian* ("Goldseekers. Itinerate degenerates bleeding westward like some heliotropic plague," or "they . . . crossed altogether into the darkness which so well became them," or "Whatever [the judge's] antecedents he was something wholly other than their sum, nor was there system by which to divide him back into his origins for he would not go"; 78, 163, 309). If McCarthy has a model for his variable use of narrative perspective in *Suttree*, it may well be found in Melville's *Moby-Dick*, in which the first-person narrator Ishmael announces himself through direct address to the reader ("Call me Ishmael") and soon defies the reader's expectations by disappearing as the first-person narrator, morphing into a flexible "omniscient" narrative perspective that may also manifest itself as the point of view of Ahab, Starbuck, or Pip or as dramatic presentation in an objective point of view—all of which suggests the blending of the character "Ishmael" and the "authorial" voice of the novel. Suttree does not disappear as thoroughly as Ishmael does, except perhaps within those chapters focused on his double Gene Harrogate. McCarthy would later employ the technique of the disappearing protagonist in *Blood Meridian*, representing the kid's experience through free indirect discourse only in its early and late chapters but without making him a narrating presence. In contrast the protean quality of the narrative stance in *Suttree* reinforces the impression that we are not only bleeding from Suttree's free indirect discourse or first-person passage into the "authorial" narrator's perspective, as many critics have suggested, but that Suttree's and the narrator's voices simultaneously invest one another or coexist, one in palimpsest under the other—are in fact twins or different manifestations of the same narrative consciousness, one contemporaneous with the action of the novel and one more retrospective.

Suttree is directly linked with the narrating voice of the frame when he advises the old ragpicker not to invite death ("He might hear you") in an echo of the prologue's and epilogue's warnings (257). The end of *Suttree*'s first chapter also strongly suggests that the narrative voice of the novel can be read as a Suttree/"authorial" hybrid, for here we find the situational repetition one might expect in the closing of a narrative frame. Suttree on the bridge in the night rain, after his lonely walk down to the river through the streets of the city, experiences approximately what the narrator leads us through in the prologue. And in his reverie on the bridge, Suttree's imagery repeats or adumbrates some of the crucial images of both the prologue and the epilogue. The *"fecal mire"* of the prologue figures in Suttree's shuddering imagination of the suicide's leap from this very bridge: *"To fall through dark to darkness. Struggle in those opaque and fecal deeps, which way is up. Till the lungs suck brown sewage and funny lights go down the final corridors of the brain"* (4, 29). He notices the downriver lightning mentioned in the prologue and makes a poetic leap in the direction of its theater imagery, reiterating its trope of the western world as a stage or as staged, and re-figuring its hounds: "A brimstone light. Are there dragons in the wings of the world?" Suttree observes the moths that "aspire in giddy coils" under the dim lamplight along First Creek, not quite establishing the metaphysical spin of the prologue, which tells us: "*There is a moonshaped rictus in the streetlamp's globe where a stone has gone and from this aperture there drifts down through the constant helix of aspiring insects a faint and steady rain of the same forms, burnt and lifeless*" (29, 4). Nor does Suttree yet connect the lifeless forms of these insects plunging back to earth through the core of the Yeatsian spiral with the theater trope, as in the prologue's "*fine rain of soot, dead beetles, anonymous small bones*" that falls with the rising of the stage curtain (5). But he sees the bridgelights in the river as "chained and burning supplicants" in a direct foretaste of the epilogue's ditch-diggers whose hands mutely beseech water in "parched supplication" (29, 470).

Such repetition of images recalls the technique McCarthy employed in the frames of "Wake for Susan" and *The Orchard Keeper*, other works which had their inception in 1959–60, in which imagery of the framing situation informs or bleeds into the narrated stories (see Luce, "'They aint the thing'"). *Suttree's* epilogue emanates from a time later than that of the novel proper, as in the earlier works, yet the prologue seems paired with the scene of Suttree on the bridge as a visionary reinscription of that specific experience that may be narrated at any time subsequent to it. However, the imagery is more elaborate in the prologue, as if with time and growth, Suttree's narrating consciousness has evolved into the authoritative/authorial guide who is our entrée to the novel, reinforcing the perception that the prologue, like the epilogue, occurs in a narrative time later than the events presented in the rest of the novel. Similarly, while in the epilogue the contiguity of Suttree's seeing the hound from the woods and the final paragraph's reference to seeing the hounds in a dream suggests that the last paragraph comes from the point of view of Suttree as character, the elaboration of imagery from Suttree's nighttime meditation on the bridge in both prologue and epilogue again strengthens the hint that we may read Suttree as an author-figure, even as the narrator of this book.[2] There is a difference, though, from earlier works in which the frames establish the book-ended narratives as hallucinated recollections, perhaps not empirical "truth" but valid visions nonetheless. In *Suttree* the hallucinated recollection pattern is not invoked in the frame but is nested within Suttree's experiences in the novel proper and is confined either to passages in which photographs, buildings, or individuals briefly prompt Suttree's imaginative visions or to literally hallucinated memories such as those he recovers under the influence of Mother She. The frame of the novel as a whole does not work from a provocative icon to the artistic invention/recovery of the past (unless the city itself may be seen as such an icon, as Marius suggests when he regards the novel as "a sort of album of a vanished past"; 121). Rather, the prologue represents the artist/protagonist performing like Dante an unsituated act of autobiographical recovery from the vantage point of greater wisdom and wholeness, presenting the dramatized lesson of his prior life to an audience conceptualized and addressed as a dear friend.[3]

Although reading the patterns of repetition as expressions of the character/narrators' consciousnesses can enrich our understanding, to read John Wesley Rattner or Suttree as protagonist/narrators of their respective books is not the same as to read, say, Quentin Compson as narrator of part 2 of *The Sound and the Fury*, where the reader's strategy is to detect the obsessions and biases of the subjective narrator. In McCarthy's "Wake for Susan" we observe the artist/narrator at work in the self-reflexive shaping of his narrative. In *The Orchard Keeper*, to recognize John Wesley as narrator is not to defraud the narrative of its autonomy by shifting our focus to his "bias," but rather, paradoxically, to invest it with greater "authority" as John Wesley's master narrative embodying the truest meaning and value of his life—even as we occasionally glimpse the constructive process. In the script of *The Gardener's Son* the "narrative" technique makes explicit the cinematic analogy that *The Orchard Keeper* had already deployed: the frame segues through the eyes (perspective) of the focalizing protagonist (I refer to William Chaffee, not Robert McEvoy) to lead us to the autonomous, dramatic perspective of the framed story. As we trace this development through McCarthy's early works, there appears some movement toward establishing the autonomy and authority of the story itself, even when it is framed within the perspective of a character/narrator. In *Suttree* the authority of the framed story is not compromised by hints of its protagonist himself as a mature narrating presence. But that recognition of Suttree as a narrative artist confirms his transcendence that we sense in the epilogue's imagery. "Old Suttee aint dead," a young boy ambiguously affirms in the novel's last chapter (470). Suttree has left his terrestrial hell, the epilogue shows us; like John Wesley Rattner, he has become the "bard of his own existence" (*CoP* 283). On the other hand, it also suggests that as we detect image patterns that cross the permeable border between the consciousnesses of the main character and the narrative voice, it is less meaningful to order the passages by strict categories of narrative authority than to observe the continuity. As in *Moby-Dick*, we find in *Suttree* a "first-person" narrative that is also omniscient.

Many scenes in the novel proper reinforce the notion of a changed Suttree, matured in wisdom, as its narrating presence: as its "authorial" narrator. The narrative voice itself identifies Suttree, when he wanders in the Smoky Mountains, as an "aberrant journeyman to the trade of wonder": an apprentice artist/philosopher who has not yet found his way (290). And as one who under-takes a quest to the underworld below the city to retrieve his lost friend, Suttree is linked with the mythic singer or poet Orpheus. As self-absorbed as Suttree often is, he possesses a highly contemplative nature and is a sensitive observer, although evidence of this is often presented with understated objectivity: walk-ing away from the corpse of the suicide, where he has just noticed "with a feel-ing he could not name that the dead man's watch was still running," Suttree rubs his "speculative jaw" (10). Whenever he encounters new people, espe-cially those he finds enigmatic, Suttree turns his speculation upon them. Shar-ing turtle stew with the reticent Michael, Suttree watches him eat: "Solemn, mute, decorous. In his crude clothes crudely mended, wearing not only the outlandish eyes but small lead medallions that bore the names of whiskeys. Sit-ting solemn and unaccountable and bizarre" (240). Sometimes Suttree's gaze is so concentrated that others react defensively. He "studied" the tattooed pros-titute Ethel, so intently reading the "blue runes" on her legs that he provokes her to hitch up her skirt with a coarse invitation (75). Indeed *study* is the verb of choice in many of these passages, suggesting that Suttree is self-apprenticed as a student of life or writer in the making. Suttree watches acutely the "elder child of sorrow"—the "smokehound" and "drinker of shaving lotion"—who, locked within himself, never speaks to his fellow prisoners. The old man catches Suttree studying him and "fell to talking to himself with a kind of secretive viciousness" (50). Similarly Suttree contemplates the ragged black woman who cries and talks to herself in Howard Clevenger's store: "Suttree standing there inclined his head to hear, wondering what the aged dispossessed discuss, but she spoke some other tongue and the only word he knew was Lord" (165). It is Suttree's concerned facial expression that draws Oceanfrog Frazer's attention to her and elicits his act of charity (167). To the degree that Suttree's move-ment is toward finding a voice, these inarticulate children of sorrow who fas-cinate him, walled away in their difficult and lonely lives, represent alternate versions of his own potential future; their presence in the novel along with the more vocal dispossessed also hints that, among other things, Suttree as narra-tor is struggling to achieve a "history" of the inarticulate, as William Chaffee is. Indeed, as Giles writes, Suttree's rejection of his middle-class heritage in favor of the city's poorer quarters "is an essential move in keeping open the possibility of dialogue with his decidedly unscholarly companions"—dialogue that thoroughly informs the artistic creation that is Suttree's story (88).

Suttree's life among the poor folk of Knoxville plays a crucial role in his education as an artist. His fumbling attempt to communicate with the deaf-mutes in Comer's, formulating and revising in their sign language, is a genial parable of the writer's quest to find a language that will speak to his audience, crossing barriers of difference and isolation—even the deafness imposed by the material factory (234). That Suttree's audience is deaf and mute does not so much criticize their disabilities as "readers" as it acknowledges that writer and reader hear and speak differently. The deaf-mutes' patient nods of encouragement and appreciative laughter when Suttree succeeds in breaking through the barriers that wall them away from one another postulate the writer/reader relationship as communion as much as communication. The story-swapping between Suttree and less-educated men brings them together in a bonding ritual and represents Suttree's efforts to master vernaculars and subcultures other than the one in which he was raised.[4] Significantly, the apprentice Suttree usually does not take the lead in the tale-swapping but rather responds in kind, as when the Jellyroll Kid tells of a pool player who cheated in drawing the pills in a check game (a version of Kelly pool), and then Suttree recounts J-Bone's being hustled by a left-handed pool player (236–37). Worm tells of the consequences "the last time" he drank J-Bone's rotgut whiskey in language that Wade Hall finds reminiscent of Knoxville newspaperman George Washington Harris's nineteenth-century Sut Lovingood tales (Hall 66): "The last time I drank some of that shit I like to died. I stunk from the inside out. I laid in a tub of hot water all day and climbed out and dried and you could still smell it. I had to burn my clothes. I had the dry heaves, the drizzling shits, the cold shakes, and the jakeleg. I can think about it now and feel bad" (*S* 26). Then he invites Suttree to go drinking at the Trocadero. Suttree declines by telling an even taller and funnier tale of "the last time" he rode with Worm: "You got us in three fights, kicked some woman's door in, and got in jail. I ran through some yards and like to hung myself on a clothesline and got a bunch of dogs after me and spotlights zippin around and cops all over the place and I wound up spendin the night in a corrugated conduit with a cat" (26).

Not only the language but also the mayhem Suttree narrates here echoes that of his namesake Sut Lovingood, that freewheeling underclass scourge of pretension and principle of the carnivalesque. The Lovingood yarns are framed by the perspective of the more literate George, who absorbs Sut's tales of his adventures with tolerant amusement and re-presents them to the reader. But Suttree, with a background more resembling George's than Lovingood's, identifies himself as a Sut figure in his own tale, echoing Lovingood's self-ironic pose as the hapless victim of the havoc that always erupts around him. George's role as Sut's interlocutor, however, is reprised in Suttree's own relationships with Gene Harrogate, Leonard, Rufus, and the ragpicker, in other examples of the multi-vocality or ventriloquism that characterizes the narrative technique of the novel and Suttree as narrator.[5]

As "reader" of the people he encounters, Suttree takes on the role of interpreter associated with the writer. When he reads the faces of his neighbors Doll and Ab Jones, his immediate perspective and the authorial perspective merge.

Suttree notices symptoms of syphilis in Doll's face: "two intersecting circles, fairy ring or hagstrack, the crescent welts of flesh. . . . Annular treponema"; in direct address the narrative voice instructs the reader and Suttree himself to "read here why he [Ab] falls in the streets," obviating the distinction between Suttree as observer and the voice of the prologue's "authorial" guide (108). Suttree similarly reads Ab's face, performing the function of the authorial narrator: "The black wiped his eyes with one huge hand. Stories of the days and nights writ there, the scars, the teeth, the ear betruncheoned in some old fray that clung in a toadlike node to the side of his shaven head" (108). Suttree reads the photo of his aunt Martha by noticing its age and Martha's wistful gaze at it rather than by recognizing her features in this image of a young girl (127). And he reads Leonard, whose uneasy and transparent inquiries about the meaning of the word *yegg* lead Suttree to the "crazy" Knoxville newspaper, the only place he has seen the word, and to the article that reveals Leonard's attempt to rob a riverboat (235).[6] Later he will ask Leonard for the "true story"—the personal version that might counter the official story encoded in the newspaper: one of McCarthy's nods to Melville's technique in *Billy Budd* or "Benito Cereno" (*S* 241). Suttree reads differently than the laughing bystanders do the acts of the "garrulous jocko" harassing a young woman: "To Suttree they appeared more sinister and their acts a withershins allegory of anger and despair" (246). Such metaphors of reading position Suttree as our stand-in and interpreter. Because the narrative voice never counters such readings from Suttree, they in effect enact the function of the omniscient narrator.

Suttree's observations, especially in his dreams and visions, often explicitly echo (or forecast) the imagery of the narrative frame, further suggesting a new Suttree as the novel's narrator, who derives the imagery of the narrative frame from his earlier experiences recounted in the novel proper. For instance, when he walks through the drawing room of Jimmy Smith's saloon, Suttree sees the poker game as a barren enactment staged upon "the remnants of a former grandeur," the poker players/actors "like shades of older times or rude imposters on a stage set," sitting in an "air of electric transiency"—picking up the theater trope and the theme of passing cultures announced in the prologue (22). The fossiled stone wall of the prologue, reminding us of the passage of eons in its evocation of "*limestone scarabs rucked in the floor of this once inland sea*," recurs with similar import when Suttree staggers homeward after a night of drunken revelry and rests on an "old retaining wall": "Looking under his hand he saw dimly the prints of trilobites, lime cameos of vanished bivalves and delicate seaferns. In these serried clefts stone armatures on which once hung the flesh of living fish." This unexpected memento of deep time and death intensifies his nausea and sends him "lurch[ing] on" (3, 82).

Earlier, as Suttree lies drunk in a junk lot, abandoned by his friends and urinated on by a disgusted bouncer, his "poisoned brain" summons "homologues of dread" that recall the prologue's speculation on the shape of the enemy within, and he sees the drop of the very theater curtain described in the prologue: "A curtain fell, unspooling in a shock of dust and beetlehusks and dried mousedirt" (80). The "*anonymous small bones*" that also unspool from the prologue's curtain echo or foreshadow Mother She's purse of bones, which she upends to read portents: "Out clattered toad and bird bones, yellow teeth, frail shapes of ivory strange or nameless, a small black heart dried hard as stone. A joint from a snake's spine, the ribs curved like claws. A bat's skull with needleteeth agrin, the little pterodactyl wingbones" (5, 281). The two experiences come together in the narrator Suttree's unspooling curtain of the prologue.

Sleeping off his inebriation in the jail cell, in a vision that prefigures Suttree's and Ab's broken ribs, Suttree dreams of a flayed man crucified on a barn door with his rib cage nailed open, and he sees an avatar of the prologue's threatening "*thing unknown*": "Beyond the flayed man dimly adumbrate another figure paled, for his surgeons move about the world even as you and I"—punning in the verb "paled" on the prologue's homophone, "*The murengers have walled the pale*" (86, 4). The surgeon of death recurs in Suttree's hallucination of the brain surgeon who saws on his "stoven" skull in a cellar and in his horror at Ab Jones's scarred body: "He looked like some dusky movie monster patched up out of graveyard parts and stitched by an indifferent hand"; this is the surgeon in the shape of the mad scientist, the false creator, even the gnostic demiurge (188, 230). Suttree has seen "another figure" in his drunken vision, and this diction is echoed in his later vision of "another hunt": in his hallucinated recollection of his Saxon forebears in his grandfather's ruined mansion, Suttree evokes the *thing unknown* as the huntsman of the frame, imagining that "beyond the muted clamor at the board there is a faint echo of another chase. . . . Down murrey fields another hunt has cried the stag. . . . Outside darkness has begun and the hounds' voices are chimes in the distance that toll seven and cease." (The darkness, the hounds, and the seven chimes are all gnostic images of the powers that rule cosmos.) Here, as in the epilogue, the waterbearer is a figure of grace who stands in opposition to the huntsman, but in Suttree's vision at the mansion, "he does not come, and does not come" (136). The huntsman reappears in other incarnations Suttree associates with the ambiguous Mother She. In dread of her, he flees her on the streets: "Give over Graymalkin, there are horsemen on the road with horns of fire, with whithy roods" (282). And in his vision under her ministrations, the hunter visits him in the shape of a "black faltress, portress of hellgate. None so ready as she. . . . He flailed bonelessly in the grip of a ghast black succubus, he screamed a dry and soundless scream" (426–27).

Suttree's Teutonic forebears, themselves linked with the huntsman and the theater of death, appear in the prologue's flood of European settlers who displaced earlier peoples on the American continent: *"old teutonic forebears with eyes incandesced by the visionary light of a massive rapacity, wave on wave of the violent and the insane, . . . lean aryans with their abrogate semitic chapbook reenacting the dramas and parables therein and mindless and pale with a longing that nothing save dark's total restitution could appease"* (4). The recurrence of these Teutonic forebears in Suttree's family mansion retrospectively glosses the prologue's settlers as Suttree's own ancestors—as well as the forefathers of American postcolonial civilization. The prologue's Teutons (in the sense of Celtic or English-speaking peoples) again resurface when Suttree, a bereaved and guilt-stricken Hamlet-figure (even if somewhat self-consciously so), summons two gravediggers to fill his son's grave, and they respond reluctantly, "shambling down across the green like ordinaries in a teutonic drama" (154). This repeated association of Teutons with dramatic enactments suggests that to Suttree human life—like that of the spiraling insects or prehistoric scarabs and trilobites—constitutes a series of stagings and restagings through the centuries of the same stories of passion and death.

When Suttree sits at night in his houseboat studying the moths attracted to his lamp, the epilogue's supplicants are linked with the prologue's image of insects spiraling toward the streetlamps. The moths are "supplicants of light," he thinks, and he has already seen the bridge lights themselves as "burning supplicants" as they are reflected in the water (89, 29). This pattern of imagery and language in the framed tale and in the frame itself thus links water with fire and human with insect supplicants in ways that emphasize spiritual aspiration and the dry futility of that aspiration. The moths spiraling in an ascending helix ironically echo the drunkenly whirling dancers at the Indian Rock roadhouse, suggesting that for humans, as for insects, the frantic spiral that ends in death is mere pointless, misdirected motion (185). The helix is associated with DNA and thus with the very foundation of life. However, through such repetition with variation, the spiral or helix ironically evokes death throughout the novel, as McCarthy yokes the double helix of DNA with the gnostic whirlpool or whirlwind as emblems of death-bound cosmic turmoil. As he helps Leonard dispose of his father's long-dead body, Suttree notices the small vortex made as his "oarstrokes coiled out through the city lights where they lay fixed among the deeper shapes of stars and galaxies fast in the silent river"—both the vortex and the fixity of the lights in the still river recalling the gnostic imagery of *Outer Dark*'s cosmic prison (S 250–51). The imagery of cosmic entrapment continues when Suttree witnesses Leonard's wrapping his unshriven father in chains, a visual echo of Marley's ghost or Hamlet's father—an echo that is reinforced later when Leonard complains that his father has risen to the surface, "draggin all them chains with him," and Suttree comments drily, "Fathers will do that" (417). Further, the association of the "coil" of water with dead fathers evokes Hamlet's meditation on shuffling off "this mortal coil" (3.2.67). In Shakespeare the mortal "coil" refers, of course, to the tumult of life, and the semantic linkage establishes images of the death-bound vortex or helix as the mortal coil, the gnostic turmoil of life. Thus do the narrative frame and narrated tale gloss one another, illustrating the evolution of the narrating Suttree's consciousness.

The prologue's helix or mortal coil is evoked on other scales in the wheeling of the constellations, the spinning of the earth, even the rotating blades of fans. The fan in Ab's saloon is a "caged windscrew the size of a plane's prop," and it subjects the drinkers to a "howling wind" in a gnostic image of oblivious human life caught in a tumultuous vortex (278). When Suttree runs from Mother She, his heavy tread stops "the fans that spun above the shopdoors" as if such flight could actually evade the helix that leads to death (282). Struck between the eyes with a hurled rock, Suttree has a sickening vision of the sky "red and soaring and whorled like the ball of an enormous thumb" (225). The immense whorled thumbprint marks him for mortality, and this personified agent of death, a recurrence of the malevolent gnostic suns of *Outer Dark* and Camus's *The Stranger*, joins the haunting archontic figures of the prologue: the carder of souls, the hunter, and the driver of the deadcart as well as the surgeons of Suttree's drunken vision in the jail cell and the black succubus of his vision at Mother She's.

Several of Suttree's midnight experiences in the city inform the prologue's trope of the city watertrucks, which leave the homeless "*washed up in the lee of walls in alleys or abandoned lots*" like trash (3). The watertrucks' sinister associations are even more pronounced in Suttree's fevered, death-haunted vision on the night he is hospitalized with a concussion: "The night is cold and colder, a fog moves with menace in the streets. . . . The watertruck goes by like a nightbeast. . . . The sweepers broom the trash along the flooded gutters, their yellow slickers bright with wet. They leap to the truck and ride with brooms aloft like figures done in lacquered wax, like hortatory gnomes" (188). The malignant watertruck that sweeps aside all life, associated with the prologue's thing inside (4), stands in opposition to the image of the blue-eyed waterboy bringing grace unbidden in the epilogue—an act that is prefigured when Mother She gives a wary Suttree ice for his wounded forehead (229). Another agent of grace, the epilogue's driver who stops for Suttree although "he'd not lifted a hand," refigures the country man who has given him an unrequested ride in the rain, which Suttree partially refuses when he leaves the car to hike across fields to his family's abandoned mansion (471, 133–34). These scenes of unexpected grace, often rejected or reluctantly accepted by Suttree, counter the novel's pattern of withheld blessings, as for instance when Suttree tries to hitchhike and no car stops or when he rides the streetcar for warmth and its surly driver refuses him the return ride from the car barn (158, 178).

Even in the sections focused on Gene Harrogate and narrated largely in free indirect discourse representing the boy's perspective, we find imagery from the narrative frame, suggesting that Gene's story is created by Suttree as "authorial" narrator in an act of imaginative recovery. As Gene seeks Suttree on his first day in the city, he picks through a junk lot of bones and charred relics and carries away with him "melted glass that had reseized in the helical bowl of a bedspring like some vitreous chrysalis or chambered whelk from southern seas" (99). The helical spring and whelk reiterate the spiral imagery of the insects, the twining vines, and the dogwhelk's shell of the prologue (3–4). And as he watches bats hunting, Gene notices the "placid life that homed to ash in the columnar light," again echoing the aspiring insect image of the prologue and of Suttree's musings (102). When Suttree watches evening fall from the vantage of Michael's cliff, he associates the bats themselves with "rough shapes of ash"—linking them with their insect prey in shared mortality (238–39). When Gene begins hunting bats, the image of them as "small replicas of the diabolic with their razorous teeth bared in fiends' grins" comes not from Gene's consciousness but from that of Suttree as narrator, and it implicitly extends the metaphor of insects homing to ash, suggesting that they are preyed upon by the diabolic, thus linking the bats/fiends with the frame's hounds (215). The same complexity of perspective holds true with the bag of bats ostensibly seen by the policeman who stops Gene: "A prefiguration of the pit. Vouchsafed a crokersack vision of hell's floor deep with the hairy damned screaming mute and toothy toward the far and heedless city of God" (215). The diabolic or damnation imagery of the bats as Gene or the policeman gazes at them represents not their interpretations but those of Suttree as narrator. The image of hell in a sack will recur in Suttree's nightmare vision of his death and damnation when he lies gravely ill with typhoid. There the harmless turtle-hunter of his childhood memory returns in the shape of the huntsman as murderous highwayman, as in *Outer Dark:* "An outlaw tollsman reeking of woodsmoke and swamp rot" who insists that the traveler peer into his sack of turtles.[7] But Suttree recoils in horror at the sight he is vouchsafed: "Those are not turtles. Oh God they're not turtles" (455).[8] In the same chapter as Gene's sackful of bats, and this time explicitly from Suttree's perspective, we find the diabolic in opposition with moths when Gene himself, bathed in the red light of his stolen street lanterns, seems "a diabolic figure across which the shadow of a moth passed and repassed like a portent" (219).

In Gene's descent into the caves beneath the city, the prologue's beast invests Harrogate's free indirect discourse. When Gene locates the sewage retaining wall, he wonders, "Were they walling in or walling out?" recalling the ambiguity of the city's ramparts and the prologue's warning that the thing is inside (263). Dynamiting the wall, Gene releases a "sluggish monster freed from what centuries of stony fastness under the city. Its breath washed over him in a putrid stench" (270). This monster of sewage with its death reek, a personification of gnostic turbid water and the leviathan of cosmos, is yet another avatar of Suttree's dreaded huntsman. Its presence is announced even before the sewage reaches him as Gene, having just been vacuumed down the tunnel "in a howling rush of air," an iteration of Suttree's vortex, hears "in the horrid darkness *shapes* emerge from the reeks and crannies, features stained with boneblack, jaws adrip," echoing the narrator's question "*can you guess his shape?*" (269, 270, emphasis added, 4–5). And shaken for once into recognition of his mortal vulnerability, Gene has a vision straight out of Suttree's imagination when he hallucinates that "little girls in flowered frocks went tripping out through stiles of sunlight and their destination was darkness as is each soul's" (270). Swallowed in darkness, Gene loses his sense of boundedness, like Melville's Pip lost in the dark immensity of the ocean (274–75). As Young observes (112), this experience echoes (and reinscribes) Suttree's own vertiginous disorientation in the wilderness, when he "scarce could tell where his being ended or the world began" (286). Four days after Gene's imprisonment, Suttree finds the city mouse "crouching" in the cave "like something that might leap up and scurry off down a hole"—an observation that links the narrative point of view with Suttree's earlier first person vision of himself as a "mouse in a grassbole crouching" (276, 80).

Suttree's complex obsession with life as a sewer, as slow seepage, an urban variation on the gnostic swamp imagery of *Outer Dark*, first becomes apparent in the prologue's images of the fecal waters of the river, echoed in Suttree's imagining that the suicide inhales sewage as he drowns (29). It receives emphasis in the opening chapter as the still unnamed protagonist floats on the river, studying "surface phenomena, gouts of sewage faintly working" and sees his reflection as a "sepia visage yawing in the scum"—an image that links sewage with the novel's prominent photograph trope (7). And it is expressed most explicitly in Suttree's memory of watching his grandfather time a racehorse. For the old man the horse's record is "a thing against which time would not prevail," but the boy Suttree "had already begun to sicken at the slow seeping of life. . . . Lives running out like something foul, nightsoil from a cesspipe, a measured dripping in the dark" (136). This memory of his childhood reaction is retrospectively invested with visual and auditory imagery from his adult experience in his houseboat moored below First Creek, where sewage drips from its conduit pipes into the river. And Suttree as narrative artist attributes his own perception of the cesspipe to Gene Harrogate, camped under the First Creek viaduct: "At night he could hear the sewage gurgling and shuttling along through the pipes hung from the bridge's underbelly overhead" (137). The ambiguity of pronoun referent in this first sentence of a new chapter, following on the heels of a chapter focused on Suttree, creates the fleeting impression that it is Suttree who hears the sewage in the cesspipes, an impression that carries a larger narrative truth even though the text soon specifies Harrogate as this section's focus.

The river on which Suttree lives and from which he makes his living, with its linear flow and its foul cargo, both organic and inorganic, is to him a giant *cloaca maxima*, a gross conduit for wasted lives that are merely "passing through" (136). With its association with digestion and excretion, the river as *cloaca maxima* suggests also the predation of the huntsman, linking the sluggish river with the very beast Suttree warns us to flee. This metaphor, elaborated in Gene's underground explorations, revisits the trope of Lester Ballard's caves as the entrails of leviathan, one that pictures the human condition as wandering in the darkness of materialism—as, in fact, a purgatorial or gnostic world. Like Lester, Gene on his avaricious quest begins "to suspect some dimensional displacement in these descents to the underworld, some disparity unaccountable between the above and the below" (262). He enters "the dark of dripping caverns, stone bowels whereon was founded the city itself, holding his lantern before him, a bloodcolored troglodyte stooped and muttering down foul corridors . . . in this nether region so gravid with seam and lode. Coming from his day's labors *slavered* over with a gray paste" (259, emphasis added). The slime of the caves is not only the clay of materialism but also the slaver of the pursuing hounds of the frame and of the predatory hunt Suttree envisions at the old mansion. In this bowel-like netherworld, Gene hears "everywhere a liquid dripping, something gone awry in the earth's organs to which this measured bleeding clocked a constantly eluded doom" (261). The auditory sensation is Harrogate's, but the focus on the measured repetition of the sound is the narrator/Suttree's registering of the clocklike "whicket" of the cradle's blade (80). The incessant metronomic sewage drip noted by Suttree, Gene, or the narrator throughout the novel originates in Suttree's death-haunted imagination.

The narrator's gnostic imagery of the caverns as viscera recurs when Suttree himself descends to rescue his young friend. Gene travels down a "stone gullet" (261); Suttree notices the "stone teeth and tongues of wet black slag" in the cave's roof, or the "ribbed palate of a stone monster comatose, a great uvula dripping rust." He hears nothing but "a distant timeless dripping." As he searches, the world above seems "gone altogether," and he passes "through black and slaverous cavities where foul liquors seeped." Finally, he finds Gene in his tattered clothes, "covered with dried sewage." "True news of man here below" he thinks, articulating the metaphorical import of the previous scenes in which the narrator describes Gene's explorations of the caves and reprising Suttree's own thought early in the novel, before he learns from Rufus where an entrance to the caves might be found, that in the caves one finds only "blind slime. As above, so it is below" (275–76, 23). Such apparent foreknowledge is actually the hindsight of Suttree as narrator of his own life.

Suttree's focus on the fecal flow of life, especially his nausea at the material impermanence of human flesh, also appears in Mother She's story of her vengeance on an enemy. By plugging a hole in a tree in which she has placed his dung, she causes his intestines to swell "like a blowed dog. . . . His stool riz up in his neck till he choken on it and he turn black in the face and his guts bust open and he die a horrible death a screamin and floppin in his own mess" (280–81). As a manifestation of Suttree's concerns, Mother She's appalling tale hints the necessity of the fecal flow, of the sequential flushing of human lives out of the material world—even though Suttree as protagonist is not yet prepared to read her story affirmatively. Only at the end of the novel will he emerge from his typhoid dreams with the consoling insight that humans are more than matter: "Listen. . . . We were never promised that our flesh, that our flesh"—a thought only partly articulated to the nurse, who wants him to cover his nakedness (459). All these patterns of repetition characterize the narrator of *Suttree* as very like, even an enlightened version of, Cornelius Suttree himself, emphasizing that the novel represents Suttree's narrative "hallucination," in which, Dante-like, he re-visions his own dream-journey, functioning as the bard of his existence with a doubleness of vision that layers his more mature understanding over his memory/dream of himself as he wandered in the purgatorial/gnostic/absurd Babylon of Knoxville.

Hallucinated Recollections: *The Album of the Dead*

Localized scenes of hallucinated recollection—memories or visions prompted by artifacts—link Suttree with McCarthy's earlier protagonist narrators—especially John Wesley Rattner, who "narrates" his own tale. However, Suttree's waking visions evoked by artifacts are usually not healing visions but manifestations of his obsessions with death and his regretted or repudiated past. The psychic and spiritual wounds of which they are expressions gradually heal as Suttree witnesses the lives of others and achieves new insights in visions induced by drugs or illness. It is not until Suttree as narrator can create the imaginative recollection we infer the whole novel to be that he is able to transform and transcend his past as John Wesley does.

The most striking pattern of hallucinated recollections occurs when Suttree studies photographs or imposes the photographic metaphor on the framed windows of moving vehicles. This pattern extends the contrast between the still photos planned for the opening of *The Gardener's Son* and the moving picture that presents the story of Robert McEvoy as recovered and imagined by William Chaffee (see Luce, "'They aint the thing'" 32–33). When Martha McEvoy tells Chaffee that she can't picture Bobby's face anymore, that it has been replaced in her mind's eye with the image captured by the official photographer, she alludes not only to the way that an individual's perception becomes modified and supplanted by the codified repetition of cultural memory but also to the replacement and effacement of the living individual by the still, dead photograph that represents him, fixing him for all time. The latter conception seems to lie behind the father's discarding his wife's photo in *The Road* (44), and in a less personal way it holds primacy in Suttree's encounters with photos: rather than effectively evoking either memories or extended hallucinated recollections of the dead, the photo more often functions for Suttree merely as a memento mori, bringing to consciousness a cognition of death that he would rather keep suppressed.

The photo album scene between Suttree and Aunt Martha in some ways re-inscribes or preinscribes the scene between William Chaffee and the aged Martha in *The Gardener's Son* (since McCarthy interrupted his work on *Suttree* to write *The Gardener's Son*, we cannot know which scene was composed first without the *Suttree* manuscripts, to which we do not yet have access). But there are crucial differences: Chaffee does not view photos of his own family, so *Suttree*'s theme of genetic repetition is not at work in the screenplay; further, the script implies that Chaffee and Martha achieve a shared imaginative transcendence of the obstacles to recovering the past, while Suttree and Aunt Martha's separate acts of recovery as they contemplate the photographs are not collaborative, and Suttree's are brief and usually abortive. Unlike Chaffee, he does not visit Martha specifically to recover his family history but to discharge a debt (probably for bail money) owed to Uncle Clayton. Thus Suttree's browsing through his maternal family photos is partly by happenstance, since Martha has been looking through them before he arrives. However, his Sunday journey downriver to Martha and Clayton's home has taken him past the imposing houses on the river's north shore, where he pauses to study "from this late vantage old childhood scenes," vividly remembers the old turtle-hunter he knew as a child and even "writes" the memory as an encounter between the turtle-hunter and "the boy" (119, 120).[9] So Suttree is in a receptive mood for such recovery, and given the opportunity he asks Martha for the photo album. Indeed this poetic, episodic novel, structured on multiple patterns of repetition, is partly organized around such incidents in which Suttree chooses more or less consciously to revisit scenes from his past: this trip past Sequoyah Hills to Martha and Clayton's and the deserted Suttree mansion, his drunken return to the Immaculate Conception Church, and his visit to his old high school. Each of these incidents reminds him of the "child buried within him" and thus of his own mortality, and each provides an opportunity for hallucinated recollection but fails to relieve his existential loneliness, his dread of death, or his obsession with uniqueness (119).

The photos of "figures out of his genealogy" function for Suttree less as reminders of valued lives than as the repetitive imagery of death. With a turn of the page, the deathbed photo of Aunt Elizabeth, dry and "cured-looking," is juxtaposed with the baby picture of Roy, recalling Suttree's association of death with the "whicket and swish" of the "clocklike blade of the cradle" in his drunken vision before he is jailed, an image that for Young captures the "working paradox of the novel" (*S* 126–27, 80, Young 103). As do many rhythmically repetitive sounds in Suttree's experience, the turning of the album pages echoes the swish of death's scythe or the ticking of the clock; the sequential images of dead kin ("I am, I am"), isolating and freezing them out of the context of their lives, begin to sicken Suttree with a perception of the redundancy and reductiveness of mortality: "The old musty album . . . seemed to breathe a reek of the vault, turning up one by one these dead faces with their wan and loveless gaze out toward the spinning world, masks of incertitude before the cold glass eye of the camera or recoiling before this celluloid immortality or faces simply staggered into gaga by the sheer velocity of time" (129). The stillness of these photos contrasts with Suttree's recurring helix image that links the gnostic turmoil of life, the mortal coil, with inevitable homing to ash. The "cold glass eye of the camera" becomes the eye of death fixing the individual forever in time, as a dispassionate collector fixes an insect on the mounting pin. Later, when Suttree sees the photo of Hoghead in the news report of his death, he thinks: "Hoghead was dead in the paper. . . . He had been shot through the head with a .32 caliber pistol and he was twenty-one years old forever" (403). Significantly, as Suttree confronts photos of his kin, mirroring images of himself, he identifies with their perspective from the album that entombs them, projecting on them his own loneliness, his recoil from the still life of the celluloid icon, his nausea at the turmoil of life as it passes. The "vortex" that has "coughed up" these dead kin is life itself, characterized by gnostic thrownness, tumultuous and brief: "Blind moil in the earth's nap cast up in an eyeblink between becoming and done" (*S* 129). Their redundancy figures the monotonous repetition of death but contrasts the unchanging redundancy of the landscapes and family homes that appear as backdrops in the photographs, "as if they inhabited another medium than the dry pilgrims shored up on them."[10] When Suttree thinks, "I am, I am," he links himself with these dead kin through an ambiguous point of view: he imagines the photographed subjects sequentially asserting their existences in an eyeblink or the turn of a page, and he simultaneously asserts his own existence and his doubleness, speaking for himself and his dead twin as he has done earlier in his drunken vision in the junk lot: "As I have seen my image twinned and blown in the smoked glass of a blind man's spectacles I am, I am" (129, 80). The repetition from the earlier scene reinforces the idea that Suttree recognizes these photos of the dead, like reflections in eyeglasses, as mirrors or doubles of himself, reflecting his own destiny; in other scenes, images framed in windows or by the camera's eye function similarly as tropes of death.[11] The phrase "an artifact of prior races," which may be read to complete Suttree's thought, "I am," is isolated in a fragment; thus it refers both to the iconic photograph and to Suttree himself in his genetic repetition and the redundancy of his shared destiny in "ultimate dark" (129, 130). As an artifact of prior races, living Suttree paradoxically becomes their dead remnant, himself the "bitter refund" of their spent lives (130).

The photographs prompt only two abortive hallucinated recollections in Suttree, neither of them achieving the narrative wholeness of Wes's, John Wesley's, or William Chaffee's, nor capturing the value of an individual life that the *gitano* of *The Crossing* claims may be accomplished through narrative in the hearts of those who love the pictured dead. Though he actually remembers some of the individuals, such as his maternal grandfather presented in a "deathbed stud[y]" and whom Suttree recalls seeing dead, he here experiences hallucinated recollections only in response to photographs of people who are essentially strangers to him, acknowledged impersonally as kin, prefigurings of himself and of his fate (129). His memories of those he has actually known are blocked until, in his literal hallucinations induced by Mother She, he "saw what had been" in a series of memories of family funerals and death watches (rather like a series of photographs), events that traumatized him as a child and to which we may trace the inception of his fear of the huntsman in any shape. In contrast, when Suttree experiences his first hallucinated recollection as he views Aunt Martha's photo album, recognizing the picture of Uncle Milo, who died at sea after a thirteen-year absence from home, it is quite likely that he remembers a family story he has heard but not any personal contact with the living—or dead—man. Suttree knows that Milo was "lost under Capricorn . . . aboard a bargeload of birdshit one foggy night off the limeslaked coast of Chile. Souls commended to the sea's salt clemency" (127–28). And the story's resonance with his vision on the bridge in the night rain prompts Suttree to revisit his imagined participation in the tumbling death of the suicide drowning in the river's "fecal deeps" in his vision of Milo's drowning, even briefly sharing Milo's underwater perspective of the strange "austral constellations," "wrinkling, fading, through the cold black waters. As he rocks in his rusty pannier to the sea's floor in a drifting stain of guano" (29, 128). Suttree's transient vision, with its evocation of the southern hemisphere, recalls the narrator's observation in the prologue of the *"gray vines coiled leftward in this northern hemisphere, what winds them shapes the dogwhelk's shell,"* a pairing of passages that evokes the mirroring of the northern and southern hemispheres and, with the implications of the mortal coil, reinforces the notion of the mirrored deaths of the suicide in the north and Milo in the south—indeed, the mirrored deaths of all (3). The constellations and the coil surface again in Suttree's brief musing on the two photographs of Aunt Elizabeth, one on her deathbed and another in her youth: "Between the mad hag's face and this young girl a vague stellar drift, the wheeling of planets on their ether trunnions" (130). The spin of the planets functions as an astronomical analogue or fractal repetition on a larger scale of the mortal coil of life on earth and thus as a memento of the relentless passage of time, with the sinister gnostic implications of the wheeling celestial spheres as hypostases of the archons that oppress and imprison the spirit in cosmos.

The second of Suttree's hallucinated recollections as he pages through the album is of the World War I soldier, and as usual his vision centers on death. Again, the soldier died before Suttree could have known him (Suttree is at most in his early thirties in the time frame of the novel, 1951 to 1955), yet he imagines himself a child among the mourners who sign for the soldier's body at the train station and bury him. In doing so, Suttree builds on family stories he has heard (as Young points out, this dead soldier may be the young Robert of Aunt Alice's recollection; 99–100), but he achieves a writer's immediacy through his imagination. Like Harry dying of gangrene in Hemingway's "The Snows of Kilimanjaro," Suttree is "writing" here: "We could not believe he was inside. Cold and dry it was, our shoes cried in the snow all the way home. The least of us tricked out in black like small monks mourning . . . with musty hymnals in our hands and eyes to the ground. . . . Pulley squeak, the mounded flowers sucked slowly into the earth. A soldier held the folded flag to Mamaw but she could not look. . . . Scoop of dirt rattling, this sobbing, these wails in the quiet winter twilight" (129–30). Suttree's recollection of Milo shares the imaginative identification with the stranger, but it is abridged as it morphs into self-concern: "What family has no mariner in its tree? No fool, no felon. No fisherman" (128). In this second instance, when Suttree identifies not with the dead soldier but with the bereaved family, he manages a more extended vision, one that only reaches closure with the return of Aunt Martha with her pitcher of tea, as Harry's visions are sometimes interrupted by the woman's attentions in "The Snows of Kilimanjaro."

Suttree's vision of the dead soldier, "one of the all but nameless who arrived home in wooden boxes," suggests that for him the picture of any unknown soldier is an image of death or of Camus's condemned man (129), and this conditions his special attention to the photo of the uniformed youth on Mother She's kitchen gallery wall. Here he projects his own death-angst on the soldier, which curtails his access to an extended imaginative vision: "A black boy in uniform who has watched the camera with some suspicion of his own expendability" (280). Suttree's contrasting reactions to these two photos of soldiers suggest that the writer must break out of the closed circuit of self-concern— fear of his own death—in order to achieve his vision of the world, and this prefigures the ultimate movement of the book, when Suttree breaks out of his self-obsessed, purgatorial circling in Knoxville, transcending his death phobia and moving on to become the narrator of this story.

Even in isolated moments we find a foreshadowing of this larger movement when Suttree's free indirect discourse encompasses shifts to the perspective of others. When he rides on trains or trolley cars, the cinematic shifts in his focus are linked with photographic images as metaphors for death. As Suttree watches the landscape pass from the window of the train taking him through the Cumberlands to his son's funeral, such a reversal in the angle of vision occurs seamlessly. The free indirect discourse describes the scenes passing before Suttree's eyes, framed in the train's window and thus a little like the photos on the turning album pages but with a filmic continuity the discrete photos lack. Then the repetitious rhythm of the railroad timbers' staccato passage enters Suttree's awareness: "They crossed a creek by an old trestle, black creosoted timbers flicking past" (149). The flicking timbers visually echo the aural "whicket and swish" of the cradle's blade and the "I am, I am" of the photo album, and abruptly Suttree's angle of vision merges with that of two boys rowing in the creek and "watching the faces pass like a filmstrip above them" (149). As Suttree sees what the boys see, isolated faces framed in the train's lighted windows, passing through and flicking into their past, he conjoins the images of photo album and film strip, with their sequential yet static representations of human lives frozen in passage, and the sound of the cradle's "whicket" (echoed by the train's clacking) in a vision of himself framed within the album of the dead. In the next sentence, the focus reverts to what Suttree literally sees: one boy's solemn salute to him, passing. But throughout, the paragraph remains grounded in Suttree's subjective experience; it closes with Suttree's visions of the dreary town on the "gray and barren plain" and of "the cold rain falling in a new dug grave" beyond (149). The grave is his son's, but as Suttree's vision of his own face passing in an isolated frame of the train/filmstrip implies, the grave is also his own.

The image of the stranger's salute to the passing other occurs earlier, when Suttree takes leave of the man who has offered him a ride in the rain, getting out of the car in the middle of nowhere, as far as the man can tell, to walk to the old family mansion. Suttree sees the man's face framed in the window of his car, studying Suttree "as if to fix him there" (134). The scene resonates with many such scenes in the Border Trilogy, where strangers watch John Grady or

Billy pass, sometimes because he is puzzling but sometimes "solely because he was passing. Solely because he would vanish" (*APH* 301). Suttree's intuition that the stranger's gaze is meant to fix him as in a snapshot prefigures the more articulated filmstrip image he perceives as he travels to his son's funeral. Even here, on the same afternoon that he pages through family photos, Suttree recognizes that as the man is framed in his car window for him, he is framed in it for the man, and he experiences a dread of the fixing gaze of the stranger, the cold glass eye of the camera that stops time and motion and thus records only death. Such dread will not be mitigated by the boy's sober salute to him as he passes on the train (the two children on the river are an image of the child Suttree and his dead twin, both of whom have already passed), but it suggests an appropriate response to the passing other: respectful recognition of the soul in transit, who stands for oneself. This is the lesson of the stranger who tells his dreams to Billy Parham in the epilogue of *Cities of the Plain:* "Every man's death is a standing in for every other. And since death comes to all there is no way to abate the fear of it except to love that man who stands for us. . . . That man who is all men and who stands in the dock for us until our own time come and we must stand for him. Do you love him, that man? Will you honor the path he has taken? Will you listen to his tale?" (288–89).

The reciprocal nature of such witness is incipient in another image of repetitious passage on Suttree's train ride. Standing between two passenger cars as the train pulls into town, he notices "staccato lights tracking in the gray frieze out there. In an upper window a man in his undershirt with his braces hanging. Across the narrow space he and Suttree looked at each other for just a moment before he was snapped away. The gray steel trusses of a bridge went past, went past, went past" (149). There is no tale, no hallucinated recollection of the other here—just the image of a man's being yanked out of one's field of vision almost simultaneously with his entering it. This further vision of the freeze-frame of death is pounded home with the whicket of the steel trusses and the repetition of "went past, went past." Later the man in braces is doubled by the man Suttree salutes with his highball from the window of the hotel room he shares with the prostitute Joyce: "a gesture indifferent and almost cynical that as he made it caused him something close to shame" (402). This moment in which Suttree cynically refuses respectful recognition of the mirroring other occurs at arguably the lowest point in his decline into despair, expressing his self-loathing projected onto the unoffending other framed in the window.

On Suttree's long streetcar ride on a bitterly cold Thanksgiving in the same autumn as his son's death, he observes "lightwires slung past in shallow convections pole to pole" (178). This image of measured repetition reprises that of his train ride to the funeral, when he sees "polewires sewing tirelessly the night beyond the cold windowglass," reminding him of his son's death and causing "loneliness [to ride] in his stomach like an egg" (148, 178). Once again, Suttree sees another through a window and imaginatively reverses his angle of vision to share in hers: "Your face among the brown bags old lady. Waiting to cross. Blinking at the transit of these half empty frames slapping past." But here he almost represses his own image windowed away in death: the woman's focus, Suttree imagines, is caught by the empty window frames rather than the one containing his image. Yet the freeze-frame death-image is implicit in the echo of the filmstrip. And Suttree next notices "beyond in a yellowlit housewindow two faces fixed aspectant and forever in some domestic vagary" with an aware-ness of the velocity of his own passing: "Rapid his progress who petrifies these innocents into stony history" (178). The momentum of the living hurtling toward death reevokes the mortal coil of insects homing to ash and suggests that the turmoil of life promotes our "fixing" others with the cold eye of the stranger, or of death. Expelled from the streetcar and hiking back to town, Sut-tree again sees the sequential freeze-frame of the filmstrip in an inbound trol-ley: "Blacks nodding in their windowstrips. A trolley of dolls or frozen dead" (179). When Suttree wakes from a drunken binge in a cemetery and trudges sullenly back to the Long house, a bus passes, its windows filled with faces. Once more, Suttree's bitter self-concern blocks his compassionate response to the passing others, and he salutes them with a gesture of his middle finger: "He shaped a curse in the air after them with a leanboned hand" (303).

Suttree's persistent meditation on death as a freeze-frame is evident too in his tendency to project photographic imagery or images of still fixity on others: after his train ride to the Cumberlands, he sees his wife's family framed by their front porch, "gathered there like a sitting for some old sepia tintype"—an image that fixes them in death but that also walls them away from him, isolated in his own grief and self-pity (150). His first vision of Reese's family is one of fixity within the vortex as they spin down the turbid river "with the next wall of the [houseboat] shack coming about and along it like plaster caryatids hung there in a stunned frieze . . . the figures of four women and two men, pale, rigid, deathless, wheeling slowly away below the bridge and gone in the mist" (307). Their deathlessness is a Keatsian illusion, of course, like the photograph that forever fixes the subject in the album of the dead.

Despite the poetic sensibility that informs Suttree's prolonged meditation on the metaphor of the photograph, his achieving only the briefest reversals in perspective with the individuals he spots from train or trolley windows implies that his capacity for imaginative identification is blocked for the time being, foiled by his compulsive imaging of his own death. The photo on Mother She's wall that most compels his attention is that of her dead grandmother, who gazes out at him from her vantage point of death, but who is his mirror image: "The hands at the neck of the creature seemed to be forcing her to look at something she had rather not see and was it Suttree himself these sixty-odd years hence?" Once again Suttree sees in the photo a projection of his own obsessions, this time specifically his own reluctance to face death. The empty space in the family portrait, the space where Mother She "never come out," suggests that she alone is exempt from the camera's cold eye of death, a condition for which Suttree longs. Yet this exemption alienates her from the rest of her family, marking her as the "ghost" among her dead kin (279). This imagery of the community of the dead hints at a potential consolation for human mortality, but Suttree cannot absorb it. As he recovers from his ordeal in the mountains, reexperiencing the dreams he has had in the wilderness and feeling as though his very spirit has been "scooped" from his chest and replaced with a cold gnostic whirlwind, he thinks that "even the community of the dead had disbanded into ashes, those shapes wheeling in the earth's crust through a nameless ether no more men than were the ruins of any other thing once living" (295).

Suttree's later insights will, however, explicitly resolve the paralyzing influence of these fixed images of mortality. Early in his journey, as Suttree gazes at photographs or at strangers passing on moving vehicles, he can only respond with nausea and fear. By the end of the novel, though, when he announces somewhat paradoxically that "all souls are one and all souls lonely," he partakes in a communion of souls in the gnostic human condition of the flesh's mortality and the spirit's terrible alienation (459). He is able to do so because he now comprehends that "nothing ever stops moving," a thought that may seem to reinforce his earlier dismay at the seeping of life but in fact expresses a modification of his obsession with the album of the dead: if nothing ever stops moving, death never fixes it (461). The freeze-frame of the photo, isolated out of time and context, is the illusion; life is more akin to the seamless motion perceived in a film or indeed all around us: the wheeling of the constellations and the motion Suttree sees from the moving train. This shift in perspective repositions Suttree within the flux of life itself, watching it move around him even as he moves in relation to others. In addition, it marks a distancing from the strictly gnostic association of the flux of life with cosmic turmoil in favor of a Camusian affirmation of earthly life itself. It may even adumbrate the view of the *gitano* in *The Crossing* that we are always alive, that we know nothing but life, because time does not exist outside of ourselves. The *gitano* tells Billy in Spanish that "we think that we are victims of time. In reality the way of the world is not fixed in any place. How could this be possible? We are ourselves our own day's journey. And therefore we are time also" (413–14). When Suttree, recovering from typhoid, tells the priest, "You would not believe what watches. . . . He [God] is not a thing. Nothing ever stops moving," he does not deny the gnostic reality of the huntsman who hounds man as he spirals down in dread of his own temporal materiality, but he also affirms a witnessing God of process: a God (perhaps the alien Good God, eternal and not time-bound) who watches the endless movement of all creation not sequentially, as in an album of the dead, but simultaneously and timelessly (461). Again Suttree's new vision resonates with the philosophical bedrock of *The Crossing*, where the priest tells Billy that "the world itself can have no temporal view of things" (148) and where the old pensioner dreams of the weaver not as Suttree's *"carder of souls from the world's nap"* but as a more benign weaver-god creating a tapestry "that was the world in its making and in its unmaking" and for whom the individual is an integral thread of this endless fabric (*S* 5, *C* 149).

"This obscure purgatory"

Even more explicitly than in *Outer Dark* and *Child of God*, the world of *Suttree* is presented in purgatorial terms. References to purgatory and hell abound, from the invocation of Virgil and Dante in the prologue to Suttree's Roman Catholic tutoring that his dead twin is "in the limbo of the Christless righteous, I in a terrestrial hell" (14) to the many descents to a "nether world." Through references to Maggeson as "some latterday Charon skulling through the fog," Suttree figures the Tennessee River as Acheron, the river marking the boundary to the first circle of Dante's inferno (*S* 107). A "fiend . . . Whose eyes were socketed in wheels of flame," Charon ferries the souls of the unrepentant dead across Acheron into hell (*Inferno* 3.107, 3.96). Dante describes him with an image McCarthy echoes both in "Wake for Susan" and in the children's cemetery in the mountains in *Suttree*, where the souls of the dead have fallen like leaves (*S* 286):

> And just as leaves swayed by the autumn winds
> Drop from the tree, each falling in its turn
> Until the branch is all despoiled and bare,
> So here did Adam's evil seed descend,
> And one by one they stepped off from the shore,
> Like hawk to hunter's call, at Charon's sign.
> (*Inferno* 3.110–15)

Maggeson, then, is one avatar of the dreaded huntsman, as is Red Callahan, who passes Suttree during the brawl at the roadhouse "smiling, . . . His busy freckled fists ferrying folks to sleep" (186). In a prescient dream Suttree invokes Acheron explicitly, but Christian symbolism not associated with Dante's infernal river modifies the reference. Suttree sees his friends drifting past him down the flooded river: "A fog . . . closed away their figures gone a sadder way by psychic seas across the Tarn of Acheron. From a rock in the river he waved them farewell but they did not wave back" (190). The dream prefigures not only the death or imprisonment to come for these friends but also Suttree's own ultimate "salvation," here conveyed in the Christian symbol of the rock rising out of the gnostic's dreadful tumultuous river—even though Suttree's spiritual growth requires him to overcome spiritual wounds inflicted by his early Christian education. Although he salutes his passing friends, Suttree's dream suggests an anxiety that may impede his quest: that finding his way will isolate him from the community of the living dead, that finding the way will mark him as the gnostic alien man or stranger, awake among the oblivious.

Other rivers in *The Divine Comedy* resonate with McCarthy's novel. Like Suttree, Dante lives by an earthly river; he tells the shades that he brings "this body from [the] shores" of the Arno in Tuscany (*Purgatory* 14.16–19). The three rivers of Dante's underworld, Acheron, Styx, and Phlegethon, flow into the depths of the inferno, where they join to form Cocytus (*Inferno* 14.109–13). The purgatorial river that corresponds to Dante's infernal Acheron is the Tiber: at death the soul falls into one river or the other, depending on its spiritual state (*Purgatory* 2.98–103). And in purgatory is Dante's version of the river Lethe, with its Platonic associations adapted to Christian mythology: "its purging flow / Affords absolution to the happy souls / Whose penance has unburdened them of guilt" (*Inferno* 14.131–33).

But the fecal waters of the Tennessee, where once could be heard packetboats "howlin on the river like souls," most evokes the dark and misty river Styx, the marsh between the fifth and sixth circles of hell that carries gnostic associations of stagnant water as darkness, the antithesis of the life of the spirit (204). In Styx the wrathful in their "filthy pond" or "sordid creek" wallow and fight each other in the "morass" (*Inferno* 7.129, 8.9, 7.110). Such stygian mire extends to locations other than the river: the drunken fight between Joyce and Suttree that ends their relationship begins in a muddy car lot outside the Redbud Room. There they "slid about and feinted in the slick red clay," and when Suttree finally strongarms Joyce into the car, their shoes are "globed with mud" (409).[12] In the *Inferno* Virgil tells Dante, "Others are deep submerged and with their gasps / Send bubbles to the surface of this ooze . . . / Fixed in the slime . . . / They gargle in their gullets" (7.118–26). Confronted by one "cloaked with slime," Virgil comments, "How many in the light of day comport / Themselves like kings who here below like pigs / Will wallow in the muck"—a passage that also resonates with Gene Harrogate's engulfment in sewage and with the several scenes focused on the pigs of the First Creek neighborhood (8.32, 8.46–48).

Across the Styx lies the walled city of Dis, "with its sad citizens and direful host" who challenge Dante and Virgil's entrance—a mythic counterpart to the ramparted city or "*encampment of the damned*" of *Suttree*'s prologue (*Inferno* 8.65–66; *S* 3). Here Virgil assures a terrified Dante, "I'll not desert you in this nether world" (*Inferno* 8.104). In Dis the heretics burn within their tombs, rich with "their wicked spoil," an aspect of the infernal city that resonates with Suttree's struggle to reject Knoxville's commercialism and social hierarchies (*Inferno* 9.130). In the spring of 1953, Suttree rows on the flooded river amid its freight of death and debris, feeling himself "yet another artifact . . . draining down out of the city . . . that no rain could make clean again," left "stunned and drying in the curing mud, the terra damnata of the city's dead alchemy" (306). Knoxville as Dis, the city of heretics, is a fallen version of the city on the hill, the Puritan hope for a city of God in America, as Canfield points out ("Dawning" 674). When Suttree makes his way down the hill to his houseboat after his break with Joyce, a separation that marks their mutual disgust with the materialism at the heart of their relationship, he notes the ruinous hardscape of the city—"all this detritus slid from the city on the hill" (411); his reference, with its ironic hindsight, is to John Winthrop's sermon, "A Model of Christian Charity," in which the Puritan leader exhorted and warned his New England–bound congregation: "We must consider that we shall be as a city upon a hill. The eyes of all people are upon us, so that if we shall deal falsely with our God in this work we have undertaken, and so cause Him to withdraw His present help from us, we shall be made a story and a by-word through the world. . . . If our hearts . . . be seduced, and worship other gods, our pleasures and profits, and serve them . . . we shall surely perish out of the good land" (118). Suttree's allusion suggests that the American enterprise has erected on the clean breast of the new world not Winthrop's city upon a hill but Dante's Dis or even Babylon, which for the gnostics was "the gross world or body" (Mead 204). It marks Suttree's full recognition—inklings of which have troubled him all along—that he has reenacted the heresy of Knoxville and America, the terrestrial city, in his seduction to pleasure and profit with the prostitute Joyce.

The bridge lights Suttree sees as "chained and burning supplicants" in the water below him recall Dante's standing dizzily on a bridge overlooking the abyss, where he sees "flickering flares" in the gulf (29). Virgil explains, "Within the fire the spirits dwell, / Each one close swathed in burning robes of flame" (*Inferno* 26.32, 26.48–49). The burning or tortured souls in hell often supplicate Dante to carry their stories back to earth, and Suttree as narrator of his novel will fulfill the same function for his fellows in infernal Knoxville. Early in the novel Suttree ascends from the river, "coming up out of this hot and funky netherworld attended by gospel music," in a passage that suggests the direction his path ultimately will take, but he cannot yet escape the purgatorial experience of the city (21). As with Culla Holme and Lester Ballard, his purgatory is an aspect of his own soul-sickness, and he carries it with him.

Stopped by the police in the city, Suttree hears a thrush and looks around at the few blackened trees, connecting this spot of sparse urban wilderness with Dante's dark wood: "this obscure purgatory" (83). The thrush, a singer in purgatory, is a metaphor for Suttree in his artistic and spiritual quest. In the market Suttree finds "whole legions of the maimed and mute and crooked deployed over the streets in a limboid vapor of smoke and fog" (168). The loiterers on the street who verbally harass a young woman recall the rabble at the portal to hell (*Inferno* 3.1–50); they appear to Suttree as "clutches of the iniquitous and unshriven howling curses at the gates and calling aloud for redress of their right damnation to a god [or gnostic demiurge?] who need be interceded with bassackwards or obliquely" (246). Finally, attracted by sewage and waste, flies beset both the river and the city, evoking Beelzebub, lord of the flies.

Even in his temporary escape from the city to the French Broad River with Reese's family, Suttree carries his obsessions and alcoholism with him, and thus his purgatory or gnostic outer dark or existential alienation. After his binge with Reese he wakes outdoors where "the sunhammered landscape veered away in a quaking shapeless hell" (341), recalling the antagonistic archontic sun of *Outer Dark*, *Blood Meridian*, and *The Stranger*. But as he recovers from typhoid fever, that purgative disease, Suttree distinguishes the objective world of McAnally Flats from the purgatorial world of his subjective experience.[13] He and Jim Long see the expressway being built over the neighborhood, and the narrator/Suttree remarks: "He knew another McAnally, good to last a thousand years. There'd be no new roads there" (463). His departure from the stygian river and "Dis-topian" city, described in the epilogue, is a symbolic departure from the purgatorial/gnostic world that has been his experience. McCarthy's deployment of purgatory as a syncretic Platonic/gnostic/Dantean metaphor for the earthly struggle for vision emphasizes that Suttree does not literally ascend into paradise, Dante's next realm, but transcends the despair, blindness, and captivity to materialism that marks the soul's earthly travail—achieving enlightenment or gnosis or its existentialist equivalent.

As narrator, Suttree projects on all contexts and characters the purgatorial and gnostic vision he finally warns us against. The crazed evangelist who calls down damnation from his high room like some perverse gnostic version of a demented and vengeful god wishes "all on to a worse hell yet" (146). Gene Harrogate, on his first day in the city, struggles in the heat, with the "sun like a bunghole to a greater hell beyond" (99). When Suttree visits Gene in his den under the First Creek viaduct, he notes that his "little grotto glowed with a hellish red from the lanterns" he has stolen from a work site; later Gene appears there like "a diabolic figure"; and when he plans his descent into the caves, the narrator/Suttree describes him as a "demon cartographer in the hellish light charting the progress of souls in the darkness below," figuring the inept, materialistic Gene as an avatar of the archontic powers (116, 219, 260). On Gene's train ride to the penitentiary in Nashville, the engine wails "like a thing damned of all deliverance," confirming the end result of his feckless descent into criminal materialism (439). Hooper, the despairing ragman, looks at Suttree through the "red flame that raged in his head"—himself a potential warning to Suttree against the despair that hounds him throughout the novel (146).

As can be seen in these image patterns, McCarthy does not reproduce and adhere to a strict Dantean geography in *Suttree*, though he associates the Tennessee River with Acheron and Styx and Knoxville with Dis. Nor is his protagonist's physical movement through the terrains of the novel a metaphor of the soul's step-by-step progress comparable to Dante's movement through the levels of the inferno and the purgatorio to the paradiso in *The Divine Comedy*, although Suttree achieves a form of gnosis by its conclusion. McCarthy does invoke both an intermittent pattern of descents as in *Child of God*—especially in Harrogate's wandering in the caverns beneath the city—and a pattern of Suttree's tethered "escapes" from the city, only to be pulled back in. But the geometry or geography most deployed in *Suttree* is that of the embedded fractal repetition of the purgatorio or inferno on greater or smaller scales, an embeddedness that alludes to the concentric spheres of archontic influence enclosing the nether world of cosmos as well as the Dantean notion of life as a purgatorial or infernal dream. The purgatory of the novel, as we are told in the prologue, is a world within a world, a subset of Knoxville; but it is also an outward projection of Suttree's inner landscape: the Knoxville he experiences reflects his inner, spiritual turmoil. The *cloaca maxima* of the river, draining its effluvium of waste out of the city, mirrors on a large scale the inner workings of the organism—such as the human—that sustains life through constant absorption of nutrients and expulsion of waste: fecal matter. Similarly the gullet and bowels of the caves through which Gene and Suttree wander figure the purgatorial experience as a journey through or imprisonment in the alimentary canal of the beast. To take the alimentary metaphor to a yet larger and more abstract scale, death itself is conceived as a river or *cloaca maxima*, cleansing the world of the material waste of mortal flesh. Implicit in this metaphor is not only Suttree's nausea at the materiality and morbidity of humankind but also the hint of the cosmos as an "organic" being, the gnostic leviathan, its continuity ensured by the regular purgation of individual bodies.

Bell reads the river as "a metaphorical condensation of the authority of the physical world" of the novel, a "radically desacralized" cosmos (*Achievement* 74). In deploying the literal meanings of purgation in his *cloaca maxima* metaphor for the river and the world, McCarthy links the state of spiritual purgatory with materialism—as he had in *Outer Dark* via the metaphor of incest and in *Child of God* through the metaphor of necrophilia. But Suttree's case reverses Lester Ballard's: whereas Lester perversely represses the hard facts of materiality and death in his love of bodies, Suttree cannot repress his hyper-awareness of the body's death and decay. From this heightened sensitivity derives what William Spencer has called the "excremental vision" of *Suttree*. Yet both Lester and Suttree are threatened with drowning in materialism, albeit with differing degrees of consciousness. Lester, in his descent into necrophilia, blindly devotes himself to oblivious materialism; Suttree, with his heightened sensitivity, fears the death-in-life of materialism and seeks to escape its pull, yet intermittently yields to it. As Spencer points out in "*Suttree:* The Excremental Vision of Cormac McCarthy," the body's physical discharges repeatedly impinge on Suttree's consciousness. They appear not only in the images of excrement that Spencer catalogues but also in discharges of other varieties: in Suttree or Gene's alcohol-induced vomiting, in Suttree's bout with the bloody flux of typhoid, in the carrion-stained bedsheets wrapping Leonard's father, in Suttree's fevered dreams of the crazed evangelist's denouncing the Huddle's "foul perverts" who "slak[e] their hideous gorges with jissom" and of being engulfed by an "enormous wattled fundament . . . , in the center a withered brown pig's eye crusted shut and hung with puffy blue and swollen lobes" from which "a white gruel welled"; in the narrator's description of the mentally retarded girl sexually abused by multiple men, her "cunt . . . like a hairclot fished from a draintrap"; even in the grotesque birth/death imagery of Suttree's hallucination in which he has a vision of being "voided by an enormous livercolored cunt" (457, 450, 416, 452).

These gross, even offensive images detail Suttree's nauseated gnostic awareness of the foul materiality of the human body and its flux: forecasts of its imminent dissolution. He sees blood, the fluid of life, as death-bent matter. In the winter of Suttree's relationship with Joyce, he walks in the snow of the city and notices "how the snow fell cherry red in the soft neon flush of the beersign like the slow dropping of blood" (386). Later he walks through another nighttime snowfall "in a light fog of alcohol" and observes the pristine snow masking the city: "It has covered up the blood and dirt and claggy sleech in gutterways and laid white lattice on the sewer grates." His image links blood with mud, the "claggy sleech"; the parallel image of sewage is intensified when he sees the creek burbling along "gorged with offal. Upon whose surface the flakes impinge softly and are gone" (403). In its purity, transience, and uniqueness, the snowflake swallowed by the flow of sewage functions as yet another of Suttree's metaphors for the individual spirit engulfed and voided by death, for the alien spirit overwhelmed by cosmic materialism.

Suttree's outrage at the material ground of human life becomes most explicit when he examines the photographs of his dead kin and poses the gnostic query,

"What deity in the realms of dementia, what rabid god decocted out of the smoking lobes of hydrophobia could have devised a keeping place for souls so poor as is this flesh. This mawky wormbent tabernacle" (130). In a Mandaean text quoted by Jonas, the spirit asks the similar gnostic question: "Why did ye carry me away from my abode into captivity and cast me into the stinking body?" (*Gnostic Religion* 63). Suttree's disgust finds a strange parallel in the twin hunters Vernon and Fernon's story of curing hounds of chasing flying squirrels by tying the body of one around the dog's neck "till it rots off"—an image that captures Suttree's sense that one lives shackled to one's own rotting corpse (359). His obsession with the fluid materiality of the flesh constitutes not only a fear of death and impermanence but also gnostic terror of metaphysical death by drowning in cosmic mire, a drowning that constitutes spiritual death and oblivion.

Suttree's dread of materialism also informs his rejection of the world of commerce and social status based on wealth, represented by the dystopia of Knoxville to which his father is apparently so acclimated. Suttree's perception that wealth creates artificial distinctions among souls is fed partly by his resentment of the disdain his father, son of a judge, bears his mother, whose family background is humble—and by extension the disdain his father bears for him. "Look," he angrily tells his maternal Uncle John, "When a man marries beneath him his children are beneath him. If he thinks that way at all. If you werent a drunk he might see me with different eyes. As it is, my case was always doubtful. I was expected to turn out badly" (19). Paradoxically Suttree is effectively an alcoholic, fulfilling his father's worst expectations and repeatedly wallowing in that form of materialism as he literally enacts the gnostic metaphor for the oblivion of the spirit in cosmos—that the spirit is drunk with cosmos. One indication of his redemption at the end of the novel is his refusing Jim Long's offer of whiskey, saying "I'd just like maybe a drink of water," a request for the Living Water associated with spiritual gnosis (463). Until he lets go of his anger at his father and ceases using his pain and alcoholism as excuses, Suttree's resentment takes the form of accusing his father of the materialism he associates with the death of the spirit. Suttree sees a dichotomy between the rich and successful, who will find it harder to enter the kingdom of heaven than it is for a camel to pass through the eye of a needle, and the poor, who will always be with us because we live in an unredeemed world. Casting his lot with the poor of Knoxville, he repudiates the middle-class materialism of his father and the social hierarchies of Knoxville (associated with judgmental archontic powers both in ancient gnosticism and in modern existentialism), indeed all people of wealth who through their industry create atmospheres of soot and landscapes of junk, those who make trash of the poor. In this sense, *Suttree* is very much a novel of the rebellious and socially conscious 1960s.

Suttree's repudiation of his father's materialism is further illuminated by his hallucinated recollection at the old family mansion, "a great empire relic," in which he associates his paternal family with a heritage of feral predation (121). Predation in all forms is a recurring feature of Suttree's purgatorial and gnostic nightmare: the material fact of predation as the foundation of human life and survival, the sublimation of humans' predatory instincts in the competitive pursuit of status and material possessions, and the predation of the archontic huntsman on human souls. In the ruined mansion of his grandfather, Suttree first remembers the old man's clocking the racehorse and his own childhood sickness at "the slow seeping of life." Then he has a vision that is more a moment of creative "writing" than a simple memory: he enters the dining room, "scene of old heraldic feasts," and segues from his grandfather's dinner parties for the now "somewhat illustrious dead" to a grim vision of the board of his preliterate Saxon forebears that unmasks a brute reality beneath the civil custom of shared bread: "Mad trenchermen in armed sortees above the platters, the clang of steel, the stained and dripping chops, the eyes sidling. Yard dogs and starving palliards contest the scraps among the straw. There is nothing laid to table save meat and water" (136). This vision, conditioned by Suttree's childhood memory of the turtle-hunter accessed earlier that same day, reconnects the act of dining with the predatory hunt that underlies it. The prey, though cooked, is torn and devoured. And the stain of man's predation is linked with the "dripping" of life—his own along with that of the animals he preys on. Suttree's vision stresses the antiquity of his ancestors' class distinction: even in medieval Europe the excluded beggars were reduced to competing with dogs for remnants from the master's table. In Suttree's imagination, this ancient heritage of social privilege hardly evokes pride: the guests are wary of one another and do not speak; they eat like primitives, and the master wipes his greasy hands in his hair. Suttree envisions his forebears in terms similar to the narrators' descriptions of Glanton's gang in *Blood Meridian* or the triune of rapacious outlaws in *Outer Dark*. The novel suggests that Suttree's family, America's colonizers and empire-builders, and humanity in general are not far removed from their feral beginnings and on a metaphoric level are avatars of the archontic powers.[14] In the mountains Suttree will think again of his "old feral fathers" (385), imagining them in a carnivalesque hallucination combining a medieval parade and a celebration of bloodletting, also associated with both the "perishability of his flesh" and the call of "illbedowered harlots": "In the rain and lightning came a troupe of squalid merrymakers bearing a caged wivern on shoulderpoles and other alchemical game, chimeras and cacodemons skewered up on boarspears and a pharmacopoeia of hellish condiments adorning a trestle and toted by trolls with an eldern gnome for guidon who shouted foul oaths from his mouthhole and a piper who piped a pipe of ploverbone and wore on his hip a glass flasket of some smoking fuel that yawed within viscid as quick-silver" (287).[15]

These scenes establish that Suttree's quest to escape the outer dark of materialism involves the repudiation of predation not so much in the literal sense (Suttree eats red meat with relish) but in its metaphorical sense as the objectifying of others in pursuit of pleasure and profit. Suttree's vision of the predatory board of his forefathers, then, reinscribes John Wesley Rattner's vision of his father as a highwayman and feral predator of another kind. Both novels stress the sons' revolt against primitive, materialistic relations among human beings and their quests for communion and communication instead. Their repudiation of their natural fathers functions metaphorically to suggest their rebellion against the dominant culture of the fatherland, America. In the prison of his purgatorial world, Suttree seeks the eyes of the indigent (59).

If in his purgatory Suttree seeks communion with his fellow humans, especially those who are most victimized by the predation of the privileged classes or of American consumer culture, the purgatory functions on a compatible level as a place of penance, as in Dante and in Roman Catholic teaching. Giles sees Suttree's descent into the slums of Knoxville as an effort "to escape the sins of his past by attempting to alleviate the problems of his outlandish circle of friends" (93). His attempt is only intermittent, however, and if this is his project, he fails to achieve a consistent commitment to it through much of the novel. Certainly he succeeds more easily in his paternal care for the men of the city than in his partnerships with women. And as Arnold observes, his most dramatic effort on behalf of another, his retrieval of Gene Harrogate from the underworld of the city, is at least partly motivated by self-concern since the resurrection is a reversal of his burying his son and a modified compensation for it ("Naming, Knowing" 60). But Giles's discussion of Suttree's repressed guilt for his transgressions against his family, especially his wife and son, suggests an interesting motive for his self-exile in this purgatory, where his penance is worked out in his gradual reconnection with the family of humanity and with his own simple human heart.

Apprentice Felons, Apprentice Predators

Aptly, this novel exploring life as a purgatory employs secondary characters as foils and lessons for the visionary sojourner. In *Suttree* as in *The Divine Comedy*, everyone with whom the protagonist interacts is in one way or another a double and a cautionary model for him and for the reader, a challenge to his compassion as well as ours. As such, *Suttree*'s secondary characters are not only finely drawn realistic and often humorous sketches of the unprivileged of East Tennessee but also emblematic figures who mimic and parody the materialistic and predatory nature of the culture that rejects them, who represent humanity in general in its gnostic oblivion. Hooper the ragman and Harvey the junkman live out their squalid lives amassing and hoarding material goods in emulation of the middle class. In doing so, they literally live in junk; in their devotion to such materialism they make themselves junk, as is suggested when the ragman, squatting in a dumpster, is showered with garbage, or when Suttree sees Harvey in his drunken stupor as "one among a mass of twisted shapes discarded here" (256, 269). Not only are they treated as waste by the upper and middle classes of the city, an idea developed in the trope of the watertrucks, but they treat themselves as waste in their oblivious devotion to materialism. Suttree perceives this with acute pain when he finds Hooper's corpse among his salvage under the bridge. In his last conversation with Hooper, Suttree has reassured him, "You're always right. . . . We're all right" (365–66).[16] This insight about the value of every man's lived experience, every man's tale, marks Suttree's emergence from the depression he suffers after Wanda's death and adumbrates early on his final assertion that "all souls are one and all souls lonely" (459). However, his fleeting insight cannot be sustained in the face of further losses, especially the police's beating of Ab Jones, which will send Suttree on a mission of vengeance. His affirmation that everyone is right does not imply that every view of reality or every philosophy is true. When Hooper dies, Suttree angrily tells his corpse, lying among the "ragged chattel of lives abandoned like his own," "You have no right to represent people this way. . . . A man is all men. You have no right to your wretchedness" (421–22). In his pain at seeing Hooper represent himself as mere trash, mere corporeality, is implicit Suttree's hope that this is a false view of mankind, a rejection of the nihilist and materialist philosophy Hooper's actual life and death have manifested (as opposed to his philosophical pronouncements).

The image of Harvey the junkman lying amid his goods prefigures the death of Hooper. Harvey not only deals in junk, but he mirrors Suttree's alcoholism and alienation from family. Harvey's hatred of his brother is grounded in his jealousy that Dubyedee (W.D.) has been more successful at junk-dealing and in his suspicion that his brother has preyed upon him: "Want to hear about that thievin son of a bitch? Want to hear how he robbed his own brother blind?" he drunkenly challenges his nephew (268). The imagery of Harvey and Hooper as two prone, "dead" men is recapitulated in the scene in which Suttree finds a decomposing corpse lying in his own cot in the houseboat: all three are allegorical representations of human life as oblivious matter that Suttree after much struggle leaves behind.

In their materialism, both Harvey and Hooper tend to view others as junk, too, and they deny responsibility and compassion for them: Harvey articulates the idea that young transgressors such as the boys who steal from his lot should be shot. "Nip em in the bud," he answers when Suttree suggests he run them off or get a watchdog because, after all, "they're just kids" (265). When Suttree asks the ragman if he has seen Daddy Watson, Hooper replies, "I never took him to raise," echoing the sentiment of the callow entrepreneur Gene Harrogate about his own mother (365, 31). From the beginning of the novel, Suttree is more often his brother's keeper: his life on the river is punctuated with scenes of his helping others, even seeking them out to check on their welfare. Suttree's intermittent care for his "brothers" is one manifestation of his repudiation of the predatory relations that he sees around him in Knoxville and that he infers is his heritage.

But Suttree is not able to sustain his compassion perfectly. For one thing it does not extend to his own family. Only at the end of his journey will he understand that he has spoken "too lightly of the winter in [his] father's heart" and acknowledge that his father, too, is a brother in the human condition (460). When Suttree is hurt physically or emotionally, his compassion, his human decency, even his manners wither. Indeed his ill treatment of others can be read as a gauge of his pain.[17] Assaulted by his mother-in-law on the day of his son's funeral, he manifests no Christlike turning of the cheek or recognition of her grief for the boy they both love; rather, he kicks the "ghastly bitch" in the head (151). On the ill-conceived mussel-brailing expedition, he is surly and disaffected except when alone with Wanda, his sexual solace. After Leonard cajoles him into helping sink the rotting corpse of his father, Suttree avoids human contact and uncharacteristically refuses charity to others: "Mine's the greater need," he tells a beseeching Smokehouse (245). And under such circumstances his salutes to others become cynical. Late in the novel, he will recognize his limited ability and inconsistent willingness to help others when he visits Aunt Alice in the state asylum and acknowledges "he'd nothing to give. He'd come to take." As he leaves, he is shocked to see Daddy Watson among the inmates, but he does not stop to speak to him (434). As the novel progresses, his idealistic rejection of materialism undergoes a gradual adjustment. At the end of the novel he still sees it as an aspect of humans' purgatorial experience on earth—still warns us to flee the predatory huntsman of death and materialism—but he comes to acknowledge it as a problem of the tragic human condition not so easily evaded. Giles observes, "Even the most gentle of McCarthy's people carry the seeds of destruction with them everywhere" (94). As Suttree recognizes and comes to terms with this, he becomes more forgiving and accepting not only of his father but of himself.

Several other friends and associates confront Suttree with the hard fact of man's predatory nature. Both Suttree and Michael make their living by fishing. Michael's fishing is partly subsistence-based: he takes from the river what he can eat or what he can convert to food through the commercial transaction. Suttree, however, does not like to eat fish, and so he is involved more than

Michael in the commercial life of the city that he disdains (205). If he is somewhat redeemed by his charity in fish, cash, or favors to the poor of the city, he
is nonetheless implicated in capitalistic predation in his competitive marketing:
he sells first to the white fishmonger, who will pay him more, and then offers
the remnants to the black grocers for lower prices. Furthermore, Suttree often
spends his fishing revenue on alcohol, miring himself in fleshly oblivion. But
his fishing is pure of spirit compared to the malevolent impulses of Willard or
the mindless entrepreneurial enthusiasm of Gene Harrogate. Willard's response
to the wildlife Suttree points out on the river is to announce that if he had a
gun he would "kill everthing up here" (321). When the boy catches a catfish,
Suttree notes the primitive aspect of the creature and thinks, "Some like spirit
joined beast and captor," associating Willard with the feral origins of humankind (355). Wanda's testimony links her brother's literally predatory inclina-
tions to the figurative, revealing that his instinct is selfish and competitive even
with his own family: "He tried to get me to hide out what pearls we found
cleanin shells and we'd slip off and sell em and keep the money" (350). And
when tragedy befalls the family, Willard abandons them—as does Suttree.

Still, Gene Harrogate is the novel's most extended, if comic, critique of
predatory materialism. For Young he represents the "acquisitive center of
the human animal" (113). A less egregious version of Lester Ballard, as Grammer has observed, he follows an escalating path of abuse of others and consequent self-destruction (42). At best, his schemes are ineffectual and minimally
rewarded. At worst, they are repulsively callous or they result in his being
injured or jailed. But in his gleeful embrace of Knoxville as the land of opportunity, the city rat parodies the American dream of wealth acquired through
cleverness and initiative (not necessarily through honesty and hard work).[18]
"In his very crudeness and naivete," Grammer writes, "Harrogate is an ideal
expression of the ethic which governs contemporary Knoxville" (41–42). He is
a predator—sometimes inept, sometimes surprisingly effective—and his predation always mires him in materialism. Hunting down Rufus's young pig, Gene
ends up covered in mud, blood, and excrement—wallowing in the mire. In its
allusion to William Golding's *Lord of the Flies*, the scene reinforces Suttree's
visions of man's innate, gracelorn predatory nature and the veneer of civilization that transparently masks it. Gene's brutal pig hunt has a more conventional parallel in the abattoir across the river, from which the sound of hogs
shrieking wafts to Suttree's ears (63). Later hunting bats for bounty, Gene corrupts the natural hunt for food into sheer commercialism at the expense of
other living creatures. As Gene plans his bank heist, he is "beset" with "phantoms" of wealth and irresistibly follows their call (263). His spiritual blindness
is similar to Lester Ballard's: wandering in his underground tunnels, Gene
pauses pondering with a "shaft of light terminating in the top of his head

without apparent pain or power of inspiration" (261). The dynamited bank vault in reality is a sewage retaining wall, and Gene's dreams of wealth again end with his engulfment in mire. "Just everthing I touch turns to shit," he ultimately tells Suttree in a rare and transient moment of self-awareness that stands as one of the novel's pronouncements on humanity's materialistic enterprise (436).

Some of Gene's ventures are also forays into the materialism of sex, and in this he parallels his older friend more than Suttree initially can recognize. Believing himself inept with girls, the adolescent Gene turns to unresisting fruit for sexual experience, reenacting on a comic plane Lester Ballard's misguided love of inert material. The persistence of the melon-fancier's material fixation is evident when he reveals the basis of his attraction to Wanda: "Boy she's got a big old set of ninnies on her" (315). Visually smitten with Wanda, he asks Suttree for advice on how to talk to girls but makes it clear that his goal is neither communion nor a loving relationship but sexual acquisition: he wants to know how to get them to take their clothes off. (Although he never transgresses as Lester Ballard does, Suttree's half-joking response that "you take them off" also resonates ominously with *Child of God;* 316.) When Gene's pay phone scheme begins to net him a little cash, he dresses up like a hip con-man (his getup is reminiscent of the jazzy pimp-garb Joyce chooses for Suttree). His ill-gained wealth brings him a new swagger, and he brags, "Shit. . . . Man has a little money about him he can get more pussy than you can shake a stick at" (420). In both Gene and Suttree, the material enterprise, a symptom of man's miring in materialism, is linked with the erotic objectifying of others.

The Prison of Erotic Attraction

Besides his frequent drunkenness, Suttree's own sexual relationships delineate most clearly his implication in the cosmic materialism he struggles to repudiate. Often caring and charitable with the men he has chosen to be surrogate father- and brother-figures, Suttree cannot so easily generate similar compassion for women, especially young women. He is kind to his aunts Martha and Alice, but he recognizes that he has nothing to offer them. In repudiating his father, he has also rejected his mother; he will have no contact with her because her grief unmans him with shame and loneliness (61–62). One senses a similar dynamic in his abandonment of his wife. It is not clear whether he leaves her before or after (and because of) his literal imprisonment, but he links her with his mother as another *mater dolorosa* for whose grief and pain he feels guilty responsibility. Yet he cannot or will not assuage their feelings. In this Suttree reprises the dynamic of Culla's flight from Rinthy. After the shameful confrontation with his wife's family on the day of his son's funeral, Suttree never sees her again. His sexual relationships during his time on the river—his one-night affair interrupted by Leonard's arrival with his father's corpse, the summer with Wanda, and the several months with Joyce—are each of sequentially longer duration, but none results in the devotion and mutual responsibility that characterize good marriages or firm friendships. Because they are tainted with materialism, they pose to Suttree the gnostic threat of entrapment. Suttree both seeks these sexual relationships and repudiates them in ways that demonstrate his psychological and spiritual confusion. Sexuality itself, with its carnal element, symbolizes the dilemma of flesh versus spirit that humans cannot evade in their earthly life. The psychic link between sexual physicality and the death of the spirit is expressed in Suttree's nightmare at Mother She's, after he has left Joyce, of being raped by a "ghast black succubus" who is the very image of death: "Black faltress, portress of hellgate. None so ready as she. . . . Dead reek of aged female flesh, a stale aridity." Engulfed by this nightmare portent, Suttree dreams his own death and reduction to the corporeal remnant: "His spine was sucked from his flesh and fell clattering to the floor like a jointed china snake"—an echo of the bones that unfurl from the prologue's theater curtain (426–27). The sexually predatory dream-hag is, according to Bell, symptomatic of "suppressed sexual fear that associates woman with biological imperatives and biology with the curse of death" (95). This gnostic nightmare marks Suttree's intuitive understanding that carnal eroticism is another manifestation of materialism, *heimarmene*, and the spirit's entrapment in oblivion, and the vision represents his terrified repudiation.

Gene points out that Wanda is his own age—much younger than Suttree. The boy's erotic attraction to her mirrors and unmasks Suttree's own. She is ripe and youthful, she smells of soap, and as Young observes, her luxuriant black hair reminds Suttree of both his wife and the "ballad-girl" of his imagination, drowned in a mountain pool—images that mark her as more dream than reality: "a perfect—and therefore either lost or unattainable—passion" (117). She is a primary reason Suttree agrees to become Reese's partner in musselbrailing for pearls although when he arrives on the French Broad River he already regrets his promises to Reese, reprising his regretted and broken promises to his wife. As Longley observes, Wanda is the pearl who attracts Suttree to this project (84). But her allure also makes him susceptible to the inept greed for wealth that characterizes Reese and that Suttree himself often warns Gene against. The other motives that attract Suttree to the French Broad, his desire to return to wilderness and the promise of family life to assuage his grief and loneliness for his rightful family, are perhaps more benign. But he arrives "with his little stained boat and his weariness" already feeling "alien and tainted. . . . As if the city had marked him" (316). In the scenes that follow, Suttree inverts the gnostic "alien man" who brings the Call, the message of mankind's true nature to those bound in the cosmic realm. Suttree bears no spiritual message for himself or for others.

Because Suttree's endeavor on the French Broad River is stained with the materialism of lust and greed, the whole enterprise is tainted (316). Suttree's self-loathing is more evident here than in any other section of the novel except his time as Joyce's kept man. The reinscription of a Narcissus-image from his earlier quest in the wilderness demonstrates his spiritual decline rather than progress. In his winter sojourn in the mountains, Suttree wanders in a dream state: "Lying on a gravel bar with the tips of his fingers in the icy water he could see his face above the sandy creek floor, a shifting visage hard by its own dark shadow. He stretched himself and bowed his lips and sucked from the passing water" (285–86). This narcissistic kiss, with its hint of unhealthy self-absorption, yet suggests a transcendental self-acceptance as Suttree drinks from this gnostic font of living water. His transient gnosis has disappeared, however, in the parallel scene on the French Broad, where Suttree spits at his "trembling visage," and rather than placing his lips to the water he soaks his feet in it (320). He begins to view himself and others as mechanical, detached from human feelings and volition: his shadow on the water looks "like a rowing marionette," and he and Reese ride into Dandridge "hunched up like puppets" beneath the deterministic hand of gnostic archons (322, 333).

Yet Suttree evaluates himself and his venture in moments of self-awareness. On his return to the camp after his debacle in town with Reese, he recognizes the embittered fearfulness of Reese's wife, an unanticipated reminder of his own disappointed spouse, and he retreats from the family, telling himself, "My life is ghastly" (348). As the family gathers at the campfire for supper, Suttree perceives that Wanda's mother "awarded to the round dark a look of grim apprehension like a fugitive," an intuition colored by his own gnostic dread, and reprising the imagery of *Outer Dark*. That night he wakes to the sound of lamentations which may be the voices of the family but which he interprets as a procession of acolytes "transgressed from a dream" or of "children who had died going along a road in the dark with lanterns and crying on their way from the world" (348). This image of the procession of souls on the dark dream-road of the cosmos reiterates Suttree's obsession with the album of the dead and the endless filmstrip sequence of souls in transit. The acolytes recall his memories of his own childhood in the Roman Catholic church, and this vision establishes Suttree's sense of himself now as a mourning child, lonely in his death-bound travels through the outer dark of earthly life and bewailing his mortality. They also mark Suttree's vision as a gnostic warning. Zosimos identifies the nonpneumatics as those who "follow in the procession of the heimarmene" and who are "in every respect its acolytes" (quoted in Jonas, *Gnostic Religion* 96). Suttree's vision here on the French Broad River in fact places him in the same mindset he will occupy in the desolate urban winter to come, when he sits at Christmastime in the Huddle with the city's other displaced souls in their procession through cosmos, "sad children of the fates whose home is the world, all gathered here a little while to forestall the going there" (386). Conceiving them all as children of the fates or *heimarmene* whose "home is the world," Suttree alludes to the gnostic idea that in cosmos the spirit is cast out from its true Home in God; the "there" to which these grieving children travel next will still be an outer dark of the spirit.

In the wilderness with Wanda's family, Suttree's physical and psychic discomfort leads him to take carnal solace in her and then ironically to reenact with Wanda his father's emotional repudiation of his mother. When Reese begins to hint that Suttree might become his son-in-law, Suttree's revulsion and fear of entrapment are such that he breaks with Wanda. This estrangement is foreshadowed before their sexual relationship even begins, in Suttree's reaction to his and Reese's failed pearl-marketing scheme. Looking at Wanda's unattractive father and brother and her despairing, work-worn mother, Suttree begins to see the lovely and innocent girl as worthless, like the Tennessee freshwater pearls that have fooled him.[19] His earlier confidence, twice-asserted, that the mussel pearls "must be worth something" parallels his idealistic affirmation of the value of all souls (334). In gnostic symbol systems, the pearl is identified with the spirit and thus is of supreme worth. In "The Hymn of the Pearl" from the apocryphal *Acts of the Apostle Thomas*, the savior is sent from his true Home into Egypt or Babel (cosmos) to recover the pearl, but once there he is confused by the Egyptians' meat and drink, and he forgets that he is "a king's son and served their king. I forgot the Pearl for which my parents had sent me" (quoted in Jonas, *Gnostic Religion* 113–14). The stern, discerning jeweler's rejection of the pearls, a parallel to Suttree's father's rejection of the poorer classes that Suttree does not consciously recognize, embarrasses him and augments his anger and frustration at Reese. The jeweler is associated with the gnostic artificer-god, and Suttree cannot easily set aside his judgment. Reese deflects his humiliation at the jeweler's with the assertion that he hates "a dumb son of a bitch like that that dont know the value of nothin," but Suttree begins to reconsider his quest for the pearls and distrust his attraction to Wanda even as he continues to experience it, and he blocks his incipient love for her (343). In this respect he mirrors Reese as well as his own father, for Reese's prurient and adulterous behavior shows that he does not value women or even his own wife, in her aging and suffering a less materially pleasing object of desire than Wanda is or than she herself once was. Allegorically the scenes suggest Suttree's drunkenness with the world, a gnostic slumber that makes him forget what is of genuine worth. This allegorical plot structure will be repeated in his relationship with Joyce.

Nevertheless, when Suttree and Wanda come together as a couple, the death imagery that so dominates his perceptions carries less direct metaphysical threat—although this may be symptomatic of his succumbing to the cosmic lure of sexuality. The material mire still appears on the French Broad in the mud Willard coats himself with when he contracts poison ivy; in the odor of the accumulating mussel shells; in the alcohol, vomit, and commercial sex of Suttree and Reese's foray into town; in the trash contaminating the clear water of the river even here. But despite the tainted motives that initially lead him to her, such metaphors do not contaminate Suttree's private scenes with Wanda. In addition, images of the helix here take on a more benign aspect. Waiting for Wanda by the river, Suttree lies "naked with his back pressed to the wheeling earth"; though he perceives the river "sucking" past and sees "stars come adrift and rifle hot and dying across the face of the firmament," he reacts not with ontological insecurity or gnostic dread but only with a feeling of "strange sweet woe" (353). As many have recognized, his nascent love for Wanda, although resisted, seems to reconcile him to the world itself and to its galactic whirling, in contrast to his earliest days on the French Broad, when he is relieved that the skies are too cloudy for the stars to "plague him with their mysteries of space and time" (332). It is as if the sexual idyll with Wanda casts a romantic fog over Suttree, muffling his perception of his enduring cosmic condition. In a less troubling permutation of the image of embeddedness, Suttree holds his ear to Wanda's womb (a gesture hinting at the procreative bond which, for the gnostic, constitutes cosmic bondage), where he hears with equanimity "the hiss of meteorites through the blind stellar depths" (358). Even when Suttree is jolted by Reese's matchmaking and slinks away from the family encampment, he looks at the turning heavens fixed in their cosmic course with uncharacteristic affirmation: "Halfmoon incandescent in her black galactic keyway, the heavens locked and wheeling. A sole star to the north pale and constant, the old wanderer's beacon burning like a molten spike that tethered fast the Small Bear to the turning firmament. . . . He was struck by the fidelity of this earth he inhabited and he bore it sudden love" (354). This passage contrasts directly with his gnostic perception in the mountains of "the cold and indifferent dark, the blind stars beaded on their tracks and mitered satellites and geared and pinioned planets all reeling through the black of space" (284). Consoled by his emerging love of Wanda, Suttree perceives no threat of archontic constraint here (although the imagery of lock and tether implies such threat dialogically) but rather the pledged constancy of nature—the steady beacon of the North Star, Polaris, that orients and guides the wayfarer. As in Plato's right response to nature and the heavenly bodies, the world's fidelity evokes Suttree's answering love, and the conjunction of such perceptions with Suttree's romantic attachment to Wanda is what makes their brief time together seem a relative idyll in this lonely man's wandering and alienated life.

But Suttree fails to sustain love and constancy in response to Wanda's fidelity although in his connection with her he comes close to transcending his initial erotic and commercial materialism and escaping his imprisoning purgatory. His fear of entrapment within a family he disdains is not the only factor that determines his holding himself aloof. As Wanda is subject to death like his son and all souls, Suttree will not accept her implicit offer of transient (because mortal) fidelity; the triumph of his gnostic repudiation and bitter realism is manifest well before Wanda's death and, it is hinted, may simply constitute a failure of courage. In retrospect we see what Suttree always intuits with dread: that camped under the impending shale cliffs, like the old pensioner in *The Crossing* who more self-consciously positions himself under the precariously poised dome of the church at Caborca, Wanda is always death's ward. Suttree's sense of this contributes to his fearful reluctance to love her. When she does die, he is nevertheless devastated—as he has dreaded he may be. Like the pensioner at Caborca, whose son has been killed in an earthquake, Wanda's bereft mother calls on God for an answer to her pain—iterating the prime gnostic question (362). Her grief for her child renews Suttree's own bereavement for his, and he runs from this scene of agony as he has already run from his growing attachment to Wanda. Floating passively downriver to Knoxville, he is "a man with no plans for going back the way he'd come nor telling any soul at all what he had seen" (363). He is at this point a Dante-figure who abandons all hope of leaving his hell or purgatory, a failed Dante who may never leave the dreamjourney to carry his message to others, a failed Orpheus who may never sing, a lapsed gnostic messenger silenced by the world. He will return to Knoxville in depression and despair, which deepen his isolation from others, witness yet more deaths and more departures of friends, and spiral down into a loveless commercial/erotic relationship with Joyce.

As in gnostic teaching, carnality, like alcohol, functions as a material distraction from Suttree's ontological anguish; until he understands that both are manifestations of the cosmic materialism and oblivion he wishes to evade, he is repeatedly drawn back to them. His initial attraction to the prostitute Joyce, like his attraction to Wanda, is complicated. The artist in him is fascinated by her jivy Yankee speech, and he follows Joyce and Margie to listen to them talk. Too, he identifies with Joyce's makeshift outlaw life; she is the female analogue of the men he befriends. But the relationship they quickly form is a carnal one in which Suttree is willingly seduced not only by Joyce's "sheer outrageous sentience" but also by her money and the physical comforts it can purchase (393). When the first envelope of her earnings reaches him, Suttree opens it, significantly, in the toilet (398).

It is no accident that this entanglement begins in the winter, when Suttree faces the difficulty of securing adequate warmth and shelter, and at Christmastime, when his loneliness for his lost family is intensified. He has just secured a dismal basement apartment, and he tells himself that although he feels "alien," he is "not unhappy" there (380). In this subterranean space he consummates his sexual alliance with Joyce. But the cellar with its leaking pipes overhead and its furnace attended by the diminished Vulcan, Nelson, is another manifestation of the netherworld caves that imprison Gene Harrogate and the cave of oblivion that constitutes Lester Ballard's purgatory. Plato's cave parable is invoked when Suttree first takes Joyce to the cellar, suggesting that both of these constricted souls will engage each other through the shadows and illusions of materiality: "Fire showed in the slotted mouth of the furnace and a wild melee of piping reeled away over the ceiling, their own shadows dipping in the slight swing of the lightbulb from its cord." The exterior world of McAnally, too, is their "shadowworld" (*S* 388). Ominously Suttree's cellar room is also reminiscent of the one in which Clegg, a Caliban-figure, imprisons the artist Miranda in John Fowles's *The Collector* (1963), a prison that brings about her suffocation with pneumonia. A collector who kills what he "loves"—butterflies, women—in the process of possessing them, Clegg parallels Lester Ballard. As an allegory of the artist imprisoned and destroyed by philistine materialism, Fowles's novel also adumbrates the Suttree/Joyce relationship.[20] Although Joyce's money allows the couple to move from cellar to hotels and then to their own apartment, where they occupy upper floors with windows, these elevated rooms remain Suttree's philistine dungeons. With Joyce, Suttree dines well and regularly, and there is no lack of drink. Their "upwardly mobile" life parodies middle-class respectability as they acquire closets (receptacles for material possessions), furnishings, rooms with views of the city's rooftops and streets, and finally Suttree's coveted Jaguar. They travel to the mountains in the luxury of a cab, and they mingle with the privileged at the Grove Park Inn, the gracious resort in Asheville, North Carolina, where F. Scott Fitzgerald—that poet and critic of American material success and of the philosophy that living well is the best revenge for the pain of life—had retreated to recuperate from tuberculosis in 1935 (Turnbull 257).

The death-in-life that this affiliation represents is clear from the very beginning. Joyce's hip urban speech is inauthentic since she was raised in Kentucky. Almost always her communication is focused on objectified sex—at least until late in their relationship, when she begins to unmask her vulnerability, despair, and longing for a more authentic connection. In a debased version of the earlier scenes in which Suttree experiments with communicating in others' familiar modes—tale-swapping or sign language, he and Joyce compete to invent "sexual slanders" about the actors in a movie, "vying to elaborate the most outrageous perversions." Ultimately Joyce usurps the artist role in their trip to the Grove Park Inn, where both are "apprentice imposters," but it is Joyce who contrives "outrageous lies" about their identities to tell the respectable guests (391, 407).

Despite their randy coupling, Suttree is infantilized and emasculated in this relationship (hence the compensatory appeal of the phallic Jaguar). In their sexual adventuring in the back seat of the taxicab, Suttree and Joyce are "like schoolchildren," implying both their immaturity and their cynical playing at innocent sexual exploration (400). Joyce mothers Suttree, calling him "Baby," telling him he looks like a little boy (392), and tucking him in (394); and he swoons passively in the "womby lassitude" (401) of their too-soft beds.[21] As she becomes his provider, the breadwinner of this unconventional and sterile family, he becomes her dependent; she feeds and clothes him.

The clothes Joyce selects for Suttree mark him as a dependent and also, as Jarrett points out, as her pimp, an accessory to her using her very person as chattel (51). In her prostitution she is analogous to Smokehouse, who subjects his body to injury in order to sue for cash settlements (201). As her pimp, Suttree recapitulates Hooper and Harvey's trafficking in junk and treats both Joyce and himself as junk by wallowing in materialism. In effect, in the act of protecting Joyce's money but not her and giving her sex and an illusion of love in exchange for material comfort, Suttree prostitutes himself.

Their rooms are in fact a gnostic prison or purgatory. In his halfhearted search for a place to rent with Joyce, Suttree perceives one landlord with his ring of keys as a "latterday gaoler" (401). And as in Suttree's cellar, the steam pipes in their rented space suggest a "horrendous foundrywork"—Vulcan's realm (394). When Suttree and Joyce approach their apartment, the light in the hallway shines "like some dim nebula viewed from the pit" (405). Finally the high rooms purchased by Joyce's prostitution are simply whorehouses, reprising *Outer Dark*'s gnostic metaphor of the world as brothel. Loftier than Suttree's cellar, these rooms are dungeons nonetheless, accessed through long dark corridors of anonymous closed doors. Such corridor imagery recurs in *Cities of the Plain*, another partly urban novel, where John Grady and Magdalena are often cast in the constricted spaces of the modern urban prison: the commercial and bureaucratic corridors of the whorehouse, the hospital, the morgue. In *Suttree*, the corridor suggests the gnostic/purgatorial constriction that expresses his spiritual blindness. And when he hears doors shut, they reverberate with all the exclusions and alienations he has ever suffered: kicked out of the restaurant in Bryson City, Suttree can "hear doors closing all back through his head like enormous dominoes toppling in a corridor" (293). The slamming of these doors reinscribes the measured repetition of death that Suttree perceives in the whicket of the cradle blade and in the filmstrip of souls' progression through the world.

Yet more constricted is the bed Suttree shares with Joyce. He is "brailed" within it—an image of sails drawn in and tied as well as a pun on the mussel-brailing venture that led him to Wanda (394). When Joyce returns to Chicago, Suttree becomes bedridden in depression and self-loathing, mesmerized by the vaguely erotic paisley pattern in the faded Persian carpet (402–3). Its head-to-tail scorpion-shapes suggest both oral sex and the yin-yang symbol of Chinese philosophy: the complementary female-male cosmic forces that combine and balance one another to form the wholeness of *chi*, the vital universal force. However, in some versions of the philosophy, including Confucianism, *chi* is specifically associated with the world of forms or the material manifestation that dissolves in death (Blackburn 62, 403). Thus in his zombie-like gazing at the carpet's pattern from the confinement of his bed, Suttree uncomprehend-ingly confronts the erotic materialism of his life with Joyce—as if mesmerized by it. During this period, his stupor is such that Michael cannot rouse him when he climbs the stairs to seek him out, in a complement to Suttree's descent into the caves to retrieve Harrogate: "The sleeper within slept deeply and after a while he [Michael] descended the stairs and went away" (404). At some unac-knowledged level, Suttree recognizes that Joyce too is imprisoned. When she tells him of her life, he perceives the city outside their window in images of walls (a pun inherent in the word *paling*) and locks: "Dawn unlocked the city in paling increments of gray" (399). In the heat of late spring he watches her sleep with "one foot trapped in a tourniquet of bedsheet" (404). But these images of Joyce's entrapment do not elicit his compassion until after he has escaped the carnal house of their affair.

In each of the dwelling-places Joyce's money leases, Suttree becomes a "sitter at windows" that might as well be barred, where he watches "like a fugi-tive" (398, 404). Framed in these windows he salutes his fellows with cynicism born of self-loathing, thus revealing his unguessed affinity with the crazed self-castrated evangelist who calls down vitriol on the heads of passersby. It is little wonder that Suttree's empathy for Joyce is blocked. Once again he repeats his father's repudiation of his mother and his own repudiation of Wanda in his negative judgments of Joyce. His lack of emotional engagement is punningly signaled when he gazes through the windows of their rooms, "a face untrue behind the cataracted glass" (398). He is ashamed of Joyce except when she manages to seem "ladylike," and he accompanies her only where her crude behavior will not be noticed: "the secondbest restaurants . . . and beer-taverns dim and rank with musk as brewery cellars. Where others kept their own coun-sel and nothing short of mayhem raised an eyebrow ever" (395, 405). When Joyce attracts attention with her drunken lewdness, he feels compelled to take her home not so much by his answering lust as by his shame (401–2). The objects on Joyce's dressing table are a mixture of "the fine with the shoddy," and analogously Suttree always perceives her as both attractive and debased, as if he views her through the gnostic lens of the spirit's mingling in matter (395). However, far from pitying her tragic human condition, as their relationship wears on he becomes less able to recognize anything fine in her at all. Wanda's cleanliness is highly appealing to Suttree, but Joyce's constant ablutions only remind him that she is his "soiled dove" (401). She refers to her ritual casually and coarsely (389), but her repetitious cleansing suggests her own obsession with her sexual stain; and her douching certainly functions for Suttree as its symbol. As he becomes increasingly disenchanted, he perceives that "she seemed always bearing her douchebag about with the hose bobbling obscenely and the bag flapping like a great bladder"—in a permutation of his excremental disgust (404).

Although enthralled by Joyce, Suttree finds it difficult to credit that she ever shared the innocence of children who look at the world through eyes of wonder. In the winter mountains, Joyce gazes "with child's eyes at this winter wonderland," but her spoken response breaks the spell: "It's fucking beautiful, she said" (399). Nevertheless, Joyce does respond to natural beauty. She gathers souvenirs of nature—a mussel shell, a veined pebble—small material treasures that hint pathetically at the child of wonder buried within. But that night, watching the lights of a fair, Suttree reveals his thoroughgoing contempt, wondering "if she were ever a child at a fair dazed by the constellations of light and the hurdygurdy music of the merrygoround and the raucous calls of the barkers. Who saw in all that shoddy world a vision that child's grace knows and never the sweat and the bad teeth and the nameless stains in the sawdust, the flies and the stale delirium and the vacant look of solitaries who go among these garish holdings seeking a thing they could not name" (408–9). Ironically Suttree's indictment applies as much to himself as to Joyce. It is he who cannot see in Joyce the value of the individual spirit he claims to honor, he who is blinded by the shoddy materialism of his own attraction to her, he who travels vacantly among the garish things of the cosmos ineffectually seeking. Joyce's response to the fireworks suggests that in fact she too is a lonely seeker struggling to transcend the world's shoddy materialism. Her tears are a sign of her grace. But because he approaches her in bad faith, Suttree does not understand why she weeps. In *Cities of the Plain*, John Grady Cole contrasts tellingly with Suttree in this respect. He sees the prostituted child Magdalena in her essential innocence, and although he implicates himself in the commercial enterprise when he purchases their time together, he takes her humanity, her spiritual nature, on good faith and repudiates others' attempts to devalue her as nothing but a whore.

Gradually it becomes clear that despite her enactment of the inauthentic role of hooker, Joyce's longing for love, purity, and acknowledgment of her essential innocence and worth underlies the gaudy show. Her tough, jaunty behavior gives way to expressions of despair at her prostitution and at the limits of Suttree's love. Finally it is the active Joyce who unmasks the basis of their affiliation and who initiates change. In petulantly damaging Suttree's Jaguar, she challenges him to recognize it as another materialistic evasion of the pain of his life, and she provokes him in a desperate bid to make him affirm their bond at a deeper level. Disappointed that her caring for him as consort and mother has not purchased his love, she behaves childishly, revealing that she is after all a wounded child, as is he. But Suttree cannot see their fundamental similarity. He responds to Joyce's attack much in the same way he responds to his mother-in-law's assault, resorting to the language of profane sexual objectification (409–10). But when Joyce tells him calmly, "It's just a car. . . . It can be fixed," she raises the issue of the right valuing of human life and relationships and clear-sightedly points to his failure. Her charge that he is "so fucking perfect" exposes her despairing realization that he will never overcome his condescension (410). And when she tears up the money, declaring that it "would never do anybody any good," she repudiates both her prostitution and the falsity of the bond it has created between them—damages that cannot be fixed (411). Ironically her repudiation echoes Suttree's own forgotten rejection of his family's wealth. Joyce, in effect, sees first and most clearly their failure to transcend materialism in their erotic attraction, and her challenges release Suttree from its imprisonment. When Suttree finds himself chasing after her torn currency in the gutters, contesting the scraps with the street urchins like the beggars at the master's table in his hallucination of his feral forebears, he comes to himself at last and stalks away from the money and from Joyce.

Released from this appalling descent into materialism, however, Suttree belatedly achieves a more compassionate appreciation of Joyce's human worth. As he walks to his houseboat on the river, he notes the detritus sliding down "from the city on the hill" in new awareness of his own failure to achieve purity of heart in his dealings with Joyce, his own repetition of the tragic failures of his forefathers throughout time to transcend the complicating clay of the human admixture. Passing the mad evangelist's house, he hears himself described as an "infidel" and as "another hero home from the whores" (412). Suttree plugs his ears against these charges, as well he might, for they echo his unvoiced self-accusations. The mad evangelist literalizes the role of the superego or, as a gnostic reading would have it, the judgmental aspects of cosmic order (guilt) introjected in psyche. Indeed the old man may well say "wars," as the expression has it, but Suttree hears "whores." This moment of self-castigation reveals that Suttree's shame at prostituting himself with Joyce coexists with his dawning sense of personal responsibility for his humiliation: that in his choice to use Joyce for her money and the physical comfort she provides, he has turned infidel to his own ideals of the value of the human spirit and the rejection of cosmic materialism.

Settled again in the poverty of his life on the river, Suttree engages in dialogue with his shadow and declares that he is "not unhappy." A repetition of his similar claim in the McAnally cellar, this assertion seems to bring him full circle, but his thoughts gathered in tranquility reveal that his experience with Joyce has brought about considerable learning and progress—unlike Culla Holme's blind circling, unlike the futile circling of the moths that orbit Suttree's lamp or the dead-end bumbling of the beetle that keeps "crashing into the windowscreen and dropping to the deck below to whirr and rise and crash again." He affirms his poverty and the unity of all souls in their suffering in life, not just in death: "I believe that the last and the first suffer equally. Pari passu" (414). Behind this revised affirmation of equality that forgives "the first" lies Suttree's recognition that humanity in its predatory and materialistic avatars does not evade suffering, that the purgatory of earthly life or the pain of the spirit's cosmic separation from its true home is universal. Implicit here is an acknowledgment of kinship not just with the poor of the world but also with Joyce and his own father, both of whom he has judged harshly for their complicity with materialism. In affirming the equality of all souls in their suffering, Suttree makes a step toward letting go of his neurotic rebellion against the human condition—his insistence on the uniqueness of his being, the uniqueness of his pain.

In addition Suttree repudiates his impulse to cope with the pain of his life by hardening his heart against his family and against his own suffering. On the bridge in rain and lightning, Suttree has called down the elements in a misguided affirmation of self-reliance and an attempt to close himself off emotionally from the pain of living: "Wrap me in the weathers of the earth, I will be hard and hard. My face will turn rain like the stones" (29). He has opened his heart in a limited way to the undervalued men of the city, but he has continued to steel it against family and against the women who offer him reconnection in familial bonds. Facing up to his failure with Joyce, however, Suttree repents the arrogance of this agenda: "I spoke with bitterness about my life and I said that I would take my own part against the slander of oblivion and against the monstrous facelessness of it and that I would stand a stone in the very void where all would read my name. Of that vanity I recant all" (414).

Rain and stone are frequently conjoined in McCarthy's works, especially in cemetery scenes, in emblems of the illusory icon man erects to his own permanence in the face of eroding natural processes. The cemetery stones prompt imaginative recovery of the dead, but they also manifest the limitations of such efforts to ensure the individual's persistence in the minds of others. When Suttree comes across the old cemetery in the mountains, he finds that rain has indeed all but obliterated the names on the stones, and despite his heightened susceptibility to visions throughout his days in the mountains, he creates no hallucinated recollection of the dead. Gravestones in *Suttree* often are merely husks of lost lives, material remnants—like bones—that may or may not preserve a name for all to read. As such they are dead things, reminders of man's mortality more than insurers of his permanence. The gravestones made into saloon tables that Suttree asks Blind Richard to read function in this way: the names bespeak the anonymity of the dead; the displacement of the stones themselves inscribes the transience of human memory of or honor for the other.[22] In this the stones function very like the salvaged photographs found by the *gitano*'s father in *The Crossing*—icons divorced from their original contexts and thus bereft of their power to evoke memory. But when the gravestones in Ab's saloon do elicit recognition, as with the name of William Callahan, they are read as predictions of death (just as Suttree hears the phrase "Suttree funeral" as a premonition of his own). More than anything, the stone is a memento mori despite the intent of those who erect it. Ironically, then, in pledging himself to stand a stone in the void, Suttree has in effect pledged himself to a kind of stasis and death by dedicating his life to a refusal of time and process—essential conditions of human existence, as Grammer has pointed out (42). In repenting of this arrogance, Suttree becomes humanized and accepts his place within the larger scheme of things. His release of his desire as an artist-figure to write his name against the slander of oblivion is also a release from the vanity of egotism that might petrify his art with narcissism.[23] He frees himself—at least temporarily—of his neurotic fear of mortality, the Medusa of materialism that can turn him to stone.

Suttree's memories of his time with Joyce acknowledge their mutual submission to the suicide of carnality and inauthenticity. He remembers "warmth in the bed with her body" and her lying "drenched . . . like a suicide" until she woke to tell him "sweet lies," but he no longer blames Joyce alone for this (414–15). Rather, he recognizes her humanity when he segues from remembering her sexual pleasure to pondering her deep grief, acknowledging for the first time her pain and despair at her abasement, opening himself at last to the implications of the razor scars on her wrists, the scar on her abdomen: a suicide attempt, a child aborted or delivered and now lost. And in her description of her orgasms he recognizes his own imagery of Milo's death by drowning: "She'd be whelmed in a warm green sea through which, dulled by the murk of it, pass a series of small suns like the footlights of a revolving stage, an electric carousel wheeling in a green ether" (415). Her imagery of wheeling constellations and her spiraling descent through tropical seas finally provokes Suttree's recognition that beneath Joyce's sweet and welcome lies, her adept playacting, has lain a deeper truth: that her carnal use of her life has been a death-in-life, a drowning from which she longs for deliverance. Further, her experience is emblematic of us all as we spin into and out of life like poor players on a revolving stage. These insights resurface in Suttree's grief at the ragman's death. It is not only Hooper but also Joyce whom Suttree addresses when he says that one has no right to represent oneself as mere material because any man or woman stands for all humanity (422).

When Suttree finally leaves the river, he will take for a talisman only the simple, vulnerable heart within. We do not see him rejoin his family or form a new one, but he has forgiven his father for the "winter" in his heart because he sees that it mirrors the iciness that congeals his own as he attempts to steel himself against the weathers of the world (460). He has also forgiven Joyce because he sees that in using herself as matter, she echoes his own stoniness. In his final affirmation of his simple human heart, Suttree opens himself more fully to honoring the hearts of others, letting go of judgment, anger, blame, and self-protection, and making room for something like grace.

The Rage for Justice

Ab Jones is yet another double whose example contributes to teaching Suttree one of the lessons he must learn before deliverance from his purgatory. A black man persecuted by racist agents of law and order, Ab girds himself against such outrages and dedicates himself to combating them. Even more than does Meursault, Ab dislikes the police. As Bell points out, "Ab's conflict with the police seems vaguely theological, as if he had displaced his resentment toward an unapparent God onto His tangible and all too willing emissaries on earth" (*Achievement* 82). Giles adds that "Jones, like Suttree, is rebelling against a cruel sentence emanating from a vindictive god and a corrupt human society" (94). Indeed the Frankenstein's monster imagery in which Suttree perceives Ab's scarred and stitched body (201, 230, 443) establishes Ab as a comparable allegorical figure of humankind set in opposition to his or her flawed maker (perhaps the gnostic artificer), a scapegoat for the unjust workings of the world. And it connects Ab with Suttree himself, whose broken head is patched by the archontic brain surgeon: "We saw you took down to the brainsurgeon's keep, deep in the cellar, under the street. Where saws sang in stoven skulls and wet bonemeal blew from an airshaft in the alleyway" (188). Ab's heart burns for revenge, an obsession he justifies with the reasonable view that his enemy, personified in the hulking figure of Tarzan Quinn (arguably his own double in his combative approach to others) is wrong. Although Quinn is a bureaucratic power-figure such as those who oppress Robert McEvoy, from another perspective he is only the latest personification of the original injustice that set Ab on the "wrath of the path" (204); in adolescence Ab was wrongfully charged with the murder of a white adversary and beaten by the police. Shocked with this early exposure to the brutal racism of the law, Ab abstracts from his experience a lifelong hatred of all police, "endless armies of the unbending pale," archontic powers who imprison him within their pale, and he engages in a fight for a principle waged with his fists, his physical being (229). Although, as Hoffmann points out (231), Ownby's resistance to governmental intrusion adumbrates Ab's, *Suttree* presents Ab's resistence more as an ontological position like McEvoy's. Ab undertakes a pseudo-gnostic/existential rebellion against oppressive cosmic powers, which becomes the repetition compulsion that structures his life. He frequently positions himself to joust against an abstracted enemy, becoming the aggressor and opening himself up to further abuse. He confesses to Suttree that he has killed but "not on purpose," a rationalization that emphasizes his impotence in the face of his compulsion and his inability or unwillingness to view himself as a morally free agent responsible for his choices (205). Only the death of Quinn will satisfy his outraged sense of justice; only his own death will end his Sisyphean quest. Ab's blindness and his seemingly gnostic rebellion both are allegorized in his nearly always appearing in darkness: Suttree's interactions with him typically occur either in Ab's dark back room, where he lies recovering from his latest injuries, or in the dark alley of his final encounter with the police, where he works out his doom in a " bloody dumbshow" against the brick walls of his prison—echoes of Plato's cave parable (442). Suttree observes that Ab adjusts his head on his pillow "as if he'd seek a darker place to rest it," a line that echoes the spiritually blind Lester Ballard's seeking "darker provinces of night" (226; *CoG* 23).

Despite his struggling in and against darkness, Ab recognizes the futility and compulsiveness of his behavior: "You aint got nothin for it but a busted head. You caint do nothin with them motherfuckers. I wouldnt fight em at all if I could keep from it" (204). Further, he articulates the emptiness of such a life: "Look up one mornin and you a old man. You aint got nothin to say to your brother. Dont know no more'n when you started" (203). Though it may seem that Ab appropriately rebels against archontic powers, his challenging of the law neither derives from nor leads to spiritual gnosis. Ab cannot break out of this cycle.[24]

Ab's comments constitute an apt warning to Suttree, who in his aggrieved alienation from his family and the world travels down the same path, receiving along the way his own series of busted heads. Ab's good advice that Suttree should "look out for you own" is ambiguous: it follows Ab's reference to Suttree's good heart, but Suttree responds instead, and somewhat defensively, to the implication that he should take care of his own family, especially his own father, rather than redirecting his care to the substitute family and fathers (such as Ab) he finds among the poor of the city. The ambiguity hints that the two options are one: that dealing compassionately and charitably with one's family, beginning at home, is the way to take care of one's own heart. But in deflecting this meaning, Suttree mirrors Ab's self-absorption and resentment. He challenges Ab to tell him where his family is, as if it is only they who have rejected him and not he who has stubbornly resisted their efforts at contact. Ab's sympathetic response about people who "piss backwards" on their friends implies his familiarity with Suttree's version of his estrangement from his father, and it derives from Ab's parallel bitterness over social class judgments. Rather than offering effective fatherly advice, then, Ab's words reinforce both men's incubation of vengefulness (203).

The nature of Suttree's heart is explored in his Christmastime retreat to the mountains, when he dreams "sad dreams and woke bitter and rueful." The dreams are of old Christmases now lost. In retrospective analysis of the self he has transcended, the narrating Suttree remarks "what a baleful heart he harbored and how dear to him" and tells us that at this stage "in his darker heart a nether self hulked above cruets of ratsbane, a crumbling old grimoire to hand, androleptic vengeances afoot for the wrongs of the world" (290). This image of Suttree's hulking, misdirected, and excessive vengefulness explicitly links him with the hulking Ab who seeks alchemical vengeance through the medium of Mother She, and it implies that Suttree's own demand for justice keeps him similarly circling in the purgatory of his nether self, the prison of his "darker heart." When Suttree and Ab together visit Mother She, she cannot tell "which of these two souls is the worst troubled" (280).

Ironically, though, Suttree has always seen quite clearly that Ab creates his own hell. When the older man remarks sardonically that "bein a nigger is a interestin life," Suttree responds, "You make it that way" (203). And when drunken Harvey predicts that Ab will be killed for his violent behavior, Suttree soberly agrees (266). But until the aftermath of his impulsive destruction of the police car, an act that affirms his loyalty to and identification with Ab, Suttree does not recognize the degree to which he mirrors Ab. Nor can he act on Ab's understanding of the futility of such a life any more than Ab himself can. Suttree's earlier encounters with the police, while not aggressive on his part, demonstrate his own deep animosity against law officers, who seem to him harassing avatars of the huntsman. Like Ab (and like the Misfit in Flannery O'Connor's "A Good Man Is Hard to Find"), he has been "imprisoned" for a crime for which Suttree does not feel responsible. His gnostic/existentialist rebellion against his father and the church is mirrored by his rebellion against the law, and his jailing functions as much on a metaphysical level as a literal one: the very order of the world, of earthly life, condemns a man to the prison-house of cosmos and places him under a death sentence that he cannot accept as just. In his rebellion against the very conditions of life, Suttree plays out the self-destructive quest for justice that the novel interrogates through the figure of Ab Jones.

The two men's angry quests resonate interestingly with Dostoevsky's *Crime and Punishment*, another novel that charts the protagonist's slow and intermittent progress toward a redemption that puts him more fully in touch with the compassionate human heart within. Cosper and Cary point to similarities between Suttree and Camus's Meursault, who enact in different ways the "revolt of the university student," of which Raskolnikov is an earlier prototype (159). Both *Suttree* and *Crime and Punishment* suggest that the self-righteous demand for earthly justice, which derives from the human capacity to imagine perfect goodness, may not only pit one against the complex darkness of life itself but also lead to the commission of grave injustices against others. The saintly young Sonya or Sophia, named for wisdom, tells the outraged Raskolnikov that her desperate stepmother Katerina Ivanovna, who has coerced her to become a whore to save her younger siblings, is not evil but good—that she believes in Justice or Righteousness: "A sort of *insatiable* compassion, if one may so express it, was reflected in every feature of [Sonya's] face.... 'You know nothing, nothing about it.... She is so unhappy ... ah, how unhappy! ... She is seeking righteousness, she is pure. She has such faith that there must be righteousness everywhere and she expects it.... And if you were to torture her, she wouldn't do wrong. She doesn't see that it's impossible for people to be righteous and she is angry at it. Like a child, like a child. She is good!'" (322). It is Katerina's demand for justice for her starving children that has led her to send Sonya into prostitution, and it is Sonya's deep empathy that makes her willing to sacrifice herself. Sonya's compassion nudges the arrogant Raskolnikov to a truer comprehension of his own mixture of goodness and evil in his arrogant judgment of the pawnbroker he murders, another violation committed partly out of an outraged sense of justice; it is Sonya's influence that brings him to seek atonement and to hope for redemption. Both novels stress that the idea of justice divorced from human compassion can lead one to rationalize the victimizing of another and thus to destroy oneself. This is the point of Suttree and Ab's battered heads, as if the ways of the world itself, or some other order working in opposition to the archontic order, admonishes against elevating rationality over compassion. As Bell points out in another context, "being 'freed' by rationality in *Suttree* is dangerously smug and naive" (*Achievement* 72). Human rationality is linked here with the most violent unleashing of human nature, as in *Crime and Punishment* and *Blood Meridian*. Tarzan Quinn the ape-man and Ab Jones the "wild man" are equally matched in this. The description of Ab as "crazed" as he turns at bay to meet the policemen he has attacked in the alley links him with the hounds who are crazed with ravening for souls in this world and reveals him, ironically, as a human avatar of the principles of death and predation—of the same dark powers he sets himself against (443). On a less starkly allegorical level, Suttree's aggrieved alienation results in his own inflicting pain on others: his father and mother, Uncle John, his son, his ex-wife and her parents, Wanda, Joyce. Like Ab, he makes his life an "interestin" one as he makes enemies of those who love him, and of life itself.

However, Mother She's gnosis selects Suttree for her ministrations rather than Ab, suggesting that although he suffers a similar blindness, he is more receptive to enlightenment. Like the psychiatrist or spiritual counselor she stands in for, she perceives that Ab is not interested in self-knowledge but only wants to see her about his enemies (278). Though Suttree initially flees her offer of self-knowledge, after Hooper dies he seeks her out. The visions he experiences under her influence are recollections that have been blocked earlier, both in his waking perusal of the photo album of the dead and in his alcoholic nightmares: he dreams the fulfillment of his own dread of mortality as his spine is sucked out of his body by the dark succubus of death, and he is shown the origin of his death trauma in his repressed memories of the deaths and funerals of several family members he witnessed as a young child—including the corpse of a baby who stands for Suttree's dead twin. The vision also fulfills the Ab / Suttree / Mother She plot strand of the novel when Suttree sees not only "what had been" but "what would come to be" in a psychic resolution to the problem of the world's injustice: he sees that Little Robert will kill Ab's enemy Tarzan Quinn, just as another man killed Ab's original enemy, the white man who shot Ab as a boy just because he, a black fourteen-year-old, had "whipped him" (428–30, 204). The vision affirms an order in the world that Suttree "had never seen before" (430). Just as he has seen that his emotionally satisfying gesture of sinking the police car will not save Ab from self-destruction or Quinn's aggression, Ab's vengeful plotting is revealed to Suttree as equally fruitless. It is not Ab in his self-will who causes the death of Quinn, but some other principle of order in the world, an order that is akin to the notion of life as process, which Suttree will articulate after his final vision in the novel. This process may sometimes employ the crazed vengefulness of others, but it releases the individual from the self-will of his own demand for justice, which is the crucial lesson. Although at this point Suttree has not yet fully achieved release from his self-imposed purgatory, the vision at Mother She's is another step in his erratic progress. This readjustment of his perception thus brings about a kind of resurrection, one that foreshadows Suttree's decision to take leave of his corpse-double in the houseboat and to embark on a new life at the end of the novel. Cocooned in his floating bed back at the houseboat as he emerges from his hallucinatory trance, Suttree lies in state like the dead Ab or like "a dead king on an altar," yet his bier is also a cradle and in it he is rocking "like the first germ of life adrift on the earth's cooling seas . . . and all creation yet to come" (430). With its hint of the moth's chrysalis, the vision reverses the direction of Suttree's obsessive cradle image: rather than the whicket of the cradle rocking the infant to death, now the rocking bier incubates new life.

"Babbling gospelarity" and the Spiritual Wound

In two buildings Suttree visits as if to invite hallucinated recollections, his church and his high school, he remembers the tainting of his education with stale dogmas, and in both he is confronted by priests who implicitly question his right to be there. Only at the Church of the Immaculate Conception does he achieve a brief recovery of his past in response to a mute artifact. He seeks the church soon after reluctantly interring Leonard's father in the river. His impulse to commend the man's spirit in some way is foiled by Leonard's indifference to such ritual and indeed to his father's death. Thus Suttree's drunken refuge in the church constitutes a subconscious hope to find succor there, despite his longstanding alienation from the religion of his own father—the religion from which, he tells a nurse, he has been "defrocked" (191). As he enters the sanctuary, he thinks "The virtues of a stainless birth were not lost on him," suggesting that it is also his revulsion from the body's carrion stains that he wishes to anneal (253).

Suttree remembers himself as a "spurious acolyte" in the church, a "dreamer impenitent" matching the oblivious or perhaps alien God who "himself lies sleeping in his golden cup." His response to the sanctuary is much like the modern's response to the architectural monuments of other cultures. He focuses on the church as artifact. His observations of the altars, statuary, and stained glass emphasize their garishness and decay, as if they are the tawdry window-dressing of a dead, alien ritual. Reminded of his reading in art history, Suttree recalls that the sculptor always leaves something unsaid, and looking at the statues of Christ and the Virgin he decides what is unsaid is that "this statuary will pass," ambiguously suggesting both the icon's transience and the heresy of its passing for or counterfeiting the represented thing itself (253).[25] The mute artifacts of the church and its iconography are the remains of a dead religion, itself a manifestation of archontic order. They do not speak to Suttree, and the scene establishes the spiritual wounding that compounds Suttree's obsession with death. Not the icons but the sounds of children playing beyond the church walls prompt Suttree's recollections of his childhood here. One memory is of his peers' less than pious response to a May ceremony, likely a first communion: the boys' spontaneous laughter when young Suttree sets another boy's hair on fire with a candle and the girls' attempts to hide their glee—"small specters of fraudulent piety"—or their feigned swoons to attract attention (254). The little girls' apparent submission to their religious indoctrination is unmasked by their subversive strategies, suggesting the principle of innate vitality underlying all children's instinctive defiance of the ritualization that threatens to deaden the spiritual impulse.

Suttree also remembers escaping with Jim Long after Mass to breakfast in the market with the poor, "this venture into the world of men rich with vitality." The boys' escape into the more vibrant city life adumbrates the adult Suttree and J-Bone's compulsive flights into Knoxville's night life and paradoxically into their alcoholism. That Suttree recognizes this himself is made clear in the ambiguous referent of his thought, "lives proscribed and doom in store." On the one hand, the doomed, proscribed lives are those of the "old men in smoky coats and broken boots" who line the roach-infested counters (254). Suttree's foreknowledge of their doom recurs when he sees the elderly men and street vendors on a winter day just before he meets Joyce: "In their faces signature of the soul's remoteness. Suttree felt their looming doom, the humming in the wires, no news is good" (381). On the other hand, the doomed are also young Suttree and Jim, who have found in their church only "doom's adumbration in the smoky censer." The boys find better sustenance (or imagine so) in the streets than in the church, where the nuns with their "orthopedic moralizing" reek of death; where the priest who wakes Suttree wears a "bland scented face"; and where the city's doomed are not welcome because they are not genteel (254). Suttree's memory is a relatively familiar indictment of twentieth-century Roman Catholicism—or more generally Christianity—as it is offered to children or withheld from the poor. The church serves no spiritual food to them. Rather, it is a "kingdom of fear and ashes," regimented, dogmatic, inspiring not hope but guilt, not spirituality but terror—a version of the gnostic nightmare (253).

These memories in and of the church accomplish none of the resolution that we find in McCarthy's early works framed as hallucinated recollections. Rather, they confirm the frustration of Suttree's hope for spiritual healing within it. Indeed his assertion, "You dont know me," to the priest who so gently expels him from the sanctuary directly echoes Robert McEvoy's alienation in Graniteville (255; *GS* 39). Suttree's words also echo Ab Jones's complaint against those who become successful and no longer "know" their friends; thus they implicitly charge the church with abandoning her people (203). When Suttree claims that the church is "not God's house," he implies that the priests expel God when they exclude the most abject of His children and that if God has a house it should be the wider world that contains us all (255). Additionally he reflects the gnostic idea that the god of the Judeo-Christian tradition is not the true Good God, who dwells unknown and unnamed outside the cosmic realm, in the spirit's true Home. Suttree's perception is of course conditioned by his felt exclusion from his earthly father's house, his having been cast forth upon the world.

Suttree's boyhood preference for the vitality of the streets over the sterility of the church seems to have prompted his father's advice that "if it is life that you feel you are missing I can tell you where to find it. In the law courts, in business, in government. There is nothing occurring in the streets. Nothing but a dumbshow composed of the helpless and the impotent" (13–14). His father may believe that Suttree is mistakenly struggling with a reductive choice between dead church and vital street life. He tries to offer his son a third alternative. But to Suttree the middle-class professional and business realms are no more vibrant than the church, being equally regimented, bureaucratic, and exclusionary; all are creations of false, archontic powers. As Guinn writes, such "institutions . . . reify meaning through a delusive ordering principle . . . of commerce and conventional progress" (106). Suttree's own quest is toward vision, communion, and voice. In seeking voice and vision, Suttree struggles to free himself from identification with his dead twin, who "neither spoke nor saw" (14). But in his brief visit to the church Suttree achieves only a negative spiritual vision, a gnostic repudiation of false gods and false religion, and only transient access to a voice in his bitter memories of his childhood there.

Before Suttree visits his high school, the other monument to his Roman Catholic education, he makes a drunken expedition to Woodlawn Cemetery, where his dead twin lies, waking there the next morning with only vague memories of the night before: "A maudlin madman stumbling among the stones in search of a friend long dead who lies here" (302). This is one of two cemetery scenes that repeat the framing situations of "Wake for Susan" and *The Orchard Keeper* and emphasize the obstacles to Suttree's consistently achieving vision. The other is his stumbling across the ancient cemetery in the mountains, where his visionary capability is blocked. Wandering there lost and starving, Suttree experiences visions that with the falling of darkness become increasingly gothic. With Rorschach-like projection, these visions sequentially rehearse the persistent obsessions of his death-haunted purgatory: the death of children, the procession of mortals to death, and humanity's history of war and predation (286–88). But earlier, when Suttree finds the ruined children's cemetery, he reads the toppling gravestones' inscriptions, words "all but perished in the weathers of seasons past." The dates tell him these are dead children, but he creates no imaginative recovery of them. Rather, he achieves only a fleeting metaphoric revisioning of the children as "small figurines composed of dust and light . . . in the broken end of a bottle, spidersized marionettes in some minute ballet there in the purple glass so lightly strung with strands of cobweb floss" (286). The condensed poetic image, a spontaneous projection of Suttree's psyche, posits the children as already inanimate, and although their makeup includes light as well as dust, the image foregrounds death, as if the dust overshadows the light, as in the gnostic conception of the tragic cosmic obscuring of spirit in clay. At this point in his progress, Suttree is tormented by his view of humanity as briefly animated dust, little more than puppets made to dance on a stage hung with cobwebs—the stage of the western world announced in the prologue.

Suttree's inebriated visit to the Woodlawn Cemetery is even less productive of vision. Although drugs or disordered physical states sometimes serve as pathways to his most revealing visions, as at Mother She's, alcohol always prevents Suttree from gaining insight, a literalizing of the gnostic metaphor of the soul's cosmic oblivion as drunkenness. Even when Suttree's drunken visions are revelatory to the reader, as when he hears the "whicket and swish" of "the clocklike blade of the cradle," they send Suttree himself spinning down the vortex of his death-obsessions (80). Here he merely sleeps drunkenly in the cemetery, oblivious among the dead. When he makes his way back to the Longs' house, where he has been recuperating from his sojourn in the mountains, he stands in its bay window at night "like a child in a pulpit in the dark of an empty church"—an image that conjoins his identities as soul-wounded child and as would-be messenger of truth, one who will eventually find his voice and audience as the narrator of this story of spiritual awakening.

The next morning, sober, Suttree makes his way to the high school, climbing its back stairs to his classroom. Here his smoldering anger at the church and its school, "where he'd been taught a sort of christian witchcraft," blocks his imagination. When Suttree notices the black figure of a priest watching him, the alien intruder, he leaves the house, pausing only to retrieve the "billikin" he had carved as a child and hidden in the chimney (304). The silent priest does not smile kindly and condescendingly as has the priest at the church; rather he seems to Suttree a "catatonic shaman who spoke no word at all." His "shape" framed in the school's bay window "like a paper priest in a pulpit or a prophet sealed in glass," he is messageless, substanceless, dead (305). Suttree links the priest with the archontic huntsman in the word *shape*, which echoes the prologue's question, *"and can you guess his shape?"* (4–5). And Suttree's imagery here links the silent priest not only with his image of himself in the pulpit of a dark church but also with the filmstrip images of the dead behind window glass. If this return is undertaken in the hopes of cultivating any creative recollection of the past, it fails. The only work of art Suttree recovers is the billikin he has actually created in the past (reminiscent of the primitive but evocative carving fashioned by the nameless whittler in *The Gardener's Son*), not any new achievement of vision or voice.

The image of the Roman Catholic priest as complacent, condescending, a relic of the past and thus spiritually dead in both his mild and his admonitory avatars is reinforced when a third priest administers Suttree's last rites as he suffers typhoid. Suttree hears him as a "maudlin voice," a "medieval ghost come to usurp his fallen corporeality," suggesting the priesthood's false claims to minister to the spirit—or even the flesh—of humankind (460). His anointing Suttree's eyelids with an "oiled thumball" evokes again the archontic thumbwhorl of death that Suttree sees when he is concussed by a rock. But if the hurled rock is to be seen retrospectively as Peter's church, this is no aggressive salvation like John Donne's invocation of a battering, ravishing God. Rather, the church and its priesthood are merely avatars of death, manifestations or creations of the dark powers that hold the cosmos in thrall. Like the well-meaning but complacent priest in *The Crossing* who presumes to minister to the heretical grieving father at Caborca, the attending priest elicits from Suttree a comparable if less forceful rebuke than the heretic's hissed "save yourself" (*C* 157) or Meursault's angry repudiation of the chaplain in *The Stranger.* When the priest patronizes Suttree with his mild "I see," Suttree quietly disputes his vision, "No. . . . You dont" (462).

Suttree's rejection of the Roman Catholic clergy as failed messengers of God's news, or worse, as agents of false gods, is matched or exceeded by his vehement rejection of the church's sleeping God—a God he views as demented, life-denying, deaf, abusive, and unjust. These characterizations of the deity, comparable to the gnostic view of the usurping demiurge or artificer god, derive from Suttree's panic at the apparently God-ordained fact of human mortality and church teachings that the dead must atone for their unrighteousness in hell or limbo. As an adult, he questions such formulations but cannot easily free himself of them. Concussed with a floor buffer, Suttree imagines waiting for him the deadcart and "perhaps the wrath of God after all" (188). Or he imagines that what waits is not "the madonna of desire or mother of eternal attendance," neither the Virgin Mary nor the Beatrice of Dante, but the "foul hag" who reappears as the succubus of death to rape him in his hallucination at the cottage of Mother She. For him the hope promised by Mother Church is entirely overshadowed by the images of death and retribution it has inculcated. And God Himself is associated with Suttree's succubus of death in his conception of the priest as "praetor to a pederastic deity" when he emerges from his near-death experience "aneled. Like a rapevictim" (460). For Suttree the fathers who sometimes abdicate their priestly responsibilities to prey like the huntsman upon their charges truly represent the Godhead Himself.

Suttree's anger at God results from his perception of an essential injustice in the way of things. He questions the justice of man's very nature, his dualistic composition of spirit and matter, light and dust. In Suttree's vision of a hydrophobic god is implied that the deity fears and eschews the very life force itself—the force He paradoxically embodies as man's creator (130). This god is a creator of death: the gnostic demiurge, not the Unknown Father of Light. Thus He sleeps, sealed away in His church, deaf to His children in their mortal pain. In one of Suttree's death visions, he evokes the irony of the slogan stamped on American currency, "In God We Trust," when the dream-revelers at the Huddle bring forth "a few pieces of Denver silver. Avowing blind faith in deaf deities" (456). Mainstream American culture, in its devotion to the commercial enterprise, mirrors its sleeping and oblivious deity, turning a deaf ear to the worth and suffering of its poorest citizens. Like the punitive, rapist God, this remote, careless God of Suttree's imagination also parallels his re-mote father and the exclusionary priests, and Suttree's anger at each father com-pounds his anger at the others. Like Hooper the ragman, Suttree doesn't like God very much because he cannot accept His ways, especially when he consid-ers the death of children: his twin's consignment to limbo, his innocent son's early death, the abrupt shearing of Wanda's young life. "Choked with bitter-ness," Suttree kneels at his child's grave and wonders about the boy's helpless fear in the face of death, "And what could a child know of the darkness of God's plan? Or how flesh is so frail it is hardly more than a dream" (154). Suttree's image of a sleeping God impassively removed from the workings of His own dark plan approaches but stops short of the nihilist "God is dead" formula because he cannot fully free himself of the influence of the church. Nor has he embraced the consolation of a transmundane God of Light such as gnostics envisioned as the spirit's true Home. Hooper's death reveals this most clearly when Suttree asks the ragman's corpse if he has followed through on his plan to quiz God about why He had him in the "crapgame" of life and then tear-fully postulates, "There's no one to ask is there? There's no. . . ." but cannot bring himself to articulate that there is no God (258, 422).[26] In his heart Sut-tree believes there is a God, but one whose workings are so unbearably opaque and impenetrable that he is left an abused orphan in cosmos.

Though deeply disaffected from the Church and its sleeping God, Suttree is far from indifferent to matters of spirit. As Bell observes, Suttree is "a kind of a secular hierophant, on watch for even waning evidence of the sacred within the profane" (*Achievement* 77). One manifestation of his watchfulness is his interest in the many fundamentalist preachers of Knoxville, as if he would sam-ple other versions of Christianity. He sees them as "God's barkers gone forth into the world like the prophets of old" and listens for "some stray scrap of news from beyond the pale" (66). He admires their crazed conviction and their willingness to take their preaching to the marketplace and the streets, contrast-ing so markedly with the complacency of the priests, who minister to the poor of the city only at the moments of their deaths.

Nevertheless Suttree does not find the answer to his spiritual yearnings in the preachers of other sects. Some share in the priests' exclusion of the poor. The minister whose service Reese's family attends in their homemade calico outfits evades the ritual of welcoming them, pointedly forgoing his pastoral greeting of the congregation on that day (313). The faithful of these sects are often sternly judgmental or self-willed in their attempts to coerce "righteous" behaviors. As Suttree watches a baptism from the riverbank and talks to two men who try to convince him to "get in that river," which with its cloacal associations he knows offers no salvation, the women nearby cast censuring looks at them, like the congregation that reproves and spurns the snuffling Lester Ballard (124). Suttree readily admits to the first man that he is not saved, and the second, a lay preacher, thereafter communicates with him only through the first—as if contact with the unsaved is incompatible with his sanctity. The lay preacher rudely dismisses Suttree's baptism-by-sprinkling, claiming "I'd rather to just go on and be infidel as that." The first man, who shares Suttree's appreciation of the erotic and humorous aspects of this rite of "total nursin," nevertheless rises to the bait when Suttree asks, "What do you think about the pope and all that mess over there?" (122, 123). His response further reveals the mindlessness of the men's repudiation of any faith that differs from their own: "I try my bestest not to think about it atall" (123). And when Suttree asks him if he has any alcohol, even this man who has been happy to talk with him edges away as if to avoid contamination.

The crazed evangelist who calls down abusive denunciations on all passersby from the "pulpit" of his high room is an extreme embodiment of the judgmental piety afflicting many of the book's religious spokesmen. And his self-castration suggests his impotence as a messenger of God. Significantly he is silenced—put to sleep like the powers of darkness after devouring the gnostic messenger—as Suttree walks past for the last time on his way out of his life in the city: "The eunuch was asleep in his chair and he stirred and mumbled fitfully as if the departing steps of the fisherman depleted his dreams but he did not wake." The misanthropy of this old "Thersites" is mirrored in one of Suttree's ancestors who on his deathbed exhorted his own dead kin "in a fevered apostrophe of invective" (469, 129). The narrating Suttree understands that "the wrath he suckled at his heart has wasted more than years," and the old man's dire nether heart is a double of Suttree's own (129). Thus Suttree's final affirmation of the unity and paradoxical loneliness of all souls offers a resolution not just to his anger at his father and family but also to his ontological isolation from the human family and from God, and it postulates in a new and more inclusive way the value of a universal kinship and communion that heals all schism—even the primal gnostic schism between man and the transmundane Divinity from which he is alienated, and to which he is kin.[27]

The elevated towers or pulpits from which some of the novel's religious figures deliver their messages, whether of judgmental hatred or bland neglect, constitute the Babel of modern religious institutions broken into schisms that further separate soul from soul and fail to connect humanity in true communion. The novel's Babel reference is most explicitly conveyed in a secular context as Suttree sees buildings being torn down for urban renewal. One half-demolished house exposes a "freestanding stairwell to nowhere" (464). The stairway is echoed by the half-constructed freeway Suttree observes as he leaves the city: "The ramp curved out into empty air and hung truncate with iron rods bristling among the vectors of nowhere" (471). The transient works of humankind, whether new or old, under construction or demolition, lead to nowhere. This includes religious institutions. Like the Tower of Babel built by Nimrod (the hunter or huntsman), these material constructions express the vanity and arrogance of human/archontic endeavor divorced from the spiritual. Knoxville itself is associated with Babel in the imagery of its buildings, which "rise into an obscurity prophetic and profound" (177). And as a near homophone of "Babylon," the Babel references evoke too the gnostic metaphor for the world and the body. In "The Hymn of the Pearl" the first-person narrative of the savior/spirit equates Babel with Egypt as the symbolic site of the spirit's captivity in matter and cosmos (Jonas, *Gnostic Religion* 113). Knoxville's Church of the Immaculate Conception is figured as a Tower of Babel in its actual topographical positioning on Summit Hill, the highest point in the city center, and facing away from the marketplace below. When Suttree and Jim escape the church to breakfast in the market, their physical descent from the towering church that turns its back to the men of the city is a departure from the tower of vain expression and a turning toward the life of humanity. Thus it foreshadows not only their temporary turn to the oblivion of drink and the pleasures of Babylon but also, paradoxically, Suttree's turn from the deadening institutional religion of the church to the spiritual search for God in the streets that he will envision in his final hallucinations and pursue when he leaves the purgatorial city. As Suttree watches demolition crews in Knoxville's slums, he perceives them as "Gnostic workmen who would have down this shabby shapeshow that masks the higher world of form" (464). (Their opposites are the parched construction crew of the epilogue, who seem to be conscripts to the cosmos of forms.) His imagery invokes the platonic underpinnings of the gnostics: the workmen repudiate the "shabby shapeshow" of the cosmos, all forms created by the artificer god(s), in favor of the "higher world of form" associated with the Light or Ultimate Truth of Plato or with the Unknown God of the gnostics. For gnostics cosmic forms did not reflect or correspond to higher forms, as Plato postulated, but blinded humanity to them, thus "masking" the higher, transmundane world. Gnostics were deemed heretics by the Roman Catholic Church partly because they stressed the individual search for spiritual insight rather than the institutionalization and perpetuation of the Church. Among other resonances, then, the gnostic reference reinforces the association of the "garish" modern church with a "shabby shapeshow" of religion, or with the

Tower of Babel, the towers "to nowhere" (253, 464). Appearing late in the book, it is further evidence that Suttree finally puts behind him the vanity of his religious teaching and rededicates himself to the pursuit of gnosis or authentic spiritual insight.

Before this, Suttree encounters several street preachers who bring their messages to the marketplace, potentially countering those who babble from their towers of isolation. But most of these street evangelists are similar failures in vision and communion, as sealed away in self-absorption from their congregations as the priest behind glass. Suttree observes one "crazed prophet in biblical sandwichboards" who delivers no good news to the man on the streets but rather "mutter[s] darkly at the heavens," carrying on some quarrel with God, like the ragman or Suttree himself (234). The female evangelist who preaches to the Jordonia prisoners seems oblivious to their presence, and they in turn seem "stricken nigh insensate by this word of God strained distaff." Suttree's recognition that her version of biblical events is inauthentic, "so altered were they from their origins," comprises an understated criticism of religious teaching that represents as indisputable and literal truth interpretations that might as well and indeed often have "come down orally" (50). When Suttree finds the Book of Mormon in the bus station in Bryson City, where he has suffered yet another expulsion, he is willing enough to read it; wrapped in his blanket and clasping the book to his breast, he himself presents the image of a "latterday crazyman" or "itinerant simonist." But Suttree can make nothing of the Mormon teachings, and "he thought he'd never read a stranger tale" (294). Locked away in his pain, Suttree mirrors the street preachers in their ironic isolation from the people they accost or merely pass by, and his incomprehension of the word he reads hints a parallel confusion of the street preachers even in their fervent exhortations.

The babble made of the gospels by all these preachers suggests Yeats's formulation of modern alienation in "The Second Coming," where "The best lack all conviction, while the worst / Are full of passionate intensity." The ragman recalls working in the carnival with street preachers who would "come off the circuit in the early summer and bark and shill with the best of em and go back to preachin in the fall" (257). And the "maddest man of God yet," stationed in the Knoxville market, whirls in a Yeatsian gyre or gnostic image of cosmic turmoil, a "revolving parody of the crucifixion," repeating the vortex of man's cosmic life as he aspires, moth-like, to ash—or to nowhere. He alone articulates Suttree's view that the way of the spirit is not in the "buyin and sellin" of the marketplace but "on your knees in the streets." And he succeeds in gaining an audience, prompting the vendors and hucksters to leave their wares to listen. One man "mad as he" even steps forth for baptism. But the baptismal water in the gutter is not the "living water" sought by gnostics but the stale waste of the watertrucks, a miniature baptism in the cloacal waters of the river; and the rites offered by this extremist are mock rituals. Like the others, this whirling "red reverend" is oblivious to the congregants he has attracted; though they are tempted to applaud his bizarre performance, they take no sustenance from his words. Suttree passes on (382–83).[28]

In quiet counterpoint to the self-absorbed babble of the novel's priests and evangelists are three men and women who in their simple humanity are truer prophets, truer communicants: the Indian Michael, the goatman, and Mother She. These three all have moments of true vision or prophecy: Michael correctly predicts that Suttree will not stay on the purgatorial river (240); the goatman who says he makes "no cures, no predictions" nevertheless recognizes Suttree's essential loneliness with a confidence that suggests second sight (200, 206); and Mother She not only sees his soul-sickness but leads him to healing visions of his past and of the future. Suttree will eventually discard the amulet Michael gives him, but not the message with which he offers it: "Dont forget about it," he tells Suttree, "You cant just put it away and forget about it" (239). Michael's admonishment is an affirmation of faith in life and the possibility of luck, an affirmation all the more striking in coming from a man who parallels Ab Jones in his pariah status within the culture that disvalues him. Michael's words suggest that the amulet works by placing its carrier in a frame of mind receptive of grace. When Suttree achieves that spiritual state at the end of the novel, he no longer needs any souvenir other than his simple human heart. He buries Michael's amulet where it "would not be found in his lifetime," reversing his retrieval of the little carved figure from his school, retrospectively associating the billikin with the simple human heart he affirms as he leaves Knoxville (468). The goatman's formal preaching does not interest Suttree, but his pastoral care for his goats is the more significant example his story offers. The policeman calls them "damned," and the goatman himself says, "You caint do nothin with em." They are somewhat analogous to the hogs of *Outer Dark* in their association with the obstinately material aspects of human nature. But unlike the archontic hog drovers, the goatman watches over his flock "paternally" (195). He has devoted his life to faithful care for his goats and for the human flock that gathers to hear him preach.

When Suttree shares his fish with the goatman, he unconsciously engages in a communion that the other accepts with grace. Similarly Michael offers communion to Suttree in the simple act of sharing his turtle stew, and when Suttree cradles the proffered bowl in two hands, he too accepts it as a grail. Suttree tells Michael he inherited his fishing from another man and that when that man left, "All he said was not to look for him back" (240). But in their roles as fishermen and their offering of communion, Michael and Suttree function as that Man's avatars. This concept of Christ in mankind is made explicit in *The*

Sunset Limited when Black affirms that if Jesus is everyman, then every man is Jesus (95). It is also manifest in *The Road*, in the father's decision not to take his son with him when he dies but rather to leave him in the destroyed world to reseed it with the spiritual fire he carries.

Despite Suttree's fear of Mother She's arcane power to confront him with what he has repressed, she too is an understated figure of ministering care, offering this strange white man ice for his wounded head, salve for his wounded soul. These three visionaries are joined by other true ministers who in their acts of kindness bless their fellow men and demonstrate their own grace. Aunt Martha, Mrs. Long, Doll Jones, and Mary Lou, who works behind the lunch counter on Thanksgiving Day, all feed Suttree and expect little or nothing in return. Not only Michael but also Blind Richard and especially Jim Long seek him out in his sickness and alienation, ministering with differing degrees of efficacy to his body and spirit. Canfield notes how after Blind Richard's visit to Suttree as he recuperates in the Long home, the dirty water flowing from the gutter pipe grows clear and the rain water on the magnolias looks clean; in such moments "the muckish water of the river yields to other, cleansing images" ("Dawning" 682). Turbid water is displaced by Living Water. The nurses and doctors who tend Suttree in his injuries and illnesses are not remote and judg-mental or mere students of the material body, as in *Child of God*, but compas-sionate healers, like the doctors who treat Rinthy in *Outer Dark*, John Grady in *All the Pretty Horses*, and Boyd in *The Crossing* and like the practicing physi-cian that the alienated John Western becomes late in "Whales and Men." For every few drivers who pass Suttree on the road, there is one who offers a ride. And Bell writes of the significance of the Josie Harrogate scene near the end of the novel, a scene that captures the "irreducible human value of the entire book" in Josie's enduring care for her feckless half-brother. "For McCarthy a belief in the reality of other people is the first principle of responsible exis-tence," Bell concludes, "and that is not a theory for him but a vision, complete in itself, expressed not in discourse but in the creation of a world that we are compelled to believe in" (114). It is not Suttree alone in this novel who enacts Christlike care for others; here, as in the Border Trilogy, *The Sunset Limited*, and *The Road*, McCarthy risks the charge of sentimentality to convey his vision that in such acts lies humanity's truest ministry, a salvific communion, simple and available to all, that paradoxically coexists with man's tendency to feral vio-lence. These understated acts of charity, overshadowed by all the pain and alienation and predation that comprise the dystopian Knoxville experience, foreshadow the grace of the waterboy and the driver in the novel's epilogue, whose acts are foregrounded there in evidence of the changed nature of Sut-tree's experience. They imply that in loving one another—not in self-absorbed preaching, nor in the dead rituals of the church—individuals bring the word of the true God and the message of humanity's true nature into the streets and minister to one another.

Suttree's fevered vision of a rebellious uprising of souls in hell clinches this insight. In a hallucination that conjoins his alienation from both his earthly father and his creator, Suttree stands accused, as Canfield says, "before the bar of the superego" ("Dawning" 689), of consorting with people and indulging in behaviors unbecoming "a person of your station." Suttree admits his "guilt" with the feeble excuse, "I was drunk," a moment that despite its humor also expresses the truth that Suttree has heretofore struggled through his life in a state of spiritual oblivion.[29] After his confession, Suttree quails temporarily at his "vision of the archetypal patriarch himself unlocking with enormous keys the gates of Hades." But he is not thrust into hell as he has been taught to fear; rather, "a floodtide of screaming fiends and assassins and thieves and hirsute buggers pours forth into the universe, tipping it slightly on its galactic axes" (457). What's more, this potentially nightmarish image quickly morphs into a vision of universal redemption as the sinners of the world, released from hell, "carry the Logos itself from the tabernacle and bear it through the streets." The triumphant uprising is permitted, even initiated, by the Patriarch Himself, who frees the rabble. It is not the good God or Christ who arraigns Suttree and humankind and "howls them down and shrouds their ragged biblical forms in oblivion" but the "absolute prebarbaric mathematick of the western world": the Greco-Roman tradition and its petrified Christian church with its archontic hierarchies, its "orthopedic moralizing," its failure of compassion and communion, and its codified and deadened spirituality (458, 254).

In this gnostic vision, Suttree repudiates and frees himself from the hell of church doctrine, even from the inferno, purgatorio, and paradiso of Dante's poetic vision, which has so informed his own experiences in Knoxville. In his near-death experience he sees both a pit where "gray geometric saurians lay snapping" and in the distance a "gold pagoda with a little flutterblade that spun in the wind" and understands that "he was not going there" (461). The line reverses Harry's death-vision of the snows atop Kilimanjaro, "unbelievably white in the sun," and his intuition that "there was where he was going" (Hemingway 27). Suttree's rejection of the nirvana of the gold pagoda along with the pit is his final repudiation of the church's division of souls in eternal torment or reward. Although it is possible to read this passage as a relinquishing only of heaven, and not of hell, the "there" to which Suttree is not going is pointedly open-ended, and his vision of the Patriarch releasing sinners from Hades establishes his rejection of hell as well. His gnostic vision of a liberating God joins his insight about the divine force as nonentropic process ("Nothing ever stops moving"; 461), and both resolve the problem of the deaf, blind, or punitive God formulated by the western tradition and the teachings of its church.[30]

Finally, his vision affirms that the true God Himself sanctions bringing the Logos into the streets, recognizing it as humanity's true nature, rather than an icon to be sealed away in the tabernacle. The transformative, healing quality of this vision is evident in Suttree's second humorous affirmation of guilt. When the priest asks him if he would like to confess, Suttree responds simply, gracefully, "I did it," mildly mocking the priest's emphasis on human guilt and penance but also affirming without terror his own human admixture of dust and light: the soot mingled in life, his cosmic nature as sut-tree (461).

Suttree is not only an Orpheus figure who guides Gene Harrogate—and himself—out of a sooty urban underworld; he is also a Lazarus figure, a type of the human spirit awakened, self-resurrected from a death-in-life, emerging from the purgatorial cave into a state of spiritual grace or gnosis. The goatman with his orthodox views of heaven and hell postulates that dead Lazarus must be in heaven if Christ selected him; this troubles the old man because he imagines that Lazarus would "hate to get to heaven and then get recalled" (199). This is one of the puzzles the goatman plans to ask Jesus about when he gets to heaven himself, a notion that interests and amuses Suttree. On one level, Suttree dismisses the biblical story of Lazarus as one of the "stories of levitation" told by the nuns of his elementary school (254). On the other hand, Suttree seriously contemplates the "strange authority" with which Lazarus is invested as an awakened initiate. Suttree also sees such authority in the inhabitants of the insane asylum, who seem "like folk who'd had to do with death some way and had come back, something about them of survivors in a realm that all must reckon with soon or late" (431). The passage is prophetic, foreshadowing Suttree's own position at the end of the novel—a strange survivor and messenger invested with special author-ity. When the prologue invokes Eliot's Prufrock as one avatar of our guide through Knoxville, we are reminded that as a Lazarus who has "Come back to tell you all," Prufrock is an ineffectual messenger unsure of his own authority. In the face of indifference or in the babble of competing voices, he drowns. Suttree, hardened in the crucible of street life and tempered by his spiritual search, is a much more assertive Lazarus. Awakened from the throes of purgative typhoid and his near-drowning of pneumonia (literally, sickness of the pneuma—or soul), he feels "like an angel" (462). He fearlessly tells the priest what he has learned in his death-experience, and he will tell us all as narrator of his story.

Suttree's physical departure from Knoxville emblematizes his spiritual release from Babylon. No longer will he live in the city attempting not to be of it, imperfectly resisting being tainted by it. Since Bell's study, a critical consensus has formed that Suttree's progress involves a reconciliation with the world, and despite the gnostic aura of his experiences in the present time of the novel and his gnostic rejection of the Roman Catholic Church, I concur with this reading. Just as Suttree's awakening love for Wanda stirs in him a love and appreciation for the natural world, not only in its beautiful manifestations but also in its entire "locked and wheeling" cosmic organization, his final recognition of the kinship of all humanity frees him to love others and to love the world itself. Early in the novel, pondering his breech birth, he has thought that like whales and bats he is a creature "meant for other mediums than the earth and having no affinity for it" (14). His repudiation of the city, the river, the sewer, all the dark matter of earth, is a gnostic rejection, and it is not just land that Suttree has no affinity for but cosmos itself. But when he leaves the site of his purgatory, he achieves a partial transcendence of the gnostic anticosmic perspective, arriving at a state analogous to John Grady Cole's recognition of the awful mixture of beauty and terror in the world and his courageous affirmation that "he felt wholly alien to the world although he loved it still" (*APH* 282). The hound still sniffs at Suttree's tracks, but he leaves the hounds and the huntsman behind with a final word of advice to the reader: "Fly them" (471). Cosper and Cary read this as a continuation of the gnostic dread of cosmos (176). But it is equally possible to read the valediction as a warning against the anticosmic mindset that has so tormented Suttree, for as the prologue tells us, the huntsman *"is not to be dwelt upon for it is by just suchwise that he's invited in"* (5). Young has gone so far as to suggest that the hound in the epilogue is now benign (120). If Suttree is no longer subject to its malignity, it is because he has transcended his gnostic soul-sickness and no longer dwells upon the cosmic prison and its wardens. Neither is he oblivious to them. But unlike Culla Holme, who circles forever in a nightmarish gnostic netherworld, Suttree moves on. His name suggests his mingled nature, soot and tree, but this is a significant variation on the tragic mingling the gnostics dwelt upon, matter and spirit. It implies an affirmation of the natural world, even a hint of the spiritual presence within nature that is foregrounded in *The Orchard Keeper* and becomes a major theme in the Border Trilogy.

The nightmare version of nature in *Outer Dark* is quietly countered there by the narrator in his ecocentric perspective, and the wild splendor of nature is the backdrop, invisible to him, against which Lester Ballard's deepening oblivion is played out. Suttree's alternating impulses to repudiate the obscene and predatory aspects of nature and to seek spiritual or psychological succor in the wilderness are implicitly resolved in his final spiritual healing. He leaves the dystopic city for the world itself, knowing its darkness and pain, yet prepared like John Grady to love it still. It is not hard to imagine this "aberrant journeyman to the trade of wonder" (290) heading west in the recovered state of child's grace he mourns earlier in the novel, the state in which we first witness Billy Parham in his attunement with the wolf and the world before his innocence is wrenched away by death. Despite his own losses, John Grady never loses his love for and wonderment at the world; Billy never regains it. Suttree is perhaps most like the blinded pensioner who in his darkness recognizes the world yet learns to listen for the Good God (*C* 292). Transcending his purgatory, he opens himself up not only to the world but also to the spirit within, and he discovers his artistic voice and vision.

Notes

Chapter 1: Landscape of Memory

1. Chilhowee Mountain is a long ridge that stretches from Sevier County southwest across Blount County to its end at the Little Tennessee River in Monroe County (*History of Blount County* 12; map 4–5).

2. Winkler died at the age of eighty-two on August 25, 1991. Thus he was thirty-two in 1941, four years older than Marion Sylder. Winkler is not a simple or absolute model for Sylder. There is no evidence he was a whiskey runner; rather, he held a job at the Jefferson Woolen Mills in Knoxville and was a member of the Vestal United Methodist Church. He had four children, one of whom was his son Hugh, who predeceased him ("Winkler, Homer"; Gibson 26). Moreover, Sylder is described as a tall man, while Winkler bore the apt nickname of "Shorty." His small stature is illustrated in a photograph accompanying an article about his fiftieth wedding anniversary, in which he is dwarfed by his wife, Cora, as they stand side by side ("Winklers Honored").

3. McCarthy's echoing of Davidson may be one reason Walter Sullivan perceived "agrarian influence" in *The Orchard Keeper* (721). Mountainous southeastern Tennessee, Unionist in the Civil War, never shared the plantation and slave culture of the deep South and thus is not identified with the culture of the Nashville Agrarians. But in his river history, Davidson defended the traditional cultures of the entire Tennessee Valley, including that of East Tennessee, sympathetically chronicling what was lost with the TVA's introduction of progressive culture; McCarthy seems to have found this compatible with his own aims in *The Orchard Keeper*. It is a mistake either to confuse East Tennessee with the plantation South or to label McCarthy a latter-day Agrarian, but if we read *The Orchard Keeper* in the context of the classic Agrarian manifesto *I'll Take My Stand: The South and the Agrarian Tradition*, we may recognize the following affinities between the two: a value placed on individualism; a value placed on ties to the land and the understanding that nature is not to be conquered; an emphasis on structuring time through awareness of natural cycles rather than through the artificial, fast-paced schedules of the mechanized world; a perception of the industrial, progressive economy as a threat to social bonds; and a perception of the spiritual deadness of those caught up in "progress."

4. The name "Tuckaleechee" is preserved in Tuckaleechee Cove. The village of Townsend is in or adjacent to the Cove (Campbell 20, map).

5. This location is approximately where McCarthy himself lived in Waldens Creek with his wife Lee in 1963 (Gibson 30).

6. Campbell later worked as a writer for the Great Smoky Mountains Conservation Association (110).

7. Initially the Park Service intended to remove all signs of pastoral life in the park, and many of the houses and farm buildings in Cades Cove were torn down as soon as they were evacuated. In keeping with Park Service policy, the lands were left for the forest to reclaim. However, in 1945 the Park Service determined that the cove warranted preservation as a historic site. They decided to maintain it as pastureland and to restore many of the remaining farmsteads to represent the human culture of the cove from 1825 to 1900 (Shields 102–3; Campbell 148). Photographs of many of these farm homes and buildings may be seen in A. Randolph Shields's *The Cades Cove Story*.

8. I located most of these articles in the biographical clipping files of the Calvin M. McClung Historical Collection of the East Tennessee Historical Center in Knoxville. I have been unable to verify complete publication information for some of them.

9. The news accounts disagree on the terms. Wilkinson says that the Park Service gave Ownby three thousand dollars and a lifetime lease for his farm (A9). McKamey reports that Ownby was offered only eight hundred dollars (C1).

10. After helping Marion Sylder out of the frigid creek in which he has wrecked his car, John Wesley stands before a "Warm Morning heater" in June Tipton's house. The heater is evidence of East Tennesseeans' "new catalog store prosperity" (105), but its use also suggests that neither the Tiptons' house in 1940 nor Lemuel Ownby's mountain home in the 1970s and '80s has central heating.

11. It also hired local people to carry out some of the TVA initiatives. For example, TVA hired East Tennessee native Marshall A. Wilson first to recruit employees for the construction of Norris Dam, then as an aide in public relations, in which position he worked closely with local families to coordinate the removal of residents and graves from the Cove Creek area that would be flooded by the dam (Wilson, 8, 19, 29ff.).

12. For Charles Joseph McCarthy's own account of TVA acquisitions, see his "Land Acquisition Policies and Proceedings in TVA—A Study of the Role of Land Acquisition in a Regional Agency," *Ohio State Law Journal* 10.1 (1949): 46–63. For discussion of Mr. McCarthy's role and his article, see Prather, "'The color of this life is water': History, Stones, and the River in Cormac McCarthy's *Suttree.*"

13. See Barbara Brickman's discussion of the cultural affinities of the people of Red Branch with the clans of Ulster in northern Ireland in "Imposition and Resistance in *The Orchard Keeper.*" Kephart relates that during the reign of James I, the British relocated the Scots-Irish from Scotland to northern Ireland, where they displaced the native Hibernian peoples but also absorbed elements of the Irish culture before emigrating to the American colonies and gradually migrating down the Appalachian chain into the mountains of Tennessee and North Carolina (150–51). Although Brickman does not discuss the historical path of Gaelic cultural transmission through the Scots-Irish from northern Ireland to East Tennessee, she recognizes in McCarthy's novel some of the cultural patterns Kephart discusses as distinctively Appalachian (for example, see Kephart's discussion of the Scots-Irish roots of the southern highlander's clan fealty, 388–91). And Brickman places the struggles of the men of Red Branch, Tennessee, in the context of a historical defiance of cultural imposition that is much earlier than East Tennessee's

resistence to modernization imposed largely from the north but that parallels it in ways that McCarthy is likely to have recognized. For Brickman, *The Orchard Keeper* "redramatizes, in the mountain community of Red Branch, Tennessee, the near destruction of Gaelic culture at the hands of English colonizers, and, in the process of mirroring that earlier conflict, he [McCarthy] celebrates the older culture and demonstrates how no conquest is complete or absolute" (55). Similarly Robert Jarrett suggests that *The Orchard Keeper* is analogous to Sir Walter Scott's Waverly novels, "in which the traditionalism of the Scottish Highlanders is viewed against the economic and social modernism of England" (29).

14. Charles G. Riddle, a retired agent for the Bureau of Alcohol, Tobacco and Firearms who worked in Cocke County, north of Sevier County, recalled that agents paid informers court-approved rewards of as much as one hundred dollars for information leading to the capture of a large still: "There might be some jealousy if one neighbor seemed to be making more money than the other, and agents used a neighbor-against-neighbor strategy. One angry moonshiner reported 18 stills and collected about $1,000" (Julian B1). For treatment of such informing in Cades Cove, see Dunn, 232–40. Dunn's discussion is perhaps not entirely objective, however, since the case he most concerns himself with is that of his own relative, John Oliver, a prohibitionist who felt that blockading contributed to ruining families and for this reason notified state and federal agents of the locations of many neighbors' stills.

15. As the local histories of Knoxville and Blount County make clear, John Kobler's *Ardent Spirits: The Rise and Fall of Prohibition* has it backward when he claims that Tennessee's four-mile rule would apply in any municipality "provided that town incorporated." On the other hand, Kobler's assessment that the rule was the Anti-Saloon League's "principal instrument for drying up Tennessee" is substantiated by the local histories (196).

16. Kephart's love and concern for the mountains led him to work in North Carolina for the establishment of the national park. Given what we know about the creation of the park, this may seem a callous decision, but Campbell relates that in North Carolina there were many fewer small landowners evicted in the acquisition of park land, since most of the acreage had been owned by logging companies (30, 36, 68).

17. William J. Schafer (106) and Natalie Grant (78) identify the installation with Oak Ridge, but the tank is clearly not part of this nuclear energy facility, which is on the northwest side of Knoxville, while the place descriptions of the novel identify Red Branch with the southeast side. The ambiguous nature of the tank certainly accommodates Oak Ridge's war-industry associations, but it also encompasses any secret military/governmental encroachment on an established community or on the natural world—intrusions also comparable to the Trinity Project in Los Alamos, which figures so importantly in the Border Trilogy. These two nuclear facilities and McCarthy's invented tank share a cynical disregard for the human and natural ecology of the invaded regions and treat them as if they were blank space.

18. The CCC built five hundred miles of trails through the Great Smoky Mountains National Park. Its presence there peaked in 1934–35, when the park housed sixteen CCC camps (Campbell 125).

19. Davidson made the same point about the first wave of northern capitalists who infiltrated the South during Reconstruction: the pioneers "who had invaded the old Indian lands had now in their turn been invaded and worsted" (2:148). Boog's fascination with the vanished Indians and their ways is a subtle reminder of the earlier culture the Celtic pioneers had displaced and the feeble quality of the usurping culture's understanding of the dispossessed.

20. For a discussion of the ways in which the narrative frame establishes John Wesley as the "author" of the story, see my "'They aint the thing': Artifact and Hallucinated Recollection in Cormac McCarthy's Early Frame-Works." In "'Like something seen through bad glass': Narrative Strategies in *The Orchard Keeper*," William Prather also recognizes "John Wesley's status as narrator (or an conarrator, along with the McCarthyean narrating intelligence)" (39). Our compatible interpretations of the novel's narration were independently formulated at about the same time, and both were published in the same edited volume. Although he is primarily concerned with the novel's spatial structure, Horton also briefly discusses John Wesley as the novel's narrator, and this assumption informs his analysis as a whole.

21. Similar issues are at stake in McCarthy's screenplay, "Whales and Men," when John Western and his girlfriend Kelly McAmon save a lion cub from being adopted as someone's pet by buying it at auction so they can send it to a preserve (20–21).

22. See Kolodny's discussion of the "phallic thrust" of man's assault on the land in *The Pioneers*, where Cooper compares it to "some sad spoiler of a virgin's fame" and describes the conspicuous roof of Judge Templeton's house as an "offensive member" jutting into the skyline (quoted by Kolodny 91).

23. The narration of this scene is disrupted, and the reader may be left with the impression that Ownby has died when the narrative focus turns to John Wesley and then to Sylder. Only after their scenes does the focus return to Ownby, when he regains consciousness. Horton notes that the Ownby scenes frame those focused on the other two, and because six days pass in the lives of Sylder and John Wesley, he suggests that Ownby has been unconscious all that time, giving the impression that the other characters' actions are "somehow embedded in a dream of the unconscious Ownby" (293). However, there is no textual evidence to support the idea that Ownby has been lying unconscious for six days. He awakes in the night with the rain still falling (184). This could be the night of the sixth day, but it seems more plausible that it is the night of the first, the same on which he is struck. The subchapter is italicized, which might indicate that it represents Ownby's memory from a later point in time. But in most cases of such memory, a narrative present and plausible context are provided in which the character recalls his past; here both are missing. More likely, the italics denote that this subchapter is a backtracking in time from the preceding one. Thus the italics are, if anything, meant to *counter* any impression that six days have passed since Ownby was injured. As Horton himself discusses, such disruptions of time to pick up the narrative strands of the three main characters at somewhat different points are relatively common. They simulate John Wesley's piecing together of a narrative out of the fragments of his memories and his imagination.

24. Other gnostic images in *The Orchard Keeper* include the "infernal sky" that "cracks and splits" the dry clay (11) and the "squadron of bullbats" that rise up against the

sunset, "harrying the dusk" (9). Both images occur in the opening pages of the novel, before the lyricism associated with the three protagonists' viewpoints comes into play. And the bullbats that harry the dusk are associated with Kenneth Rattner, the dark stranger who harries the roads but whom Sylder soon expels from Red Branch.

25. His rebellion is adumbrated in McCarthy's second apprentice story, "A Drowning Incident," published in the March 1960 issue of the *Phoenix*, the literary magazine of the University of Tennessee. The unnamed boy protagonist of the story similarly escapes the claustrophobia of his oppressive home by venturing out of doors. His alienation from his parents culminates in an act of rebellion after he discovers that his father has drowned the puppies of his dog Suzy. In retaliation for his father's violent abnegation of stewardship for the pups, the boy pointedly places the decaying body of one puppy in the crib of his baby sister, with whose care he has been charged. For further discussion of "A Drowning Incident," see Wallach's "Prefiguring Cormac McCarthy: The Early Stories" (18–20) and Arnold's "Disgust in the Early Works of Cormac McCarthy" (69–72).

Chapter 2: Cosmic Estrangement

1. In "'And there shall be weeping and gnashing of teeth': Cormac McCarthy's *Outer Dark* as a Vision of Retribution in a World without Grace through Christ," William D. Taylor mentions two other passages concerning outer darkness in Matthew 13:11 and 22:13 and offers yet another Christian reading, arguing (too schematically and reductively, in my view) that Psalms 109:6–13 is a template for the novel's plot. Robert Jarrett appropriately links the novel's imagery of light and darkness to the first epistle of John, one of the most gnostic of the apostles (22), and in an early version of his book manuscript, Guillemin identified biblical parallels in the Revelation to John, the most striking of which is the verse that reads "and the sun became black as sackcloth" (Revelation 6:12; also Revelation 6:2–8; Guillemin, "Desolation" 149).

2. I have emphasized Bell and Arnold's points of dispute here to demonstrate the range of reactions to the novel's metaphysics and because Metress attempts to mediate between their positions as stated in 1988 and 1992 (when Arnold's "Naming, Knowing" was first published). By 1995 both scholars had modified their positions in ways that demonstrate they are not really so far apart. In his review-essay of *All the Pretty Horses*, Bell wrote that "McCarthy is a genuine—if somehow secular—mystic" ("'Between the wish'" 926). And in "The Mosaic of McCarthy's Fiction," first published in 1995, Arnold reaffirmed his belief that McCarthy "is no nihilist" but also stated, "I don't want to turn McCarthy into an overtly Christian writer; although he makes compelling use of western Christian symbology, I suspect his own belief system embraces a larger and more pantheistic view" (7–8).

3. Jonas makes it clear that the gnostics employed *soul* in the same contexts in which they might use *psyche* and that they did not mean by this the transcendent spirit. Having established this, Jonas himself sometimes uses the term *soul* when he means the pneuma or transcendent spirit. In this chapter I use the term *spirit* to imply the transcendent element within humankind. The term *soul* appears only when I quote others. When Jonas occasionally translates a gnostic passage referring to the psyche or the pneuma as *soul*, I provide interpolations to clarify which idea is meant.

4. When Rinthy prepares to begin her quest, she turns her face to the sun-washed sky, "bestowing upon it a smile all bland and burdenless as a child's" (53). Bell seems to read this passage as an uncomplicated sign of her grace, yet he observes that her simple identification with light "becomes progressively more ambiguous and ironic as her status in the world does—and as her hopes become frayed" (*Achievement* 47).

5. Fire (desire) and wind (counterspirit) are the upper elements, yet still components of cosmos (Jonas, *Gnostic Religion* 204–5).

6. Ann Fisher-Wirth's Kristevan reading, "Abjection and 'the Feminine' in *Outer Dark*," provides an interesting alternative approach to the imagery of mire. She links the images of mud and blood as signs of the abject and of the "feminine" in the Kristevan sense: "that realm of experience or existence that lies outside what Jacques Lacan calls the symbolic order, and that must be repressed or repudiated if the subject is to retain his illusion of autonomy, of identity" (125–26). Thus she argues that, especially with regard to Culla, the novel's plot "enacts one long flight from, and one long arrival at, the 'mire'" and that the landscape imagery "serves as a projection of its subjects' psyches"— points with which I agree (128). If applied to the psychological underpinnings of gnostic myth, the Kristevan/Lacanian psychoanalytical approach might intriguingly deconstruct this ancient anticosmic religion. Both recognize the "terror of the whole physical world" that Fisher-Wirth and I find dominating Culla (129). But it is important to recognize essential differences that make them difficult to reconcile in a reading of *Outer Dark*. Gnostics distrusted all aspects of psyche as manifestations of darkness and forces of spiritual alienation, so they placed a negative value on the "symbolic order." (Their own myth-making they saw as spiritual gnosis, emanating from a transcendent, spiritual order.) Gnosticism found no respite in religious, moral, or legal codes, regarding these aspects of the symbolic order as signs of man's deep involvement in cosmos and even assigning them the status of something rather like the abject. For the gnostic the individual's progress was not marked by the strength of his or her psychological identity or autonomy but by the liberation of the spiritual identity from its gross entanglement in flesh and psyche.

7. Fisher-Wirth claims that in *Outer Dark* "all men are blind, and this road toward the 'vulvate welt' is the only road there is," but she writes in the context of her psychological argument, which nowhere considers the spiritual element evoked in the novel (128).

8. After his first experience with the triune, Culla reverses his choice when he is threatened by their avatars, the hog drovers. This time he chooses the river and joins the hogs and the maddened horse in casting himself into it. Pagels quotes a description of the oblivious man from *The Teachings of Silvanus* in the Nag Hammadi find: "He is like a ship which the wind tosses to and fro, and like a loose horse which has no rider" (*Gnostic Gospels* 127).

9. Allusions to the gnostic artificer god are connected with several of McCarthy's works: the reference to Melville's deafened weaver-god in director Richard Pearce's research newsletters about "The Gardener's Son" (chapter 4, p. 178); the jeweler who refuses Reese and Suttree's pearls (see *S* 333–34, and chapter 5, p. 241); the cold-forger dream in *Blood Meridian* (310); the draftsman Judge Holden; and perhaps the Vulcan-like

blacksmith of *Child of God* (70–74). In *The Crossing* the weaver-god is reinscribed as a truer god in the heretic's vision (149).

10. Mead, however, cites Irenaeus' description of a gnostic system that formulated a trinity of Father, Mother, and Son (188). An early system described by Hippolytus also postulated a triad of the Good or Deity (God), the Father (the creator), and the World-Soul, which was figured as feminine above the waist and a serpent below (Mead 194). Pagels discusses how trinities that included the feminine were repudiated by the early church in favor of its male-gendered formulation of Father, Son, and Holy Spirit (*Gnostic Gospels* 52).

11. Guillemin writes that Culla's inherited rifle is a "phallic symbol of paternal omnipotence [which] exemplifies his psychic crisis. Culla's failed identification with an absconding father figure . . . indicates his internalization of the patriarchal ethos that terrorizes his ego into abjection" (*Pastoral Vision* 67). The rifle's "return" as an attribute of the triune suggests similar implications in relation to the counterfeit father, the world-ruler: internalized within Culla, as an aspect of *heimarmene*, is the archontic ethos which terrorizes him.

12. In the realm of morality, the gnostics' anticosmic vision led in two directions: asceticism or libertinism. The ascetic gnostic rejected all things worldly: material wealth, food, sexuality, home, and family. The libertine rejected cosmic law and authority in assertive rebellion against the world rulers. See Jonas, *Gnostic Religion* 46.

13. After the tinker refuses to return her child, Rinthy keens, "You won't never have no rest. . . . Not never." The tinker understands this as a curse directed at him, and he responds, "Nor any human soul" (194). But it is uncertain that Rinthy means this as a threat. Earlier, we have seen Culla guiltily projecting on her a "female invective" that has nothing to do with her essential serenity (33). It seems likely that Rinthy foresees her endless quest for her son: that she herself will never find rest.

14. Commenting on St. Paul's terminology for the transcendent spirit, Jonas writes, "It is remarkable that Paul, writing in Greek and certainly not ignorant of Greek terminological traditions, never uses in this connection the term '*psyche*,' which since the Orphics and Plato had denoted the divine principle in us. On the contrary, he *opposes*, as did the Greek-writing Gnostics after him, 'soul' and 'spirit,' and 'psychic man' and 'pneumatic man.' Obviously the Greek meaning of *psyche*, with all its dignity, did not suffice to express the new conception of a principle transcending all natural and cosmic associations that adhered to the Greek concept" (*Gnostic Religion* 124).

15. The gnostic conception of the counterfeit god of cosmos in his role as repressive judge is one of the intimations underlying the appalling figure of Holden as "the judge" in *Blood Meridian*.

16. McCarthy puns on pneuma or spirit when he gives his spiritually lost or struggling characters respiratory diseases. Culla's only illness is whooping cough, Lester Ballard dies of pneumonia, Suttree suffers from pneumonia as well as purgative typhoid but recovers, and the man of *The Road* dies of coughing out the bitter ashes of the world.

17. Fisher-Wirth sees Rinthy as "nothing but body and patience," and she reads Rinthy's milk and blood as signs of the abject which express "her transformation into she who has been ruptured, outraged, rendered bereft" (132, 133). Such conclusions

might be compatible with the gnostic context of the book, but in rather different ways than Fisher-Wirth means: Rinthy's bodily expressions of her need (her body manifesting her psyche), and her seeming reduction to nothing but body and psyche mark the outrage to which her submerged spirit has been subjected, ruptured from its origin in the transcendent realm and bereft of its true identity and its transmundane Father. Fisher-Wirth associates Rinthy with body and Culla with psyche and the symbolic order, roughly reversing Bell's identification of Rinthy with word and Culla with flesh (clearly Fisher-Wirth's symbolic order is not the same thing as Bell's understanding of word as *logos*). My reading emphasizes the mingling and confusion of spirit in body and psyche in both siblings, although I stress the greater ascendency of the suppressed spirit in Rinthy, which does indeed allow her to chart "a path . . . *around* the symbolic order," as Fisher-Wirth says (133), and to remain relatively immune to temptations of the flesh as Bell observes.

18. Even more affirmative is the man in McCarthy's apocalyptic novel *The Road* (2006), whose love for his son and for the lost world of nature is an aspect of the spiritual "fire" that is the answer to the gnostic view of the world (234). The good God is in this man, who so loves the world, even in its lost and diminished state, that he gives his son to it rather than take him with him when he dies.

19. According to Jonas, since the alien Messenger, "a divine figure dwelling in the world in a . . . tragic role as victim and savior at once[, . . .] is the prototype of man, whose destiny . . . he suffers in his own person (frequently his name is Man . . .), we are justified in taking the first-person accounts of his suffering as projections of the experience of those [narrators] who make him speak thus" (*Gnostic Religion* 65). Such concepts inform the association of both the father and son with the divine in *The Road*.

20. Seeking that culminates only in the recovery of bones figures in other McCarthy novels as well. John Wesley Rattner's "search" for his father in *The Orchard Keeper* results in the hallucinated recollection of his father's death and reduction to bones in the pesticide pit. The gnostic epilogue of *Blood Meridian* contrasts the true Seeker with those who do not seek or who seek only bones. In *The Crossing*, Billy Parham's quest to recover the bones of his brother Boyd is implied to be pointless in any spiritual sense because "*La cáscara no es la cosa*" ("The husk is not the thing"; *C* 411). Even the state's recovery of the corpses of Lester Ballard's victims in *Child of God* is similarly undercut.

21. Terri Witek focuses on the cage as "some dwelling for a small animal who has vanished," and she links the image to the pattern in McCarthy's work of male flights from domestic spaces, leaving behind the sorrowing woman ("Reeds" 140). Coexisting with and somewhat tempering the alternative dark implications of the birdcage that Witek and I address is the faint suggestion in the empty cage of the spirit as a flown bird, transcending its cosmic prison.

22. The tinker inverts the significance of Arthur Ownby, who follows Thoreau's advice in living so unencumbered that he is able to pile his entire wealth onto his sledge for a quick escape from the madness of the law run amok. McCarthy's depiction of the tinker echoes another passage in "Walden," in which Thoreau challenges men's assumptions that they must accumulate material goods: "It is the same as if all these traps were buckled to a man's belt, and he could not move over the rough country . . . without dragging

them—dragging his trap. . . . If I have got to drag my trap, I will take care that it be a light one and do not nip me in a vital part. But perchance it would be wisest never to put one's paw into it" (288).

23. Similarly Hoffmann notes that the noise of the tinker's wares "strangely [parallels] the dementedness of the outer world" (225).

24. Compare the similar passage in Judges 19:7: "And the old man lifted up his eyes and saw the wayfarer in the street of the city; and the old man said to him, Where are you going? And whence do you come?"

25. According to Mead, the class of humans dominated by their physical or material nature were designated "the bound" in the Naassene system of thought (199).

26. In *The Crossing*, the blind pensioner tells Billy, *"En este viaje el mundo visible es no más que un distraimiento. . . . Ultimamente sabemos que no podemos ver el buen Dios. Vamos escuchando. Me entiendes, joven? Debemos escuchar."* ("In this journey the visible world is no more than a distraction. . . . Ultimately we know that we cannot see the good God. We go listening. You understand me, young man? We should listen"; 292).

27. However, in other gnostic speculations, the "Hymn of the Pearl" and the *Pistis Sophia*, the serpent is associated with the "earth-circling dragon of the original chaos, the ruler or evil principle of this world" (Jonas, *Gnostic Religion* 116). This connotation is evoked when Rinthy departs from the farmer's house into the outer dark under the constellation of the water serpent (211).

28. The word *camera*, denoting a judge's private office, also associates the grandmother, who remains hostile to Rinthy, a young woman traveling alone, with the triune as archontic powers in their aspect as judges.

29. This detail links him with the archon-like judge of *Blood Meridian*, who roots out the "small life" hiding in the folds of his monstrous flesh (93).

30. In his study of pastoralism in McCarthy's fiction, Guillemin finds *Outer Dark* "a gothic more than a pastoral novel even though its Southern setting is marked by a rusticity bordering on the primitive" (*Pastoral Vision* 54). As Leo Marx points out, the pastoral mode is identified "not so much [by what the setting] *is* as what it *means*, especially the moral and metaphysical import of its various sectors"—among other factors ("Pastoralism" 52).

31. Similarly Guillemin observes that the novel's "surrealist adaptation of Southern stock images seems to create a virtual Southern microcosm"; however, he focuses not on the ecological dislocations but on the imagery of "pastoral decay [which] escalates into universal desolation." He ascribes these images of decay to the "narrator's pastoral nostalgia . . . gone berserk to the point that it seeks desolation of the garden rather than acceptance and sublimation of the loss of the pastoral dream" (*Pastoral* 58, 68). The universal or cosmic desolation we both perceive in the novel derives, in my view, from its gnostic perspective on the natural world and on human nature. In a reading of the gnostic stance of *Outer Dark*, what may appear as pastoral longing for an ideal middle ground now absent or lost in the past is understood instead as gnostic longing for the transmundane realm of wholeness and unity with the divine, a spiritual longing that, like the pastoral impulse, is marked with profound nostalgia. The narrator's "berserk" seeking for the desolation of the garden may be perceived rather to derive from his proper

recognition of the spiritual desolation that is the demiurge-created world of cosmos—
and his longing for its end.

32. Hoffmann verges on a gnostic reading when he writes, "Human evil and
grotesqueness in *Outer Dark* correspond with a 'dead' landscape and a 'stony earth' that
reflect and extend human dementedness into the universe" (224). The gnostic would
emend his statement slightly to assert that both human evil and the dead landscape are
creations and reflections of the cosmic artificers.

33. As with the timber or mountain rattlesnake that Ownby finds dead in *The Orchard
Keeper*, McCarthy has taken care to locate his rattlesnakes realistically in *Outer Dark*.
The size and swampy habitat of this huge snake identify it as a diamondback (*Crotalus
adamanteus*), native not to Tennessee but to "pine swamps and hummock lands" of
"lower or coastal regions" of the South. The diamondback can reach eight feet in length.
If the snake-buyer hopes to keep the snakes alive, he is disappointed because diamond-
backs are "morose" in captivity and often refuse to eat. Also indigenous to such swampy
and coastal areas is the smaller canebrake rattler (*Crotalus horridus atricaudatus*), which
grows four to six feet long (Ditmars 133–35).

34. Muir's account of his experience with rattlesnakes in Yellowstone and Yosemite
includes an archetypal environmentalist's repentance narrative of his killing a snake out
of ignorance: "At that time, thirty years ago, I imagined that rattlesnakes should be
killed wherever found. . . . Persecuted, tormented, again and again he tried to get away,
bravely striking out to protect himself; but at last my heel came squarely down, sorely
wounding him, and a few more brutal stampings crushed him. I felt degraded by the
killing business, farther from heaven, and I made up my mind to try to be at least as
fair and charitable as the snakes themselves, and to kill no more save in self-defense"
(206–7). In his *Field Book of North American Snakes* (1939), Raymond L. Ditmars endorses
Muir's ethical perspective on snake hunting: "I have seen these big reptiles [diamond-
back rattlers] shot and held up for exploitation; but I have always felt a kind of regret on
such occasions. . . . It concerned the wiping out of an impressive form of life—dangerous
as it was" (134). Repentance narratives such as Muir's are common in ecological writing, following in the tradition of American guilt over the rape of the land or assault
against her creatures as examined by Kolodny (see, for instance, her discussions of
Woolman, 22–24; Audubon, 80; Cooper, 102–3; and Simms, 126–27). Aldo Leopold
would later create his own similar parable centering on his youthful killing of another
animal coded as a dangerous pariah in the southwest—the wolf. He prefaces his story
by echoing Muir: "In those days we had never heard of passing up a chance to kill a
wolf." But when he sees the "fierce green fire" die in the eyes of the she-wolf he and his
companions have shot, he regrets his act because he begins to see it as an assault against
nature itself (130). For a discussion of how such repentance narratives in works by Leopold, Ernest Thompson Seton, and Barry Lopez influence McCarthy's treatment of
wolf hunting in *The Crossing*, see my essay "The Vanishing World of Cormac McCarthy's
Border Trilogy."

35. One of Perry's best illustrations, from the Chicago Historical Society, is of a current ferry on the Colorado River at the Yuma crossing—not Dr. Lincoln's jury-rigged
ferry of two wagon boxes (*BM* 253) but a later one of more sophisticated design (Perry
141). In this illustration the bank-to-bank cable apparatus is clearly visible.

36. Similarly Grammer sees the triune as a "kind of Murrell gang," linking them to the nineteenth-century outliers who waylaid travelers on the Natchez Trace in Mississippi and Tennessee and who figure in several of Faulkner's novels (36). Edwin Arnold has linked them to the Harpes of Tennessee in his unpublished article, "Madison Jones's *Forest of the Night* and McCarthy's *Outer Dark*," presented at the Cormac McCarthy Society conference in 2001. Both the Harpes and the Murrell gang are treated in Robert M. Coates's *The Outlaw Years: The History of the Land Pirates of the Natchez Trace* (1930). McCarthy could also have read brief accounts of the Harpes, who settled near Knoxville in 1797, in Davidson (1:218) and MacArthur (12); and Arnold makes a strong case for the influence on *Outer Dark* of Jones's *Forest of the Night* (1960), a novel haunted by the ghost of Wiley Harpe.

37. McCarthy's scene may also be influenced by Kephart's musings on the mountaineers' half-wild razorback hog, who is "bold and crafty": "The razorback has a mind of his own; not instinct but *mind*. . . . He thinks. Anybody can see that when he is not rooting or sleeping he is studying devilment. He shows remarkable understanding of human speech, especially profane speech, and even an uncanny gift of reading men's thoughts, whenever those thoughts are directed against the peace and dignity of pig-ship. He bears grudges, broods over indignities, and plans redresses for the morrow or the week after. . . . And at the last, when arrested in his crimes and lodged in the pen, he is liable to attacks of mania from sheer helpless rage" (47).

38. In conversation Ken Hada has told me that elsewhere in the Appalachians hog drovers used staves, so it may be that McCarthy took this detail from another, as yet unidentified, source.

Chapter 3: The Cave of Oblivion

1. Carrying one victim to his cave, Lester performs a feat similar to Alessandro's— one which he must have performed many times—yet the imagery stresses that he is over-burdened both physically and metaphysically by the gross material body he has sought to possess: "Scuttling down the mountain with the thing on his back he looked like a man beset by some ghast succubus, the dead girl riding him with legs bowed akimbo like a monstrous frog" (153).

2. Information provided by the Registrar's Office of the University of Tennessee.

3. For a study of the texts and history relating to nineteenth-century whitecapping in East Tennessee and other related topics, see my "White Caps, Moral Judgment, and Law in *Child of God* or, the 'wrong blood' in Community History." If McCarthy researched the White Caps in Sevierville when he lived there in 1963, his meditation on the abuses possible within legal systems and the law cases related to White Cap history likely informed the themes of law and justice in both *Outer Dark* and *Child of God* and blended with the gnostic antinomianism about which he was reading during the same period.

4. Similarly, when Culla Holme is arrested for trespassing, he is made to march bare-foot to the Justice of the Peace. Such images always convey the helplessness of human-kind before the archontic powers that regulate their lives.

5. The image of these three mysteriously haunting the murder site echoes provoca-tively with *Outer Dark*'s triune.

6. Sources McCarthy could have consulted for the story of Ed Gein include newspaper accounts in the *Milwaukee Journal* and articles in *Time* and *Life* magazines. These are the sources I cite in my discussion. My attention was first called to the possibility of an affinity between *Child of God* and *Psycho* when Christian Kiefer delivered his paper, "God's Lonely Child: Necrophilia as a Delineator of Character in Cormac McCarthy's *Child of God*," at the Southern Writers / Southern Writing Conference sponsored by the University of Mississippi in July 1996. The epigraph to Kiefer's paper is from Harold Schechter's *Deviant*, and in discussion Kiefer noted that there were some similarities between Lester Ballard and the notorious Ed Gein, the model for Norman Bates. McCarthy could not, of course, have known Schechter's 1989 book, and there is no evidence that Schechter knew *Child of God*. Still, Schechter's popular account, *Deviant* (New York: Pocket Books, 1989), provides full but undocumented treatment of the Gein story based on the contemporary newspaper and other sources. See also Robert Bloch's brief nonfiction account, "The Shambles of Ed Gein."

7. The character is named Mary Crane in Bloch's novel, Marion Crane in the film.

8. Persons responsible for various versions of *Psycho* recognized the aesthetic problem of the scene in which the "glib psychiatrist . . . verbally unravels Norman's psychological peccadillos for . . . any audience member rusty on his Freud" (Rebello 66). During the shooting, this was known among crew members as the "headshrinker-explains-it-all" scene, but according to Rebello both Hitchcock and Stefano considered the scene "'obligatory': a chance for the audience to catch its collective breath while the 'logic' buffs among them got their fill of the facts." Hitchcock's strategy was to "enliven the action with slick camera moves" and by casting a notorious scene-stealer, Simon Oakland, as the psychiatrist (127). Nevertheless, the scene was singled out for criticism by novelist Robert Bloch, who told Rebello, "It could have been done in about one-third of the time, been perfectly clear to audiences, and given final momentum to the finale" (144).

9. In a press interview, Chicago psychiatrist Edward J. Kelleher surmised, based on the early and unofficial reports of Gein's activity, that his pathology was a rare combination of transvestism, fetishism, and voyeurism. Paraphrasing Kelleher, the *Milwaukee Journal* reported that Gein's "desire to be a woman was expressed in an extreme form of fetishism that involved dressing himself in a vestlike garment made from a woman's torso skin, leggings from skin of women's legs, a woman's face removed from a head and other female body parts" ("Doctor" 1–2).

10. Another photo, of a residential street in downtown Sevierville in the flood of 1965, is printed in *Sevier County* (130).

11. According to Jonas, "The gnostic systems compounded everything—oriental mythologies, astrological doctrines, Iranian theology, elements of Jewish tradition, whether biblical, rabbinical, or occult, Christian salvation-eschatology, Platonic terms and concepts" (*Gnostic Religion* 25).

12. Lester's motive, however, is self-protection: his search for her remains is to ensure that his transgression will not be discovered. And he learns opportunistically from this fire how to cover his traces when he murders the retarded child and his sister/mother.

13. Lester trades in stolen watches across the mountain in neighboring Blount County, where the men gathered companionably around the store's stove openly cheat

Lester as the outsider he so clearly is; but their treatment of Lester does not significantly differ from what he experiences in Sevier County, reinforcing the idea that he is the designated outsider or stranger everywhere.

14. Christine Chollier observes that Lester as outsider is excluded from the monetary exchange system and that he does not try to amass money. As a boy, he worked just long enough to earn the money for his rifle (700 fenceposts' worth), and then he quit (Chollier 172). But this may be as much a cultural characteristic as a personal one. Kephart indicates that the independent mountaineer disliked working for others: "Generally he will stay on a job just long enough to earn money for immediate needs; then back to the farm he goes" (382). It does seem that Lester, raised as a mountain farmer, is not oriented toward the accumulation of cash. When he finds the asphyxiated couple, he steals their money as an afterthought (*CoG* 89). And whenever he comes into a few dollars this way, he immediately exchanges them for food or for alluring clothing to enhance his sexual illusions. But Lester's rifle and ammunition themselves become means of exchange when he shoots targets for stuffed animals at the fair and when he hunts human victims. He does aim to accumulate material goods. The abstraction of money means less to him because money cannot buy the inert material he most wants. For Lester a well-placed bullet has more currency.

15. See Holloway for further discussion of the novel's treatments of property relations, scarcity, and commodification, especially of Lester "as McCarthy's early (and ultimately abortive) sketching of the existential self saturated in market logic" (125–32, quotation 130).

16. Jarrett writes, "Unlike Thoreau at Walden Pond, Ballard's isolation in nature neither regenerates nor restores a lost innocence; it corrupts this contemporary inversion of the American Adam" (41). Jarrett's phrasing meshes more with the gnostic conception of nature as an alienating aspect of cosmos than with the Platonic view of nature as an avenue to transcendence.

17. More than he will admit, Lester is akin to the man in a nearby cell who has been convicted of killing people and eating their brains (193). Although he was not a cannibal, it is in such materialistic "consumption" of the body that the horror of Ed Gein lies.

18. Other images reinforce Lester's self-destructiveness. Just as he is overburdened by his possessions, including the corpse of a girl who rides him like a succubus (see note 1), Lester bears his "rifle on his neck like a yoke" or carries it on his lonely night vigils "hanging in his hand as if it were a thing he could not get shut of" (25–26, 41)—images that recall the gnostic traps of the tinker and shackles of the farmer yoked to his plow in *Outer Dark*, emblems of the spirit's entrapment in matter.

19. Bartlett finds in this scene an "enigmatic conversion" that causes Lester to return to the hospital, an act which, whether "resignation or repentance . . . is a kind of suicide" (15). Bartlett's reading leads one to recognize parallels between Lester's return to the hospital and the kid's return to the judge at the end of *Blood Meridian*. However, I find the church bus scene even more ambiguous as to its effects on Lester and question whether it *causes* either a conversion or his return to the hospital, where he is already headed. When he emerges from his entombment in the cave, where he has envisioned his own death, he deliberately sets out for Sevierville. The hospital, too, is a prison, but there he has been physically cared for and nourished. In both the jail and the hospital,

he can count on food that is "not bad" (53). Thus his intention is to provide for his material needs: to eat of the world and to thrive at least materially. He may finally recognize, however, that his life is a prison no matter where he sleeps. His return to society seems, then, a kind of submission to the world. In his discussion of Lester as a "nomad," Brian Evenson argues that Lester's declaration "I'm supposed to be here" (*CoG* 192) signals his acceptance of the community's view of him (55). I see it rather as an ironic sign of his submission, crippled, weak and threatened with execution, to the power structure of the community and of cosmos, his recognition that his physical needs may best be met from within the social/cosmic order that judges and would regulate his behavior. In its affirmation of belonging, it also obliquely comments on the expelled Lester's commonality with the rest of humankind—and ours with him.

20. Bartlett was the first to emphasize the importance of the voyeurism trope in the novel, but his observation that "the recurrent image of the voyeur in *Child of God* is that of a hunter who focuses on a presence or a scene of actual or potential death" is only sometimes accurate, as I hope my discussion of variations on the image shows (4). Indeed many scenes of voyeurism foreground not the hunter's focused eye but the oblivious perspective of Ballard's neighbors—Bartlett's second level of narrative "proximity to Ballard"—and Ballard's own obliviousness, especially to himself (4). The mirroring images always suggest doubling of Ballard by others, but this doubling is seldom recognized by any of the characters.

21. Relevant here is the 1989 letter from McCarthy paraphrased by Garry Wallace. Challenging Wallace's scientific skepticism, McCarthy wrote to the effect that "the mystical experience is a direct apprehension of reality, unmediated by symbol" and that "our inability to see spiritual truth is the greater mystery" (138). For commentary on the importance of "the world itself" in McCarthy's works, see my "The Road and the Matrix: The World as Tale in *The Crossing*" and J. Douglas Canfield's "Crossing from the Wasteland into the Exotic in McCarthy's Border Trilogy."

22. Even the gnostically inspired environment of *Outer Dark* is presented as "the counterpart" of Culla, Rinthy, or the tinker's own character. One is reminded of Culla Holme's choice of evasion, which becomes the pattern that keeps him circling in darkness. In *Suttree*, too, the protagonist's experiences are presented as an out-picturing of his spiritual condition, the "counterpart of his own character." In the Border Trilogy, the repetition compulsions that lead to so much of the sorrow in Billy Parham's long life, and even more so in John Grady Cole's brief one, can also be viewed from this Platonic perspective.

Chapter 4: A Stranger in the Garden of Industry

1. For a discussion of the play's historical background, see my "Cormac McCarthy's First Screenplay: 'The Gardener's Son.'"

2. About the silencing of the looms, Canfield makes the similar point: "It is as if Robert has shot the factory itself, the very system, in the abdomen, bringing capitalism's exploitation of its workers to a temporary halt" ("Oedipal" 19).

3. The "Timekeeper" or supervisor, Mr. Giles, plays a much more ominous role in the screenplay itself than does his son, the "Old Timekeeper" of the frame, who counsels

the young man, a descendent of the Greggs who has come to recover the story of his family, that the documents in his care will provide inadequate access to the "fugitive" past (*GS* 3, 5).

4. In *A Happy Death*, Camus also links the two as dual aspects of the oppressive life Mersault finds in Breslau: "The city looked like a forest of factory chimneys and church steeples" (76).

5. The cast of characters specifies that the doctor might be "somewhat cadaverous," but in the filmed version, the rather beefy Earl Wynn is cast in the role, which he plays in a decidedly uncongenial manner (vii). Both versions suggest, albeit in differing ways, that the doctor is an intimidating and unsympathetic presence.

6. For an astute discussion of Oedipal conflict and phallic imagery in the screenplay, see Canfield, "Oedipal Complexities" (17–21). Canfield's treatment indirectly recognizes the gnostic/existential aura of the work: he discusses Robert's revolt, observing that he "implicitly rebels against his father's complicity with the system" and glosses Robert's murder of James thus: "Robert shoots him where poetic justice dictates, in his lubricious abdomen. Robert has castrated his rival, momentarily seizing the phallus from the agent of hegemonic power" (18, 19). Of Robert's scapegoating, he asks, "To whom or what are these sacrifices made? To another apparently absent Father, whose ways remain inscrutable?" (21).

7. Camus rejects suicide as a response to the absurdity of the world; instead, the man of existentialist lucidity values life and courageous awareness. This position is manifest in his philosophical essay *The Myth of Sisyphus* (see especially 53–65) and in Mersault's striving to live until the end with "eyes open upon death" in his novel *A Happy Death* (150).

8. In another parallel the Arab has threatened Meursault's friend, Raymond, and Gregg has insulted Robert's sister, Martha. However, the screenplay is ambiguous about whether Robert knows of the insult. Martha tells Mrs. Gregg that she would never tell Robert that James offered her money, but Robert tells Martha, "I *know* he insulted you" (81). His knowledge seems an intuition based in his awakened conception of the world's nature. In the shooting script, Robert's assertion has been softened to "I know what he was" (120). This revision may have been prompted by McCarthy's wish to avoid too literal an explanation for Robert's violence against James.

9. The last phrase is borrowed from Dale Cosper and Ethan Cary's treatment of gnosticism and existentialism in *Suttree*.

10. The gnostically influenced Camus was critical of Dostoevsky's choice to end *Crime and Punishment* with Raskolnikov's seeking atonement, and his own Meursault approaches his death affirming his "rightness."

11. See Tom E. Terrill's "Murder in Graniteville" for the historical background. Terrill was historical advisor for the film project. He points out that the judgment against Robert McEvoy was also complicated by the white elite's "desperation" before the 1876 elections "to reassert their dominance clearly and finally over blacks, in particular, but also over the lower orders of whites," a social and political reality that meshes with the gnostic/existentialist perspective of the screenplay, which makes the Reconstruction power structure emblematic of the archontic world powers oppressing humankind (211).

12. Canfield suggests that these are hired mourners ("Oedipal" 18). If so, that would emphasize the inauthenticity of the community's expectations for the conventional display of grief and of Patrick's initial compliance with such expectations.

13. Patrick delays the burial because he is more vitally concerned with preserving his son's life, and perhaps because he, too, is finally shocked out of his complacency and now agrees with Robert that Mrs. McEvoy and the rest of the family do not belong to the mill. Certainly his despairing act of burning her body in its coffin evades the conventional and still feasible solution of interring her on mill grounds. As Canfield observes, Patrick "defies the company *and* Catholic doctrine by cremating Mrs. McEvoy's rotting corpse" ("Oedipal" 21). His unexpected and belated response to the constable's warning is not so much a concession to the sensibilities of his neighbors as his own act of existential rebellion, an act that is paralleled in his stolid refusal to sign for his son's body in the filmed version of the screenplay and his interring Robert in a place hidden from the community but where, he tells Martha with unconscious irony, "God would know where to hunt him" (91).

14. The phrase is from Richard Pearce's research newsletter of October 8, 1975, in which he implies that creating such a history is one goal of the film.

Chapter 5: Prisoner in Babylon

1. Perhaps because of Suttree's interest in the destruction of McAnally Flats near the end of the novel and his thought that "he knew another McAnally, good to last a thousand years," it is a common misconception appearing in many studies of *Suttree* that the riverfront area where Suttree, Ab Jones, Harrogate, and Rufus live is in McAnally Flats and that the novel is principally set in McAnally (463). Actually only a few scenes are set there, the most important of which is Suttree's winter retreat from the river to a cellar apartment in that neighborhood.

2. Similarly William Prather suggests that "it certainly would not be surprising to learn that Suttree had gone on to become an artist, a writer possibly" and that *Suttree* can be read as "to some extent a *Kunstlerroman*, chronicling the struggles and growth of an absurd artist" ("Absurd" 151n3).

3. This is another way of considering Cosper and Cary's observation that "the world view of the narrator and that of Suttree are not the same in the course of the novel, but they coincide in the last pages" (168). John Vanderheide reads the novel similarly. "On the thematic level the protagonist figures as an earlier, but now discarded, self of the narrator," he writes. "The protagonist is thus an ontological phase the narrator passed through in the stream of becoming" (177). Models for this can be found in Rainer Maria Rilke's *The Notebooks of Malte Laurids Brigge* and in James Joyce's *Ulysses*, where the protagonists "are perhaps more obviously inchoate artists than Suttree," but nevertheless Vanderheide finds that the narrator invests Suttree with "many authorial qualities" (179). Canfield queries, "Can we *paradoxically* view *Suttree* as Suttree's first novel, the telling of his story of enlightenment?" He continues, "The narrator of *Suttree* is, of course, not Suttree, though the narrator's and Suttree's consciousnesses often seem to blend. But I suggest that we can productively . . . *reread* the novel in the light of Suttree's final enlightenment, that we can reread the abject for signs of what Kristeva calls

jouissance." For Canfield, then, the novel represents Suttree's achievement of an "art that shares the experience of the human heart as it confronts abjection." Earlier, he observes, "And what this individual who has gained identity-in-community seems to do is dedicate himself, celibate, not to his father's world of law, business, and government but to the world of art. He tells his own story, as it were, in the novel *Suttree*" ("Dawning" 685–86, 666).

4. See Nell Sullivan's "Cormac McCarthy and the Text of *Jouissance*" for discussion of the way that vernacular language "infiltrates" Suttree's discourse when he confronts the crossbow-hunter in the woods, even when he is in an altered state of consciousness (157).

5. John Grammer comments briefly on the Sut Lovingood connection, arguing that like Sut, Suttree learns that "plannin and studdyin am ginerly no count" (Harris 67; Grammer 40–41). Hall extends the connection somewhat. He points out that like McCarthy, Harris was born elsewhere but grew up in Knoxville, thus bringing something of the outsider's perspective to his realistic portrayal of "the often crude and violent backwoods life of East Tennessee." McCarthy shares with Harris and other humorous writers of the Old Southwest "his depiction of a mostly masculine society . . . and his use of authentic regional dialect" (65).

6. A *News-Sentinel* headline of June 9, 1952, reads, "Yeggs Get $300 from Car Lot" (9). The *Oxford English Dictionary* notes that this American word derives from the surname of a particular burglar and safecracker.

7. The tollsman is a version of the gnostic/existentialist gatekeeper. In a Mandaean text, the messenger tells Adam, "The way that we have to go is long and endless. . . . Overseers are installed there, and watchmen and toll-collectors sit beside it" (quoted in Jonas, *Gnostic Religion* 87). See also Josephine Donovan's discussion of the "cosmic gatekeepers" in Kafka's Parable of the Law in *The Trial* (171–73).

8. Canfield reads the turtles as "the abject . . . reminders of death, of our materiality," a reading that suggests a link between this sack and *Outer Dark*'s gnostic image of the creature held captive in a bag ("Dawning" 670).

9. The north shore is also the location of the Sequoyah Hills neighborhood, where McCarthy's family lived before they moved to Vestal when McCarthy was eight or nine. The house at 118 Cherokee (now Noelton) belonged to H. E. Christenberry Sr. and then to his son, H. E. Christenberry Jr. when the McCarthys lived there from 1938 to 1941 (Knox County Register of Deeds, City-County Building, Knoxville, Tennessee). In 1993 Jack Neely described it as a "two-story house on Noelton Drive, just barely off of Kingston Pike, near Western Plaza: in this well-tended, almost-wealthy neighborhood at the fringe of Sequoyah Hills, a once-white frame house rots behind a fence" and a keep-out sign warns intruders away (135).

The novel suggests that Suttree's childhood was spent in the affluent section of Sequoyah Hills or a similar north-shore neighborhood and that his father chose to move there rather than occupy the old family mansion on the south shore—hinting at an alienation between Suttree's father and grandfather similar to Suttree's own estrangement from his father.

10. McCarthy returns to this idea in his unfilmed screenplay, "Whales and Men," where Peter Gregory makes a similar observation about the procession of family members

against the same backdrop in his family album: "I find old photographs a bit unsettling. They do seem to accuse somehow. They're not like paintings. They're a more successful illusion. There are photos here of my great great grandparents going back a hundred and thirty years. They were taken in front of the house and in the photographs the house is exactly the same. It has not changed at all. . . . I find it. . . . The fact that we are sequential beings in a sense. . . . That their most enduring reality—and mine—should take the form of a small square of tin or cardboard. Like a form of taxidermy, really. . . . It's just unnatural in some way" (46).

11. Other passages employ similar verbal repetitions. These are presented in various contexts, but always there is a faint echo of the whispered assertion of the album of the dead: "I am, I am." Cf. "went past, went past, went past" (149); Vernon and Fernon's "howdy howdy" (359); "if you can, if you can" (366); "she said, she said" (415); "another door closed, door closed, door closed" (452); and "like me like me" (453).

12. Cf. the fight in the mudlot between the kid and Toadvine in *Blood Meridian* (9–11), where mud and feces again are emblematic of man's gnostic dualism: his materiality cloaking his spirituality. The lot in which the kid almost smothers in mud borders on the outhouse, and the scene forecasts his death in the jakes at the hands of the judge.

13. In 1952 a *News-Sentinel* article warned readers not to swim in the creeks or river to avoid contracting typhoid. A city health official reminded citizens that there were typically four or five cases per year in Knoxville, especially in the summer ("Typhoid"). Suttree's illness thus results both realistically and metaphorically from his close association with the turbid waters of Knoxville. And the purgation of the disease frees him of the influence of the cosmic mire.

14. If removed at all. Following Young, Matthew Guinn notes McCarthy's tendency to depict humanity as atavistic. Like the writers of the Southern Renascence, he argues, "McCarthy, too, employs the past to establish continuous patterns of human behavior." But McCarthy breaks with them in that "His evocation of the past is antinostalgic; rather than presenting a lost stability, it emphasizes an elemental primitivism that humanity retains" (94). Guinn finds in *Suttree* McCarthy's "mythoclastic and atavistic strains in full flower" (96).

15. In his discussion of the carnivalesque in *Suttree*, Canfield stresses the grotesque humor of these fantasies and points out that often Suttree smiles to see them. In these visions, he writes, the abject becomes carnivalesque, and thus the dreams are not nihilistic but salvific ("Dawning" 688). Canfield's article builds on Bell, who argues that Suttree's existence in the city is itself carnivalesque because this is the nature of the world.

16. Suttree's response to Hooper also echoes Meursault's claim that in his rebellion "I'd been right, I was still right, I was always right" (151).

17. In this Suttree is comparable to the depressed and death-seeking White of *The Sunset Limited*, who daily curses his fellow travelers in his heart (88–90).

18. For Bell the optimism of such characters as Harrogate and Reese "collaborates with other influences that move . . . [Suttree] off the dead center of his nihilistic immobility" (*Achievement* 81). Bell reads Harrogate as a more benign character than I do, but some of his conclusions are similar: "Harrogate's story is preeminently a celebration of ingenuity, an episodic parody of imagination striking back against reality" (*Achievement*

85). Bell acknowledges that Gene's final schemes, his telephone scam and his robbing a store have become more conventional, and thus he is in a sense defeated because bereft of his "exuberantly resourceful" innocence even before his arrest (*Achievement* 84, 89).

19. The issue of value is inherent in Donald Davidson's account of gathering mussels on Tennessee rivers. He writes that unlike the Indians, who ate mussels, European descendants have always discarded the meat and used only the shells to make buttons and gathered the freshwater pearls (1.23). However, Davidson is vague about the market value of the pearls: his informant in 1942 received thirty-two dollars a ton for the shells, but of the pearls Davidson remarks only that they "bring something" (2.353).

Interestingly, Davidson's judgmental descriptions of the mussel-gathering Indians, antecedents of the Caucasian mussel-brailers, also raise issues of human value. He judges them as "distinguished from other Indians by their slothful craving for mussels. . . . As they ate, they tossed aside the empty shells, and therefore lived in the midst of, or even on top of, the vast middens, or heaps of shell refuse accumulated by their insatiable appetites. They must have been surrounded by a bad smell of unholy proportions, but they were primitives and did not mind bad smells. . . . They finally gave way to more enterprising Indians, of a much superior stage of culture. . . . Except for their extraordinarily permanent shell mounds, the mussel-eating Indians left no impression upon the Valley, and they seem hardly worth remembering" (1.22).

One of the Fugitive writers, Davidson expresses a mixture of progressive interpretation of white settlement and antebellum culture in Tennessee and conservative skepticism about the TVA and its introduction of a "northern" culture that threatened to displace the southern one. McCarthy's works reject Davidson's partisan view of the successive displacements of peoples and cultures throughout human history and articulate more respect for each displaced group.

Davidson's detailed technical description of the workings of the mussel brails and the rigging of the mussel boat based on his 1942 expedition on the river meshes in every way with McCarthy's description except one: Davidson writes that mussel-brailing is "lazy, easy fishing" (2.353). For an engraving of the mussel boats outfitted with their brails, see Theresa Sherrer Davidson's illustration (Davidson 2.352).

20. In 1965 *The Collector* was released as a film directed by William Wyler; the lead roles were acted by Terence Stamp and Samantha Eggar. Wyler, Eggar, and screenwriters Stanley Mann and John Kohn all received Academy Award nominations for their work on the project. McCarthy's knowledge of *The Collector* may derive from the novel, the film, or both.

21. Some of the novel's black characters also call Suttree "baby," suggesting his relative innocence in the ways of the world and perhaps the childishness of his solipsistic quest, despite his chronological age. See his interchanges with Oceanfrog Frazer (110, 446) and Trippin Through the Dew (468).

22. The displacement is an understated but direct reference to TVA programs that transformed the river valley through social and topographical engineering. The Tennessee River of the 1950s on which Suttree and Ab live has already been altered by the construction of the Fort Loudoun Dam below Knoxville in 1943. As it dammed the rivers, the TVA displaced the earlier cultures of the mountain and valley people. Thus

Ab's reused tombstones implicitly function for Suttree not only as a memento mori but also as reminders of the predatory quality of cultural "progress" as the usurping culture chews up its antecedents.

The TVA tried to make its intervention respectful of the Tennessee people and their traditions even as it displaced them and their dead. Graves were relocated and bones reinterred whenever possible. Usually new caskets were provided, but the old tombstone might either be reused or replaced with a "new one of a standard model" (Davidson 2.259); thus until Suttree and Richard's subversive act of recovery, Ab's salvaged tombstones are dissociated from their original purpose of honoring or evoking memory of the dead. For further discussion, especially of the role McCarthy's father played in relocating families and cemeteries for the TVA, see Prather's "'The color of this life is water': History, Stones, and the River in Cormac McCarthy's *Suttree*."

23. Consistent with his skeptical reading of the character, Young interprets this passage as Suttree's repudiation of the vanity of "the artistic sensibility," of his "habitual conversion of experience into the language of thought" (121, 117). Young's discussion of this seems admirably prophetic in light of McCarthy's later treatments, in "Whales and Men" and *The Crossing*, of humankind's tendency to replace the world with language, which I have treated at length in "The Road and the Matrix: The World as Tale in *The Crossing*." But as I argue there, *The Crossing* valorizes the human need for narration even as it recognizes the secondhandedness of language, and, as my treatment of Suttree emphasizes, I see him as evolving into the narrative artist as he repudiates egotism but not narration.

24. Shelton also recognizes Ab's suicidal behavior but reads it as an active, existentialist assertion of his dignity and thus as a more positive model for Suttree than the passive will to death exhibited by Hooper the ragman: "Suttree never becomes as active or as resolute a character as Ab, but near the end of the novel his attitude shifts from the passive nihilism of the ragpicker to the more purposeful rebellion of Ab Jones" (80).

25. The passage is echoed in the kid's dream of the cold-forger, whose agenda is to counterfeit a coin that "will pass" (*BM* 310). Both can be read as artifices of the demiurge.

26. Spencer points out that Hooper's metaphor "implies an existential emphasis on chance but also further suggests that 'crap' is somehow the essence of life" ("Excremental" 2). From the gnostic perspective, the crapgame of life is the cosmic experience of the spirit mired in matter and subject to *heimarmene*.

27. Giles suggests that Suttree's father, hinted to be "autocratic, harsh, and judgmental" is "a kind of sane, secular version of the mad evangelist" (90). Synthesizing Arnold's insight that for McCarthy's characters earthly fathers are often projections of the divine ("Mosaic" 7) with the gnostic tendency to read all cosmic creatures as reflections of the cosmic artificers, I would suggest that all of the novel's preachers and evangelists function as archontic figures in their judgmental or complacent relations with the people they exhort and that like the many other figures of power and judgment in the novel, so does Suttree's father, especially in Suttree's dream, in which his father appears as a "dark figure against the shadowed brick" who holds him in his "bone grip" and accosts him with a knife but with dispassionate and "rancorless intent" (28).

28. Canfield reads this "clownish" reverend somewhat more affirmatively: "Does the real Logos remain in the marketplace, among the dispossessed of the world . . . ? Does it rise from the filthy gutter water to be cleansed and transformed into gratuitous water from the cup of the new Aquarius? Is there a clownish, comic 'billikin' hidden in the ashes of organized religion? Can he not sing!" ("Dawning" 693).

29. Cosper and Cary (162) appropriately link Suttree's "I was drunk" with Meursault's "It was the sun." Both are in fact serious gnostic explanations for the "evil" acts of mankind.

30. In *The Crossing*, McCarthy again implies that the church and its priests are heretical in their alienation from the pain and suffering of humanity and in their complacency that blocks them from the spiritual search. The ex-priest at Huisiachepic does, however, eventually achieve true compassion for the heretic who challenges both him and God, and he finally repudiates his own heresy of complacency. In "Whales and Men" the Roman Catholic Mother Teresa is held up as a model of spiritual compassion when she is quoted, "[God] didnt call upon me to be successful. He just called upon me to be faithful" (24). Her ministry in the streets exemplifies Suttree's new vision.

Works Cited

"94-Year-Old Man, One of Smokies' Last Residents, Dies." *Knoxville Journal* 18 January 1984: C12.

Alighieri, Dante. *The Divine Comedy*. Tr. and ed. Thomas G. Bergin. Arlington Heights, Ill.: Harlan Davidson, 1955.

"All That Gein Owned Auctioned; $5,000 Proceeds Held in Trust." *Milwaukee Journal* 31 March 1958: 2.

Ambrosiano, Jason. "Blood in the Tracks: Catholic Postmodernism in *The Crossing*." *Southwestern American Literature* 25.1 (Fall 1999): 83–91.

Arnold, Edwin T. "Blood and Grace: The Fiction of Cormac McCarthy." *Commonweal* 4 November 1994: 11–16.

———. "Disgust in the Early Works of Cormac McCarthy." *Profils Américains* 17: Cormac McCarthy (2004): 61–87.

———. "'Go to sleep': Dreams and Visions in the Border Trilogy." Arnold and Luce, *Cormac McCarthy Companion* 37–72.

———. "McCarthy and the Sacred: A Reading of *The Crossing*." Lilley 215–38.

———. "The Mosaic of McCarthy's Fiction." Hall and Wallach 1:1–8.

———. "Naming, Knowing, and Nothingness: McCarthy's Moral Parables." Arnold and Luce, *Perspectives* 45–69.

———. "The World of *The Orchard Keeper*." Holloway 1–5, 7.

Arnold, Edwin T., and Dianne C. Luce, eds. *A Cormac McCarthy Companion: The Border Trilogy*. Jackson: University Press of Mississippi, 2001.

———, eds. *Perspectives on Cormac McCarthy*. 1993. Rev. ed. Jackson: University Press of Mississippi, 1999.

"Author Lives in Blount." *News-Sentinel* [Knoxville, Tenn.] 6 October 1968: F5.

Barksdale, Don W. "You Can Help Control Flooding." *Tennessee Conservationist* 45.4 (July/August 1979): 22–23.

Barr, Thomas C., Jr. *Caves of Tennessee*. Nashville: Tennessee Department of Conservation and Commerce, Division of Geology, 1961.

Bartlett, Andrew. "From Voyeurism to Archaeology: Cormac McCarthy's *Child of God*." *Southern Literary Journal* 24.1 (Fall 1991): 3–15.

Bell, Vereen M. *The Achievement of Cormac McCarthy*. Baton Rouge: Louisiana State University Press, 1988.

———. "'Between the wish and the thing the world lies waiting.'" *Southern Review* 28 (Autumn 1992): 920–27.

Berry, K. Wesley. "The Lay of the Land in Cormac McCarthy's Appalachia." Lilley 47–73.

Berwick, Sandy, comp. *Reflections on Sequoyah Hills.* [Knoxville]: Kingston Pike-Sequoyah Hills Association Historical Committee, 1997.

Blackburn, Simon. *The Oxford Dictionary of Philosophy.* New York: Oxford University Press, 1994.

"Blevins Has Quit Counting Days after Spending 2 Years in Jail." *Chattanooga Daily Times* 11 May 1965: 11.

"Blevins to Await Appeal on Venue." *Chattanooga Daily Times* 24 August 1963: 1, 9.

"Blevins v. The State." No. 22821. Supreme Court of Georgia. 23 February 1965. *South Eastern Reporter.* 2nd ser. 141:426–31.

Bloch, Robert. *Psycho.* 1959. New York: Tom Doherty, 1989.

———. "The Shambles of Ed Gein." *The Quality of Murder: Three Hundred Years of True Crime Compiled by Members of the Mystery Writers of America.* Ed. Anthony Boucher. New York: E. P. Dutton, 1962. 216–25.

Bourne, Frank E. Letter. *Metro Pulse* [Knoxville] n.d. http://metropulse.com/dir_zine/dir_2001/1113/t_letters.html (accessed 27 May 2001).

Bowles, Jay. "Blevins Awaits Freedom Ruling." *Chattanooga Daily Times* 3 November 1966: 2, 7.

———. "Blevins, Now a Free Man, Ready to Rebuild His Life." *Chattanooga Daily Times* 5 November 1966: 1, 4.

Brecht, Bertolt. *Mother Courage and Her Children: A Chronicle of the Thirty Years' War.* New York: Grove, 1963.

Brewer, Carson. "Last Smokies Park Lifer, Ownby, Dies." *News-Sentinel* [Knoxville] 17 January 1984: B2.

———. "This Is Your Community." *News-Sentinel* [Knoxville] 21 January 1973: F1.

Brewer, Hazel. "Memories of Waldens Creek." *Sevier County, Tennessee and Its Heritage.* 119.

Brickman, Barbara. "Imposition and Resistance in *The Orchard Keeper.*" Wallach 55–67.

Brooks, Tim, and Earle Marsh. *The Complete Directory to Prime Time Network and Cable TV Shows, 1946–Present.* 7th ed. New York: Ballantine, 1999.

Broome, Harvey. "Nineteen Hundred Thirty to Nineteen Forty-Six." Rothrock 355–59.

Burnett, Edmund Cody. "Hog Raising and Hog Driving in the Region of the French Broad River." *Agricultural History* 20 (April 1946): 86–103.

Butterworth, D. S. "Pearls as Swine: Recentering the Marginal in Cormac McCarthy's *Suttree.*" Hall and Wallach 1:131–37.

Campbell, Carlos C. *Birth of a National Park in the Great Smoky Mountains.* 1960. Rev. ed. [Knoxville]: University of Tennessee Press, 1969.

Camus, Albert. *A Happy Death.* 1971. Tr. Richard Howard. New York: Vintage, 1972.

———. *The Myth of Sisyphus and Other Essays.* 1955. Tr. Justin O'Brien. New York: Knopf, 1957.

———. *The Stranger.* Tr. Stuart Gilbert. New York: Vintage, 1954.

Canby, Henry Seidel, ed. *The Works of Thoreau.* Boston: Houghton Mifflin, 1946.

Canfield, J. Douglas. "Crossing from the Wasteland into the Exotic in McCarthy's Border Trilogy." Arnold and Luce, *Cormac McCarthy Companion* 256–69.

———. "The Dawning of the Age of Aquarius: Abjection, Identity, and the Carnivalesque in Cormac McCarthy's *Suttree.*" *Contemporary Literature* 44.4 (2004): 664–96.

————. "Oedipal Complexities in Cormac McCarthy's *The Stonemason* and *The Gardener's Son.*" *Cormac McCarthy Journal* 2 (2002): 12–22.

Carberry, Michael. *Historic Sites in Blount, Cocke, Monroe and Sevier Counties.* Knoxville: East Tennessee Development District, 1973.

Chandler, Charles. "Structure of Catholic Has Changed while Mission Remains Same." *News-Sentinel* [Knoxville, Tenn.] 8 January 1991.

Chollier, Christine. "'I aint come back rich, that's for sure,' or the Questioning of Market Economies in Cormac McCarthy's Novels." Wallach 171–76.

Ciuba, Gary M. "McCarthy's Enfant Terrible: Mimetic Desire and Sacred Violence in *Child of God.*" Hall and Wallach 1:93–102.

Confirmation Register. Immaculate Conception Catholic Church, Knoxville, Tennessee.

Cooper, Alfred J. "Flood Control in the Tennessee Valley River Basin." M.S. Thesis. University of Tennessee, 1951.

Cosper, Dale, and Ethan Cary. "*Suttree* and *L'Etranger:* The Hounds of Gnosticism." *Studies on Lucette Desvignes and the Twentieth Century* 6 (1996): 155–76.

"Crowd Visits Gein's Farm." *Milwaukee Journal* 24 March 1958: 8.

Daugherty, Leo. "Gravers False and True: *Blood Meridian* as Gnostic Tragedy." Arnold and Luce, *Perspectives* 159–74.

Davidson, Donald. *The Tennessee.* 1948. 2 vols. Southern Classics Ser. Nashville: J. S. Sanders, 1992.

Davis, Donald Edward. *Where There Are Mountains: An Environmental History of the Southern Appalachians.* Athens: University of Georgia Press, 2000.

Deaderick, Lucile, ed. *Heart of the Valley: A History of Knoxville, Tennessee.* Knoxville: East Tennessee Historical Society, 1976.

Ditmars, Raymond L. *A Field Book of North American Snakes.* Garden City, N.Y.: Doubleday, 1939.

"Doctor Calls His Complex First of Kind." *Milwaukee Journal* 22 November 1957: 1–2.

Donoghue, Denis. "Teaching *Blood Meridian.*" *The Practice of Reading.* New Haven: Yale University Press, 1998. 259–77.

Donovan, Josephine. *Gnosticism in Modern Literature: A Study of the Selected Works of Camus, Sartre, Hesse, and Kafka.* New York: Garland, 1990.

Dostoevsky, Fyodor. *Crime and Punishment.* Tr. Constance Garnett. Evanston, Ill.: Harper and Row, 1965.

Dumas, Jim. "Fabled Lem Ownby Finally Leaves Park." *Smoky Mountain Star* 19 January 1984.

————. "Lem Ownby Lives the Simple Life." *The Mountain Visitor* [Gatlinburg] n.d. [1978]: sec. 1:12.

Dunn, Durwood. *Cades Cove: The Life and Death of a Southern Appalachian Community, 1818–1937.* Knoxville: University of Tennessee Press, 1988.

Dykeman, Wilma. *The French Broad.* 1955. Newport, Tenn.: Wakestone, 1992.

Eliot, T. S. "The Love Song of J. Alfred Prufrock." *The Complete Poems and Plays, 1905–1950.* New York: Harcourt, Brace and World, 1971. 3–7.

Evenson, Brian. "McCarthy's Wanderers: Nomadology, Violence, and Open Country." Hall and Wallach 1:51–59.

Ezzell, Patricia Bernard. *TVA Photography: Thirty Years of Life in the Tennessee Valley.* Jackson: University Press of Mississippi, 2003.

"Father of 3 Charged in Assault-Slaying." *News-Sentinel* [Knoxville] 8 May 1963: 1.

Faulkner, William. "A Rose for Emily." *Collected Stories of William Faulkner.* New York: Random, 1950. 119–30.

Fields, Pat. "Knoxville Author Gets Award for Writing." *Knoxville Journal* 19 May 1965: 13.

———. "Lifetime LeConte Resident Celebrates 92nd Birthday." Unattributed newspaper clipping. [February or March 1981]. Biographical clipping file, Calvin M. McClung Historical Collection, East Tennessee Historical Center, Knoxville.

Fisher-Wirth, Ann. "Abjection and 'the Feminine' in *Outer Dark.*" Lilley 125–40.

Fox, John. "March 26, 1965: Sevierville's Last Great Flood." *Mountain Press* [Sevier County] 26 March 1984: A5.

Frost, Robert. "'Out, Out—.'" *The Poetry of Robert Frost.* Ed. Edward Connery Lathem. New York: Holt, Rinehart and Winston, 1969. 136–37.

Gallant, Grady. "Spied on Lovers, Blevins Admits." *Chattanooga Daily Times* 20 May 1965: 1, 40.

"'Gardner's [sic] Son.' on PBS This Week, Written by Louisvillian." *News-Sentinel* [Knoxville, Tenn.] 2 January 1977: G7.

"Gein Confesses Two Killings; Cleared in Hartley Girl Case." *Milwaukee Journal* (final), 20 November 1957: 1.

"Gein's Story True; Two Graves Empty." *Milwaukee Journal* 25 November 1957: 1, 8.

The Gentle Winds of Change: A History of Sevier County, Tennessee, 1900–1930. 2nd ed. Sevierville: Smoky Mountain Historical Society, 1989.

"Ghoulish Acts Were Stirred by Her Death." *Milwaukee Journal* 21 November 1957: 1, 3.

Gibson, Mike. "Knoxville Gave Cormac McCarthy the Raw Material of His Art. And He Gave It Back." Hall and Wallach 1:23–34.

Giles, James R. *Violence in the Contemporary American Novel: An End to Innocence.* Columbia: University of South Carolina Press, 2000.

"Goat Man's Son Found Dead of Gunshots." *Atlanta Constitution* 10 June 1988: B6.

Grammer, John M. "'A thing against which time will not prevail': Pastoral and History in Cormac McCarthy's South." Arnold and Luce, *Perspectives* 29–44.

Grant, Natalie. "The Landscape of the Soul: Man and the Natural World in *The Orchard Keeper.*" Hall and Wallach 1:75–82.

"Graves Probe Brings Relief." *Milwaukee Journal* 23 November 1957: 3.

Gray, Aelred J., and Susan F. Adams. "Government." Deaderick 68–144.

Grimstad, Kirsten J. *The Modern Revival of Gnosticism and Thomas Mann's* Doktor Faustus. Rochester, N.Y.: Camden House, 2002.

Guillemin, Georg. "Desolation in the Garden: The Pastoral Vision of Cormac McCarthy." Typescript.

———. *The Pastoral Vision of Cormac McCarthy.* College Station: Texas A&M University Press, 2004.

Guinn, Matthew. *After Southern Modernism: Fiction of the Contemporary South.* Jackson: University Press of Mississippi, 2000.

Gunther, John. *Inside U.S.A.* New York: Harper and Brothers, 1947.

Hall, Wade. "The Human Comedy of Cormac McCarthy." Hall and Wallach 1:61–73.

Hall, Wade, and Rick Wallach, eds. 1995. *Sacred Violence.* 2nd ed. 2 vols. El Paso: Texas Western Press, 2002.

Harris, George Washington. *Sut Lovingood: Yarns Spun by a "Nat'ral Born Durn'd Fool."* New York: Dick and Fitzgerald, 1867.

Hemingway, Ernest. "The Snows of Kilimanjaro." *The Snows of Kilimanjaro and Other Stories.* New York: Charles Scribner's Sons, 1970.

The History of Blount County, Tennessee, and Its People: 1795–1995. [Maryville]: Blount County History Book Committee, 1995.

Hoffmann, Gerhard. "Strangeness, Gaps, and the Mystery of Life: Cormac McCarthy's Southern Novels." *Amerikastudien / American Studies* 42.2 (1997): 217–38.

Holloway, David. *The Late Modernism of Cormac McCarthy.* Westport, Conn.: Greenwood Press, 2002.

———, ed. *Proceedings of the First European Conference on Cormac McCarthy.* Miami: Cormac McCarthy Society, 1999.

Holmes, Tony. "Tennessee's Many River Ferries." *Appalachian Life Magazine* 43 (May 2000): 3–4 [incomplete].

Hooper, Ed. *Images of America: Knoxville.* Charleston, S.C.: Arcadia, 2003.

Horton, Matthew R. "'Hallucinated Recollections': Narrative as Spatialized Perception of History in *The Orchard Keeper.*" Lilley 285–312.

"House of Horror Stuns the Nation." *Life* 2 December 1957: 24–31.

Howard, T. L. "The Justice of the Peace System in Tennessee." *Tennessee Law Review* 13 (December 1934–June 1935): 19–38.

Jarrett, Robert L. *Cormac McCarthy.* New York: Twayne, 1997.

Jenkins, Peter. "Lem to Lamar: 'I Ain't Never Heard Nothing on You Yet.'" *Smoky Mountain Star* 19 January 1984.

Jonas, Hans. *The Gnostic Religion: The Message of the Alien God and the Beginnings of Christianity.* Boston: Beacon Press, 1958.

———. "Epilogue: Gnosticism, Existentialism, and Nihilism." *The Gnostic Religion: The Message of the Alien God and the Beginnings of Christianity.* 3rd ed. Boston: Beacon Press, 2001.

Jones, Robbie. *The Historic Architecture of Sevier County, Tennessee.* Sevierville: Smoky Mountain Historical Society, 1996.

Josyph, Peter. "Tragic Ecstasy: A Conversation with Harold Bloom about Cormac McCarthy's *Blood Meridian.*" Hall and Wallach 2:205–21.

Julian, Harold. "Moonshining Was Big in These Parts." *News-Sentinel* [Knoxville] 20 February 1984: B1.

Jung, C. G. *Aion: Researches into the Phenomenology of the Self.* 1951. Tr. R. F. C. Hull. Ed. Herbert Read et al. Vol. 9, part 2 of *The Collected Works of C. G. Jung.* 1959. 2nd ed. Princeton: Princeton University Press, 1968.

Keebler, Robert S. "Our Justice of the Peace Courts—A Problem in Justice." *Tennessee Law Review* 9.1 (December 1930): 1–21.

Kelley, Buzz. "The Late Master Sheddan's Lumps." *Metropulse.* March 2001. http://metropulse.com/dir_zine/dir_2001/1111/t_letters.html (accessed 27 May 2001).

Kephart, Horace. *Our Southern Highlanders: A Narrative of Adventure in the Southern Appalachians and a Study of Life among the Mountaineers.* 1913. Rev. ed. Knoxville: University of Tennessee Press, 1984.

Kienitz, Richard C. "Find Two Graves Empty." *Milwaukee Journal* (final), 25 November 1957: 1.

———. "Gein Facing Sanity Tests." *Milwaukee Journal* 24 November 1957: 1, 16.

———. "Gein's Ghoul Story Verified at Graves." *Milwaukee Journal* 26 November 1957: 1–2.

———. "Robbed Graves, 'Butcher' Claims." *Milwaukee Journal* 19 November 1957: 1–2.

Kobler, John. *Ardent Spirits: The Rise and Fall of Prohibition.* New York: G.P. Putnam's Sons, 1973.

Kolodny, Annette. *The Lay of the Land: Metaphor as Experience and History in American Life and Letters.* Chapel Hill: University of North Carolina Press, 1975.

Knoxville City Directory, 1951. Knoxville: City Directory Co. of Knoxville, 1951.

Lang, John. "Lester Ballard: McCarthy's Challenge to the Reader's Compassion." Hall and Wallach 1:103–11.

Leonard, Richard H. "Murder Farm Horror Grows." *Milwaukee Journal* 18 November 1957: 1, 12, 17.

Leopold, Aldo. *A Sand County Almanac and Sketches Here and There.* New York: Oxford University Press, 1949.

Lewis, Sanford. "Blevins Case Due to Jurors Today." *Chattanooga Daily Times* 21 May 1965: 1, 26.

———. "Blevins Cleared by Jury after Two Years in Jail, but Faces Second Count." *Chattanooga Daily Times* 22 May 1965: 1, 5.

———. "Blevins Defense Expected Today." *Chattanooga Daily Times* 18 May 1965: 1, 11.

———. "Blevins Is Found Guilty with Sentence of Death Scheduled This Morning." *Chattanooga Daily Times* 6 May 1964: 1–2.

———. "Blevins on Witness Stand Invokes Fifth Amendment." *Chattanooga Daily Times* 15 May 1965: 1, 9.

———. "Blevins' Trial Opens Monday." *Chattanooga Daily Times* 9 May 1965: 1, 71.

———. "Blevins Upheld by Former Wife." *Chattanooga Daily Times* 19 May 1965: 1, 13.

———. "Ex-Wife Reports Blevins Told Her of Seeing Couple." *Chattanooga Sunday Times* 3 May 1964: 1, 37.

———. "Hairs from Suit Worn by Blevins Linked to Victim." *Chattanooga Daily Times* 2 May 1964: 1, 11.

———. "Jury Due to Get Case of Blevins Sometime Today." *Chattanooga Daily Times* 5 May 1964: 1, 9.

———. "Trial of Blevins to Resume Today." *Chattanooga Daily Times* 17 May 1965: 3.

Lilley, James D., ed. *Cormac McCarthy: New Directions.* Albuquerque: University of New Mexico Press, 2002.

Linn, Beulah. Letter to the author. 16 August 2000.

"Little Progress Is Seen in Probe of Twin Slaying." *Chattanooga Sunday Times* 28 April 1963: 1.

Longley, John Lewis, Jr. "Suttree and the Metaphysics of Death." *Southern Literary Journal* 17 (Spring 1985): 79–90.

Luce, Dianne C. "Cormac McCarthy's First Screenplay: 'The Gardener's Son.'" Arnold and Luce, *Perspectives* 71–96.

———. "Suttree's Knoxville / McCarthy's Knoxville: A Slide Presentation." Holloway 6–17.

———. "The Road and the Matrix: The World as Tale in *The Crossing*." Arnold and Luce, *Perspectives* 195–219.

———. "'They aint the thing': Artifact and Hallucinated Recollection in Cormac McCarthy's Early Frame-Works." Wallach 21–36.

———. "The Vanishing World of Cormac McCarthy's Border Trilogy." Arnold and Luce, *Cormac McCarthy Companion* 161–97.

———. "White Caps, Moral Judgment, and Law in *Child of God* or, the 'Wrong Blood' in Community History." *Cormac McCarthy: Uncharted Territories / Territoires Inconnus.* Ed. Christine Chollier. Reims, France: Presses Universitaires de Reims, 2003. 43–59.

MacArthur, William J., Jr. "Knoxville's History: An Interpretation." Deaderick 1–67.

Marius, Richard. "*Suttree* as Window into the Soul of Cormac McCarthy." Hall and Wallach 1:113–29.

Marx, Leo. *The Machine in the Garden: Technology and the Pastoral Ideal in America.* 1964. New York: Oxford University Press, 1967.

———. "Pastoralism in America." *Ideology and Classic American Literature.* 1986. Ed. Sacvan Bercovitch and Myra Jehlen. Cambridge: Cambridge University Press, 1987. 36–69.

Masters, R. E. L., and Eduard Lea. *Sex Crimes in History: Evolving Concepts of Sadism, Lust-Murder, and Necrophilia—from Ancient to Modern Times.* New York: Julian Press, 1963.

McCarthy, C. J. [Cormac]. "A Drowning Incident." *Phoenix* [University of Tennessee *Orange and White* Literary Supplement] March 1960: 3–4.

McCarthy, C. J., Jr. [Cormac]. "Wake for Susan." *Phoenix* [University of Tennessee *Orange and White* Literary Supplement] October 1959: 3–6.

McCarthy, Cormac. *All the Pretty Horses.* 1992. New York: Vintage, 1993.

———. *Blood Meridian, or the Evening Redness in the West.* 1985. New York: Vintage, 1992.

———. *Child of God.* 1973. New York: Vintage, 1993.

———. *Cities of the Plain.* 1998. New York: Vintage, 1999.

———. *The Crossing.* 1994. New York: Vintage, 1995.

———. *The Gardener's Son: A Screenplay.* Hopewell, N.J.: Ecco Press, 1996.

———. "The Gardener's Son." Shooting script typescript. Richard Inman Pearce Collection. South Caroliniana Library. University of South Carolina.

———. *No Country for Old Men.* New York: Knopf, 2005.

———. *The Orchard Keeper.* New York: Vintage, 1993.

———. *Outer Dark.* 1968. New York: Vintage, 1993.

———. *The Road.* New York: Knopf, 2006.

———. *The Sunset Limited: A Novel in Dramatic Form.* New York: Vintage, 2006.

———. *Suttree.* 1979. New York: Vintage, 1992.

———. "Whales and Men." Unpublished typescript. Cormac McCarthy Papers, Southwestern Writers Collection, Albert B. Alkek Library, Southwest Texas State University, San Marcos.

McKamey, Jeannine. "Lem Still Has His Bees." *Knoxville Journal* 18 August 1978: C1.

McKnight, Lynn. "Down on the Farm." *Smoky Mountain Star* 6 March 1982.

Mead, G. R. S. *Fragments of a Faith Forgotten*. 1900. New Hyde Park, N.Y.: University Books, 1960.

Melville, Herman. *Billy Budd, Sailor (An Inside Narrative)*. Ed. Harrison Hayford and Merton M. Sealts Jr. Chicago: University of Chicago Press, 1962.

———. *Moby-Dick*. Ed. Harrison Hayford and Hershel Parker. New York: W. W. Norton, 1967.

"Mental Test to Determine Sanity Sought." *Milwaukee Journal* 22 November 1957: 1, 3.

Metress, Christopher. "*Via Negativa:* The Way of Unknowing in Cormac McCarthy's *Outer Dark.*" *Southern Review* 37.1 (Winter 2001): 147–54.

"Miss McCarthy Marries Mr. James A. Jaques [Jacques] III." *Knoxville Journal* 10 June 1963: 6.

"More Rain Likely Tonight." *News-Sentinel* [Knoxville] 5 February 1957: 1, 10.

Morgan, Wesley G. "Red Callahan in *Suttree:* The Actual and the Fictitious." *Cormac McCarthy Journal* 5 (Spring 2005): 210–19.

———. "'A season of death and epidemic violence': Knoxville Rogues in *Suttree.*" *Cormac McCarthy Journal* 5 (Spring 2005): 195–209.

Muir, John. *Our National Parks*. Boston: Houghton Mifflin, 1902.

Nash, Roderick. "Preface to the Third Edition." *Wilderness and the American Mind*. 1967. New Haven: Yale University Press, 1982.

———. *Wilderness and the American Mind*. New Haven: Yale University Press, 1967.

Neely, Jack. *Knoxville's Secret History*. 2nd ed. Knoxville: Scruffy City, 1999.

O'Regan, Cyril. *Gnostic Return in Modernity*. Albany: State University of New York Press, 2001.

Pagels, Elaine. *The Gnostic Gospels*. 1979. New York: Vintage, 1989.

Palmer, David J. "Corinthians." Ed. David Lyle Jeffrey. *A Dictionary of Biblical Tradition in English Literature*. Grand Rapids, Mich.: William B. Eerdmans, 1992. 162–63.

Pearce, Richard. Foreword. *The Gardener's Son*. By Cormac McCarthy. Hopewell, N.J.: Ecco, 1996. [v–vi].

———. Research newsletter, received 7 April 1975. Richard Inman Pearce Collection. South Caroliniana Library. University of South Carolina.

———. Research newsletter, 8 October 1975. Richard Inman Pearce Collection. South Caroliniana Library. University of South Carolina.

Perry, John. *American Ferryboats*. New York: Wilfred Funk, 1957.

"Portrait of a Killer." *Time* 2 December 1957: 38–40.

Prather, William. "Absurd Reasoning in an Existential World: A Consideration of Cormac McCarthy's *Suttree.*" Hall and Wallach 1:139–51.

———. "'The color of this life is water': History, Stones, and the River in Cormac McCarthy's *Suttree.*" *Cormac McCarthy Journal* 4 (Spring 2005): 30–59.

———. "'Like something seen through bad glass': Narrative Strategies in *The Orchard Keeper.*" Wallach 37–54.

Psycho. Dir. Alfred Hitchcock. Paramount, 1960. Screenplay by Joseph Stefano. Based on Robert Bloch's *Psycho*.

Rebello, Stephen. *Alfred Hitchcock and the Making of Psycho.* New York: Dembner Books, 1990.

Rothrock, Mary U., ed. *The French Broad–Holston Country: A History of Knox County, Tennessee.* 1946. Knoxville: East Tennessee Historical Society, 1972.

Schafer, William J. "Cormac McCarthy: The Hard Wages of Original Sin." *Appalachian Journal* 4 (Winter 1977): 105–19.

Sevier County, Tennessee and Its Heritage. [Waynesville, N.C.: Walsworth, 1994.]

"Sevierville Land Use Plan." Knoxville: Tennessee State Planning Commission, East Tennessee Office, 1964.

Shakespeare, William. "Hamlet, Prince of Denmark." *The Complete Works of Shakespeare.* Ed. Hardin Craig. Glenview, Ill.: Scott, Foresman, 1961, 903–43.

Shelton, Frank W. "Suttree and Suicide." *Southern Quarterly* 29.1 (Fall 1990): 71–83.

Shields, A. Randolph. *The Cades Cove Story.* Gatlinburg, Tenn.: Great Smoky Mountains Natural History Association, 1981.

Simmons, Jessica. "Crossing Gendered Borders: Transsexualism in *Suttree.*" *Cormac McCarthy Journal* 2 (Spring 2002): 56–58.

Simpson, Lewis P. *The Dispossessed Garden: Pastoral and History in Southern Literature.* Athens: University of Georgia Press, 1975.

Simpson, Philip L. *Psycho Paths: Tracking the Serial Killer through Contemporary American Film and Fiction.* Carbondale: Southern Illinois University Press, 2000.

"Slain Girl Assaulted Repeatedly." *News-Sentinel* [Knoxville] 27 April 1963: 3.

"Smoky Streams on Rampage." *News-Sentinel* [Knoxville] (home ed.) 1 February 1957: 1, 14.

Spencer, William C. "Cormac McCarthy's Unholy Trinity: Biblical Parody in *Outer Dark.*" Hall and Wallach 1:83–91.

———. "*Suttree:* The Excremental Vision of Cormac McCarthy." Unpublished paper.

Stefano, Joseph. "Psycho." Photocopy of the revised screenplay, dated December 7, 1959. Thomas Cooper Library, University of South Carolina, Columbia.

Stewart, J. A. *The Myths of Plato.* 1904. Ed. G. R. Levy. London: Centaur Press, 1960.

Sullivan, Nell. "Cormac McCarthy and the Text of *Jouissance.*" Hall and Wallach 1:153–61.

———. "The Evolution of the Dead Girlfriend Motif in *Outer Dark* and *Child of God.*" Wallach 68–77.

Sullivan, Walter. "Worlds Past and Future: A Christian and Several from the South." *Sewanee Review* 73 (Autumn 1965): 719–26.

"Suspect Held to Jury in Killing of Couple." *News-Sentinel* [Knoxville] 23 May 1963: 35.

Taylor, William D. "'And there shall be weeping and gnashing of teeth': Cormac McCarthy's *Outer Dark* as a Vision of Retribution in a World without Grace through Christ." *Carson-Newman Studies* 8 (Fall 1994): 33–39.

Tennessee Historical Records Survey Division of Community Service Programs, Works Projects Administration. *Blount County (Maryville).* Inventory of the County Archives of Tennessee Ser. 5. Nashville: Tennessee Historical Records Survey, 1941.

Terrill, Tom E. "Murder in Graniteville." *Toward a New South? Studies in Post–Civil War Southern Communities.* Ed. Orville Vernon Burton and Robert C. McMath Jr. Westport, Conn.: Greenwood, 1982. 193–222.

"Three Men Held in Slaying of Couple." *News-Sentinel* [Knoxville] 26 April 1963: 5.

Thoreau, Henry David. "Civil Disobedience." Canby 789–808.

———. "Paradise (To Be) Regained." Canby 774–88.

———. "Walden." Canby 245–465.

Turnbull, Andrew. *Scott Fitzgerald*. New York: Charles Scribner's Sons, 1962.

"Typhoid Cases Bring Swimming Warning." *News-Sentinel* [Knoxville] 23 June 1952: 12.

Vanderheide, John. "The Process of Elimination: Tracing the Prodigal's Irrevocable Passage through Cormac McCarthy's Southern and Western Works." Wallach 177–82.

Vincent, Bert. "Strolling." *News-Sentinel* [Knoxville] 15 April 1963: 13.

———. "Strolling." *News-Sentinel* [Knoxville] 2 June 1968: F1.

Wallace, Garry. "Meeting McCarthy." *Southern Quarterly* 30.4 (Summer 1992): 134–39.

Wallach, Rick, ed. *Myth, Legend, Dust: Critical Responses to Cormac McCarthy*. Manchester: Manchester University Press, 2000.

———. "Prefiguring Cormac McCarthy: The Early Short Stories." Wallach 15–20.

"We Just Pass This Way One Time." *Sevier County Observer* 1 August 1974: 3.

White, C. P. "Commercial and Industrial Trends since 1865." Rothrock 220–25.

Wilkerson, Worth. "Girl's Parents Take out Warrant in Dual Murder." *Chattanooga Daily Times* 8 May 1963: 1, 9.

———. "Spied on Couple Near Death Site, Blevins Asserts." *Chattanooga Daily Times* 23 May 1963: 1–2.

Wilkinson, Diane. "The Last of the Smoky Mountaineers: 'I Wouldn't Live Anywhere Else.'" *Smoky Mountain Star* 22 June 1972: A9.

Williams, Don. *101 Places off the Beaten Track: What to See in East Tennessee and How to Get There*. Maryville, Tenn.: Outback, [1982].

Wilson, Marshall A. *Tales from the Grass Roots of TVA, 1933–1952*. N.p., 1982.

Winchell, Mark Royden. "Inner Dark: or, The Place of Cormac McCarthy." *Southern Review* n.s. 26 (April 1990): 293–309.

"Winkler, Homer Garland (Shorty)." *Knoxville Journal* 27 August 1991: 9A.

"Winklers Honored at Buffet Dinner." *News-Sentinel* [Knoxville] 6 September 1978: A13.

Winthrop, John. "A Model of Christian Charity." Ed. Nina Baym, *et al. The Norton Anthology of American Literature*. Shorter 5th ed. New York: Norton, 1999. 107–18.

Witek, Terri. "Reeds and Hides: Cormac McCarthy's Domestic Spaces." *Southern Review* 30.1 (January 1994): 136–42.

Woodward, Richard B. "Cormac McCarthy's Venomous Fiction." *New York Times Magazine* 19 April 1992: 28–31+.

Yeats, William Butler. "The Second Coming." *The Collected Poems of W. B. Yeats*. New York: Macmillan, 1956. 184–85.

"Yeggs Get $300 from Car Lot." *News-Sentinel* [Knoxville] 9 June 1952: 9.

Young, Thomas D., Jr. "The Imprisonment of Sensibility: *Suttree*." Arnold and Luce, *Perspectives* 97–122.

Acheron, 86, 226–27, 230

Adam (biblical), 115, 120, 124. *See also* gnosticism and Adam

Alcoa Aluminum, 2–3, 49

alcohol regulation. *See* prohibition; whiskey blockading

Alexander, Lamar, 18

Alighieri, Dante, *The Divine Comedy*, 62–64, 71–72, 75, 84–87, 93, 159, 198, 203, 207, 217, 226–30, 234, 243, 260, 267; and Dis, 227–28, 230; rivers in, 226–27, 230

Allegheny Mountains, 23–24, 26

Ambrosiano, Jason, 65

American Civil War, 14, 125–26, 271n3

American Revolution, 13, 50

Anderson, Jerry, 2

antinomianism, 37, 43–52, 54–56, 58–61, 111, 176, 183, 185–89, 252–53, 255, 281n3. *See also* officers and bureaucrats

Appalachian Mountains, 6, 11, 24, 272n13; Southern Appalachians 4–6, 23, 27, 44. *See also* Allegheny Mountains, Great Smoky Mountains

Arnett, Foster, 17

Arnold, Edwin T., 2–3, 53, 64–65, 73–74, 85–86, 93, 96, 98, 100–102, 107, 110, 112, 234, 275n25, 275n2, 281n36, 290n27

Asheville, N.C., 136, 244

Babylonian theology, 89

Barksdale, Don W., 155

Barr, Thomas C., Jr., 156

Bartlett, Andrew, 283n19, 284n20

Bell, Vereen M., ix, 64, 79–80, 98, 100, 102, 106, 108, 111–112, 114, 161, 165, 169, 198, 200–202, 230, 239, 251, 254, 261, 266, 268, 275n2, 276n4, 277–78n17, 288n15, 288–89n18

Berry, K. Wesley, 7, 156

Berwick, Sandy, 126

Bible, 67; Corinthians, 64, 101–102; Genesis, 124; John, 275n1; Judges, 279n24; Luke, 131; Mark, 131; Matthew, 64, 131, 157, 275n1; Paul, 101–2, 277n14; Peter, 260; Psalms, 275n1; Old Testament, 83; Revelations, 64, 107, 275n1

Birth of Iron Myth, 172–73

Blackburn, Simon, 246

Blackmun, Harry, 17

Blevins, James Melvin (historical person), 136, 138–44, 153, 157; and Jimmy Blevins (in *All the Pretty Horses*), 142; sources for, 138

Blevins, Patricia Ann, 139, 141, 143

Bloch, Robert, 282n8; *Psycho*, 136–37, 146–47, 149–53, 282n7; "The Shambles of Ed Gein," 282n6

Bloom, Harold, 65

Blount County, Tenn., 1–5, 11, 14–15, 26, 49, 51, 271n1. *See also* Maryville, Tenn.

Boehme, Jacob, 65

bounty themes, 34, 57, 60, 122, 124, 237

Bourne, Frank E., 2

Bowles, Jay, 143–44

Brecht, Bertolt, *Mother Courage*, 105–6

Brewer, Carson, 16–18

Brewer, Hazel, 154

Brickman, Barbara, 272–73n13

Brooks, Tim, and Earle Marsh, 50

Broome, Harvey, 3–4, 10, 12, 19

Brown, Irving, 158

Brown Mountain (Tenn.), 1–3

Bryant, William Cullen, *Picturesque America*, 126

Bryson, Daddy, 15

Bultmann, Rudolph, 67

bureaucrats. *See* officers and bureaucrats

Burnett, Edmund Cody, 131–33

Butterworth, D. S., 201

Cades Cove, Tenn., 10, 12–15, 26, 272n7, 273n14

Campbell, Carlos C., 9–16, 21, 32, 271n4, 272n6, 272n7, 273n16, 273n18

Camus, Albert, 159, 176, 181, 199–200, 221, 225; and condemned man, 189–90, 221; "Entre Plotin et Saint Augustin," 177; and gnosticism, 187, 190; *A Happy Death*, 185, 190, 285n4, 285n7; *L'Homme Révolté*, 198; *The Myth of Sisyphus*, 191, 198–99, 285n7; and nature, 164, 177, 190; *The Stranger*, 65, 151, 178, 180, 182–93, 198–99, 254, 260, 285n8, 285n10, 288n16, 291n29; sun imagery in, 183–85, 189, 213, 229

Canfield, J. Douglas, 65, 179, 191, 199–200, 228, 266–67, 284n21, 284n2, 285n6, 286n12, 286n13, 286–87n3, 287n8, 288n15, 291n28

Carberry, Michael, 5

Catholic High School (Knoxville, Tenn.), 194–95

Catlett, Bob, 15

caves, 156–58, 166, 174–75, 216–17

Chandler, Charles, 195

Chapman, Col. David C., 10

Charleston, S.C., 131

Charon, 87, 226

Chattanooga Daily Times, 138, 140–43

Chicago Tribune, 137

Chilhowee Mountain, 1, 271n1

Chollier, Christine, 60, 283n14

Christianity, 64–65, 146, 201–202; and angels, 80; and body as clay or dust, 85; Christian allegory, 104; and Creator, benevolent, 181–82; and communion, rite of, 75, 91, 256, 265–66; and dominion over animals, 123; and God's providence, 109, 123–24; and gnosticism, 66–68, 83, 101, 109–110, 277n10, 282n11; and heaven, 159; and piety, 183, 192; and Platonic tradition, 171; and the rock (symbol), 226–27; and serpent, 86, 123; and sin and atonement, 75, 98, 160, 186, 190; symbology and terminology of (in McCarthy's works), 109–110, 275n1; and trinity, 88–90, 277n10; and wilderness, 113–14, 123. *See also* Adam; Bible; Dante; Eden; Eve; Jesus; Jonah; Lazarus; Puritanism; Roman Catholicism; Virgin Mary

Ciuba, Gary M., 151, 161

Civilian Conservation Corps (CCC), 32, 34, 273n18

class hierarchies, conflict, 179, 182, 232–35, 241, 253, 257–58

Clemens, Samuel, *Huckleberry Finn*, 31

Clement of Alexandria, 107

Coates, Robert M., *The Outlaw Years*, 281n36

Collector, The, (film), 289n20

Condon, David deL., 18

Cooper, Alfred J., 154

Cooper, James Fenimore, 280n34; *The Pioneers*, 36, 40, 47, 274n22

Cooper, James W., 21

Corinth, 102

Cormac McCarthy Society, 3, 281n36

Cosper, Dale, and Ethan Cary, 65, 199, 201, 254, 269, 285n9, 286n3, 291n29

Cove Creek, Tenn., 21–22, 272n11
Crane, Stephen, *The Red Badge of Courage*, 118
cultural displacement, imposition, 32, 37, 40, 44–45, 47–52, 210, 212, 272–73n13, 274n19, 289n19. *See also* Great Smoky Mountains National Park; Tennessee Valley Authority

Dante. *See* Alighieri, Dante
Daugherty, Leo, 65, 67–68
Davidson, Donald, 4, 18–22, 37, 126–27, 271n3, 274n19, 281n36, 289n19, 289–90n22
Davidson, Theresa Sherrer, 126–27, 289n19
Davis, Ann, 9, 11
Davis, Donald Edward, 4–7, 9, 11, 19, 21–23, 26, 132
Davis, Willis P., 9
De Fontaine, F. G., 126–27
Deaderick, Lucile, 196
Depression, 2, 6–7, 14–15, 19, 27, 32, 50, 52, 156
Dickens, Charles, "A Christmas Carol," 203, 213
Dis. *See* Alighieri, Dante
Ditmars, Raymond L., 280n33, 280n34
Donne, John, "Batter My Heart, Three-Personed God," 260
Donoghue, Denis, ix
Donovan, Josephine, 176–77, 181–83, 185, 187, 189, 191, 199, 287n7
Dostoevsky, Fyodor, *Crime and Punishment*, 151, 185, 194, 254, 285n10
Douglas Reservoir (Tenn.), 154–55
dreams, nightmares, visions 41, 62–63, 72–74, 78–79, 82, 92–96, 111–12, 172, 204, 210–11, 214, 217, 225–27, 230, 239–40, 255, 258, 288n15, 290n27. *See also* hallucinated recollection
Dumas, Jim, 5, 15–18
Dunn, Durwood, 10, 12–15, 26, 273n14
Dykeman, Wilma, 5–7, 131–33

East Tennessee, 1, 3, 12, 29–31, 271n3; and Depression, 15; and farming, 15, and tourism, 10; attitudes toward federal government of, 14; cultural change in, 4; environmental change in, 4–5; ferries in, 125–26; floods in, 136, 153–55, 282n10; northern influence on, 4; and local prohibition laws, 27; and whiskey production, 26; and wilderness, 117. *See also* Tennessee Valley Authority
ecological themes, 28–37, 39–42, 45–46, 57–58, 60, 119–24, 273n17, 274n21, 274n22, 280n34
economic themes, 57, 59, 162, 185, 236–38, 283n14, 283n15, 284n2. *See also* class hierarchies, conflict
Eden, Garden of, 115, 124, 179
Eliot, T. S., "The Hollow Men," 86; "The Love Song of J. Alfred Prufrock," 203, 268; "The Waste Land," 67, 86
Elkmont, Tenn., 12–13, 15–16
Eve, 115, 124
Evenson, Brian, 283–84n19
existentialism, 37, 53–54, 65, 166; and alienation, 176–77, 181, 183, 191, 198; and archontic powers, 176, 180, 183; and authenticity, 176–77, 181, 190; and the condemned, 181; and gnosis, lucidity, 177, 182–83, 191, 199; and gnosticism, 110, 176–78, 199; and God, 176; and the lie of the world, 181, 185–89, 191; and revolt, 180–87, 198–99. *See also* Camus, Albert; Heidegger, Martin; Kafka, Franz; McCarthy, Cormac, works—*The Gardener's Son, Suttree*; Nietzsche, Friedrich; Sartre, Jean-Paul
Ezzell, Patricia Bernard, 21

Faulkner, William; *As I Lay Dying*, 86; and Natchez Trace outlaws, 281n36; "A Rose for Emily," 146, 151; *The Sound and the Fury*, 207

Fenn, Harry, 126
ferries, 125–27
Ficino, 167
Fields, Pat, 17, 136–37
Fisher-Wirth, Ann, 91–92, 102–103, 118, 200, 276n6, 276n7, 277–78n17
Fitzgerald, F. Scott, 244; *The Great Gatsby*, 31
Forbidden Caverns (Tenn.), 154, 156
Fort Loudoun Dam, 21, 289n22
Fowles, John, *The Collector*, 134, 244; film, 289n20
Fox, John, 154
French Broad River, 5–6, 125, 126, 131, 154
Freud, Sigmund, 88, 93–94
Frost, Robert, "'Out, Out—,'" 181

Gallant, Grady, 142–43
Gatlinburg, Tenn., 12
Gein, Ed, 136–38, 144–53, 155, 282n9, 283n17; sources for, 137, 282n6
Gentle Winds of Change, The, 5, 26
Georgia (state), 138, 141; Bureau of Investigation (GBI), 140–41; Court of Appeals, 140; Supreme Court, 140–41, 143
Gibson, Mike, 2–3, 153, 195–96, 271n2, 271n5
Giles, James R., 201–202, 208, 234, 236, 251, 290n27
Gilpin, William, 31
Gleason, Frank M., 139–41, 143
gnostic imagery and McCarthy's use of artificer god, 87–88, 173, 182, 241, 251, 260, 276–77n9, 277n15; Babel, Babylon, 228, 262–64, 268; brothel, 103–104, 245; the Call, 108, 178, 239–40; darkness, 72–73, 184, 252; dwelling or inn, 73; Home, 108–109, 241, 257; horse, loose, 276n8; light, 80–82; mingling, 85, 92, 102–104, 165, 246–47, 258–59, 268–69; noise, 105, 178–80; oblivion, drunkenness,

sleep, 73–75, 78, 83–84, 92, 101, 166, 175, 184, 232, 237, 241, 259, 262, 267; pearl, 241; planets and stars, 79, 169–70, 221, 242; poison, 74–75, 91–92, 114–15; prison, trap, captivity, 75–76, 81–82, 103–105, 119, 157, 166, 185, 189, 201, 212–13, 242, 245–46, 278n21, 283n18, 283–84n19, 287n8; shadow, 72, 75–78, 96, 179; stranger, estrangement, 103–104, 176–77; sun, 53–54, 72, 78–80, 82, 179, 213, 229; tollsman, 287n7; thrownness, 84, 109, 219; water, living versus turbid, 83–87, 102, 131, 166, 215–16, 224, 227, 232, 240, 264–66, 288n13; the Way or Path, 110; wind, whirlwind, 80, 212–13, 225, 264. *See also* leviathan
gnostic manuscripts: *Corpus Hermeticum*, 72, 161; "Gospel of Truth," 92–93, 107–108; "Hymn of the Pearl," 74, 91, 103, 241, 263, 279n27; Nag Hammadi manuscripts, 66, 75, 276n8; *The Origin of the World*, 75; *Pistis Sophia*, 72, 279n27; "Poimandres" of Hermes Trismegistus, 86, 89, 166; *The Teachings of Sylvanus*, 276n8; Turfan manuscripts, 66, 108
gnosticism, 53, 65–121; and Adam, 84–85, 178, 287n7; and Alien (transcendent, transmundane, True) God, Unknown Father, Unknown Light, 68, 72, 79, 87–88; and Alien Man (Messenger, Primal Man, Savior, Traveler), 69, 74, 85, 91–92, 103, 109–110, 278n19; and alienation, 79, 94, 98, 101, 103, 108, 111, 113–114, 168, 176–77; and archons (demiurge, world-artificers, world-rulers), 68–69, 71, 78, 87–91, 94, 98, 115, 173; and body, 69, 85, 105, 232; Christian, 68–69, 89; and Christianity, 66, 68, 109–110, 186, 257, 263; and cosmos, 68, 71, 73, 83–84, 92–93, 158–59, 176, 182, 200, 232; and dualism, 68, 112; and

embedded worlds, 68, 71, 175; and existentialism, 110–11, 176–78, 199; and gnosis, 69, 99–101, 108, 115, 177, 276n6; and *harmonia*, 78, 89; and history 70–71; and human condition, 79, 92–93, 104, 167–68, 225; and human nature, 69, 89, 92–100, 146, 153, 167, 171, 201, 279–80n31; Iranian, 67–68; and Judaism, 65, 68, 83, 87, 89, 98–99, 109, 124; and the lawsuit concerning the world, 85–86, 232; Mandaean, 67, 80–81, 83, 232, 287n7; Manichaean, 67–68, 91, 108, 111; McCarthy's sources of, 66–67; and mingling of spirit with matter, 72, 83–84, 160, 277–78n17; Naassene, 279n25; and nature, 69, 113–21, 165, 177, 279–80n31, 283n16; and nihilism, 66, 111–13; and oblivion, ignorance, unknowing, 74, 91, 100, 160, 167; and outer dark, 71–72; and morality, 277n12; and Platonic tradition, 100, 158–60, 169–71, 263; and *pneuma* (spirit), 69, 94, 98–99, 107, 171, 177; and *psyche* (soul), 69, 75, 94–95, 99, 172, 200, 248, 275n3, 276n6; and reunification with the divine, 69, 71, 101, 103, 159; and salvation, 91–92, 98, 101; and serpent, 86, 115, 123–24, 279n27; and sexuality, 102, 161, 239, 242; and sin, 79, 85, 98, 160; and Sophia, 75, 103–104; Syrian-Egyptian (Valentinian), 67–68, 83, 92–93, 105; tenets of (overview), 68–69; and "thrownness," 78, 92, 109, 111–112, 176–77, 232; and transcendence, 65; and Zosimos, 240. *See also* gnostic imagery; gnostic manuscripts; *heimarmene*

god, weaver, 178, 180, 203, 226, 276n9
Golding, William, *Lord of the Flies*, 237
Grammer, John M., 64, 69–71, 90, 161, 169, 237, 250, 281n36, 287n5
Graniteville Mill (historical), 37

Graniteville, S.C., 188, 285n11
Grant, Natalie, 273n17
Grant, Robert M., 67
Gray, Aelred J., and Susan F. Adams, 27
Great Smoky Mountains, 4, 32; and chestnut blight, 6; and logging, 9. *See also* logging industry
Great Smoky Mountains Conservation Association, 10–12, 272n6
Great Smoky Mountains National Park, 3, 5, 9–16, 18–21; and economic development, 9–10; and infrastructure, 32; and historic preservation, 9, 272n7; and land acquisition, 11–16; legislation for, 12–13; and natural preservation, 9–10; and park versus forest debate, 10
Great Smoky Mountains National Park Commission, 12–16
Gregg, William (historical), 179, 185
Grimstad, Kirsten J., 66–68, 71, 199
Guillemin, Georg, 29, 38, 41–42, 70, 115, 124, 275n1, 277n11, 279n30, 279n31
Guinn, Matthew, 124, 198, 258, 288n14
Gunther, John, 27

Hada, Ken, 281n38
Hades, Sheol, 71–72, 87, 157, 160, 166, 174, 267
Hall, Wade, 209, 287n5
hallucinated recollection, 37, 59, 62, 206, 211, 217–21, 233, 249–50, 256–57, 278n20
Harmon, W. F., 139, 141
Harpe brothers, 281n36
Harris, George Washington, 209, 287n5
Heidegger, Martin, 65, 111–12, 176–77
heimarmene (necessity), 88–92, 94–96, 98–99, 101, 105–106, 108, 110, 113, 119–20, 124, 170, 180, 184, 187, 190, 239–40, 277n11, 290n26
Hellenism, 67, 109, 111, 159
Hemingway, Ernest, "The Snows of Kilimanjaro," 221, 267

Hippolytus, 277n10
History of Blount County, Tennessee, and Its People: 1795–1995, The, 1, 11–13, 271n1
Hitchcock, Alfred, 137; *Psycho*, 136–38, 146–53, 165, 168, 282n8
Hoffmann, Gerhard, 103, 114, 201–202, 252, 279n23, 280n32
hogs, 85–86, 116, 227, 237, 265, 281n37; and hog drives, 131–33, 281n38
Holloway, David, 65, 166, 169, 199, 283n15
Holmes, Tony, 125–26
Hooper, Ed, 27
Horton, Matthew R., 274n20, 274n23
Howard, T. L., 128–30
the Hurricane (Tenn.) ("Harrykin"), 1, 5

Immaculate Conception Catholic Church (Knoxville, Tenn.), 195–96, 263
Indians, 289n19
Industrial Revolution, 176, 178–79
industrialization, 18, 32, 179, 271n3 *See also* logging industry; Tennessee Valley Authority
Irenaeus, Bishop, 66, 103–104, 277n10

Jarrett, Robert L., 151, 163, 170–71, 245, 272–73n13, 275n1, 283n16
Jefferson, Thomas, 24; Jeffersonian agrarianism, 29
Jenkins, Peter, 16
Jesus, Christ, 69, 107, 170, 265–68
Jonah, 157, 174
Jonas, Hans, 66–70, 72–75, 78–81, 83–86, 89, 91–95, 98–105, 107–108, 110–113, 115, 158–59, 161, 166, 169–71, 175–76, 178, 199, 232, 240–41, 263, 275n3, 276n5, 277n12, 277n14, 278n19, 279n27, 282n11, 287n7
Jones, Madison, *Forest of the Night*, 281n36
Jones, Ralph, 139–40
Jones, Robbie, 32, 154

Josyph, Peter, 65
Joyce, James, *Ulysses*, 194, 286n3
Judaism, 159. *See also* gnosticism and Judaism
Julian, Harold, 26, 273n14
Jung, C. G., 67, 93–94; *Aion* 76–77, 95–96; "Seven Sermons to the Dead," 68
Justice of the Peace (J.P.) system, 128–30

Kafka, Franz, *The Trial*, 287n7
Kalewala, 172–73
Keebler, Robert S., 128–30
Kelley, Buzz, 196
Kephart, Horace, 8–9, 23–27, 31–32, 35, 37, 43–44, 47, 50, 272n13, 273n16, 281n37, 283n14
Kiefer, Christian, 282n6
Kienitz, Richard C., 144, 147, 149
Knott, Jack, 140–41
Knox County, Tenn., 1, 3–4, 51, 136, 287n9
Knoxville, Tenn., 4, 21; and alcohol, 27–28; Chamber of Commerce, 9, 13; and flooding, 136, 155; and promotion of the Great Smoky Mountains National Park, 9–13; in *Suttree*, 194–97; and the TVA, 18–19, 52; typhoid fever in, 288n13. *See also* McAnally Flats, Sequoyah Hills
Knoxville *News-Sentinel*, 135, 138, 140, 155, 196, 287n6, 288n13
Kobler, John, 27, 273n15
Kolodny, Annette, 30, 34, 36, 38–42, 57, 113, 121–22, 274n22, 280n34
Kristeva, Julia, 92, 200, 276n6, 286–87n3

Lacan, Jacques, 276n6
Lang, John, 168
Lazarus, 268
Leonard, Richard H., 144
Leopold, Aldo, 123–24, 280n34

Lethe, 83, 158, 166, 173, 227
leviathan, 180; as Gnostic symbol, 91,
 157, 174, 215, 230; and Jonah 157
Lewis, Sanford, 139–43
Life, 136, 145, 148, 150–51
Linn, Beulah, 135–36
Little Pigeon River, Tenn., 154–55
Little River Lumber Company, 5, 11–13,
 16
Little River Railroad, 5
Locke, John, 70
logging industry, 16, 19; cultural impact
 of, 4, 6–8, 29, 37–38; environmental
 impact of, 4–6, 8–9, 13, 31, 39; and
 Great Smoky Mountains National
 Park, 11–12; and railroads, 4–6; and
 wages, 5; and war industry, 9
Long, James (historical), 196
Longley, John Lewis, Jr., 198, 239
Lookout Mountain (Ga.), 138–39
Los Alamos, N.Mex., 60, 273n17
Luce, Dianne C., 132, 194, 206, 218,
 274n20, 280n34, 281n3, 284n21,
 284n1, 290n23
Lula Lake (Ga.), 138–39
lumber industry. *See* logging industry

MacArthur, William J., Jr., 9–12, 18–19,
 27–28, 52, 281n36
Machiavelli, Niccolb, 70
Mann, Thomas, *Joseph* tetralogy, 68
Marion, Francis, 50
Marius, Richard, 194–98, 207
Marx, Leo, 28–29, 31–33, 113, 117,
 279n30
Mary. *See* Virgin Mary
Maryville, Tenn., 2, 12, 15, 27
Masters, R. E. L., and Eduard Lea, *Sex
 Crimes in History*, 134–35, 145, 147,
 162
materialism, 47, 106, 134, 148, 159–63,
 168–69, 174, 197, 201, 216, 228–40,
 243–50
Matthews, Larry E., 156

McAnally Flats (Knoxville, Tenn.), 195,
 286n1
McCarthy, Anne DeLisle, 153, 195
McCarthy, Charles Joseph, Sr., 21–22,
 52, 272n12, 289–90n22
McCarthy, Cormac, biographical information, 1, 4, 31, 126, 136–38, 141–42,
 153–54, 176, 194, 218, 271n5, 287n9;
 characters, doubling of, 51, 53–55,
 86, 88, 95, 97–98, 105, 163, 198, 205,
 208, 219–20, 223–25, 234–39, 245–46,
 251–55, 262, 284n20; ontological
 place metaphors, use of, 63, 72,
 156–57, 159, 178–79, 197, 226–30
McCarthy, Cormac, works:
 All the Pretty Horses, 54, 142, 159, 198,
  222–23, 266, 269–70
 Blood Meridian, 31, 34, 62–64, 88, 96,
  131, 178, 189, 233, 254, 277n15,
  279n29, 280n35, 283n19, 290n25;
  gnosticism in, 53–54, 66–67, 78,
  92–94, 159, 174, 229, 276n9, 278n20,
  288n12; narrator of, 202, 205; protagonist of, 205
 Border Trilogy, 28, 30, 35, 170,
  194–95, 222–23, 266, 269–70,
  284n22
 Child of God, 1, 63, 66, 83, 86, 90, 93,
  176, 178, 197, 216, 230–31, 237–38,
  244, 252, 262, 266, 269, 278n20,
  281n3; Lester Ballard, 56, 134–35,
  142, 145, 150–52, 155–57, 160–72,
  174–75, 228, 231, 277n16, 282n12,
  282–83n13, 283n14, 283n18, 283–
  84n19; blacksmith, 173, 276–77n9;
  and Blevins case, 136, 138–44, 153;
  and Gein case, 136, 144–146,
  151–53; and gnosticism, 144, 146,
  153, 157–62, 164–71, 173–75; and
  Narcissus myth, 165–69; and Platonic mythology, 65, 157–75; and
  Psycho, 146–53; narration of, 151,
  163–65, 169, 202, 204–205; setting
  (time and place) of, 154–56

McCarthy, Cormac, works (*continued*)
  Cities of the Plain, 9, 28, 54, 61–62,
    103–104, 120, 204, 207, 223, 245,
    247
  Crossing, The, 28, 34–35, 37, 65, 190,
    220, 225–26, 243, 250, 260, 266,
    269, 276–77n9, 278n20, 279n26,
    290n23, 291n30
  "Drowning Incident, A," 275n25
  Gardener's Son, The, 37, 53, 151, 197,
    199, 203, 251, 257, 259, 284–85n3;
    and existentialism, 176–93, 286n13;
    factory, machinery, 178–80, 185–86,
    189; and gnosticism, 176–78, 180,
    182, 184, 187–89, 193; James Gregg,
    179, 185–86; Mrs. Gregg, 179–82;
    historical background of, 179, 183,
    185, 188, 285n11; Patrick McEvoy,
    179, 186–87, 286n12, 286n13;
    Robert McEvoy, 180–86, 188–89,
    191–93, 285n6, 285n8; metaphors
    in, condemned man, 189–93; Dr.
    Perceval, 181; shooting script of,
    176, 178–79, 181, 188, 191, 193,
    204, 207–208, 218, 220, 285n8;
    W. J. Whipper, 186–87. *See also*
    god, weaver
  No Country for Old Men, 64, 120
  Orchard Keeper, The, 83, 113, 117,
    120–22, 136–37, 194–95, 206, 234,
    252, 258, 278n20; biographical back-
    ground of, 1–3; ecocentric stance
    of, 28–37, 269; and gnostic imagery,
    274–75n 24; historical background
    of, 3–28, 37, 272–73n13; narrator
    of (John Wesley Rattner), 38, 56,
    59–60, 62, 203, 207, 217, 220,
    274n20, 274n23; Arthur Ownby,
    37–49, 274n23; John Wesley Rattner,
    55–61; Kenneth Rattner, 52–55,
    274–75n24; Marion Sylder, 49–55
  Outer Dark, 34, 53, 142, 144, 150,
    153, 157–59, 161, 168, 174–75,
    178–79, 183–84, 203, 212, 214–15,
  229–30, 233, 238, 245, 249, 265–66,
    281n4, 281n5, 283n18, 284n22,
    287n8; blind man, 79, 107, 109–110,
    112; child, 91–92; dream structure
    of, 62–64, 87, 124, 204; ecocentric
    stance of, 119–124, 269; and gnosti-
    cism, 65–124; historical background
    of, 124–33, 281n3; Culla Holme,
    72–79, 81–82, 84–87, 89–92, 95–101,
    104–110, 112, 228, 277n11, 277n16;
    Rinthy Holme, 73–74, 77–83, 101–
    105, 109, 116, 170, 276n4, 277n13,
    277–78n17; narrator of, 72, 204–
    205, 279–80n31; as road narrative,
    63; Squire Salter, 100–101; tinker,
    73–74, 105–106, 278n22; trinity in,
    88–90; triune, 63–64, 73, 87–91,
    95–99, 109; and unknowing, theme
    of, 100–110
  Road, The, 62–63, 72, 159, 170, 178,
    218, 266, 277n16, 278n18
  Sunset Limited, The, 54, 159, 170, 178,
    189, 265–66, 288n17
  Suttree, 1, 21, 34, 63, 83, 136–37,
    178, 181–84; and existentialism, 65,
    176–77, 198–202, 221, 229, 232,
    252–53; and gnosticism, 66–67,
    199–204, 211–12, 216–17, 219, 221,
    225–27, 229–32, 234–35, 239–43,
    245–46, 249, 252–53, 258, 260–64,
    267–69, 276n9, 290n26; goatman,
    265, 268; Gene Harrogate, 237–38,
    288–89n18; Harvey the junkman,
    235–36; historical background for,
    194–97, 289n19, 289–90n22; Hooper
    the ragman, 235–36; and huntsman,
    181, 199, 204, 211–12, 214–16, 220,
    225–26, 233, 236, 259–60, 263, 269;
    image patterns in, 197–98, 205–206,
    210–17, 229–30, 239–40, 242, 245,
    249–50, 255–56, 259; Ab Jones,
    251–55, 290n24; Joyce, 244–48,
    250–51; Michael, 265; Mother She,
    211, 265–66; narrative frame of,

203–207, 210–15; narrator of, 94, 202–17, 220–22, 228–30, 253, 259, 268, 286n3; and photographs, film strip, 215, 217–26, 240, 245, 259; and predation, 233–34, 236–37, 254; and Platonism, 229, 242, 244; and Protestant preachers, 261–62, 264–65, 290n27, 291n28; and Roman Catholicism, 226, 257–61, 267–68; and sexuality, 238–51; structure of, 197–98, 218–219;; Suttree, 112, 159, 190, 198–226, 228–70, 277n16, 284n22, 289n21

"Wake for Susan," 203–204, 206–207, 220, 226, 258

"Whales and Men," 35, 266, 274n21, 287–88n10, 290n23, 291n30. *See also* gnostic imagery, McCarthy's use of

McCarthy, Lee Holleman, 136, 153, 271n5

McCarthy, Maryellen, 136

McCartney, Ches (Goat Man), 196

McDonald, Jeanne, *Voices from the Valley,* 196

McEvoy, Robert (historical), 178, 188, 285n11

McEvoy family (historical), 183

McKamey, Jeannine, 16–17, 272n9

McKnight, Lynn, 16–17

Mead, G. R. S., 66–67, 103–104, 157, 228, 277n10, 279n25; and Theosophical Society 66

Meeman, Edward J., 11–12

Melville, Herman, "Benito Cereno," 210; *Billy Budd, Sailor,* 191, 210; *Moby-Dick,* 31, 134, 157, 178, 180, 205, 207, 215, 276n9

Metress, Christopher, 64–65, 68, 85, 100, 110, 275n2

Milwaukee Journal, 137, 145, 148–49, 153, 282n6

Mitchell, Broadus, 185

Moneymaker, Berlen, 156

Morgan, Wesley G., 3, 196

Mormon religion, 264

Mother Teresa, 291n30

moths, 82–83, 206, 212, 214, 224, 249

Muir, John, 123–24, 280n34

Murrell gang, 281n36

Muscle Shoals, Ala., 19, 51

mysticism, 38–40, 43, 64–65, 275n2, 284n21. *See also via negativa*

Nag Hammadi Library, 67

Narcissus, in *Child of God,* 165–69; in *Suttree,* 240

Nash, Roderick, 10–11, 30–33, 41, 113–15, 117–18, 121, 123

Nashville Agrarians (Fugitives), 4, 19, 271n3, 289n19

Neal, John Randolph, 196

necrophilia, 90, 134–35, 144–48, 160–64, 166, 168–69, 230–31

Neely, Jack, 287n9

New Deal, 14, 18, 32

Newell, Carolyn, 138–43

Nietzsche, Friedrich, 112

nihilism, 64–65, 100, 198, 235, 261, 275n2, 288n15, 290n24. *See also* gnosticism and nihilism

Nimrod, 263

Norris Dam, 19, 21–22, 51, 272n11

North Carolina, 5, 10, 12, 24, 131, 272n13, 273n16

Oak Ridge, Tenn., 3, 60, 273n17

Oates, Joyce Carol, *Zombie,* 162

O'Connor, Flannery, "A Good Man Is Hard to Find," 253

officers and bureaucrats, 36, 43, 45–47, 52, 55, 61, 99, 128, 176–77, 180, 183, 189–90, 200, 251, 253, 258

Oliver, John, 13–15, 273n14

O'Regan, Cyril, 70–71

Orpheus, 208, 243, 268

Orphics, 65, 277n14

Ownby, Lemuel, 5, 15–18, 272n9, 272n10

Pagels, Elaine, 66–67, 71, 276n8, 277n10
Palmer, David J., 102
Pascal, Blaise, 111–112
Patton, Darryl, *America's Goat Man*, 196
Pearce, Richard, 151, 176, 178, 276n9, 286n14
Peay, Austin, 13
Perry, John, 125–27, 280n35
Petree, Edgar, 51
Plainfield, Wis., 136, 145, 148–49
Plato, 65, 71–72, 204; and appetitive soul, 171–72; Cave Parable, 160, 174, 244, 252; and choice, prenatal, 166–67, 174; and daimon, 171; "Discourse of Diotima" (*Symposium*), 160–61, 163–64; and good and evil, 172–74; *Gorgias*, 158, 172; and human condition, 168; and human nature, 171–72; and immortal soul (psyche), 171–72, 277n14; "Myth of Er" (*Republic*), 174; and nature, 164–65, 170, 242, 283n16; *Phaedrus*, 164; *Politicus*, 172; and purgation, purification, 158–59; and reincarnation, 158, 172; *Timaeus*, 169, 171–72.; and Truth, 158, 167, 170, 172; and vision, blindness, illusion, 159–61, 163, 167, 169–70, 175; Tartarus. *See also* Lethe; McCarthy, Cormac, works: *Child of God, Suttree*
Plotinus, 166, 177
Prather, William, 22, 56, 61, 65, 198–99, 272n12, 274n20, 286n2, 289–90n22
prohibition: national, 25–27; local, 27
Psycho (film). *See* Hitchcock, Alfred
Psycho (novel). *See* Bloch, Robert
purgatory, 72, 75, 87, 159, 197–98, 226–30, 234, 243–45, 269. *See also* Tartarus
Puritanism, 113–14, 157, 228
Pythagoras, 170

race, racism, 122, 186–88, 251–52
Rebello, Stephen, 137, 149, 282n8

Reconstruction, 24, 187–88, 274n19, 285n11
Reed, Jerry, 2
Rilke, Rainer Maria, *The Notebooks of Malte Laurids Brigge*, 286n3
Roman Catholicism, 65, 137, 158, 189, 192, 291n30; and burial practices, 286n13; and purgatory, 75, 159, 234. *See also* McCarthy, Cormac, works: *Suttree* and Roman Catholicism
Roosevelt, Franklin Delano, 12, 14

Sartre, Jean-Paul, 111, 177, 199
Schafer, William J., 64, 273n17
Schechter, Harold, *Deviant*, 282n6
Scots-Irish, 23–24, 44, 272n13
Scott, Sir Walter, 272–73n13
Sequoyah Hills (Knoxville, Tenn.), 126, 287n9
Sevier County, Tenn., 1, 3, 6, 11, 26, 131, 135–36, 138, 153–56, 161; courthouse, 154. *See also* White Caps
Sevier County, Tennessee and Its Heritage, 154–55, 282n10
Sevierville, Tenn., 153–55, 282n10
Shakespeare, William, 203; *Hamlet, Prince of Denmark*, 212–13
Sheddan, John, 196
Shelton, Frank W., 65, 198, 290n24
Shields, A. Randolph, 7, 13, 26, 272n7
Simmons, Jessica, 197
Simms, William Gilmore, 50, 280n 34; *The Forayers*, 34
Simpson, Lewis P., 69–71
Simpson, Philip L., 162, 169
Smith, Warn, 3
Smoky Mountains. *See* Great Smoky Mountains
snakes, 34–35, 116, 122–24, 280n33, 280n34. *See also* gnosticism and serpent
Southern Agrarians. *See* Nashville Agrarians
Southern Appalachian National Park Committee, 10

Spencer, William C., 88, 95, 231, 290n26
Steele, Orville (Pete), 138–41, 143
Stefano, Joseph, *Psycho* (script), 146–47, 149–51, 153, 282n8
Stewart, J. A., 158–61, 166–67, 169–74
Stewart, Potter, 17
Stewart, V. D., 140–41
Sullivan, Nell, 74, 163, 287n4
Sullivan, Walter, 271n3
"Swamp Fox" (television series), 50

Tartarus, 158, 160, 172–73, 175
Taylor, William D., 275n1
Tennessee (state), 12, 14, 24; Code of Laws, 129; four-mile law, 27, 273n15; Pendleton Bill, 27; Supreme Court, 14–15
Tennessee Historical Records Survey, 2, 14, 27, 49
Tennessee River, 18, 21, 127; in Knoxville, 126, 195
Tennessee Valley Authority (TVA), 2–3, 14, 18–23, 29–32, 37–38, 49, 51–52, 126, 154, 272n11, 289–90n22
Terrill, Tom E., 285n11
Theodotus, 107
Thoreau, Henry David, 37, 159; "Civil Disobedience," 46–49; "Paradise (To Be) Regained," 43; "Walden," 46–48, 55, 164, 278–79n22, 283n16
Time, 136, 145, 151, 282n6
Tipton, William ("Fighting Billy"), 13–14
Townsend, Col. W. B., 5
Townsend, Tenn., 5, 13, 271n4
trinity. *See* Christianity
Trinity Project, 273n17
Tuckaleechee, Tenn.. *See* Townsend, Tenn.
Turnbull, Andrew, 244
TVA. *See* Tennessee Valley Authority
Twain, Mark (Samuel Clemens), *Huckleberry Finn*, 31

Tyson, Lawrence D., 13
United States, 14
U.S. Alcohol, Tobacco and Firearms Bureau, 26, 273n14
U.S. Congress, 12, 18
U.S. Constitution (Eighteenth Amendment), 26
U.S. Department of the Interior, 12
U.S. Internal Revenue Service, 24–25
U.S. National Park Service, 11–12, 15–16, 272n7, 272n9
U.S. National Park Service Act of 1916, 10–11
University of South Carolina, 176
University of Tennessee, 136–37, 194, 275n25, 281n2

Vanderheide, John, 286n3
Vestal, Tenn., 1–2, 194, 287n9
via negativa, 65, 68, 100
Vincent, Bert, 27–28, 195–96
Virgin Mary, 103, 260
Voegelin, Eric, 69–70
Volstead Act, 26
voyeurism, 135, 138, 142, 144, 148–50, 153, 160–61, 165–68, 170, 282n9, 284n20
Vulcan, 244–45, 276–77n9

Waldens Creek, Tenn., 153–54, 271n5
Walker County, Ga., 139–42
Wallace, Garry, 158, 284n21
Wallach, Rick, 275n25
Walland, Tenn., 5, 13
Washington, George, 24
Wear's Valley, Tenn., 5, 13
weaver god. *See* god, weaver
Weston, Jesse, *From Ritual to Romance*, 67
whiskey blockading, 23–28, 43, 50; economy of, 23–27; informers about, 273n14; penalties for, 25; Scots-Irish roots of, 23–24
Whiskey Rebellion, 24

White, C. P., 3

White Caps, 15, 125, 138, 150, 154, 281n3

wilderness, 6, 11, 30–33, 36–42, 45–46, 49–50, 60, 113–118, 121, 123–24, 239, 269

Wilkerson, Worth, 138–40, 142

Wilkinson, Diane, 16–17, 272n9

Williams, Don, 154

Wilson, Marshall A., 21–22, 51, 272n11

Winchell, Mark Royden, 50

Winkler, Homer Garland, 3, 271n2

Winkler, Hugh, 2–3, 271n2

Winthrop, John, "A Model of Christian Charity," 228

Witek, Terri, 108–109, 114, 278n21

Woodward, Richard B., 135–36

World War I, 9, 16, 29

World War II, 16, 21, 60, 155–56

Yeats, William Butler, 66; *Purgatory*, 93; "The Second Coming," 264

Young, Thomas D., Jr., 200–201, 215, 219, 221, 237, 239, 269, 288n14, 290n23